# NEW POSSIBILITIES FOR THE PAST

# NEW POSSIBILITIES FOR THE PAST
Shaping History Education in Canada

Edited by Penney Clark

**UBC**Press · Vancouver · Toronto

© UBC Press 2011

All rights reserved. No part of this publication may be reproduced, stored in a retrieval system, or transmitted, in any form or by any means, without prior written permission of the publisher, or, in Canada, in the case of photocopying or other reprographic copying, a licence from Access Copyright, www.accesscopyright.ca.

21 20 19 18 17 16 15 14 13 12    5 4 3 2

Printed in Canada on FSC-certified ancient-forest-free paper (100% post-consumer recycled) that is processed chlorine- and acid-free.

Library and Archives Canada Cataloguing in Publication

New possibilities for the past: shaping history education in Canada / edited by Penney Clark.

Includes bibliographical references and index.
Also issued in electronic format.
ISBN 978-0-7748-2058-5 (bound); ISBN 978-0-7748-2059-2 (pbk.)

1. Canada – History – Study and teaching. 2. History – Study and teaching – Canada. I. Clark, Penney

FC155.N49 2011              971.0071              C2011-903545-6

e-book ISBNs: 978-0-7748-2060-8 (pdf); 978-0-7748-2061-5 (e-pub)

Canada

UBC Press gratefully acknowledges the financial support for our publishing program of the Government of Canada (through the Canada Book Fund), the Canada Council for the Arts, and the British Columbia Arts Council.

This book has been published with the help of a grant from the Canadian Federation for the Humanities and Social Sciences, through the Aid to Scholarly Publications Program, using funds provided by the Social Sciences and Humanities Research Council of Canada.

This volume is the first major publication of The History Education Network/Histoire et éducation en réseau (THEN/HiER).   **THEN HiER** the history education network / histoire et éducation en réseau

UBC Press
The University of British Columbia
2029 West Mall
Vancouver, BC V6T 1Z2
www.ubcpress.ca

# Contents

Acknowledgments / ix

Introduction / 1
*Penney Clark*

## Part 1: History Education: Contested Terrain

**1** A Brief Survey of Canadian Historiography / 33
*Margaret Conrad*

**2** Teaching Canadian History: A Century of Debate / 55
*Ken Osborne*

**3** The Debate on History Education in Quebec / 81
*Jocelyn Létourneau*

**4** Teaching History from an Indigenous Perspective:
Four Winding Paths up the Mountain / 97
*Michael Marker*

## Part 2: Orientations toward Historical Thinking

**5** What It Means to Think Historically / 115
*Stéphane Lévesque*

**6** Assessment of Historical Thinking / 139
*Peter Seixas*

**7** History Education as a Disciplined "Ethic of Truths" / 154
*Kent den Heyer*

## Part 3: Classroom Contexts for Historical Thinking

**8** Historical Thinking in Elementary Education:
A Review of Research / 175
*Amy von Heyking*

**9** Historical Thinking in Secondary Schools:
Zones and Gardens / 195
*Tom Morton*

**10** The Shape of Historical Thinking in a Canadian History
Survey Course in University / 210
*Gerald Friesen*

**11** History Is a Verb: Teaching Historical Practice to
Teacher Education Students / 224
*Ruth Sandwell*

## Part 4: Other Contexts for Historical Thinking

**12** Historical Thinking in the Museum: Open to
Interpretation / 245
*Viviane Gosselin*

**13** Creating and Using Virtual Environments to Promote
Historical Thinking / 264
*Kevin Kee and Nicki Darbyson*

**14** Obsolete Icons and the Teaching of History / 282
*Peter Seixas and Penney Clark*

## Part 5: Perspectives on Historical Thinking

**15** Ethnicity and Students' Historical Understandings / 305
*Carla Peck*

**16** Learning and Teaching History in Quebec: Assessment, Context, Outlook / 325
*Marc-André Éthier and David Lefrançois*

**17** Historical Thinking and Citizenship Education: It Is Time to End the War / 344
*Alan Sears*

Contributors / 365

Index / 371

# Acknowledgments

I gratefully acknowledge the generous support of the Social Sciences and Humanities Research Council of Canada (SSHRC) for the Strategic Knowledge Clusters Grant, which has supported the work of the History Education Network/Histoire et éducation en réseau (THEN/HiER) since 2008. This collection is the first major scholarly publication of the network, and I take note of the wisdom, encouragement, and enthusiasm of the network's Executive Board: Jennifer Bonnell, Margaret Conrad, Anne Marie Goodfellow, Viviane Gosselin, Jan Haskings-Winner, Kevin Kee, Jocelyn Létourneau, Stéphane Lévesque, Ruth Sandwell, Alan Sears, Peter Seixas, and Amy von Heyking.

I extend a special thank you to my colleague Peter Seixas for his unwavering encouragement. Professor Mario Carretero of Autonoma University of Madrid offered generous and invaluable scholarly support, as did Margaret Conrad, who acted in an advisory capacity that extended far beyond her role as chapter contributor. Darcy Cullen, Laraine Coates, and Holly Keller, editors at UBC Press, were always generous with their time. The anonymous reviewers offered detailed and thoughtful feedback, which sparked new insights. Ulrike Spitzer at the Centre for the Study of Historical Consciousness provided technical and administrative assistance. I also wish to acknowledge the Faculty of Education at the University of British Columbia – in particular, Dennis Sumara, former head of the Department of Curriculum and Pedagogy. Finally, I thank my patient family members, Ian, Emily, and Robert, who bring me much joy and make it all worthwhile.

# NEW POSSIBILITIES FOR THE PAST

# Introduction

PENNEY CLARK

This collection explores and articulates the landscape of history education research and practice in Canada. It does this to help define and refine the research agenda in history teaching and practice, which at the present time take place against a backdrop of public concern about Canadians' abysmal knowledge of their own history and a perceived need for more, and then even more, Canadian history in schools. It is crucial that scholarly research be pursued thoughtfully and in a cohesive manner and that classroom practice be informed by the findings of this research.

## Debates

History is contentious in Canada, as it is in most countries. The debates today are not new. They disappear only to reappear over the way. History has been contentious in the public arena, among academics, and in classrooms at every level. The ways we interpret the past to create official (and unofficial) narratives, how we use those narratives and for what purposes, and the place of history in the school curriculum have all sparked debate in Canada time and again.

Recent examples of debate in the forum of public opinion abound. The cancellation of plans to mark the 250th anniversary of the Battle of the Plains of Abraham in Quebec City by re-enacting the event comes quickly to mind; as does the two-year (2005-7) storm of criticism over the representation of the Allied bombings of Germany during the Second World War at the Canadian War Museum; and the 2001 controversy around the depiction of the colonization of British Columbia in murals located in the provincial legislature building.[1]

Academic history is also contentious. Canada has had its own version of the "history wars" that have taken place in the United States and Australia.[2] From the 1960s through the 1990s, new subjects were introduced to the historical canon, in the process challenging traditional assumptions about what was worth investigating and what was worth knowing. First women, gender, race, class, and regionalism, then other subjects such as sexuality, masculinity, youth, the family, and the environment joined the list; with the result that the unified, politically based historical narrative was, according to some, "sundered" beyond repair.[3]

In a groundbreaking 2000 article, historian Ian McKay proposed a "third paradigm," one that would replace the traditional national and sociocultural history narratives with what he called a liberal order framework, which would involve not a synthesis but a "reconnaissance" of history. By this McKay meant that the study of Canada should be about the expansion of liberalism rather than "an essence we must defend or an empty homogeneous space we must possess."[4] This paradigm, which McKay first proposed in the *Canadian Historical Review Forum,* has met with an extensive and diverse response.[5]

Christopher Dummitt and Michael Dawson, in their 2009 edited volume *Contesting Clio's Craft: New Directions and Debates in Canadian History,* suggest that the questions that dominate debate among academic Canadian historians in the first decade of the twenty-first century include these: Why is the public so ignorant about Canadian history? And who is to blame? Is Canadian history "dead"? If so, who killed it? Are we naively clinging to empirical ideas about truth and a knowable past in the face of post-structuralism, discourse analysis, and our postmodern condition? Such questions have generated vigorous debate, but Dummitt and Dawson argue that they are overused and even stale because they have not changed over the past twenty years. They suggest that other debates are beginning to take their place, some of which are tackled in their collection.[6] For example, Dummitt argues in his chapter that the clarion call of social history for an ever more inclusive history has lost its intellectual originality and that it is time to move on.[7] Adele Perry disagrees, arguing that the task is to rethink "the past through the categories of race, ethnicity, class, gender, region, sexuality and colonization."[8] Magda Fahrni asks how we can explain the increasing reluctance of English Canadian scholars to study Quebec and what the place of Quebec ought to be in current historical writing on Canada.[9] Andrew Smith investigates the link between Canada's imperial past and the fact that this country is seen internationally as a success story.[10] Michael Dawson and Catherine Gidney probe the dilemma of how the decisions we make around periodization shape our version of the past. Finally, Dummitt and Dawson ask whether the very notion of Canadian history is now passé.[11] Such questions are intriguing and provide a glimpse of possible future directions.

If history is contentious, history in schools is a battleground. Canadians are asking: Are we historically illiterate as a nation? Why aren't history teachers more effective? What academic preparation should history teachers have? Why must we have a separate and different history curriculum in every province? Should we have a national curriculum for Canadian history? How can we best teach national history in a nation that is culturally and ethnically divided? Why are history textbooks so boring? How should we assess students' historical literacy? Why do our children seem to know so little about Canadian history? Are we teaching them enough about their past to enable them to make informed judgments about the best course for their futures? How should schools be using new technologies to teach history?

Notwithstanding what appears to be an acute current crisis, three issues emerge as perennial sources of contention: inadequate or inaccurate representations of the past in authorized textbooks; the stature and place of history as a school subject; and its purposes and pedagogy.

Although we cannot assume that the content of a prescribed textbook neatly encapsulates what teachers teach and students learn, the textbook has been central to history instruction and until mid-twentieth century served as de facto curriculum. Textbooks have often been located at the centre of controversy.[12] In January 1920, for example, historian W.L. Grant's *History of Canada* was abruptly removed from British Columbia classrooms and teachers were directed to teach civics for the remainder of the year because no alternative history textbook was available. Criticism centred on two issues. The first stemmed from the divide between anglophones and francophones. There were objections to Grant's tolerant treatment of the actions of the Métis during the 1869 and 1885 armed resistances against the Canadian government. He was also criticized for not being sufficiently laudatory about British actions during the First World War, nor sufficiently critical of the Germans. Overall, he was accused of being anti-British, anti-Protestant, pro-German, and pro-French Catholic. This occurred despite his impeccable credentials as a historian, his having been decorated for his wartime service, and his position as head of the prestigious – and very British – Upper Canada College in Toronto. A somewhat similar controversy took place in New Brunswick around Myers's *General History Textbook*.[13]

There has been major concern about the very different depictions of Canadian history in the textbooks used by francophone students in Quebec and those used by anglophone students in the rest of Canada.[14] In a 1970 study sponsored by the Royal Commission on Bilingualism and Biculturalism, Marcel Trudel and Genevieve Jain commented that after 1760 the texts "do not even seem to be talking about the same country! The English-speaking authors do their best to give an overall history of Canada, while the French authors ... hardly talk about anything but the history of Quebec and its expansion beyond its borders."[15] This "socialization into discord" was corroborated by later studies conducted by Paul Lamy, J.P. Richert, and Marshal Conley and Kenneth Osborne.[16]

During the 1970s and 1980s, attention turned to the depictions of Aboriginal peoples, women, and ethnic groups other than English and French. A 1971 study sponsored by the Ontario Ministry of Education and the Ontario Human Rights Commission examined 143 history textbooks authorized in Ontario. In their report, *Teaching Prejudice*, the authors, Garnet McDiarmid and David Pratt of the Ontario Institute for Studies in Education (OISE), concluded that "we are most likely to encounter in textbooks devoted Christians, great Jews, hardworking immigrants, infidel Moslems, primitive Negroes, and savage Indians."[17] This study was followed by others, many of them carried out by provincial human rights commissions.[18] As a result of these studies, some textbooks were removed from provincially authorized lists and textbook selection criteria were mandated in every province. Such criteria continue to be used by authors and publishers during the textbook development process, as well as by provincial textbook selection committees when textbooks to support the curriculum are being authorized.

The second perennial source of contention in the schools concerns the stature of history in the curriculum and its presumed demise, its place assumed by social studies. Canada's ten provinces and three territories have control over their own school curricula, and most have chosen the interdisciplinary subject of social studies over the discipline of history.[19] Social studies encompasses history but also embraces elements of geography, sociology, anthropology, and other social science disciplines. In some provinces, at particular times, it has taken an issues or values approach, incorporating history only as it is relevant to the consideration of contemporary problems of public or personal concern. Social studies became increasingly prominent in the 1930s, at a time when progressive education influences were coming to the fore. Its interdisciplinary nature placed it at the core of "enterprise" or activity-oriented project-based curricula in elementary schools, especially in Alberta, British Columbia, and Ontario.

Opposition to the place of social studies in the curriculum was eloquently expressed by historian Hilda Neatby in *So Little for the Mind* (1953), which achieved bestseller status. Famously condemning social studies as "the truly typical part of the progressive curriculum with its obsession for indoctrination," Neatby noted that it was "taught not only without the classic distinctions between geography, history and politics, but also without the logical arrangement of place, time, and causation ordinarily considered to be inherent in these disciplines."[20] More recently, a 1996 issue of *Canadian Social Studies: The History and Social Science Teacher* examined the state of history and social studies in Canada. Ken Osborne, an eminent history educator and historian of history education, concluded his article in that issue with this dramatic statement: "The downgrading of history ... is neither an aberration nor an accident. It is part of a wider move to sweep the very idea of democratic citizenship aside."[21]

Perhaps the strongest expression of the presumed demise of history was historian J.L. Granatstein's *Who Killed Canadian History?* (1998; 2nd ed. 2007).[22] This bestselling polemic blamed the end of history as a school subject on a range of lethal causes, including these: the interdisciplinary subject of social studies, which had resulted in a diluted version of history in many provinces; the limited research focus of many historians; an overemphasis on teaching skills rather than content; and the success of determined interest groups in getting their narrow agendas into the curriculum, which had resulted in a fragmentation of the national narrative and an overemphasis on negative aspects of our history. Granatstein's most potent vitriol, though, was heaped on social studies. Response to his book was swift and heated on both sides of the debate.[23]

Over the past decade, the Dominion Institute, a charitable organization formed in 1997 with the purpose of helping "Canadians connect in meaningful ways with the country's history, shared citizenship and democratic institutions and values,"[24] has administered tests of Canadians' knowledge about people and events in our past. People have performed poorly. In 2009 the institute assessed provincial history and social studies curricula and found their history content wanting. Its Report Card, which assessed the amount – and to some extent the quality – of Canadian history in the curriculum in each of Canada's provinces and territories, awarded marks ranging from B+ to an F.[25] The institute has been skilful in handling the media, and announcements of the knowledge surveys and the Report Card have garnered a great deal of attention, resulting in much wringing of hands over Canadians' lack of knowledge of their history.[26]

The third perennial debate is centred on the purposes of history as a school subject and how it should be taught. The assumption underlying the Dominion Institute quizzes is that the more knowledge people possess about events, people, and places in Canada's past, the stronger their sense of identity with their nation. The implied purpose for the teaching of history, then, is to build a strong sense of national identity. There are two problems with this reasoning. The first is that we do not *know* that more information leads to a stronger sense of identity. A recent study by Jack Jedwab, President of the Association for Canadian Studies, indicates the opposite.[27] Second, there is no agreement that a sense of national identity should be the raison d'être for teaching history in schools. Many teacher education faculty members, provincial curriculum developers, historians, teachers, and students would disagree with such a goal. History educator Peter Seixas, for example, has argued for a "critical disciplinary history" – that is, a history that challenges students to ask questions about historical evidence and the construction of historical accounts.

To date, there is not a great deal of empirical data about what actually happens in history (or social studies) classrooms, though there are anecdotal accounts, such as the following:

> Mr. Norris Belton taught social studies. A man with a grey brushcut, who wore glasses that magnified his eyes, rumpled blue blazers and grey flannels, his teaching style was to have the class underline important phrases in the social studies textbook. His classes consisted of forty minutes of his reading a few pages, and stopping every few words so kids could underline an important phrase. What happened of course was that you became an expert underliner. You'd underline some phrases with single lines and some with double lines, and quickly got the knack of whipping out your ruler and drawing perfect lines. What the lines were under didn't sink in very far.[28]

*What Culture? What Heritage?* published in 1968, is still the only pan-Canadian investigation of history (and civics) education as it is taught in schools ever conducted in Canada. This study criticized classroom history as a "bland, consensus story, told without the controversy that is an inherent part of history ... a dry-as-dust account of uninterrupted political and economic progress," and history pedagogy as a matter of consigning students to the role of "bench bound listeners."[29] It is doubtful whether this pedagogical approach would achieve either national identity goals or the goals of a critical disciplinary history. The report sparked debate in at least one provincial legislature, was widely covered in the media, and as with *So Little for the Mind*, achieved bestseller status.[30]

## A Way Forward

Since 1996, a remarkable confluence of events has created an agenda for history education research. That year, Peter Seixas of the University of British Columbia published "Conceptualizing Growth in Historical Understanding" in *The Handbook of Education and Human Development: New Models of Learning, Teaching, and Schooling*. In this groundbreaking article, Seixas articulated a framework for the field of history education, mapping out six concepts of historical thinking: significance, epistemology and evidence, continuity and change, progress and decline, empathy (perspective taking) and moral judgment, and agency.[31] This article, which built on and reinterpreted work by Peter Lee, Rosalyn Ashby, Christopher Portal, and others in the United Kingdom, established a research agenda for Canadian scholars.[32]

The next event of central importance was the "Giving the Past a Future" Conference, sponsored by the McGill Institute for the Study of Canada in January 1999. Touted as the largest Canadian conference ever on the teaching and learning of history, it had 750 people in attendance. This conference marked the beginning of what is now a decade-long biennial series of national conferences on history education sponsored by the Association for Canadian Studies, often in conjunction with provincial history and social studies teachers' associations.

Perhaps the most unique aspect of this conference was the remarkable array of people and organizations it brought together. These included historians; history education scholars; provincial Department of Education curriculum officials; public historians, including museum educators and curators; some schoolteachers; and representatives of a variety of organizations, including the National Film Board of Canada, Veterans Affairs Canada, and the Bronfmann Foundation, producer of the popular *Heritage*

*Minutes*. Another organization present at the conference was Canada's National History Society, now called Canada's History, established in 1994 with the aim of popularizing Canadian history. This organization has become increasingly influential in history education. It now publishes not only *Canada's History* (formerly *The Beaver: Canada's History Magazine*) but also *Kayak: Canada's History Magazine for Kids;* and it recognizes six teachers each year with the Governor General's Awards for history teaching. In the autumn of 2009, it published its first special education version of *The Beaver*.

The 1999 conference also marked the beginning of Historica, which, until its merger with the Dominion Institute in 2009, sponsored summer institutes for secondary school teachers and Heritage Fairs for upper elementary and middle school students; and produced the *Canadian Encyclopedia Online* as well as *Historica Minutes*, an iteration of the Bronfmann Foundation's *Heritage Minutes*. In 2006, Historica provided support for the launching of the Benchmarks of Historical Thinking Project under the auspices of the Centre for the Study of Historical Consciousness. The purpose of this project was articulated as

> to have a more clearly articulated conception of the qualities of historical knowledge and thinking that Historica – and organizations and institutions, including ministries of education, with similar goals – are actually trying to promote. Of immediate and direct benefit to Historica will be a basis for assessing the impact of existing programs as well as providing criteria for making decisions about future programs. Furthermore, such benchmarks could provide the basis for the revision and supplement of provincial (as well as local and school-based) curriculum materials, assessment, and professional development.[33]

The Benchmarks project involves research and practice sites across the country, where secondary school teachers and history educators explore the challenges of teaching a critical disciplinary history using concepts of historical understanding. This approach has already begun to influence textbooks, curriculum development, and teacher education programs. (See Seixas, Chapter 6, and Morton, Chapter 9.)

The first decade of the new millennium has been marked by four key publications that, together, have begun to move the research agenda forward. The first of these was *Knowing, Teaching, and Learning History: National and International Perspectives* (2000), edited by Peter Stearns, Peter

Seixas, and Sam Wineburg. The second, *Theorizing Historical Consciousness* (2004), edited by Seixas, was an outcome of the presentation of theoretical papers by Canadian and international scholars at an inaugural symposium marking the establishment of the Centre for the Study of Historical Consciousness at the University of British Columbia, under Seixas as director. *To the Past: History Education, Public Memory, and Citizenship in Canada* (2006), edited by Ruth Sandwell, serves as concrete recognition of increased public interest in history, since, except for one chapter, it represents public lectures by academics, broadcast as part of the CBC's *Ideas* series. The final publication in this remarkable list is *Thinking Historically: Educating Students for the 21st Century* (2008) by Stéphane Lévesque, a former graduate student of Seixas. This book provides a rich exploration and explication of historical thinking concepts.[34]

These collections decidedly do *not* call for the dissemination of more historical information through the school social studies or history curriculum, as the Dominion Institute does. Nor do they call for greater reliance on stirring narratives to engage children in the "story" of history, as Mark Starowicz, producer of the CBC film series *Canada: A People's History* has done.[35] Taken together, these collections are an investigation of – and ultimately a call for – what Peter Seixas calls a "critical disciplinary" history education. This approach has been criticized as too dry and "academic." In fact it is not, as the present book will show.

A significant increase in research funding offered through the Social Sciences and Humanities Research Council (SSHRC) and other granting agencies has helped move the research agenda forward. For example, Quebec scholar Jocelyn Létourneau's Canadian University Research Alliance (CURA) grant "Canadians and Their Pasts" (2006-2011) has enabled him and his team of seven academic researchers and nineteen collaborators to complete a pan-Canadian survey designed to probe the historical consciousness of Canadians. They ask these questions: What role does the past play in the everyday lives of Canadians? How does history help define individual and collective identities? Is history dead, or does it shape Canada's future?[36] This survey will facilitate comparisons with similar projects undertaken in Europe, the United States, and Australia. "Simulating History," another SSHRC-funded research project, this one at the Centre for Digital Humanities, Brock University, and led by historian Kevin Kee, investigates the "best potential" for educational computer simulations (sometimes called computer "serious games") to teach Canadian history.

The History Education Network/Histoire et éducation en réseau (THEN/ HiER) is a SSHRC-funded project that has a significant funding commitment over a seven-year period (2008-15). The aims of this project are to encourage new research about history teaching and learning and to mobilize and disseminate existing research among the various constituencies involved in history education in Canada, including academic historians; history education scholars in faculties of education; public historians in universities, museums, archives, and historic sites; practising teachers; and curriculum developers and policy makers. The goal is teaching informed by research – not only in classrooms at every level, but also in museums and other venues where history education takes place formally or informally – as well as research informed by teaching.

The network began in 2005, under the direction of Ruth Sandwell, OISE/ University of Toronto; John Lutz, University of Victoria; and Peter Gossage, Université de Sherbrooke. These historians recognized the need for researchers and practitioners to speak to one another across the divides separating them. As Ruth Sandwell has so aptly put it: "From the vantage point of elementary and secondary school history teachers, the work of professional historians in the post-1960 period has been increasingly 'academic' in the worst sense of the word: irrelevant, pretentious, and frequently unreadable. For historians, the work of history teachers has been seen as, at best, facile and irrelevant, and at its worst a more or less benign form of government propaganda."[37]

Representatives of the various constituencies involved in history education were invited to a first meeting of the network in January 2005 at OISE/ University of Toronto. This was followed by a second meeting at the University of British Columbia in April 2006 and by a third at the University of Saskatchewan in 2007.

In 2008 the project gained significant momentum with the award of a SSHRC Strategic Clusters Grant of $2.1 million to pursue its goals over a seven-year period, under the direction of Penney Clark of the Department of Curriculum and Pedagogy, University of British Columbia.[38] In a very early meeting following receipt of the grant, it was agreed that a first major project would be the development of an edited volume that would document the state of history education research in Canada as a baseline for future work. This is that book.

Knowledge mobilization travels in both directions. The motto of the History Education Network is "practice-informed research and research-informed practice." As Alex and David Bennet point out, knowledge mobilization is "situated within the paradigms of theory, praxis and action. It combines knowledge gained from research, the accumulated knowledge and experience of researchers, the specialty knowledge of change agents and organizational or community development specialists, and the knowledge acquired from the lived experience of community leaders and citizens."[39]

## The Collection

This collection, the first in a series to be developed by THEN/HiER, represents the state of history education research and practice in Canada ten years into the new millennium. History education is experiencing a revival in this country. It is said that alcoholics have to hit bottom before they can begin to heal. Perhaps that is what has happened with history education in Canada, given that little more than a decade ago there was pervasive despair about its very existence as a school subject, inside or outside social studies.

Since concepts of historical thinking are becoming so central to history education in Canada, and since they have such a significant place in the pages of this book, I will take space here to describe them as they are currently defined by Peter Seixas. Note that Seixas has modified his conceptual framework since first proposing it.[40] Such frameworks are mutable. They will vary over time as well as from one theorist to another. It is interesting that both in his own book and in Chapter 5 of this volume, Stéphane Lévesque has chosen to elucidate the original framework offered by Seixas in 1996.

Seixas highlights these concepts: historical significance, primary source evidence, continuity and change, cause and consequence, historical perspective taking, and the ethical dimension. Historical *significance* refers to what is considered worth including in accounts of the past and the criteria for choosing one event, trend, issue, or person over an infinite number of others. The simplest criterion relates to the extent of the impact. More complex cases involve the place of the event, issue, or person in a larger narrative constructed by a historian. As Seixas notes, "historical significance does not inhere in the past itself, but rather, is created out of the relationship between the historian and the past."[41] *Primary source evidence* is comprised of the traces used by the historian to create an account or argument about life in the past. Again, the relationship between the historian and the past is central. What becomes evidence is determined by the questions the historian asks of the traces of the past. *Continuity and change* is about what has changed and what has remained the same over time. There is a value dimension here that involves consideration of which changes involve progress and which decline, and from whose perspective in each case. (Note that in Seixas's original framework, progress and decline were treated separately from continuity and change.) *Cause and consequence* involves isolating those events that most closely and crucially precipitated or followed from other events in which the historian is interested. Causes and consequences can be both long term (economic, social, political) and immediate. A particular event can have many causes and many consequences. The historian asks this question: Which are most crucial to the account being created? *Historical perspective taking* involves a recognition that people of the past operated in a milieu different from the one in which we function today. Their expectations of themselves and others were different, and so were their values and their ways of experiencing the world. Therefore, we should not expect people of the past to behave as we might. As Seixas notes: "It is not just that they didn't dress in our styles of clothing or that they did not have our electronic gadgets: their whole way of experiencing the world, their whole way of thinking, and perhaps even feeling, were different in ways that are a challenge for us to imagine."[42] The *ethical dimension* concerns how we judge people's actions in the past. Historians must exercise a great deal of caution in this regard; they must try to avoid judging from contemporary ways of viewing the world.[43] However, we do expect our understanding of past events to help us understand and make decisions about contemporary dilemmas.

These concepts are becoming increasingly central to the ways in which curriculum documents, textbooks, pedagogical handbooks, and classroom instruction are being framed. Hence, they are central to the discussions in this book, which examines the state of history education in Canada today. As of early 2011, the Benchmarks of Historical Thinking Project has held three national meetings (the last two sponsored by THEN/HiER) that have involved many history education stakeholders, including teachers, textbook publishers, academic historians, history education scholars, public historians, and representatives of provincial education ministries. The purpose of these meetings is to discuss strategies for incorporating historical thinking concepts into provincial history and social studies curricula, authorized textbooks, and classroom practice.

This volume builds on the important work that has appeared since 2000; but it also takes a significant leap beyond that work. Representing collaboration among leading Canadian researchers and theorists in the field, it opens up discussions that will set new parameters for research, theory, policy, and practice in history education. It addresses the questions that Canadians are asking about history and history education. It brings together a diverse group of authors who represent the constituencies listed above. Each is a passionate and influential history educator who has worked tirelessly toward the betterment of history education in Canada. Together, they have sought to accomplish this in a range of ways in both academe and the broader community: conducting research and disseminating findings; teaching graduate, undergraduate, and elementary/high school history courses and courses in teacher education programs; contributing to provincial curriculum development; creating teaching materials, including traditional textbooks and Web-based resources; contributing to teacher professional development activities; designing museum exhibitions; speaking in public forums; and making their voices heard in public media.

This book speaks across several great divides. As with any setting where groups develop their own cultures in pockets, different dialects develop. Instead of assuming that the meanings of the labels we have chosen to describe different groups will be immediately clear to every reader, I will define them here.

We refer to history teachers, history educators, and historians. *History teachers* includes those who teach in an elementary or secondary school setting. *History educators* refers to those academics who teach and conduct research in a teacher education or graduate education program. *Historians*, in this volume, means academic researchers who teach history at the university undergraduate or graduate level. *Public historians*, in this volume, refers to those who work in universities, museums, archives, or historic sites.

We also need to distinguish between history, historiography, and history education. *History* is the study of the past. The past is not history. The past is everything that has happened, whereas history is composed of accounts constructed by historians using the remains of the past. *Historiography* describes the efforts at understanding the enterprise of producing history. Historians shape our memory of the past according to theories and methods of historical inquiry that are subject to change. Most professional historians now recognize that their interpretations, like those of their predecessors, are shaped by present-day biases and interests. As a result, they are more modest in their claims to objectivity. Good historians now strive to examine their own motivations, take pains to understand the context of earlier efforts to write the history of their topic, and concede that exploring the past from a variety of perspectives is the closest they can come to the ideal of objectivity. In other words, they are both historiographers *and* historians. Finally, *history education* is about teaching and learning history. It involves investigating ways that history teachers and other educators can make history understandable and usable for their students.

The third distinction is the one between citizenship and civics education. While these terms can be used interchangeably, *citizenship* is often used in a broader sense. Ken Osborne defines it as including the following: "First, a sense of identity with some wider community, usually defined as the nation; second, a set of rights and entitlements, such as the right to vote and to be represented; and, third, a corresponding set of obligations, such as obedience to the law."[44] *Civics* often has a narrower focus and involves the teaching of politics, law, and government. It is worthwhile noting, however, that history is used as a vehicle for achieving both civics and citizenship goals. For example, Alan Sears in Chapter 17 points to the work of American researchers Keith Barton and Linda Levstik, who contend that teaching history can contribute to building democracies that are "participatory, pluralist, and deliberative." They also argue that "it is possible to teach history in a way that both develops a sense of national identity and explores the contested and complex nature of that identity; and that opens discussions of difference, exclusion, and inclusion" (in Sears, Chapter 17, p. 355). Ken Osborne, in "The Teaching of History and Democratic Citizenship," posits ten understandings about Canada and eight about the world that students should know by the end of their years in school (including one concerning the characteristics of Canada's parliamentary democracy), in order to acquire abilities necessary to engage in democratic citizenship. He suggests that the task of acquiring these understandings should be approached through history: "Perhaps the most important reason for approaching this task through history is that it is a powerful way of helping students to see themselves as part of a tradition, connected to those who have gone before them and to those who will come after."[45] History, citizenship, and civics, he argues, are inextricably connected.

**History Education: Contested Terrain**
In the first chapter of Part 1, Margaret Conrad explores interpretations of the purposes of history and historiography in Canada from the perspectives of historians and in public discourse. Ken Osborne and Jocelyn Létourneau continue the discussion, applying it to the school curriculum. Osborne looks at influences on provincial curricula, tracing trends over time; Létourneau considers the relatively new and controversial history

and citizenship curriculum in Quebec. In the final chapter in Part 1, Michael Marker explores history, historiography, and history education from an Aboriginal perspective.

Margaret Conrad offers a history of Canadian historiography, sketching the broader intellectual terrain in which school history has been conceptualized and taught. She surveys the distinct historiographic traditions of First Nations; the differing narratives of English and French Canadians; the movement from political to social history; the parallel roads taken by amateur and professional historians; and the impact of region, as well as cultural factors such as class, ethnicity, gender, race, and religion, on the writing of history. She concludes her chapter by pointing to the possibilities presented by the recent work of two Canadian historians, Gerald Friesen and Ian McKay, who have offered new and thought-provoking frameworks for addressing questions about Canada as a historical enterprise in a globalizing world.

Ken Osborne continues the discussion with a focus on the formal curriculum and the teaching of Canadian history in schools. He shows how the political and military history that Conrad described found its way into a "nation-building" narrative evident in school curriculum and textbooks through to the 1960s. Echoing Conrad's discussion of the new emphasis on social history beginning in the 1960s, he describes curriculum projects in Canada and the United States which have reflected that emphasis. He notes the perilous place of history in the 1980s, which resulted in a lively debate in the 1990s over why and how history should be taught. Finally, he identifies two new approaches that emerged in the 1990s: one that views history as part of education for democratic citizenship, and another that teaches students to think historically.

Jocelyn Létourneau examines the controversial reshaping of Quebec's national history curriculum into a history and citizenship course in 2006. He describes an intensely political process, situating the curriculum shift in the tensions and ambiguities experienced by the broader Quebec society as it attempts to reconcile its ancient founding myths with new myths that are jockeying for a place in the public space. He ends with a provocative question: "What kind of history does the future of Quebec hold – and for whom, and created with what aim and what collective meaning?"

Michael Marker discusses indigenous perspectives on the teaching of history, elaborating on "four themes of indigenous historical consciousness that travel outside of ways that history courses are constructed and taught." The first theme is a circular concept of time versus a linear one, a view that contradicts the Eurocentric sense of progression of people and ideas in time. The second is a view of plants and animals as being unsegmented from humans. This differs from the economic context in which they are presented in Canadian history textbooks – a context that presents them as economic commodities in resource industries such as the fur trade. The third highlights indigenous attention to local concerns and the relationship between these concerns and concepts of protection of traditional territory and land claims. The fourth theme concerns colonization, including misunderstandings that stemmed from different world views. Indigenous people responded to colonization in ways that the colonizers did not always clearly understand. For example, many amalgamated Christianity into traditional spiritual beliefs, which were confusing for missionaries but which functioned effectively for indigenous people in their efforts to cope with the complex realities of colonization. Marker concludes by urging that indigenous perspectives be included in history courses and textbooks.

Several major themes emerge in Part 1. There is the tension – continuing into the present – between a scientific approach to history and history education and nation-building narratives intended to promote national identity. There is the tension between interdisciplinary social studies and history as a distinct discipline in the schools. There are tensions around pedagogy, with perennial debates over whether the teacher should deliver the content directly rather than having students actively engage with historical sources. Finally, there are tensions between indigenous and Eurocentric world views that make Aboriginal students' participation in history courses difficult.

All four authors end their contributions with a future-oriented stance by pointing to the crucial place of the discipline of history with regard to citizenship education and informed citizenship. The differences among them lie in the breadth of their conceptions. Conrad points to a more global citizenship; Osborne, to a "national" one in the context of the country of Canada; and Létourneau, to a "national" one in terms of the province of Quebec. Marker points out that Aboriginal people are often concerned with the local, but his discussion also has implications for national identity and global ecology. Conrad stresses the centrality of history as a means to help us understand the place of human beings in the world and as an aid in identifying, interpreting, and sharing "the values on which civil society depends." Osborne points out that "the exercise of citizenship depends in part on our understanding of the state and society of which we are citizens." Létourneau's focus is on identity; he asks which version of the past is most fitting to transmit to the students of the present, given the recent transformation of Quebec society. Marker calls for the inclusion of indigenous world views in school history – a move that may help "reconfigure our relationships to the ecologies of our communities and revise our thinking about how to live sustainably in the future."

**Orientations toward Historical Thinking**

In Part 2, we have two authors who are in substantial agreement and one who offers a different perspective. In terms of Ken Osborne's categories, the chapters by Stéphane Lévesque and Peter Seixas are concerned with teaching students to think historically and to make reasoned judgments; whereas the chapter by Kent den Heyer is concerned more explicitly with concepts of ethics and social action.

The section begins with a chapter by Stéphane Lévesque, who provides a nuanced analysis of what it means to think historically. He takes five historical thinking concepts and dissects each one; for example, he asks which criteria are used to determine whether an event is significant. He suggests that those criteria are as follows: how deeply people are affected by an event; the number of people affected; the event's durability (i.e., its legacy); its relevance to today; its relevance to personal vantage point; its symbolic significance; and its usefulness as a lesson. Lévesque's other concepts are as follows: continuity and change; progress and decline; evidence; and historical empathy. He cautions that if students are not taught how to apply a critical lens to history, they will be left with a naive acceptance of whatever is presented to them by authorities, be they political leaders, movie producers, parents, or teachers. He points to the urgent need for a theory of progression in historical learning. "We know what experts do and how they do it, but we need a clearer scaffolded vision of what it is to progressively develop expertise, in both substantive and procedural knowledge of history, with realistic attainable targets."

Peter Seixas examines the assessment of historical thinking, building on the work of his Benchmarks of Historical Thinking Project.[46] He outlines how four components are applicable to the assessment of historical thinking. The first, which is implicit in all assessment, is the assumption that it is measuring progress toward particular goals. The goals of historical thinking that he articulates here were outlined earlier in this discussion. The second involves a model of cognition and learning. He defines this as "the ideas we have about how students confront problems that are central to the discipline of history, and the multiple paths by which they learn more sophisticated ways to do so." The third and fourth involve, respectively, assumptions about tasks that will elicit demonstration of that cognition and assumptions about how to interpret the evidence drawn from those demonstrations. Using one historical thinking concept – historical perspective taking – he explores the developmental approach to assessment that he is positing, laying out what this concept would look like at the basic, intermediate, and advanced levels.

In the final chapter of Part 2, Kent den Heyer points to several shortcomings he sees in what he calls the "disciplinarian" approach to history education, an approach exemplified in the work of Seixas and Lévesque. His central concern is that their approach is not equipped to achieve democratic purposes because it fails to place ethics and social action at its core. He also criticizes their approach for its rationality, arguing that using "reasoned judgments" is only one way to engage with the past. In his view, their "best practices" ignore people's "subjective relationships to their doing of history." He suggests that "disciplinarians" fail to "judge the social-political context" and students' own positionalities: "It is as if the historical concepts were extracted in labs from people without histories, hopes, fantasies, or racialized, gendered, classed, and desiring bodies and without political intelligence." He argues that their approach is based on a deficit model that perceives young people as in need of disciplinary treatments rather than an active engagement with history. He calls for a more affirmative model that would incorporate a more explicit acknowledgment that certain interpretations of the past are privileged while others are marginalized.

In this section, we have moved from the broad sweep of history and history education over time, in order to focus on a particular approach to history education in the present. Lévesque provides a detailed account of historical thinking concepts; Seixas demonstrates how we can assess students' abilities to use these competencies as well as measure their progress; and den Heyer rejects their approach out of hand, calling it "disciplinarian" in a pejorative sense.

## Classroom Contexts for Historical Thinking

In Part 3, Amy von Heyking, Tom Morton, Gerald Friesen, and Ruth Sandwell explore the teaching and learning of historical thinking in four classroom settings: elementary and secondary schools; undergraduate Canadian history survey courses; and a pre-service teacher education course. These four chapters capture the authors' personal perspectives. Von Heyking introduces her review and analysis of the literature on historical thinking with a description of her own experiences as a researcher observing elementary school children as they interacted with primary source materials. The three chapters that follow hers are highly personal accounts of the authors' own experiences as they have faced the challenges of "walking the walk" of putting historical thinking into action in the instructional settings in which they work.

Researchers have long rejected the idea that elementary school children cannot grasp historical concepts. In her chapter, von Heyking provides an overview of history topics and requirements in Canadian elementary school curricula, reviews research into the nature of children's historical thinking, and considers implications of that research for teaching and learning in Canadian classrooms. She emphasizes that students' progress in their historical understandings is not necessarily related to age and that the quality of teaching is crucial. She points out here that children need breadth and depth of instruction, including opportunities to examine a range of primary and secondary resources, in order to become more sophisticated thinkers. She notes that students have their own personal or family historical narratives, which teachers can use as reference points to encourage engagement with history. (This is in keeping with Carla Peck's point that students' ethnic identities influence their ascriptions of historical significance; see Chapter 15.) Finally, echoing Jocelyn Létourneau's earlier comments about history education in Quebec (see Chapter 3), she observes that thinking historically means "seeing oneself in time, as both an inheritor of the legacies of the past and as a maker of the future."

Tom Morton takes the theoretical discussions of historical thinking concepts offered by Lévesque and Seixas into the high school classroom. He cautions that we must establish a complex alignment of institutions, politics, research, official curriculum, and assessment toward common goals if we are to successfully connect research with practice. He describes the challenges of teaching history using this approach, given the exigencies of a high school setting, which includes heavy curriculum content, externally imposed student assessment, and a school culture that does not encourage teacher collegiality. He uses the image of "craft knowledge" to examine teachers' knowledge of history, knowledge of ways to teach it, and knowledge of how students learn it. He turns to the metaphor of "victory gardens" – that is, the backyard vegetable gardens cultivated during the Second World War – to highlight various sites in Canada where teachers are working on projects incorporating historical thinking concepts as part of the Benchmarks of Historical Thinking Project. He also addresses what he calls "zones of uncertainty," or areas of challenge. For an example, he uses his own work with grade eleven students on a project that involved creating videos on the historical significance of the First World War, outlining his aims, procedures, use of resources, and challenges.

Gerald Friesen uses descriptions of their practice by two experienced university professors, as well as reflections on his own teaching practice, to define "the shape of historical thinking" as it would ideally appear in an undergraduate Canadian history survey course – and, by implication, in classrooms at other levels. He points to the importance of conveying content (the transmission of a body of data), developing particular skills, and nurturing good work habits; the latter broadly interpreted as respect for learning, openness to ideas, and accountability for the quality of one's own work. He concludes by noting that the procedural concepts of historical thinking, such as "using primary sources, discussing historical context and historical significance, identifying decisive moments of change, debating evidence, uncovering uncertainty about meaning, considering morality and ethical choices will endure"; and he implies that they should do so. However, he issues two caveats. First, teachers have an obligation to inspire a sense of wonder in their students. Effective history education must be more than a series of sterile academic exercises. In this regard, he elaborates on the need to incite students' imaginations and to "kindle an infectious delight in the classroom." Second, it is important to avoid reifying historical thinking concepts: "The basic approach of historians changes over time and any attempt to crystallize the basic questions asked by 'historians' will probably be misleading within several decades." These are cautions worth heeding.

Ruth Sandwell would no doubt welcome Gerald Friesen's students into her history education course, given her lament that students view history as a static body of facts that is not subject to interpretation. She describes how her teacher education course evolved as she explored ways to construct a "catwalk across the great divide"[47] – that is, between history courses in departments of history and history education courses in faculties of education. She wants to provide her students with experiences that actually allow them to *be* historians instead of passive readers of the historical accounts that historians have produced. She emphasizes that this approach involves more than teaching content and skills in a more interesting way; it is based on a different understanding of what history actually *is*. She takes the reader carefully through the construction and reconstruction of this course, in the end offering what is essentially a blueprint for anyone who wishes to teach a history education course in a similar manner.

Each of these authors is committed to an approach to history education involving engagement with the raw materials of history. All of them desire to offer students opportunities to enter into the messy world of the historian, a world in which events are not already selected and organized into a sequential narrative tidily wrapped up with crisp beginnings and endings and carefully defined causes and effects. This approach requires some courage because it comes with challenges, as is clear from each author's account. Students are not always receptive, and it is not an "efficient" way to teach. The learning does not arrive in bite-sized chunks with key ideas in boldface defined in a glossary. But these authors view the approach as central to successful history education.

**Other Contexts for Historical Thinking**
In Part 4, the authors venture beyond the classroom to examine historical thinking in museum exhibitions, virtual environments, and public institutional settings. In venturing out, these authors embrace the possibility of including a wide and democratic array of people within the scope of their examination. These are sites that anyone may enter.

Viviane Gosselin examines the potential of museum exhibitions to foster historical meaning making, as well as the limitations of this approach. She contends that this process is inhibited because, while museum exhibitions have adapted to show the influence of social history – and to some extent, critical history – they continue to base their narratives on substantive knowledge and provide few clues about the process used to construct the historical narratives they present. As a consequence, the public's belief is sustained that museums' interpretations are about uncovering a *truer* picture of the past. Gosselin contends that museums should provide "conceptual historical wayfinders" ("strategic elements in the exhibition that orient visitors spatially") in order to engage visitors more critically with historical accounts. For example, a wayfinder could provide different interpretations of the same objects to stimulate visitors to consider the interpretive nature of historical accounts. Gosselin calls for a research agenda that acknowledges the dialogical relationship between the museum and its audience and that recognizes the ways museum visitors' conceptions of history influence how they engage with exhibitions.

Kevin Kee and Nicki Darbyson explore the possibilities of virtual environments (VEs) for supporting the teaching and learning of historical thinking. These researchers point out that the concept of "learning games" is especially appealing for twenty-first-century youth, who are "digital natives," and that VE games can be especially useful for students who perform poorly in other kinds of classroom activities. In this way, students experience history not as historians sifting through documents and examining artifacts (see the chapters in Part 3), or as readers of textbooks (as might be seen in many classrooms), but rather as people who are "present" in a historical environment that has been constructed for them. In such an environment, users "explore and play," as Kee and Darbyson put it. In this way, students both gather historical information and engage in historical practices. For example, assuming the role of a historical character requires that a student take a historical perspective, seeing events through the eyes of that character. Students can also build historical environments. As an example, while constructing the environment for Kee's undergraduate course on the War of 1812, students "encountered the high ratio of churches to residences, the segregation of new immigrants from established ethnic groups, and the possibilities, and limitations, of nineteenth-century travel. The act of creation requires that students determine how the environment, and the characters inside it, are different from the present." VEs are not commonly used in elementary or secondary schools, or in university undergraduate history courses, for that matter. Nor has much research been done on their effectiveness. However, it is clear from this chapter that this is an important area for further investigation.

Peter Seixas and Penney Clark examine British Columbia secondary school students' reasoning, recorded in a Canadian history competition, regarding solutions to a public history controversy. The controversy centred on four murals depicting the province's colonial period, but painted in 1935, and located prominently in the rotunda of the BC legislature. The murals, titled *Justice, Enterprise, Labour, and Courage*, depicted Aboriginal and European people interacting in various ways. Students responded in writing to a question that asked them what should be done about the murals, given the objections that had been raised about their depictions of Aboriginal people. Seixas and Clark found that, while students understood the interpretive nature of the murals, and while most understood that historical representations can be controversial, they did not necessarily see the messages the murals, as monuments, were attempting to convey in light of the historical context in which those messages had been constructed. The authors end the chapter with a discussion of the pedagogical implications of their findings and by considering ways to make students' reasoning richer and more sophisticated. They argue that history courses should not be limited to the recounting of mythic, foundational narratives, but should include opportunities for students to participate in public debates, for such opportunities will help them learn to make reasoned judgments about contemporary moral dilemmas.

Each of these chapters ventures beyond the bounded walls of the classroom into unique and largely unexplored environments. Each is concerned with pedagogy and offers approaches to teaching history concepts and procedures in those places. Gosselin offers the possibility of wayfinders to help visitors see the interpretive nature of museum content; Kee and Darbyson explore the possibilities of artificially constructed historical environments; and Seixas and Clark examine a specific controversy and then explore the ways in which controversies like it can be used to teach a critical disciplinary history.

**Perspectives on Historical Thinking**
The authors in Part 5 argue across a "great divide," as Ruth Sandwell did in her earlier chapter, but this time the great divide is the one often seen as separating history education from citizenship education. These authors explore aspects of citizenship and citizenship education in terms of their relationship to history education. In the process, they consider the relationship between students' ethnic identities and their historical understandings; the nature of the new history and civics curriculum in Quebec and the classroom contexts in which it is being implemented; and approaches to meeting the goals of both historical thinking and citizenship.

Carla Peck's research provides a cautionary note with regard to generalized notions of "the student." She explores how contemporary theorists employ the concepts of "ethnicity" and "ethnic identity"; she examines current research on the relationship between ethnic identity and students' historical understandings; and she discusses her own research into how students ascribe significance to historical events in the Canadian context. This research goes beyond simply attempting to correlate ethnic identity with ascriptions of significance; it does so by asking students to reflect on how they believe their ethnic identity influences the ways they ascribe significance. She has found that students bring complex identity-related frameworks to their study of history, and she calls for recognition of these differences on the part of both researchers and educators who teach history and citizenship.

Marc-André Éthier and David Lefrançois examine the highly contentious 2006 history and civics curriculum in Quebec, analyzing its strengths and weaknesses as well as its challenges. They also examine the textbooks that support the curriculum; approaches to student assessment; teachers' education and views on the reform; typical classroom practices and teaching conditions; and current research on Quebec students' abilities to think historically. They point out that the Programme de formation de l'école québécoise (Quebec Education Program) posits that the predominant mission of schools is to train autonomous individuals capable of acting as engaged, critical citizens and that this is largely what makes it so controversial.[48] They then analyze the curriculum for the conception of citizenship inherent in it. They conclude that the implicit expectation is that students should learn to base their opinions and civic consciousness on historical foundations, which should in turn help them become aware of their responsibilities as citizens. A danger of the curriculum is that it presents the institutions of the current Quebec parliamentary system in an unproblematic way, "almost as if they constituted the standard for liberal democracy." This chapter reveals that students' historical thinking is a rich area of research in Quebec. Researchers outside of Quebec have been largely unaware of this work because it is in French. It is imperative that we explore opportunities for its translation and dissemination.

In the final chapter of this volume, Alan Sears, a noted scholar of citizenship education, brings the discussion back to the goals of history education. He agrees with American history education researchers Keith Barton and Linda Levstik that some form of identification is necessary for democratic life. He argues that national identity should be acknowledged as a significant part of that identity, because democratic citizenship is most often lived out in a specific context that gives it both form and function and the nation state will provide that context for the foreseeable future. He then demonstrates how the fostering of agency, the development of understanding of the "Other," and the enhancement of public discourse are shared goals of both historical thinking and citizenship education. He notes that recent research into cognition has called for a truce between advocates for citizenship education – who work most often through the school subject of social studies – and advocates for history education. He contends that the fostering of civic competence is a key purpose of history education; and that, instead of engaging in fruitless turf battles, proponents in each field should join forces to achieve their common goal of a more vibrant education for citizenship.

These three final chapters venture into new territory. Carla Peck argues for granting students' identity-related frameworks a more central place in history education research – a change that, she contends, will benefit both students and the research itself. The other two chapters support Ken Osborne's argument favouring a central place for history in citizenship education. Éthier and Lefrançois describe an actual curriculum that attempts to combine the goals of teaching for citizenship with those of history education. Sears suggests that these goals are already synchronized; speaking directly to civics educators, he argues that they need to take into account the goals of history education. Éthier and Lefrançois point to the rich research into historical thinking that is presently being carried out in Quebec.

John Lewis Gaddis talks about the landscape of history: "For if you think of the past as a landscape, then history is the way we represent it, and it's that act of representation that lifts us above the familiar to let us experience vicariously what we can't experience directly: a wider view."[49] The current collection maps the landscape of history education research in Canada at the end of the first decade of the twenty-first century. This exercise in mental cartography has revealed questions that history education scholars have asked as well as the topics pursued, the books produced, and the understandings we have about how teachers teach and how students learn. We have seen where we have been, and we can see where we are at this time. We have also seen the new questions that are being raised and the directions in which they are pointing. For example, Amy von Heyking calls for more research – especially with elementary school children – into how students develop historical thinking abilities, so that we can better cultivate those abilities. Stéphane Lévesque takes this a step further, calling for investigations into progression – that is, how students progressively develop expertise in both substantive and procedural knowledge of history. Viviane Gosselin proposes a research agenda that explores the heuristic potential of a historical thinking framework with regard to museum exhibition production and reception. Highlighting the importance of museums as public institutions with a mandate to facilitate lifelong learning about the collective past, she points out that we know little about how this medium nurtures historical thinking or how visitors' conceptions of history influence how they engage with museum exhibitions.

Ruth Sandwell points to a gap between how historians conduct research and how they approach the teaching of their undergraduate students. When they stand behind a lectern at the front of a lecture theatre, they seem to forget the painstaking gathering of evidence and the time spent authenticating it, developing different explanations and trying them on for size, and so on. To their own students, they deliver a polished, chronological, tidy, one-thing-leads-to-another kind of account. She asks why this is so, and she calls for a bridge across the divide between historians and history teachers. We need to conduct research on the structural factors, such as post-secondary institutional promotion policies, that lead to this. We also need to find out more about the favoured teaching strategies of history professors. We have our own experiences, and we have anecdotal information, but what do we actually *know?* Is Gerald Friesen's approach an exception, or is it more typical than we realize? Why are there not more history education preparatory courses, such as the one taught by Ruth Sandwell?

All of the above are areas for fruitful research.

The endeavour of looking at history education in a historical context inevitably turns our gaze toward the future. As Gaddis reminds us: "Studying the past is no sure guide to predicting the future. What it does do, though, is to prepare you for the future by expanding experience, so that you can increase your skills, your stamina – and, if all goes well, your wisdom."[50] History education may not be on a trajectory toward becoming less contentious, but with a coherent research agenda, we will with time be equipped to take positions that are more informed in terms of what students understand and how they understand it, how we might reasonably expect them to progress, and how to best foster and assess that progress.

Over time, landscapes change; sometimes gradually, and at other times more dramatically, spurred by cataclysmic events. In the case of history education, change has been relatively gradual so far. Even so, if this book had been written ten years ago, the terrain would have been very different. Research will allow us to develop new insights into how students best learn history; and these, in turn, will lead to adaptations of classroom practices and resources. We cannot foresee what these new insights and changes in classroom practice will be, but we know they are coming because the momentum for change has become formidable. It is impossible to predict where we will be a decade hence.

## NOTES

1 See "Organizers Cancel Mock Battle of the Plains of Abraham," 17 February 2009, http://www.cbc.ca/canada; Victor Rabinovitch, "Narrating Public History and the Bomber Command Controversy (2005-07)," http://www.cha-shc.ca/public_history; Peter Seixas and Penney Clark, "Murals as Monuments: Students' Ideas about Depictions of Civilization in British Columbia," *American Journal of Education* 110, 2 (2004): 146-71 and Chapter 14 in this volume.

2 For the United States, see Edward T. Linenthal and Tom Engelhardt, eds., *History Wars: The Enola Gay and Other Battles for the American Past* (New York: Henry Holt, 1996); and Gary B. Nash, Charlotte Crabtree, and Ross E. Dunn, *History on Trial: Culture Wars and the Teaching of the Past* (New York: Vintage, 2000). For

*Introduction*

Australia, see Keith Windschuttle, *The Killing of History: How Literary Critics and Social Theorists Are Murdering Our Past* (Sydney: Macleay Press, 1994); and Stuart McIntyre and Anna Clark, *The History Wars* (Melbourne: Melbourne University Press, 2003).

3   Michael Bliss, "Privatizing the Mind: The Sundering of Canadian History, the Sundering of Canada," *Journal of Canadian Studies* 26, 4 (Winter 1991-92): 5-17. For responses to Bliss, see *Journal of Canadian Studies* 27, 2 (1992).
4   Ian McKay, "The Liberal Order Framework: A Prospectus for a Reconnaissance of Canadian History," *Canadian Historical Review* 81, 4 (December 2000): 617-45.
5   See Jean-François Constant and Michel Ducharme, eds., *Liberalism and Hegemony: Debating the Canadian Liberal Revolution* (Toronto: University of Toronto Press, 2009).
6   Christopher Dummitt and Michael Dawson, eds., *Contesting Clio's Craft: New Directions and Debates in Canadian History* (London: University of London, Institute for the Study of the Americas, 2009).
7   Christopher Dummitt, "After Inclusiveness: The Future of Canadian History," in *Contesting Clio's Craft*, 98-122.
8   Adele Perry, "Nation, Empire, and the Writing of History in Canada," in *Contesting Clio's Craft*, 123-40.
9   Magda Fahrni, "Reflections on the Place of Quebec in Historical Writing on Canada," in *Contesting Clio's Craft*, 1-20.
10  Andrew Smith, "Canadian Progress and the British Connection: Why Canadian Historians Seeking the Middle Road Should Give 2½ Cheers for the British Empire," in *Contesting Clio's Craft*, 75-97.
11  Michael Dawson and Catherine Gidney, "Persistence and Inheritance: Rethinking Periodisation and English Canada's 'Twentieth Century,'" in *Contesting Clio's Craft*, 47-74.
12  For a more detailed discussion of textbook controversies in Canada, see Penney Clark, "'The Most Fundamental of All Learning Tools': An Historical Investigation of Textbook Controversies in English Canada," in *Auf der Suche nach der wahren Art von Textbüchern*, ed. Angelo Van Gorp and Marc Depaepe (Bad Heilbrunn: Klinkhardt, 2009), 123-42.
13  See Charles W. Humphries, "The Banning of a Book in British Columbia," *BC Studies* 58 (Winter 1968-69): 1-12; and Frances M. Helyar, "A Crisis in History Education: The Life Story of Myers' General History Textbook in New Brunswick Schools (1910-1949)," master's thesis, University of New Brunswick, 2003.
14  Canada and Newfoundland Education Association, "Report of the Committee for the Study of Canadian History Textbooks," *Canadian Education* 1 (October 1945): 2-34; A.B. Hodgetts, *What Culture? What Heritage? A Study of Civic Education in Canada* (Toronto: OISE, 1968), 25, 45.
15  Marcel Trudel and Genevieve Jain, *Canadian History Textbooks: A Comparative Study*, Royal Commission on Biliguanlism and Biculturalism, Staff Study No. 5 (Ottawa: Queen's Printer, 1970).
16  Paul Lamy, "Political Socialization of French and English Canadian Youth: Socialization into Discord," in *Socialization and Values in Canadian Society*, vol. 1, ed. Elia

Zureik and Robert M. Pike (Toronto: McClelland and Stewart, 1975), 263-80; J.P. Richert, "The Impact of Ethnicity on the Perception of Heroes and Historical Symbols," *Canadian Review of Sociology and Anthropology* 8 (May 1974): 159-63; Marshal William Conley and Kenneth Osborne, "Political Education in Canadian Schools: An Assessment of Social Studies and Political Science Courses and Pedagogy," *International Journal of Political Education* 6 (1983): 65-85.

17 Garnet McDiarmid and David Pratt, *Teaching Prejudice: A Content Analysis of Social Studies Textbooks Authorized for Use in Ontario* (Toronto: OISE, 1971), 124.

18 L. Paton and J. Deverell, *Prejudice in Social Studies Textbooks* (Saskatoon: Saskatchewan Human Rights Commission, Modern Press, 1974); Nova Scotia Human Rights Commission, *Textbook Analysis – Nova Scotia* (Halifax: Queen's Printer, 1974); Manitoba Indian Brotherhood, *The Shocking Truth about Indians in Textbooks* (Winnipeg: Textbook Evaluation and Revision Committee of the Manitoba Indian Brotherhood, 1977).

19 Most provinces have social studies courses or a combination of social studies, social science, history, geography, and Canadian studies courses. History is an important component of mandatory social studies curricula, and most provinces offer elective history courses, which may be taken in addition to the mandatory social studies program. For example, British Columbia offers an elective world history course and a First Nations history course. See http://www.thenhier.ca for curriculum links to all provinces and territories.

20 Hilda Neatby, *So Little for the Mind* (Toronto: Clarke, Irwin, 1953), 162-63.

21 Ken Osborne, "The Changing Status of Canadian History in Manitoba," *Canadian Social Studies* 31, 1 (1996): 30.

22 J.L. Granatstein, *Who Killed Canadian History?* (Toronto: HarperCollins, 1998).

23 A.B. McKillop, "Who Killed Canadian History: A View from the Trenches," *Canadian Historical Review* 80, 2 (June 1999): 269-99; Graham Carr, "Review Essay: Harsh Sentences: Appealing the Strange Verdict of *Who Killed Canadian History?*" *American Review of Canadian Studies* (Spring-Summer 1998): 167-76.

24 Historica-Dominion Institute, http://www.historica-dominion.ca/en/about.

25 "The Canadian History Report Card: Curriculum Analysis of High Schools in Canada," http://www.newswire.ca/en/releases/archive.

26 Sahm Adrangi, "The Latest Canada Day Quiz Shows Many of Us Are in the Dark about War and Peace," *Globe and Mail*, 1 July 2003, A3; Shawn McCarthy, "Political History Not Our Forte," *Globe and Mail*, 11 January 2002, A4.

27 Jack Jedwab, "Does Knowledge of Canadian History Reinforce National Identity?" *Knowing Ourselves: The Challenge of Teaching History in Canadian Official Minority Language Communities*, presentation to Association for Canadian Studies Conference, Moncton, 5 November 2009.

28 Melinda McCracken, *Memories Are Made of This* (Toronto: James Lorimer, 1975), 79.

29 Hodgetts, *What Culture?* 25, 45.

30 See John N. Grant, "The Canada Studies Foundation: An Historical Overview," in *The Canada Studies Foundation*, ed. John N. Grant, Robert M. Anderson, and Peter L. McCreath (Toronto: 1986), 11.

*Introduction*

31 Peter Seixas, "Conceptualizing the Growth of Historical Understanding," in *Handbook of Education and Human Development: New Models of Learning, Teaching, and Schooling*, ed. David Olson and Nancy Torrance, (Oxford: Blackwell, 1996), 765-83; and refer to http://www.historybenchmarks.ca.

32 Alaric Dickinson, Peter Lee, and Peter Rogers, eds., *Learning History* (London: Heinemann, 1984); Christopher Portal, ed., *The History Curriculum for Teachers* (London: Falmer Press, 1987); Alaric Dickinson, Peter Gordon, Peter Lee, and J. Slater, eds., *International Yearbook of History Education* 1 (London: Woburn Press, 1995).

33 "Benchmarks 2006 Symposium," proposal, Peter Seixas personal files.

34 Peter N. Stearns, Peter Seixas, and Sam Wineburg, eds., *Knowing, Teaching, and Learning History: National and International Perspectives* (New York: New York University Press, 2000); Peter Seixas, ed., *Theorizing Historical Consciousness* (Toronto: University of Toronto Press, 2004); Ruth W. Sandwell, ed., *To the Past: History Education, Public Memory, and Citizenship in Canada* (Toronto: University of Toronto Press, 2006); Stéphane Lévesque, *Thinking Historically: Educating Students for the 21st Century* (Toronto: University of Toronto Press, 2008).

35 Mark Starowicz, *Making History: The Remarkable Story behind* Canada: A People's History (Toronto: McClelland and Stewart, 2002); Penney Clark, "Engaging the Field: A Conversation with Mark Starowicz," *Canadian Social Studies* 36, 2 (2003). http://www.quasar.ualberta.ca.

36 http://www.canadiansandtheirpasts.ca.

37 Ruth W. Sandwell, "Introduction: History Education, Public Memory, and Citizenship in Canada," in *To the Past*, 3-10.

38 The principal applicant was Penney Clark, University of British Columbia. The co-applicants were Margaret Conrad, University of New Brunswick; Kevin Kee, Brock University; Jocelyn Létourneau, Université de Laval; Stéphane Lévesque, University of Ottawa; Ruth Sandwell, OISE/University of Toronto; Peter Seixas, University of British Columbia; and Amy von Heyking, University of Lethbridge.

39 Alex Bennet and David Bennet, *Knowledge Mobilization in the Social Sciences and Humanities: Moving from Research to Action* (Frost: MQI Press, 2007). Other books dealing with a similar theme are Etienne Wenger, *Communities of Practice: Learning, Meaning, and Identity* (Cambridge, MA: Cambridge University Press, 1998); and Etienne Wenger, Richard McDermott, and William M. Snyder, *Cultivating Communities of Practice: A Guide to Managing Knowledge* (Cambridge, MA: Harvard Business School Press, 2002).

40 These concepts have been defined many times. These particular definitions were based on those provided in Peter Seixas, "A Modest Proposal for Change in Canadian History Education," *Teaching History* 137 (December 2009): 26-30.

41 Ibid, 28.

42 Ibid, 29.

43 Ibid.

44 Ken Osborne, "The Teaching of History and Democratic Citizenship," in *The Canadian Anthology of Social Studies: Issues and Strategies for Teachers*, ed. Roland Case and Penney Clark (Vancouver: Pacific Educational Press, 1997), 30.

45 Ibid., 35.
46 Carla Peck and Peter Seixas, "Benchmarks of Historical Thinking: First Steps," *Canadian Journal of Education* 31, 4 (2008), http://www.csse-scee.ca/CJE.
47 G. Williamson McDiarmid and Peter Vinten-Johansen, "A Catwalk across the Great Divide: Redesigning the History Teaching Methods Course," in *Knowing, Teaching, and Learning History*, 156.
48 MÉQ (Quebec Ministry of Education), *Programme de formation de l'école québecois Enseignement secondaire – 1$^{er}$ cycle* (Quebec: 2004), 4.
49 John Lewis Gaddis, *The Landscape of History: How Historians Map the Past* (New York: Oxford University Press, 2002), 5.
50 Ibid., 11.

PART 1

# HISTORY EDUCATION: CONTESTED TERRAIN

# A Brief Survey of Canadian Historiography

MARGARET CONRAD

Most professional historians in Canada today understand that the past is not history; it merely provides the raw materials they use to study the past. Since historians shape our memory of the past according to theories and methods of historical inquiry that are subject to change, it is important to grasp what is meant by the word "history" at any given time and place. Scholars use the word "historiography" to describe this effort at understanding the enterprise of producing history.[1]

In recent years, the lines between history – the study of the past – and historiography – the study of how history has been perceived and constructed – have begun to blur. Historians now recognize that their interpretations, like those of their predecessors, are shaped by present biases and interests. As a result, they are more modest in their claims to objectivity. Good historians strive to examine their own motivations, take pains to understand the context of earlier efforts to write the history of their topic, and concede that exploring the past from a variety of perspectives is the closest they can come to the ideal of objectivity. In other words, they are both historiographers and historians.

For Aboriginal societies in what is now Canada, historical memory was created mainly through oral testimony that could be modified as stories were passed from one generation to the next. Early European immigrants also relied on oral tradition, but they also brought with them written historical texts. Although interpretations of the past were often revised in written accounts, earlier texts could be used to show how research methods and perspectives on the past changed over time. The potential for comparative analysis eventually led to historiographical inquiry. Presumably, oral history could also be challenged by critical listeners, but few vocal critiques have survived the passage of time.

Canadian historiography as it pertains to written texts has its own rhythms and preoccupations that are embedded in the cultural traditions of the Western world. Historiography as a field of study arose in the nineteenth century, when university-based historians in Europe and North America began to dominate the production of history. In earlier periods, written history was largely the preserve of educated men, often priests or politicians, who wrote history to serve broader religious and political purposes. Professional historians were also mostly men and were preoccupied with political and military topics, but unlike their "amateur" predecessors, they developed methods of inquiry that reflected scientific principles of the time with regard to accuracy, objectivity, and predictability. For students of history, this meant spending an ever-expanding period in rigorous university training before "becoming" historians – that is, professionals who not only possessed factual information about the past and where to find reliable sources of information, but also were trained in assessing historical evidence and explaining the causes of change over time. In the twentieth century, the number of professional historians working both within and outside the academy expanded dramatically while the scope of history broadened to include economic, social, cultural, intellectual, and environmental topics.

At the same time that professional historians were honing their craft, the production of history continued outside the academy. Oral transmission of historical knowledge flourished, especially in families and small communities, and enthusiastic amateur historians often proved as adept as their academic counterparts at finding, assessing, and interpreting historical sources. As literacy increased, the public's interest in history grew, and this led to the founding of local history societies, the publication of popular history books, and the public commemoration of historical events. Meanwhile, governments at all levels tried to sustain historical memory for civic purposes by supporting the building of monuments, museums, and historic sites, and by encouraging the teaching of national history in the schools.

By the end of the twentieth century, the public's enthusiasm for history had intensified for reasons that are not altogether clear. It seems that a number of factors contributed to the "historical turn," including the rapid pace of change, which required people to reassess their identities; the explosion of new media, television and the Internet most notably; and the expansion of leisure time. The past suddenly became a vast reservoir for activists, fiction writers, film producers, genealogists, hobbyists, journalists, politicians, and tourism promoters. Although critics complained that this enthusiasm for heritage bore little resemblance to the practice of academic history, the distinction between history and heritage proved difficult to sustain. Many public historians, including curators at museums and historic sites, were academically trained, and academic historians had long claimed that their research had relevance beyond the ivory tower. As the Internet made academic research more accessible to a wider audience, professional historians found that they, too, were public historians, and they were being called upon to communicate in ways that would make their work more accessible to those not trained in the field. The distinction between public history (representations of the past for public consumption) and academic history (what professionals produce for one another) still holds, but there is a lot of overlap between the two approaches.

What role history will play in the future is anybody's guess. Some critics lament the fracturing of professional history into narrow specialties; others predict the "end of history" – that is, thinking with a historical perspective – as we hurtle toward the future-fixated Information Age. Still others rejoice at the expanding scope and popularity of history, which now finds an audience at historic sites and museums, on television channels devoted entirely to historical programming, in bookstore sections dominated by history books, and in the virtual universe of the World Wide Web. The recent scholarly preoccupation with the study of historical consciousness, historical memory, and public uses of the past suggests that we are entering a new phase in our understanding of history, one that not only acknowledges the limits of the truth-seeking goals of historical inquiry but also addresses – sometimes in unsettling ways – the role that history plays in shaping present identities and imagining future goals.

Any examination of Canadian historiography at the beginning of the twenty-first century must take into account several factors besides the philosophical positions of individual historians. These include the distinct historiographical traditions of First Peoples, English Canadians, and French Canadians; the parallel roads taken by amateur and professional historians; and the impact of cultural factors such as class, ethnicity, gender, race, region, and religion in the writing of history. Only a few aspects of these complex historiographical matters can be explored here.

## Aboriginal History and Oral Tradition

Before the 1960s, Canadian history texts generally began with the "discovery" of the "New World" by European explorers. Historians argued that the discipline of history was restricted to archival sources and therefore to literate peoples; this left the study of pre-contact Aboriginal societies to anthropologists and archaeologists. Fortunately, these rigid boundaries between disciplines have begun to break down. By piecing together evidence from Aboriginal oral accounts, European observations, anthropological studies, archaeological evidence, and relevant data provided by meteorologists, biologists, and other scientists, ethnohistorians have managed to understand more clearly what life was like for the early peoples who lived in the area that we now call Canada.[2]

Each Aboriginal nation has its own version of its pre-contact history and of its relations with newcomers to the continent. The tradition of handing down history orally from one generation to the next was firmly established long before the Europeans arrived, yet only relatively recently have professional historians lent much credence to this approach to the past. Historians trained in the European tradition (i.e., to analyze written documents) contended that oral history merely recreated the past with present-day interests in mind; in other words, it took views that were currently fashionable and projected them back in time so that they appeared to be eternal truths. It is now widely recognized that oral traditions are more reliable than text-bound historians formerly believed and that written documents are also shaped by biases. Scholars generally accept that all sources used by historians to understand the past must be placed in their contexts and subjected to critical scrutiny.

The question of whether oral history traditions are as valid as the written record is more than academic. By the late twentieth century, courts were being forced to address the competing claims of Aboriginal oral traditions and the written records of government officials. In 1991 a Justice of the Supreme Court of British Columbia issued a verdict in *Delgamuukw* that rejected the land claims of the Gitskan-Wet'suwet'en First Nation, whose case relied heavily on oral history. That decision was appealed to the Supreme Court of Canada, which, in a 1997 ruling, explicitly affirmed the admissibility of oral history in efforts by Aboriginal peoples to establish their rights in court.[3]

A useful discussion of indigenous approaches to the past is found in the *Report of the Royal Commission on Aboriginal Peoples* (1996). Before proceeding with their inquiry, the commissioners were obliged to sort out the issues relating to historical method. In contrast to the Western historical tradition, the Aboriginal approach was perceived to be

> neither linear nor steeped in the same notions of social progress and evolution. Nor is it usually human-centred in the same way as the western scientific tradition, for it does not assume that human beings are anything more than one – and not necessarily the most important – element of the natural order of the universe. Moreover, the Aboriginal historical tradition is an oral one, involving legends, stories, and accounts handed down through the generations in oral form. It is less focused on establishing objective truth and assumes that the teller of the story is so much a part of the event being described that it would be arrogant to classify or categorize the event exactly or for all time.[4]

These subtle distinctions are important for understanding how perceptions of the past influence the present. For further discussion of these points, see Michael Marker's chapter in this volume.

## Writing History

When Europeans arrived in North America, they brought with them written texts that they called histories. The Bible served for many Europeans as the model history text – indeed, the Reformation sparked by Martin Luther in the early sixteenth century focused on the reading and interpretation of biblical texts – but secular histories were also becoming popular as the Renaissance in learning and culture spread throughout Europe. By reconnecting to the societies of Ancient Greece and Rome, Europeans developed a complex sense of a linear past that stretched back several millennia. Eighteenth-century European scholars, who saw themselves as more advanced than their forebears, began to present history as a story of progress to a better world than had hitherto existed and drew a line between religious and secular approaches to the past.

In the early years of European settlement of North America, narratives called "histories" were little more than travel accounts intended to satisfy curiosity about the "new world," or to promote commercial investment and settlement. F.X. Charlevoix's *Histoire et description general de la Nouvelle France* (1744) is one of the best of these early descriptive accounts. A Jesuit priest who visited New France in the early eighteenth century, Charlevoix had a clear eye for detail and documented political, military, and religious developments in the colony. The genre continued into the nineteenth century with, for example, Peter Fisher's *Sketches of New Brunswick containing an account of the first settlement of New Brunswick* (1825), T.C. Haliburton's two-volume *An Historical and Statistical Account of Nova Scotia* (1829), and Joseph James Hargrave's *Red River* (1871).

The rise of nationalism in the nineteenth century in the Western world inspired an unprecedented interest in the past as historians rushed to chart the origins and characteristics of emerging nation-states.[5] In the United Province of Canada (today's Quebec and Ontario), two works in this tradition are particularly noteworthy: François-Xavier Garneau's *Histoire du Canada depuis sa découverte jusqu'à nos jours*, published in four volumes (1845-52); and John Mercier McMullen's *The History of Canada from Its First Discovery to the Present* (1855). Garneau was inspired to write by the comment made in Lord Durham's *Report* (1839) that French Canadians were "a people with no history, and no literature"; McMullen wrote to celebrate his belief that English Canadians had both. Influenced by French historians of the time, Garneau fixed upon "racial" – by which he meant cultural – antagonism as the driving force of history, arguing that the central theme of French Canadian society was the struggle for survival against outside forces, which included French imperialists and British conquerors. This view continued to inspire francophone historians well into the twentieth century. McMullen looked to the colonial past to foster a spirit of Canadian nationalism among British North Americans. Maintaining that his was the best of times, McMullen saw material progress and responsible government in the British Empire as the twin pillars upon which the United Canadas – effectively Canada West – would achieve their national destiny.

Following Confederation in 1867, the liberal themes emphasized by McMullen were expanded in English Canada to encompass the entire nation, most notably by William Kingsford, who produced an eccentric ten-volume *History of Canada* (1887-98). More accessible to general readers were the biographies of Canada's "founding fathers" served up in the twenty volumes of the *Makers of Canada* (1902-8). In Quebec, the influence of the Roman Catholic Church ensured that the liberal ideology reflected in the first edition of Garneau's *Histoire* would be superseded by an emphasis on the providential mission of French Canadians to pursue a religious destiny in North America. Much of the history written in Quebec after Confederation was produced by priests such as Henri-Raymond Casgrain (1831-1904), who focused on larger-than-life figures in a heroic, albeit embattled, French Canadian past.

For most of the nineteenth century, Canadian historians were educated amateurs who came to the field out of enthusiasm rather than formal training. Haliburton and Garneau were lawyers, McMullen was a businessman and journalist, and Kingsford was an engineer. Even historian-priests who held college degrees were educated in theology, not in the methods of the new academic history that was rapidly gaining ascendancy. Pioneered by Leopold von Ranke in his seminars at the University of Berlin, the new academic history emphasized archival research, careful documentary analysis, and accuracy – portraying the past "exactly as it was." By the end of the nineteenth century, universities in Europe and the United States were teaching courses in history, and a few even offered doctoral degrees in the subject.

## The Professionals

In Canada's fledgling universities, history was rarely taught as a discipline separate from theology, classics, and literature until the 1890s. The appointment of Oxford-trained scholar G.M. Wrong to the newly created Chair of History at the University of Toronto in 1894 is usually taken as the beginning of the new academic history in English Canada. Three years earlier, Queen's University had appointed Adam Shortt to its Sir John A. Macdonald Chair of Political Science, and from that position he began to explore the economic and social history of Canada. In Quebec, Thomas Chapais and Lionel Groulx are credited with laying the foundations for a more academic approach to historical inquiry. Chapais wrote biographies of Jean Talon and the Marquis de Montcalm; he also published *Cours d'histoire du Canada* (8 vols, 1919-34), which covered the conquest to Confederation. Abbé Lionel Groulx's lectures in Canadian history at the Montreal campus of Laval University (now Université de Montréal) in 1915 led to his appointment as the first full-time professor of Canadian history in a francophone university.[6]

These men were not charting new directions in a vacuum. The creation of the Public Archives of Canada (now Library and Archives Canada) in 1872, under the direction of Douglas Brymner, testified to the growing interest in collecting historical documents, while the formation of the Royal Society of Canada in 1882 gave a few academic and public historians a forum in which to disseminate their archival research.[7] The historian Carl Berger notes that after its founding in 1882, the Royal Society and its affiliates became major outlets for "enthusiasm for recovering the past and the literary departments of its *Transactions* in both French and English were dominated by historical studies."[8] Of the thirty-six organizations affiliated with the

Royal Society in 1900, two-thirds were historical in character; they included a group from the Six Nations as well as two women's historical societies. Until the middle of the twentieth century, the line between academic and amateur historians remained blurred. When the Canadian Historical Association (CHA) was founded in 1922, academic historians and archivists made up less than one-seventh of its membership.[9]

Although their work reflected the same moral issues, romantic nationalism, and ethnocentrism that preoccupied their predecessors, Wrong and Groulx are credited with laying the foundations for new professional directions. Wrong established *Review of Historical Publications Relating to Canada*, the precursor of *Canadian Historical Review* (1920) in 1896; he also participated in the founding of the Champlain Society in 1905 as a vehicle for publishing historical documents; and he was a founding member in 1922 of the CHA. Groulx convened conferences on Quebec history in 1925 and 1945, was instrumental in the creation of history departments at both Laval and Montreal, and helped establish the Institut d'histoire de l'Amérique français in 1946 and the *Revue d'histoire de l'Amérique français* the following year.

By that time, the new academic history was making its mark in English Canada. Adam Shortt and Arthur Doughty, Brymner's successor at the Public Archives, produced a twenty-three-volume series, *Canada and Its Provinces* (1913-17), that showcased archival research and what they believed to be objective analysis. Reflecting their own preoccupation with the triumph of industrial capitalism and the evolution of Canada as an independent nation-state, they abandoned romantic notions about Canada's role in the British Empire, substituting instead hard-headed economic and political analysis. They were also sensitive to regional differences. Both men were broadly liberal in their sentiments and emphasized Canada's march toward liberalism in its institutional and intellectual development.

As Canada moved along the road to independence within the British Empire and into the economic orbit of the United States following the First World War, academic historians shifted their focus to the geographic, demographic, and economic forces underlying continental ties, increasingly taking their cue from south of the border. In the interwar years, Frank Underhill adapted a progressive political approach, pioneered by American scholar Charles Beard, in his critique of Canadian elites; other scholars wrestled with the implications of Frederick Jackson Turner's claim that the frontier had been instrumental in shaping the American democratic spirit. The "frontier thesis" informed the thinking of many of the historians who contributed to the twenty-five-volume Carnegie-sponsored series on Canadian-American relations that appeared between 1936 and 1945. The chief adviser for the project was Canadian-born historian J.B. Brebner, who, from his base at Columbia University, produced two books on the impact of Massachusetts on Nova Scotia in the eighteenth century: *New England's Outpost* (1927) and *The Neutral Yankees of Nova Scotia* (1937). He also wrote a highly influential study titled *North Atlantic Triangle: The Interplay of Canada, the United States, and Great Britain* (1945).

Inspiration and financing for historical scholarship may have come from outside the country, but the findings soon began to reflect nationalist tendencies within Canadian borders. The most widely regarded of this new crop of scholars was Harold Innis, a political economist based at the University of Toronto. In his groundbreaking books *The Fur Trade in Canada* (1930) and *The Cod Fisheries* (1940), Innis rooted Canada's political distinctiveness in its economic history. He argued that the export of staple, or primary, products – first fish and fur, later timber, wheat, and minerals – to more mature economies had laid the foundations for Canada's east-west political boundaries. The "staples thesis" found an enthusiastic audience among Canadians seeking a national identity separate from that of their powerful southern neighbour; it also inspired a generation of historical research. Arthur Lower, who taught history at Wesley College in Winnipeg from 1929 to 1947 before moving to Queen's University, explored the timber trade in three books published during the 1930s. Donald Creighton, a historian at the University of Toronto, identified Canada's major waterway as the environmental determinant of Canadian unity in *Commercial Empire of the St. Lawrence, 1760-1850* (1937). Creighton's "Laurentian thesis" led him to explore political themes, including the background to Confederation and the career of Canada's first prime minister, John A. Macdonald.[10] Meanwhile, one of Creighton's colleagues, J.M.S. Careless, turned his attention to the metropolitan dominance of the St. Lawrence heartland and to the career of George Brown, founder of the *Globe* and leader of the Reform Party of Canada West.[11] Before 1960 only a few Canadian historians – most notably W.L. Morton in two books, *The Progressive Party of Canada* (1950) and *Manitoba* (1957); and Margaret A. Ormsby in *British Columbia: A History* (1958) – had focused their attention on the regions of Canada neglected by the Laurentian historians.

Nationalist themes also shaped the thinking of academic historians in Quebec, many of whom had been trained in the United States. Most of the young men who taught Canadian history at Laval (Marcel Trudel, Fernand

Ouellet, Jean Hamelin) and Montreal (Michel Brunet, Guy Frégault, Maurice Séguin) rejected Groulx's interest in the miraculous cultural survival of French Canadians after the conquest, turning instead to examinations of the historical roots of their economic inferiority. By the 1960s, distinct schools of historical thought had developed at Laval and Montreal. The Montreal historians tended to lay blame for Quebec's economic inferiority on the British conquerors. In *La guerre de la Conquête* (1954), Frégault emphasized the "normal" state of colonial development before the conquest; Brunet in *Canadians and Canadiens* (1954) lashed out at his compatriots for their worship of rural life and their acceptance of imperial domination in its British *and* Canadian manifestations. Brunet pointed to the "decapitation" of the social structure when elites returned to France following the conquest as a key element in creating a colonized people. At Laval, Trudel and his colleagues drew inspiration from the *Annales* school in France, whose practitioners studied long-term geographic, economic, and social forces. Hamelin, in his *Économie et société en Nouvelle-France* (1960), emphasized structural flaws in colonial society under the old regime; Ouellet in *Histoire économique et sociale du Québec, 1760-1850* (1966) rigorously charted economic and social trends that he claimed had more to do with the fate of Quebec than with the fact of the conquest. As the Quiet Revolution ran its course, these positions took on direct political implications: the Montreal perspective called for special status or even independence for Quebec; the Laval perspective called for working within the system to achieve desired ends.

There was little room in university history departments for women or for men from minority cultures. As happened in many professions, history became the preserve of a small cadre of white men, who took pains to police the boundaries of their craft. The few women who were admitted to graduate studies or who were hired by history departments – among the latter were Margaret Ormsby, Hilda Neatby, and Margaret Prang – often faced blatant discrimination. Female students were excluded from the Historical Club at the University of Toronto when it was founded in 1904, and meetings of the CHA sometimes included social events at clubs to which women were denied access.[12] As a result, female scholars such as Isabel Skelton and Esther Clark Wright often pursued solitary careers as historians.[13]

## The New Social History

In the 1960s and 1970s, the academic study of history underwent a sea change: university history departments grew in numbers of students and faculty; graduate programs proliferated across the nation; new ideologies – Marxism, feminism, and multiculturalism in particular – challenged the prevailing orthodoxies; new methodologies, many of them inspired by the social sciences, suggested different approaches to exploring the past; new technologies, most notably the computer, made it possible to process huge amounts of information; new funding bodies, such as the Canada Council (est. 1957) and its academic successor the Social Sciences and Humanities Research Council (est. 1978), fuelled research activity; and new history journals (such as *Acadiensis, BC Studies, Canadian Bulletin of Medical History, Historical Studies in Education, Histoire Sociale, Labour/Le Travail, Northern Review,* and *Urban History Review*) were launched to focus on regional and social topics.

As in the past, the directions were inspired by developments in Europe and the United States, but the applications were distinctly Canadian. Not surprisingly, the old history produced by professional elites – most of them ensconced in the larger universities in Quebec and Ontario – was found wanting. Nevertheless, two of these establishment figures, Ramsay Cook and J.M.S. Careless, were among the first to urge historians to take up what became known as the "new social history" by exploring Canada's "limited identities" of region, class, and ethnicity.[14] Women and racialized minorities – First Nations and African Canadians in particular – soon added their voices to the chorus demanding a more inclusive approach to the past.[15] In short order, an explosion of research on the history of the working class, women, cultural minorities, and neglected areas of the country began to appear in journals, anthologies, and monographs. The new social historians knew they had arrived when their work began spawning survey texts to disseminate the findings in their prolific subfields. Examples include Bryan Palmer's *Working-Class Experience: The Rise and Reconstitution of Canadian Labour, 1800-1980* (1983); Jacques Rouillard's *Histoire du syndicalisme Québécois* (1989) on labour and working-class history; Micheline Dumont and colleagues' (Le Collectif Clio) *L'Histoire des femmes au Québec depuis quatre siècles* (1982); Alison Prentice and colleagues' *Canadian Women: A History* (1988) on women's history; J.R. Miller's *Skyscrapers Hide the Heavens: A History of Indian-White Relations in Canada* (1989); and Olive Patricia Dickason's *Canada's First Nations: A History of Founding Peoples from Earliest Times* (1992) on Aboriginal history. Other subfields took on new life when explored through the lenses of class, culture, gender, and region.[16]

It was in this context that the history of education itself came under intense scrutiny.[17] In 1970 J.D. Wilson, Robert M. Stamp, and Louis-Philippe Audet published a volume of essays informed by the view that "educational history should be regarded as social history."[18] The field of social history was insufficiently developed in 1970 to enable the authors to advance too far beyond the classic survey by C.E. Phillips, *The Development of Education in Canada* (1957), but it was not long before articles and monographs offering a critical perspective on education began pouring off the presses. While it is impossible to do justice to all of the research inspired by the new social history, several highly influential books suggest the range and depth of analysis that forever changed how the history of education was perceived: Alison Prentice focused on issues of class, gender, and race in *The School Promoters: Education and Social Class in Mid-Nineteenth-Century Upper Canada* (1977); Harvey J. Graff offered a new understanding of literacy in *The Literacy Myth: Literacy and Social Structure in the Nineteenth-Century City* (1979); Jean Barman explored the world of private schooling in *Growing Up in British Columbia: Boys in Private Schools* (1984); Chad Gaffield tackled religion and language in *Language, Schooling, and Cultural Conflict: The Origin of French-Language Controversy in Ontario* (1987); and historical sociologist Bruce Curtis brought notions of governance developed by European scholars Antonio Gramsci and Michel Foucault to two remarkable volumes: *Building the Educational State: Canada West, 1836-1871* (1988); and *True Government by Choice Men? Inspection, Education, and State Formation in Canada West* (1992). Every level of education was analyzed, including high schools, teachers colleges, Aboriginal residential schools, and universities.[19] In 1986 George S. Tomkins explored curriculum development in *A Common Countenance: Stability and Change in the Canadian Curriculum* (1986), a study so comprehensive that it was reissued in 2008. Meanwhile, the output of journal articles and essay collections on the history of education reached such a torrent in the latter decades of the twentieth century that writing a new synthesis to supersede Phillips was like shooting at a moving target. Nevertheless, Paul Axelrod managed to capture the major themes in *The Promise of Schooling: Education in Canada, 1800-1914* (1997). Kenneth Osborne's *In Defence of History: Teaching the Past and the Meaning of Democratic Citizenship* (1995) offered a timely reflection on the role of history in schools and in society generally.

In Quebec, the new social history was widely embraced and found expression in a highly influential two-volume synthesis, *Histoire du Québec contemporain* (1979 and 1986), produced by Paul-André Linteau, René Durocher, and Jean-Claude Robert. This trio turned their focus away from the conquest to the post-Confederation period, which they claimed revealed Quebec to be a "normal" industrializing society, with all the trends – class antagonisms, migration, secularization, and urbanization – found in other societies undergoing a similar transformation. By taking this perspective, they reflected the new optimism of francophone Quebecers who had come of age during the Quiet Revolution, when a sense of defeat and demoralization gave way to purpose and ambition.

Beginning in the 1960s, the Atlantic region, the West, and the North – the "other" of the metropolitan thesis – also began to inspire serious historical scholarship. Growing discontent with the political and economic domination of Confederation by Ontario and Quebec meant that there was an enthusiastic audience for historical studies that explored the causes of the colonial condition of people living in the St. Lawrence hinterland. Gerald Freisen and Jean Barman were among the many historians who began to offer a new Western perspective on events.[20] David Alexander, Ernest R. Forbes, and P.A. Buckner penned thoughtful critiques of a "national" historiography that ignored developments in Atlantic Canada.[21] In *Eastern and Western Perspectives* (1981), edited by David Bercuson and P.A. Buckner, the margins briefly came together to examine aspects of their common predicament. The North, too, attracted scholarly interest, much of it from academics based in southern Canada. With *Northern Visions: New Perspectives on the North in Canadian History* (2001), edited by Kerry Abel and Ken Coates, a northern historiography was established. Attempts to incorporate social history into a survey text for university students yielded a run of new English-language textbooks, two of which appeared with similar titles underscoring their social history perspective: J.M. Bumsted's *The Peoples of Canada* (2 vols., 1992); and Margaret Conrad, Alvin Finkel, and Cornelius Jaenen with Veronica Strong-Boag, *History of the Canadian Peoples* (2 vols., 1993).

## Postmodernism

By the century's end, historians of all political stripes were reeling under the impact of "postmodern" theories that called into question any claims to truth and objectivity in the production of historical accounts. Postmodern philosophy is a form of skepticism that recognizes that knowledge is not simply a reflection of reality, but, rather, that reality is created in the process of knowing it. Drawing on the insights of European scholars such as Roland Barthes, Jacques Derrida, Jacques Lacan, and Michel Foucault, postmodernists deconstruct meaning – often through processes of close textual analysis – and underscore the importance of language and differing interpretations of words by those who hear or read them.[22] Of course, such questioning of the fundamental nature of historical knowledge was not new, nor was it particularly Canadian in origin, but it came at a time when the coherence of nation-states generally and of Canada in particular was coming under the dual threat of globalization and cultural pluralism. With a growing independence movement in Quebec, and with national boundaries seemingly dissolving under the impact of free trade agreements, international institutions, and new communications technologies, history was soon being called into service to "save" the nation.

A few historians in English Canada, mistaking the effect for the cause of social change, and conflating the new social history with postmodern theory, accused their colleagues of contributing to the chaos by abandoning "national" topics for narrow, particularistic interests.[23] In his widely read critique *Who Killed Canadian History?* (1998), J.L. Granatstein accused his academic colleagues of "professing trivia" at the expense of the national narrative.[24] Charting the major themes in the nation's political and military history, he argued, was infinitely more important than exploring such insignificant developments as "housemaid's knee in Belleville." This dismissal of the new social history brought sharp responses from many scholars, most notably from A.B. McKillop, who not only affirmed the value of household labour in Canadian economic development but also made a compelling case for the work that social historians do in helping Canadians understand past developments that had contributed to challenges facing the country.[25]

In Quebec, where history had long been a staple in the school curriculum and in defining francophone identity, the debate took a somewhat different turn, focusing on what kind of historical narrative was appropriate in preparing Quebecers to situate themselves in a globalizing world. In this debate, Jocelyn Létourneau took a postnationalist approach, arguing that the time had come to abandon the preoccupation with the sorrows and grievances of the past and imagine a new history that would better serve Quebec as it moved into the future.[26] His arguments raised considerable controversy, pitting him against neo-nationalist Gérard Bouchard, who, in a number of influential publications, emphasized the experience of Quebecers from the point of view of their separate and still embattled *national* identity in North America.[27] As was the case earlier in the twentieth century, these positions were seen to reflect federalist and separatist sentiments, which continued to compete for ascendancy in the province.[28]

## History in Public

While university-based historians slugged it out on issues of theory, method, and content, interest in Canadian history among the general public continued to grow. In the second half of the twentieth century, the histories published by journalists such as Pierre Berton, Sandra Gwyn, and Peter C. Newman commanded a much larger readership than most academic monographs. In Quebec, Jacques Lacoursière became a household name with his popular books, films, and television programs on Quebec history. The CHA, meanwhile, launched a booklet series in 1953 specifically to appeal to a wider readership. To everyone's surprise, these booklets proved remarkably popular. G.F.G. Stanley's *Louis Riel: Patriot or Rebel/Louis Riel: Patriote ou rebelle?* for example, sold 67,077 copies in English and 18,917 in French between 1954 and 2004. Academic historians also participated in two bilingual, multi-volume projects – the *Centenary Series,* and the *Dictionary of Canadian Biography* – designed to synthesize scholarly research for a larger audience. Volumes from these initiatives began to appear in time for Canada's one hundredth birthday, an anniversary that further inspired popular interest in Canada's past.

In the 1990s, the debates among university-based historians intersected with a growing public concern that Canadians knew little about their history. Most Canadians, polls revealed, were unable to name Canada's first prime minister and were as likely to name an American historical figure as a Canadian one in answer to basic questions about their nation's history. Granatstein's controversial book was only one of many initiatives designed to raise history from its deathbed. Others included the founding of three organizations to promote Canadian history – the CRB Foundation (1986), which morphed into Historica (1999); the National History Society (1994); and the Dominion Institute (1997) – all initially funded by major Canadian corporations. In addition, the CBC, under the energetic leadership of Mark Starowitz, launched an ambitious CBC/Radio Canada millennium project to chronicle the history of Canada on film in *Canada: A People's History;* and in January 1999, McGill University's new Institute for the Study of Canada, under the direction of Desmond Morton, hosted the first in a series of conferences on "Giving the Past a Future." If nothing else, these initiatives demonstrated that history was entering the twenty-first century as a powerful force.[29]

This truth became painfully obvious when historical representations in public institutions became embroiled in controversy. At the Royal Ontario

Museum, an exhibition on African history was criticized by some African Canadians for sacrificing sensitivity to academic perspectives. Interpretations of Canada's involvement in the strategic bombing of Germany during the Second World War in the film *The Valour and the Horror* (1992) and at the new Canadian War Museum (2005) drew fierce criticism from some veterans and their supporters, which prompted two Senate hearings. In challenging representations of the past in this way, Canadians were putting history to civic uses different from those envisioned by politicians and educators, who saw history as a vehicle for building national coherence. As a resource for shoring up imperilled imagined communities in a period of great change, history offered many Canadians a resource for establishing identity, morality, immortality, and agency. This had long been the case, but public controversy had rarely been so protracted.

Inevitably, academic historians began to examine public engagement with the past in all its complexity. The pioneering research on imagined communities, historical memory, and historical consciousness by European scholars such as Benedict Anderson, Pierre Nora, and Jörn Rüsen was read with great interest by Canadian historians who shared with their European counterparts a preoccupation with national narratives.[30] Canadians have yet to experience the kind of historical revisionism that prevailed in Russia and Germany following major regime changes; that said, the example of those countries underscores the instability of interpretations of the past in periods of political and social transformation. Peter Seixas, who in 2001 established the Centre for the Study of Historical Consciousness, and Jocelyn Létourneau have played leading roles in bringing this new historiographical approach to Canada.[31]

Reflecting the growing popular interest in history, a new subfield called public history emerged to train historians in the skills of producing and communicating in public venues. Public historians are usually defined as those working *outside* the academy – in archives, museums, history sites, historical societies, government departments, private firms, and the various media. For the most part, these practitioners require the same awareness regarding content, theories, and methods of historical inquiry as those toiling in the academic stream, but academic historians do their work in university settings, writing often – but not exclusively – for one another, whereas public historians conduct their research and teaching outside academic milieux, often using methods other than written texts when presenting their work to a diversified audience.[32]

## What's Next?

By the turn of the twenty-first century, Canadian historians were being influenced by comparative, transnational, and Atlantic perspectives inspired by general globalizing trends. A sampling of historiographical approaches by a new generation of Canadian scholars appeared in Christopher Dummitt and Michael Dawson, eds., *Contesting Clio's Craft: New Directions and Debates in Canadian History* (2009). As the first volume since Carl Berger's *Contemporary Approaches to Canadian History* (1987) to focus on new historiographical directions in a comprehensive way, it suggests what might lie ahead in the field of Canadian history.

Notwithstanding the proliferation of approaches to Canada's past and a drift from national frameworks, there has been a lingering interest in understanding what Canada is about as a historical enterprise. Two historians, Gerald Friesen and Ian McKay, developed provocative new ways of addressing this question. In *Citizens and Nation: An Essay on History, Communication, and Canada* (2000), Friesen fixed on the dominant means of communications as a way of understanding Canada. His approach linked social history with the later work of Harold Innis and of Innis's student Marshall McLuhan in communications history, demonstrating how distinct political economies based on oral traditions, print texts, and screens defined succeeding epochs. By focusing on communications and human agency, Friesen helped his readers situate themselves in a world that was being transformed rapidly by the new information and communications technology represented by the Internet.

McKay, meanwhile, suggested that historians take a new look at the ideologies that have defined modern Canada. In an influential article published in *Canadian Historical Review* in 2000, he argued that the achievement of responsible government and Confederation were early steps in what he called the "project of liberal rule." Although he singled out individualism, rule of law, civil liberties, and property rights as key components of this ideology, he also maintained that liberalism is "something more akin to a secular religion or a totalizing philosophy than to a manipulated set of political ideas." The success of the liberal world view, he argued, makes it difficult for Canadians to see its manifestations clearly, but he emphasized "the enormity of what the Canadian liberal undertook – the replacement, often of antithetical traditions and forms that had functioned for centuries, and even millennia, with new conceptions of the human being and society."[33] Not surprisingly, historians have disagreed about the extent to which the liberal order has prevailed in Canada, either in the mid-nineteenth century or later. Jerry Bannister, for example, has noted that older aristocratic–loyalist notions have remained an essential feature of the Canadian story (a monarch is still the head of state, for example), and Ruth Sandwell has argued that communal values as expressed in families have complicated the embrace of liberalism by many Canadians, especially by women.[34] This discussion will no doubt percolate for some time, bringing historians back – though with a much different lens – to the theme of liberalism, which informed historical inquiry in the late nineteenth and early twentieth centuries.

The timeliness of McKay's call for a revision of Canada's past in a world where liberalism is in retreat, and of Friesen's focus on the individual in the face of revolutions in communication, underscores the value of the discipline of history as a way of understanding the place of human beings in the world. Along with literature, history has long been central to identifying, interpreting, and sharing the values on which civil society depends. This kind of knowledge, much discounted in a society driven by stock market swings, the clash of civilizations, and doomsday scenarios, is important and perhaps even crucial to our well-being as a species on this planet.[35]

**NOTES**

This chapter is an expanded version of an entry on "historiography" in *Encyclopedia of Literature in Canada*, ed. William New (Toronto: University of Toronto Press, 2002) and benefits greatly from comments by members of the THEN/HiER collective.

1 For discussions of the general trends in historiography, see Norman J. Wilson, *History in Crisis? Recent Directions in Historiography*, 2nd ed. (Upper Saddle River: Pearson/Prentice Hall, 2005); and George G. Iggers, ed., *Historiography in the Twentieth Century: From Scientific Objectivity to the Postmodern Challenge* (Hanover: University Press of New England, 1997).

2 Toby Morntz discusses the problems associated with trying to reconcile different historical approaches in "Plunder or Harmony? On Merging European and Native Views of Early Contact," in *Canada and Europe in Decentring the Renaissance: Multidisciplinary Perspective*, ed. Germain Warkentin and Carol Podruchny (Toronto: University of Toronto Press, 2001), 48-67. For a discussion of Aboriginal oral history in the Canadian context, see Winona Wheeler, "Reflections on the Social Relations of Indigenous History," in *Walking a Tightrope: Aboriginal Peoples and Their Representations*, ed. Ute Lischke and David T. McNab (Waterloo: Wilfrid Laurier University Press, 2005), 189-213. Julie Cruikshank has played a leading role in advancing the use and understanding of the complicated genre of indigenous oral history in three important books: *Life Lived as a Story: The Life Stories of Three Yukon Native Elders* (Vancouver: UBC Press, 1992); *The Social Life of Stories: Narrative and*

*Knowledge in the Yukon Territory* (Vancouver: UBC Press, 1998); and *Do Glaciers Listen? Local Knowledge, Colonial Encounters, and Social Imagination* (Vancouver: UBC Press, 2005).

3   See "Aboriginal Title: The Supreme Court of Canada Decision in *Delgamuukw v. British Columbia*" (2000) http://www.parl.gc.ca.

4   Royal Commission on Aboriginal Peoples, *Part One: The Relationship in Historical Perspective* (1996), http://www.ainc-inac.gc.ca.

5   Early developments in the writing of Canadian history are discussed in M. Brook Taylor, *Promoters, Patriots, and Partisans: Historiography in Nineteenth-Century English Canada* (Toronto: University of Toronto Press, 1989); and Serge Gagnon, *Quebec and Its Historians: 1840-1920* (Montreal: Harvest House, 1982). See also A.B. McKillop, "Historiography in English"; and Pierre Savard, "Historiography in French," in *The Canadian Encyclopedia* http://www.thecanadianencyclopedia.com.

6   On the rise of professional history in Canada, see Carl Berger, *The Writing of Canadian History: Aspects of English Canadian Historical Writing Since 1900*, 2nd ed. (Toronto: University of Toronto Press, 1986); Donald Wright, *The Professionalization of History in English Canada* (Toronto: University of Toronto Press, 2005); and Ronald Rudin, *Making History in Twentieth Century Quebec* (Toronto: University of Toronto Press, 1997).

7   Danielle Lacasse and Antonio Lechasseur, *The National Archives of Canada, 1872-1997*, Canadian Historical Association, Historical Booklet No. 58 (Ottawa, 1997); Carl Berger, *Honour and the Search for Influence: A History of the Royal Society of Canada* (Toronto: University of Toronto Press, 1996).

8   Berger, *Honour and the Search for Influence*, 26-27.

9   Ibid., 32.

10  Donald G. Creighton, *John A. Macdonald*, 2 vols. (Toronto: Macmillan, 1952-55).

11  J.M.S. Careless, *Brown of the Globe*, 2 vols. (Toronto: Macmillan, 1959).

12  Wright, *The Professionalization of History in English Canada*, 36; Beverly Boutilier and Alison Prentice, eds., *Creating Historical Memory: English Canadian Women and the Work of History* (Vancouver: UBC Press, 1997), 3.

13  Terry Crowley, "Isabel Skelton: Precursor to Canadian Cultural History"; and Barry M. Moody, "A View from the Front Steps: Esther Clark Wright and the Making of a Maritime Historian"; both in Boutilier and Prentice, *Creating Historical Memory*, 164-93, 233-53. See also Terence Crowley, *The Marriage of Minds: Isabel and Oscar Skelton Reinventing Canada* (Toronto: University of Toronto Press, 2003).

14  Ramsay Cook, "Canadian Historical Writing," in *Scholarship in Canada, 1967: Achievement and Outlook*, ed. R.H. Hubbard (Toronto: University of Toronto Press for the Royal Society of Canada, 1968), 71-81; J.M.S. Careless, "Limited Identities in Canada," *Canadian Historical Review* 50, 1 (March 1969): 1-10.

15  A collection of historiographical articles covering many of the topics touched by the new social history can be found in Carl Berger, ed., *Contemporary Approaches to Canadian History* (Toronto: Copp Clark Pitman, 1987).

16  Alison Prentice, *The School Promoters: Education and Social Class in Mid-Nineteenth-Century Upper Canada* (Toronto: University of Toronto Press, 1977). Prentice reflects on her scholarly career in "Workers, Professionals, Pilgrims: Tracing Canadian

Women Teachers' Histories," in *Telling Women's Lives: Narrative Inquiries in the History of Women's Education*, ed. Kathleen Weiler and Sue Middleton (Buckingham: Open University Press, 1999).

17 This topic is covered in detail in Paul Axelrod, "Historical Writing and Canadian Education from the 1970s to the 1990s," *History of Education Quarterly* 36, 1 (Spring 1996): 19-38; see also J. Donald Wilson, "Some Observations on Recent Trends in Canadian Education History," in *An Imperfect Past: Education and Society in Canadian History* (Vancouver: Centre for the Study of Curriculum and Instruction, University of British Columbia, 1984), 7-29.

18 J. Donald Wilson, Robert M. Stamp, and Louis-Phillippe Audet, eds., *Canadian Education: A History* (Toronto: Prentice-Hall, 1970).

19 See, for example, R.D. Gidney and W.P.J. Millar, *Inventing Secondary Education: The Rise of the High School in Nineteenth-Century Ontario* (Montreal and Kingston: McGill-Queen's University Press, 1990); Thérèse Hamel, *Un siècle de formation des maitres au Quebec: 1836-1939* (Montreal: Hurtubise HMH, 1995); J.R. Miller, *Shingwauk's Vision: A History of Native Residential Schools* (Toronto: University of Toronto Press, 1995); and A.B. McKillop, *Matters of the Mind: The University in Ontario, 1791-1951* (Toronto: University of Toronto Press, 1994).

20 Gerald Friesen, *The Canadian Prairies: A History* (Toronto: University of Toronto Press, 1984); Jean Barman, *The West Beyond the West: A History of British Columbia* (Toronto: University of Toronto Press, 1991).

21 David G. Alexander, "New Notions of Happiness: Nationalism, Regionalism, and Atlantic Canada," in *Atlantic Canada and Confederation: Essays in Canadian Political Economy*, ed. Eric W. Sager, Lewis R. Fischer, and Stuart O. Pierson (St. John's/Toronto: Memorial University/University of Toronto Press, 1983); E.R. Forbes, *Challenging the Regional Stereotype: Essays on the 20th Century Maritimes* (Fredericton: Acadiensis Press, 1989); Phillip A. Buckner, "'Limited Identities' and Canadian Historical Scholarship: An Atlantic Canada Perspective," *Journal of Canadian Studies* 23 (Spring-Summer 1988): 177-98.

22 One of the most rigorous attacks on postmodernism as an approach to scholarship was penned by Bryan Palmer, who in *Descent into Discourse: The Reification of Language and the Writing of Social History* (Philadelphia: Temple University Press, 1990) underscored the absurdity of postmodernism if carried to its logical conclusion.

23 The most lucid articulation of this position is Michael Bliss, "Privatizing the Mind: The Sundering of Canadian History, the Sundering of Canada," *Journal of Canadian Studies* 26, 4 (Winter 1991-92): 5-17.

24 J.L. Granatstein, *Who Killed Canadian History?* (Toronto: HarperCollins, 1998), 51-78.

25 A.B. McKillop, "Who Killed Canadian History? A View from the Trenches," *Canadian Historical Review* 80, 2 (June 1999): 269-99.

26 See, for example, Jocelyn Létourneau, *A History for the Future: Rewriting Memory and Identity in Quebec Today* (Montreal and Kingston: McGill-Queen's University Press, 2004); *Le Québec, les Québécois: Un parcours historique* (Montreal: Fides/Musée de la civilisation, 2004); and *Que veulent vraiment les Québécois? Regard sur*

*l'intention nationale au Québec (français) d'hier à aujourd'hui* (Montreal: Boreal, 2007).

27 Bouchard's views are most fully expressed in *La Nation au futur et au passé* (Montreal: VLB, 1999); and *Genèse des nations et cultures du nouveau monde: Essai d'histoire comparée* (Montreal: Boréal, 2000). The latter appeared in English as Gérard Bouchard, *The Making of the Nations and Cultures of the New World* (Montreal and Kingston: McGill-Queen's University Press, 2008). For other major contributions, see Jacques Beauchemin, *L'Histoire en trop: La mauvaise conscience des souverainistes québécois (*Montreal: VLB, 2002); and Joseph-Yvon Thériault, *Critique de l'américanité: Mémoire et démocratie au Québec* (Montreal: Québec-Amérique, 2002).

28 For a discussion of how these positions have been the focus of controversy around the teaching of history in Quebec schools, see, in this volume, Jocelyn Létourneau, "Teaching History, Memory, and Identity: The Debate on History Education in Quebec."

29 These and other matters relating to public history are discussed in Margaret Conrad, "Public History and Its Discontents, or History in the Age of *Wikipedia*," *Journal of the Canadian Historical Association, Saskatoon 2007* (2008): 1-26.

30 Benedict Anderson, *Imagined Communities: Reflections on the Origins and Spread of Nationalism* (London: Verso, 1991); Pierre Nora, *Realms of Memory: The Construction of the French Past*, trans. Arthur Goldhammer (New York: Columbia University Press, 1996); "Les lieux de mémoire," *Representations* 26 (1989): 7-25; Jörn Rüsen, *Studies in Metahistory* (Pretoria: Human Sciences Research Council, 1993); *History: Narration, Interpretation, Orientation* (New York: Berghahn Books, 2005), and his edited volume *Western Historical Thinking: An Intercultural Debate* (New York: Bergahn Books, 2002).

31 See Peter Seixas, ed., *Theorizing Historical Consciousness* (Toronto: University of Toronto Press, 2004); and Ruth Sandwell, ed., *To the Past: History Education, Public Memory, and Citizenship in Canada* (Toronto: University of Toronto Press, 2006).

32 The field of public history is most advanced in the United States, which supports a journal, *The Public Historian*, and as many as one hundred programs to train practitioners. See David Glassberg, "Public History and the Study of Memory," *Public Historian* 18, 2 (Spring 1996): 7-23, and "History and Memory: Roundtable Responses to David Glassberg's 'Public History and Public Memory,'" *Public Historian* 19, 2 (Spring 1997): 31-72. See also two special issues of journals: "The National Council on Public History: Reflections on a Twentieth Anniversary," *Public Historian* 21, 3 (Summer 1999); and "L'histoire 'publique': Un enjeu pour l'histoire," special issue of *Revue d'histoire de l'Amérique française* 57, 1 (Summer 2003); as well as James B. Gardner and Peter S. LaPaglia, eds., *Public History: Essays from the Field*, rev. ed. (Malibar: Kreiger, 2004).

33 Ian McKay, "The Liberal Order Framework: A Prospectus for a Reconnaissance of Canadian History," *Canadian Historical Review* 81, 4 (December 2000): 617-45.

34 Jerry Bannister, "Canada as Counter-Revolution: The Loyalist Order Framework in Canadian History," in *Liberalism and Hegemony: Debating the Canadian Liberal*

*Revolution*, ed. Jean-François Constant and Michel Ducharme (Toronto: University of Toronto Press, 2008); Ruth Sandwell, "The Limits of Liberalism: The Liberal Reconnaissance and the History of the Family in Canada," *Canadian Historical Review* 83, 3 (September 2003): 423-50.

35 For a lucid commentary on the value of history as a discipline, see Kenneth Osborne, "'To the Past': Why We Need to Teach and Study History," in *To the Past*, 103-31.

# Teaching Canadian History
## A Century of Debate

KEN OSBORNE

This chapter explores the main developments in the teaching of Canadian history in Canada's schools from the 1890s to the present. Until the 1950s, most provinces also taught British and European history – and since the 1960s, world history or modern world problems. In what follows, however, I concentrate on the teaching of Canadian history. History education has been the subject of occasional public and professional debate in Canada over the past hundred years, but that debate has almost always focused on the teaching of Canadian, not world, history.[1]

Briefly stated, my argument is as follows. From the 1890s to the 1970s, Canadian history education in English-speaking Canada was dominated by the theme of nation building, intended to instill a sense of pan-Canadian identity in the young. This took a different form in francophone Quebec, where the focus was on the history of Quebec and its relationship with the rest of Canada; but in both anglophone Canada and francophone Quebec, the central theme of history textbooks and curricula was nation building, even if two different conceptions of nationhood were in play. Nation-building history always had its critics, but only in the 1960s did it begin to lose its power. In the 1960s and 1970s and beyond, Canadian history education entered an experimental phase. The established nation-building orthodoxy never totally disappeared, but a number of innovative curriculum projects were created. Some were devoted to teaching history as a form of values education; some were organized around exploring history as a form of disciplined inquiry; some tied history to the analysis of contemporary social problems; some organized history around concepts and themes; and some merged history into an interdisciplinary social studies.

These innovations generated some controversy, especially when they were seen as threatening the long-established place of history in the school curriculum – a development that was further hastened in the 1980s, when policy makers harnessed education to the goals of economic policy. The result was a lively debate in the 1990s over why and how history should be taught in schools. At the same time, two new approaches to history education emerged in Canada in the 1990s. One made history part of a renewed conception of education for democratic citizenship; the other emphasized teaching students to think historically.

## Nation-Building History

Until the 1970s, to teach the history of Canada – at least in English-speaking Canada – was to tell the story of how the Canadian nation came to assume its present form. Its purpose was to instill in students a historically rooted sense of Canadian identity and a reasoned pride in the Canadian past. Above all, it was a story of progress, of challenges met and overcome, be they geographic, economic, political, international, or any other. Textbook titles told the story: *Building the Canadian Nation; From Colony to Nation; Canada: A Nation and How It Came to Be; The Canadian Pageant; Challenge and Survival.*

The task of nation building was not left to Canadian history alone. Before the 1950s, British and European history also had a part to play. Most Canadian educationists took pride in Canada's membership in the British Empire and valued the imperial connection for providing protection against Americanizing pressures. In addition, many Canadian institutions were rooted in the British past. Not surprisingly, therefore, Canadian students were required to study the main events of British history. By the 1950s, however, largely in response to the post-1945 realignment of world politics, British history was rapidly losing its place in the curriculum. Educationists still thought that Canadian students should study the British origins of Canadian institutions, but they increasingly believed that this was best done in the context of Canadian history rather than through courses in British history. They also believed that Canadians needed to appreciate the wider Western tradition on which Canada was founded. Thus, as part of the nation-building project, Canadian students were taught the main elements of European history. Beginning in the 1960s, this narrative of the western European past was enlarged to include the study of world history, usually in the form of a survey course in junior high school and elective courses in world problems in senior high.

Even so, for most students, the content of the nation-building narrative was predominantly Canadian. In the words of a 1926 textbook: "The prime need of the student is for an unbiased account of how Canada came to be what she is to-day and the main object of writing this book has been to provide such an account." At the same time, this 1926 text proclaimed its intent to "instil in those who read it a thorough-going spirit of patriotism which, while not wholly ignorant of the mistakes of the past, may yet express itself in a proper and predominant love of country, based on a healthy pride in its past record and a firm belief in its future greatness."[2] In other words, history was to be taught as the authoritative story of what happened in the past, with no reference to questions of evidence or interpretation, in the belief that this would automatically promote patriotism and national pride while also equipping students to continue the nation-building work that previous generations had begun. Curricula and textbooks portrayed Canada as a work in progress whose continuing development depended on the commitment of historically informed citizens.

There was, however, a lack of fit between the stated goals of history curricula and what happened in the classroom. According to a 1953 survey, "responsibility as a citizen" was the primary goal of Canadian history curricula, followed by "loyalty, patriotism, nationalism or unity" and then by understanding "the importance of the past for the present" and "critical thinking." Commenting on the survey, the University of Manitoba historian W.L. Morton noted the "great discrepancies" between the stated goals of curricula, which were all about citizenship, and their content, which was "academic in spirit" and valued knowledge "for its own sake."[3] Morton was pointing to a larger problem. While pleased to see their subject enjoying a prominent place in the curricular sun, some historians worried that enlisting history in the cause of citizenship risked turning it into patriotic propaganda. A University of Toronto historian argued in 1910 that the study of history must be devoted to developing students' powers of imagination and reason, and not become "an expanded form of 'Rule Britannia' [or] a passport to citizenship."[4] In 1923, another University of Toronto historian, Charles Cochrane, argued that there were "grave dangers in assuming too readily that history is a natural medium for teaching either patriotism or internationalism."[5] As Quebec's Parent Commission on educational reform argued in 1965: "It is important to dissociate history from patriotic justification; the first aim in the teaching of history is not the development of a civic, patriotic or religious conscience. This confusion can only be harmful to history, patriotism and to religion. The teaching of history aims to develop the human mind by the objective and honest study of the past, based on documents."[6]

The question was whether or how the conception of history as an intellectual discipline worthy of study in its own right could be reconciled with the schools' mandate to produce national citizens, especially in a culturally diverse, bilingual, and federally organized country such as Canada, which had to accommodate strong regional identities and in which education remained firmly under provincial control. As Ontario's Minister of Education George Ross put it in 1892: "The question we ask ourselves today is: 'Are we going to be provincial in our education or are we going to be national?'"[7]

Rejecting existing history textbooks as merely "provincial" in their approach, Ross asked: "Can't we agree upon certain broad features common to the whole of this Dominion with which we can indoctrinate our pupils, so that when a child takes up the history of Canada, he feels that he is not simply taking up the history of Canada such as the old Canada was, but that he is taking up the history of a great country?"[8] It was in this spirit that the Dominion Education Association organized a contest in the 1890s to produce a national history textbook that would be acceptable to all provinces. The winner, W.H.P. Clements's *History of the Dominion of Canada,* was published in 1898. Though it was not endorsed by all provinces, it established the basic nation-building narrative that endured into the 1960s and beyond.[9]

From the 1890s through the 1960s, Canadian history curricula in English-speaking Canada took the form of a chronological and descriptive narrative organized around four principal axes: (1) European exploration and settlement, primarily in central Canada (New France, the Loyalists, British immigration in the early nineteenth century, and so on) but also in the West with an emphasis on European settlement on the Prairies; (2) pre-Confederation political and constitutional developments, from the 1763 Proclamation to the achievement of responsible government in the 1840s; (3) Confederation itself; and (4) the shaping of Canada after 1867 (Macdonald's National Policy, railway building, the opening of the West, the winning of autonomy in international affairs, and so on).

French-language history curricula in Quebec described a somewhat different version of the Canadian past. They spent much more time on the history of New France and placed considerable emphasis on the role of the Church in Quebec's history. They devoted fewer pages than did English-language texts to post-Confederation history and generally focused not so much on a pan-Canadian panorama of the past but on Quebec's struggle to maintain its French and Catholic identity in an anglophone and materialist British North America.[10] In the 1970s, following the recommendations of the 1965 Parent Report, Quebec curricula adopted a more dispassionately secular tone, though still with a focus on Quebec and its relationship with the rest of Canada.[11] When a group of historians in 1967 published a text that deliberately set out to present a pan-Canadian perspective, under the title *Canada: Unity in Diversity*, in Quebec it appeared as *Canada: Unité et Diversité*.[12] The distinction between "in" and "et" speaks volumes.

## Criticisms of Nation-Building History

From its beginnings, critics of nation-building history objected to what they saw as its restrictive view of just who the nation builders were. Some pointed to its stereotypical and limited portrayal of the First Nations. In western and Atlantic Canada, objections were raised to its central Canadian "Laurentian" bias. Feminists pointed to the male biases of the nation-building story. Agrarian radicals criticized its urban and capitalist tendencies. Socialists and labour activists rejected its class bias. Internationalists and pacifists condemned its emphasis on war and conflict. To take only a few examples, in 1924 the historian Isabel Skelton observed that though women were nearly half the population, "historians, absorbed in the annals of war and politics and business, tell us little of the part they played. The women's stage was not set in the limelight, but in the firelight."[13] Writing in 1946, the Manitoba historian W.L. Morton contended that "no more than French Canada can the West accept a common interpretation of Canadian history or a cultural metropolitanism."[14] Agrarian radicals were equally critical. Mary McCallum of the Grain Growers' Association told an audience of Winnipeg teachers in 1919 that history was too often taught as "only a recital of facts in chronological order" devoid of any "social interpretation."[15] This accusation that history courses were ideologically slanted in favour of the status quo was a favourite theme of socialists and labour groups. In 1934, the Maritime socialist Roscoe Fillmore penned the standard left-wing critique:

> In the past our children have been taught history that was a pack of lies and jingo ravings. The doings of lecherous and cut-throat kings and lords and

ladies who rode on the backs of our forefathers and enslaved them were dished up as history ... History as taught reflected little of man's discoveries and achievements and never so much as hinted that progress was the result of the struggles carried on by various classes at various times, against the tyranny of kings, landlords, etc.[16]

Internationalist critics, especially between the two world wars, chastised nation-building history from another angle. In the 1920s, H.G. Wells, who was much quoted in Canadian education journals in these years, argued that nation-building history must inevitably become the "poison" of nationalist history, "one long record of the wars, invasions, usurpations, betrayals, murders, and persecutions" that comprised the conventional historical narrative and that had created the belligerent patriotism that led to the First World War. What was needed, he argued, was a truly global history that ignored national boundaries and that viewed humanity as one interconnected species. Most provincial departments of education between the wars endorsed a mild internationalism, requiring history teachers to teach about the League of Nations and holding up the British Empire as a perfect example of international cooperation in action, but they never came close to Wells's vision of a one-world, supranational history.[17]

A different kind of objection was voiced in Quebec, where English-speaking Canada's version of nation-building history was seen as an assimilative threat to Quebec's distinct identity. Most Quebec educationists saw Canada as a union of two founding peoples and believed that any pan-Canadian nation-building narrative must inevitably sell Quebec short. In the late 1930s, a Laval University historian, Arthur Maheux, accused history textbooks of setting anglophone and francophone Canadians against each other by dwelling excessively on incidents and issues that divided them. Maheux's critics countered that to describe English-speaking Canada's many attempts to curtail Quebec's rights was not to foster division but to describe historical reality. One investigation of the texts in question concluded that they were too dull to teach anything. Another found that the problem was not the inculcation of animosity but the existence of a state of mutual ignorance.[18]

Whatever the facts, there was general agreement that the teaching of history had done as much to drive the two Canadas apart as to bring them together. A 1944 Senate debate on history teaching ended in an appeal to historians to identify those facts that all Canadians should know so that a unifying national textbook could be written; but, though the Canada and

Newfoundland Education Association produced a model history curriculum in 1945, neither historians nor provincial departments of education took up the call. The idea of a uniform national history textbook was the subject of some debate in the late 1940s and early 1950s, but even those few who were attracted to it concluded that it was not a practical proposition. The result, according to a 1968 survey, was that anglophone and francophone students learned two "sharply opposed views" of Canada's history, with all the predictable political consequences.[19]

There were also those who rejected nation-building history on pedagogical grounds. As they saw it, it turned what should have been a thinking subject into a test of memory in which narrative swamped analysis. These critics wanted to replace textbooks with collections of sources, thereby turning history into the investigation of problems rather than the memorization of facts. To quote one of the most fervent exponents of this view, the historian Fred Morrow Fling of the University of Nebraska, writing in 1906: "Let our pupils be taught that proof must be insisted on in historical work, and that when proof ends history ends. Teach them that no matter how long a story has been believed nor by how many people it has been accepted as true, if it does not rest on trustworthy evidence it is not a historical fact and cannot be classed as history."[20] Before the 1970s, this conception of history never attracted much support in Canada, but it offered a clear alternative to any conception of history education as the recital of an authoritative narrative of the past.

It was generally agreed by the early 1900s that students under the age of fourteen were too immature to understand real history. What was needed, therefore, was a curriculum centred on the tangible phenomena of everyday life that students would find familiar and intelligible, especially in the elementary grades. Properly taught, there was a good deal of history to be learned from a bar of soap, a lump of coal, or the fire brigade. And such things were best taught not through history alone but through the medium of interdisciplinary projects (often called by the British term "enterprises" in Canada). As for civics, this was best taught through the investigation of contemporary problems at the local level. The result was that in the 1930s and 1940s, Canadian schools merged history into an interdisciplinary social studies in the early grades. In the 1940s, there was talk of pushing the social studies approach into high schools; but before the 1970s, only Alberta actually did so.[21]

Some saw salvation, not in social studies, but in a reformed history teaching. In 1904 a Manitoba school inspector, S.E. Lang, suggested that history should be taught backwards, beginning with the present and working back into the past. Others urged a turn to a kind of social history of everyday life. The influential textbook publisher Lorne Pierce argued in the 1930s that history should be taught as a series of "quests" (for justice, for security, for happiness, and so on) that would appeal to adolescents' search for meaning while also turning history into a process of inquiry. According to another critic, the central theme of Canadian history was not politics but the "battle of the wilderness," and teaching it in this way would inject romantic adventure and intellectual challenge into an otherwise sterile subject.[22]

Perhaps the most damaging criticism of nation-building history was that it was not doing its job. A 1923 report concluded that many history teachers faced a "hopeless task." A 1930 report observed that curricula placed unrealistic demands on hard-pressed teachers. A 1933 inquiry found history textbooks to be depressingly dull – a finding endorsed by two other reports in 1941. A 1953 report criticized history curricula as "factualized to the point of boredom." A 1962 report was scathing in its assessment of history teaching:

> It does not train the mind; it leaves only a slight deposit on the mind after a few months or a few years; it does not help the student to think abstractly, to look at evidence, or to consider relevance, which we have argued are the main contributions that the study of history can be expected to make to the intelligence of the adult and the merit of the citizen.

A 1968 investigation concluded that history, as generally taught, was "almost useless as a stimulating school subject."[23] In short, nation-building history simply was not working.

In fact, nation-building history was rarely ever taught. Teachers defined their task not as shaping citizens but as getting students through the provincial examinations that governed high school graduation. And across Canada, provincial examinations said nothing about nation building. They were remorselessly factual, "mere tests of mechanical memorization," according to the University of Saskatchewan historian Hilda Neatby, writing in 1944. Some reformers wanted to eliminate examinations altogether; but most observers called, not for their abolition, but for their reform, urging that examinations test for "organized thought and expression" and not memory work.[24] The problem was that such examinations could not be marked cheaply and uniformly on a province-wide basis, whereas purely factual questions could be.

Nonetheless, from the 1890s onwards, there was general agreement that history ought to be an "education" and not merely an "information" subject and that its educational value lay in its power to stimulate students' imagination and reason. For reformers, this meant that (1) effective history teaching depended on studying fewer topics in depth rather than covering many topics more superficially; (2) history was best taught not as a definitive narrative but as the investigation of problems, be they substantive ("What caused the War of 1812?"), evidentiary ("What is the evidence for the story of Dollard des Ormeaux at the Long Sault Rapids, and how credible is it?"), or interpretative ("Was Confederation an act or a pact?"); (3) students should work with primary and secondary sources; and (4) students should learn to think historically while also acquiring the "historic sense" that enabled them to situate the present in the context of a transition from a more or less known past to an unknown but desired future.[25]

In the 1900s, source work enjoyed a certain popularity, though more so in the United States and Britain than in Canada. In the 1910s, history teachers were urged to adopt "laboratory" methods whereby history would become a form of problem solving. In the 1920s and 1930s, the problem-centred "project" and "enterprise" methods were the centre of attention. In the 1940s and beyond, child-centred progressivism became the new orthodoxy. Most history classrooms, however, remained true to what a Toronto school inspector in 1932 called "the memorization method."[26] In 1968, Hodgetts reported that the typical history student was little more than "a bench-bound listener."[27] Thirty years later, in Quebec, Martineau found that lecture and textbook coverage ("le discours magistral") remained the norm.[28]

This is not to say that all history classrooms were stuck in a pedagogical rut. Teachers' magazines contained many descriptions of imaginative history lessons. Innovative teachers experimented with local and family history projects, with source work, and with poetry and drama; they created classroom museums and turned to the new technologies of radio and film. Beginning in the 1930s, the Public Archives, the National Film Board, the Canadian Historical Association, and the CBC produced classroom resources. In 1940 the University of Toronto's George Brown published a Canadian history source book designed specifically for school use; in 1952, Guy Frégault and Marcel Trudel did the same in Quebec. This suggests that enough history teachers were incorporating sources into their teaching to constitute a viable commercial market.[29] This said, however, it seems that for the most part, history was often not taught as well as it might have been. Teachers at all grade levels faced difficult working conditions and lacked both time and resources to employ the innovations that were being pressed upon them; high school teachers were further constrained by memory-based provincial examinations.

## The Erosion of Nation-Building History in the 1960s

None of its critics succeeded in shaking nation-building narrative history's overall domination of the Canadian curriculum, but in the 1960s they gained a certain credibility. Quebec's Quiet Revolution posed new challenges to Confederation; Canadian nationalists worried about what they saw as the increasing Americanization of Canada; and the growing assertiveness of the women's movement and the First Nations, together with the heightened political salience of human rights issues, raised questions about the nature of Canadian democracy. In 1968 the Royal Commission on Bilingualism and Biculturalism urged that Canadian history curricula pay much more attention to the English-French duality of Canada – a view that stimulated Canadians who were not of English or French descent to press for greater attention to the wider multicultural diversity of Canadian society.[30]

In these circumstances, it was hardly surprising that the 1967 centennial of Confederation stimulated debate over just how history might contribute to a renewed sense of citizenship. Did Canada's past have any lessons for its citizens of the future, or were Canadians so historically uninformed that Canada's first century was likely to be its last, as Donald Creighton and George Grant feared?[31] According to some historians, Canadians should accept that Canada was a society of limited identities. According to Quebec sovereignists, Canada's first hundred years had been "cent ans d'injustice." Multiculturalists pressed for a treatment of history that would place more emphasis on cultural diversity – less a history of the Canadian people, in the singular, than of the Canadian *peoples,* in the plural. Women, the First Nations, and others restated their long-standing complaints that they were largely excluded from Canada's history books. In 1971 an analysis of Ontario social studies texts (quickly followed by similar studies in other provinces) concluded that their omissions and biases meant they were teaching, not history, but "prejudice."[32] In Quebec, the long-standing survivalist narrative of Quebec nationhood came under attack for numbing the minds of students with its "sinistres platitudes," "sottises," "les erreurs plus évidentes," "énormités," and "fadaises," all enlisted in the cause of a false and romanticized patriotism ("un patriotisme lyrique et faux").[33] And as we have seen, in 1965, Quebec's influential Parent Commission on school reform dismissed any attempt to enlist history in the cause of patriotism or identity, calling instead for the subject to be taught as a form of detached intellectual inquiry.

These developments called into question the value of nation-building history, at least as conventionally taught. There had always been those who advocated reform, but only in the 1960s did suggestions for change command a wide hearing. Before the 1960s, such suggestions went largely unheeded; and in the high school grades, political and constitutional history, with a dash of economic development (primarily immigration and railways), formed the backbone of the nation-building narrative. In the 1960s, some observers suggested that this might be precisely the problem – that schools were still teaching "a white, Anglo-Saxon, Protestant political and constitutional history" dominated by textbook recitation, "a bland consensus story, told without the controversy that is an inherent part of history."[34]

In the 1960s (see Conrad, Chapter 1 in this volume), such a controversial history became increasingly accessible. A new type of social history (though perhaps not as new as some of its proponents believed) began to make its presence felt. It dealt with the historical experience of those who had been largely ignored by the established nation-building narrative: women, workers, children, minorities, "ordinary" people, and – more radically – those whose experience of nation building had been negative rather than positive. Surprisingly quickly, beginning in the 1970s, history curricula and textbooks incorporated this new social history into their descriptions of the Canadian past. In doing so, they highlighted incidents that the older history had passed over in silence, such as the Winnipeg General Strike of 1919, Indian residential schools, and the more racist aspects of immigration policy. From the 1970s onwards, such topics became part of history curricula in all provinces, to the point that by the 1990s some commentators were beginning to complain that history had become "victimology."[35]

More fundamentally, the founding assumptions of nation-building history came under question. Perhaps the study of society and culture was more important than the study of political and economic development. Perhaps the invention of aspirin or ready-to-wear clothing was more important in people's lives than the Rebellion Losses Bill and the many other staples of the conventional nation-building story. Perhaps the Canadian story was one of the articulation of limited identities, not the construction of a single overarching national identity. Perhaps the complexities of the Canadian past could not be described in any single story. Perhaps history was not the recital of any kind of single authoritative narrative, but rather a kaleidoscope of competing narratives. Perhaps the very concept of narrative needed to be re-examined and its assumptions and operating procedures deconstructed.

Or perhaps history simply could not be taught to children and adolescents except in so simplified a form that it lost any resemblance to history as an intellectual discipline. In the 1960s, researchers in the developmental Piagetian tradition claimed that most students simply could not understand history, even in the high school grades. According to a British psychologist, E.A. Peel, most students were "context-bound" or "describer" thinkers who could not move beyond whatever information they had at their disposal; whereas history required "possibility invoking" or "explainer" thinking that demanded an ability to pose hypotheses and test them against relevant evidence. There was little disagreement that most students were in fact "describer" thinkers; but there was some debate as to whether this reflected an immutable developmental reality or was simply a reflection of the kind of chalk-and-talk teaching that characterized many history lessons. Even if the research described the reality of students' thinking, was it not possible that this thinking could be improved by better teaching?[36]

Whatever the case, in the 1960s and 1970s, it seemed to be an open question whether history was a teachable subject in schools. If it was not, then another question obviously followed: What should replace it? If nothing else, this opened the door for the extension of interdisciplinary social studies from the elementary schools into the high school grades. Its emphasis on the problems of the here and now might make it more accessible and more interesting to students and provide a more effective education for citizenship.

In the 1960s, it was more than just history that was changing. So also was the process of curriculum design and development. Jerome Bruner's *The Process of Education* appeared in 1960 and quickly exerted a powerful influence on curriculum making across Canada. Briefly put, Bruner argued that school subjects should reflect the "structure" of the intellectual disciplines on which they were based. Curricula should be based on the study of "concepts" and the "mode of inquiry" of the various disciplines. A British philosopher of education, Paul Hirst, said much the same thing, arguing that school curricula should embody the "forms of knowledge" of which the academic disciplines were a reflection. In Canada, though, Bruner was much more influential.[37]

The impact of Piaget and Bruner, and many others like them, reflected an important shift. Before the 1960s, university-based historians had played a key role in history education in Canada. They wrote many of the textbooks, set and marked provincial examinations, and worked closely with teachers, most of whom were their former students. By the 1960s, however, historians increasingly saw themselves as researchers rather than educators and left education to the educationists. Moreover, the elimination of provincial examinations in the late 1960s meant that universities lost their main mechanism of control over school curricula. At the same time, the study of education was becoming more academically specialized. Faculties of education were staffed by scholars with specialist degrees in education and assumed responsibility for the undergraduate education of teachers; teachers increasingly took graduate training in education rather than history or the liberal arts. Curriculum development and design became the province of educational experts. As a result, from the 1960s onwards, history education became the concern of teachers and educationists and not of historians. Only a few people managed to bridge the growing divide.

### Years of Experiment and Innovation: The 1970s and Beyond

The erosion of support for nation-building history in the 1960s occurred at the same time that alternatives to its unidimensional narrative were increasingly available. In the United States, the Amherst History Project required high school students to investigate historical problems through the use of primary sources. The American historian Edwin Fenton and others promoted the cause of the "new history" and the "new social studies," which focused on organizing curricula around interdisciplinary concepts and the "mode of inquiry" distinctive of the social science disciplines.[38] In Britain, the influential Schools Council History 13-16 Project (now the Schools History Project), founded in 1972, rejected history as chronological narrative, whether of nation building or anything else, and instead introduced students to history as a form of evidence-based inquiry.[39] In Canada, textbooks began to include source extracts; and historiographical exercises and "kits" of documents, source books, simulations, videos, and other resources became increasingly available. By the 1970s, the question increasingly became, not how many historical facts students knew or how patriotic they felt, but what the study of history could do for their intellectual development.

More ominously for history, dissatisfaction with nation-building narratives and their associated chalk-and-talk didacticism hastened moves to blend history into an interdisciplinary social studies that drew on all the social sciences as needed. After the Canada Studies Foundation was founded in 1970, the new interdisciplinary subject of Canadian Studies became part of many provinces' curricula, often at the expense of history as a stand-alone subject. As Bob Davis observed, sociology seemed likely to replace history as the core of the social studies curriculum.[40] These trends were reinforced by the provinces' adoption of the credit system for high school graduation and the resulting tendency to make history an elective rather than a compulsory subject, so that it competed with law, sociology, Canadian Studies, psychology, and other subjects.

This move from history to social studies was part of a wider trend that tied history more directly than ever before to a present-oriented education for citizenship. What was important about the past, it was widely agreed, was what it told us about the present. Some preferred to focus on the immediate problems of the present, arguing that this was the most effective way of educating for citizenship since students would presumably find such problems interesting. Others concentrated on "persisting" issues that were inherent in any organized society, past, present, or future, as, for example, in the case of the balance between private interests and public duty, or between majority rule and minority rights. Following the example of the Harvard Social Studies Project, the OISE-based Canadian Public Issues Project rejected both Bruner's emphasis on the structure of the disciplines and Fenton's preference for the mode of inquiry, arguing instead that the demands of citizenship in a democracy called for an approach that taught students the skills and values necessary for tackling controversial public issues.[41]

Any investigation of public issues, persisting or otherwise, usually involves the examination of values, and by the end of the 1960s there were plenty of value issues to discuss: Quebec sovereignty; Aboriginal treaty rights; gender equity; human rights; health care; racism; the Vietnam War; apartheid in South Africa; civil rights in the United States – these and similar topics put values squarely on the public and political agenda. Not surprisingly, in view of the long-standing connection between history/social studies and education for citizenship, this concern for values quickly became part of the effort to reshape the teaching of history, though only Alberta adopted values education in any explicit way, when, for a few years in the 1970s, it made values clarification the basis of its social studies curriculum. At UBC, the Association for Values Education and Research devised a model for analyzing value issues and published a series of classroom resources that, while not strictly historical, drew on historical materials. At OISE, the Values Education Project produced classroom materials based on Lawrence Kohlberg's theory of moral reasoning, while the Canadian Public Issues Project emphasized the analysis of contemporary issues, arguing that "the problems of today and tomorrow should take priority over the problems of yesterday." Clearly, history was under threat.[42] Moreover, in the 1980s, history came under further pressure as policy makers emphasized science, literacy, and such "generic" skills as problem solving and decision making as keys to competitive success in the emerging high-tech global economy.

## The History Debates of the 1990s

In the 1990s, fear that history was losing its place in school curricula created a certain level of public interest in the state of history education in Canada's schools. Not least, failed attempts at constitutional reform and Quebec's drive for constitutional change and perhaps some form of independence raised new questions about Canadian unity and national identity. Supporters and opponents of the Meech Lake Agreement of 1989 and the Charlottetown Accord of 1992 seemed to believe they could have won the day if only Canadians had known their history. Joe Clark, point man for the unsuccessful Charlottetown Accord, concluded that "if we are serious about keeping and building a large Canada, we must encourage more schools to teach more facts about the history and nature of our country. It should not be propaganda, because that is not who we are. But it should tell the Canadian story honestly and reasonably fully, and in the same way in every part of Canada." For Keith Spicer, chairperson of the Task Force on National Unity, Canada's apparent disunity was due in part to the fact that "Canadian schools outside Quebec teach almost no Canadian history at all before late high school."[43] The fact that this assertion was demonstrably wrong did nothing to diminish the feeling that the teaching of Canadian history had much to answer for.

In 1991 a University of Toronto historian, Michael Bliss, sharpened this line of argument when he accused historians of abandoning the role of "interpreters of the evolution of the public community." With its emphasis on the personal experience of daily life, the new social history had "privatized" history as a discipline. The result was the erosion of any sense of national community based on shared historical experience. In 1998 another historian, J.L. Granatstein, stripped this argument of its nuances, charging that Canadian history was dead, having been killed by indifferent educationists, misguided social historians, and divisive multiculturalists. Instead of pointing to the nation's achievements, historians now highlighted its failings. Educationists had smothered history in the suffocating embrace of social studies. Teachers had been seduced by the false charms of student-centred teaching methods. Whatever the accuracy of these claims, they attracted considerable public attention and brought to a head a variety of concerns that had been bubbling ever since the late 1980s.[44]

In addition, Canada was affected by the same forces that were leading many countries to search for some sort of collective memory and sense of shared heritage as a hedge against the mutually reinforcing forces of globalization and regionalism. At the same time, a plethora of politically charged historical anniversaries in other countries – the bicentennials of British settlement in Australia and of the French Revolution; the quincentennial of Columbus's first voyage to the Americas; the fiftieth anniversary of the bombing of Hiroshima and Nagasaki; and others – drew attention to the role of the past in shaping the present. For their part, as described by Margaret Conrad in this volume, historians debated the relative merits of old-style political history and the new social history that successfully challenged it, lamenting the fragmentation of their discipline and looking uneasily at what most of them saw as the emerging threat of postmodernism. In addition, debates over the teaching of history elsewhere washed over into Canada, raising questions about the place of history in Canada's schools. The United Kingdom's creation of a national history curriculum, like the creation of national history standards in the United States, led some to wonder why Canada could not follow a similar path.

Briefly stated, the debates of the 1990s revolved around six charges.[45] The first was that history was disappearing from school curricula, either by being merged into an interdisciplinary social studies or by being displaced by supposedly more vocationally useful subjects. The second was that, even where they survived, Canadian history curricula no longer told a coherent national story and thus were failing to implant a sense of national identity in students. The third was that history courses dwelt unduly on gender inequities, social injustice, racism, class conflict, and other "negative" aspects of the Canadian past. The fourth was that schools had abandoned the pursuit of knowledge and instead were emphasizing the acquisition of "generic" skills, such as critical thinking and problem solving, that were not specific to any particular subject. The fifth was that most students did not know even the most basic facts of history. The sixth was that too many teachers defined their task as meeting the "needs" of children rather than pursuing rigorously academic standards (though other critics claimed that, in reality, too many teachers still equated history with textbook coverage and chalk-and-talk didacticism).

The first of these criticisms was accurate: by the early 1990s, history was in danger of losing its accustomed place in school curricula, whether by being converted from a compulsory course into an elective credit or by being absorbed into social studies. The second and third criticisms were obviously matters of value judgment. What some commentators saw as the negative effects of "history from below," others welcomed as breathing new life into the study and teaching of history generally. The fourth criticism had some empirical foundation: educationists in the 1980s increasingly spoke of "process" rather than "product," of "learning how to learn," and the like. In their search for a flexible and adaptable workforce, many employers agreed with this approach. What was important, they said, was not carrying facts in one's head, but learning how to find them as needed in some convenient database. The fifth criticism similarly was based in reality. During the 1990s, the Dominion Institute published surveys that regularly revealed how little Canadians remembered of the historical facts they had been taught in school. Educationists pointed out that this was neither new nor unique to Canada. They also argued that history was more than the memorization of facts and pointed to errors and ambiguities in the surveys. But such responses did not allay widespread worries that Canadians did not know their history and that this must have some impact on the quality of citizenship. The sixth criticism, like the second and third, was more a matter of personal judgment than of empirical reality, since no one knew just what went on in Canada's history classrooms.

If nothing else, the debates of the 1990s had one concrete result: they halted the erosion of history's place in school curricula that had begun in the 1980s, though no province went as far as Quebec, which made history and education for citizenship a compulsory subject in all grades after grade three. A 2003 survey found that all the standard topics of Canadian history were being taught in all provinces and territories, albeit at different grade levels and in different ways, so that there was a de facto national history curriculum in Canada.[46] In addition, the 1990s saw the creation of three organizations devoted to improving the status and the teaching of Canadian history: the Dominion Institute, the CRB (later the Historica) Foundation, and Canada's National History Society (Historica and the Dominion Institute merged in 2009). In 1999 the Institute for the Study of Canada at McGill University organized the first ever truly national conference on the teaching of Canadian history, a conference that has met biennially ever since. In short, by the end of the 1990s, history's place in school curricula seemed stronger than it had been for some years.

In terms of curriculum content, textbooks, and teaching methods, though the 1970s interest in values education evaporated, the innovations of the 1970s and 1980s largely remained in place. Most provinces continued to blend history into social studies instead of treating it as a stand-alone discipline. Social history and multicultural diversity continued to be part of the curriculum. Teachers were encouraged to treat history as the exploration of themes and the investigation of issues rather than as a chronological narrative of events. Discovery and inquiry methods of teaching remained in favour, now buttressed by constructivist theories of learning that saw students, not simply as receivers of information, but as active meaning makers in their own right.

At the same time, history education assumed a different sort of national focus. It was now seen as important, not so much for any contribution it might make to the consolidation of national unity or national identity, but rather for its contribution to a participatory, activist, and democratic citizenship. This conception of citizenship as democratic problem solving pervaded all Canadian history curricula by the end of the 1990s, with Quebec in effect creating a new subject by combining history and education for citizenship into a single entity. Other provinces used slightly different language, but this 2003 Alberta statement is typical, both in its wording and in its ambitions: "Social studies develops the key values and attitudes, knowledge and understandings and skills and processes necessary for students to become active and responsible citizens, engaged in the democratic process and aware of their capacity to effect change in their communities, society and world."[47]

Though the history debates of the 1990s captured media attention, the more significant developments in history education escaped public notice. There were two in particular: one was a surge of new research into how students actually understand history; the other, as demonstrated by many of the chapters in this volume, was the emergence of a professional consensus that the central goal of history education should be the cultivation of historical thinking.

The new research into students' historical thinking discredited the Piagetian-derived research of the 1960s and 1970s that claimed that children and adolescents simply could not understand history. It also demonstrated that even in the elementary grades, children could think about history in relatively sophisticated ways, provided they were taught appropriately. No one suggested that students could become skilled historians, but they could at least learn to grapple with those fundamental historical questions: How do we know what we think we know? How reliable is our knowledge? What does it really tell us, and why does it matter anyway?[48]

If students are to be taught to think historically, it is obviously important to have a clear idea of just what historical thinking involves. It was increasingly accepted in the 1990s that "substantive" knowledge of facts is necessary but not sufficient. Students also need to master "disciplinary" or "procedural" knowledge so that, at the same time that they study a specific topic, such as the War of 1812 or the Winnipeg General Strike, they also explore how its history came to be researched and written, why it matters, and what arguments and interpretations it embodies.[49] In the United States in the mid-1990s, the National History Standards spoke of understanding chronological sequence and other conventions of historical time; of historical comprehension; analysis and interpretation; research skills; and issues analysis and decision making. In the United Kingdom, the initial version of the National History Curriculum (1992) spoke of historical knowledge and understanding; interpretation; and using historical sources. In Canada, as described in this volume, Peter Seixas constructed a model of historical thinking and ways of teaching it that are now being incorporated into provincial curricula. This emphasis on historical thinking was not altogether new. In the 1890s, for example, the American Historical Association rejected the idea that learning history meant only memorizing facts, insisting instead that the development of "historical mindedness" was the most important goal. Others spoke of developing the "historic sense" or "historical judgment" or "historical culture."[50]

Two things were new in the 1990s: (1) the growing agreement that historical thinking is an indispensable goal of history teaching; and (2) the sustained attempt to define just what historical thinking is and to design appropriate teaching strategies for its attainment. For some, this meant that the central goal was not the consolidation of national identity but an understanding of history as a form of disciplined inquiry, sometimes in a national context, sometimes not. For others, this disciplinary approach to history was important not only for what it did for students, but for what it did for the quality of citizenship. In the words of Quebec's 1996 Lacoursière Report, "Because the methods and operations of historical thought are substantially the same as those used in making reasoned personal decisions and in making a contribution to collective decisions at whatever level of life in society, history is a form of civic education."[51]

## History Education Today

Though old-style nation-building narrative has lost much of its appeal since the 1960s, it still commands a certain following. In 2006, for example, as described by Jocelyn Létourneau in this volume, some Quebec nationalists created a political storm when they objected to a new history curriculum that, in their view, did not pay sufficient attention to the traditional names, dates, and events of Quebec's history and that strayed too far from what they saw as Quebec's national narrative.[52] In English-speaking Canada, occasional complaints are heard that schools no longer teach the kind of unifying, heritage-celebrating history that its proponents believe society badly needs. This no doubt helps explain why J.L. Granatstein's 1998 polemic *Who Killed Canadian History?* was revised and republished in 2007, still insisting on its central claim that "Canadian students rarely learn anything of their country's past or its place in world history."[53] What is most notable about all such episodes, however, at least outside Quebec, is how little public and media attention they attract compared to similar episodes in the 1990s. For the time being, at least, the history wars seem to be over.

Today all but the most die-hard defenders of history-as-factual-narrative allow some place for the teaching of historical thinking, though they disagree over just what that entails. Similarly, all but the most ardent proponents of historical thinking endorse the teaching of some form of national history. What they object to is not the history of Canada but its reduction to a single supposedly authoritative story that says nothing about the nature of history as a form of disciplined inquiry. It is obvious that historical thinking cannot occur in a vacuum. Students must think historically about something, and in the Canadian setting, part of that something needs to be Canada. To extend a metaphor used by the historian Desmond Morton, Canadian history is a "'user's manual' to help the current residents to take advantage of the country with the least damage to themselves and their fellow citizens."[54]

In short, historical knowledge and historical thinking are two sides of the same coin, though there has not been much discussion of just what historical knowledge Canadian schools ought to teach. There are occasional calls for a national history curriculum, but there have been few attempts to delineate what such a curriculum might actually contain.[55] To date, there has been nothing in Canada to compare with Australia's 2009 plans for a national history curriculum that would combine national and global history while incorporating the elements of historical thinking. In any case, it is far from certain that a national curriculum, however defined, would do anything for the actual teaching of history in the classroom. Jocelyn Létourneau's research suggests that, despite the best efforts of historians and history educators, Quebec students continue to internalize the old nation-building view of Quebec's history with its emphasis on *la survivance*.[56] In the United Kingdom, it is not clear that the national history curriculum, with its proliferation of attainment targets and accountability measures, has had a positive impact on history teaching. In the United States, the evidence suggests that the National History Standards have not as yet improved students' knowledge and understanding of history, while the back-to-the-basics thrust of the No Child Left Behind legislation has had a deleterious effect on the subject. In Canada, a 2008 survey conducted for the Association for Canadian Studies found that the more history Canadians knew, the less proud they said they were of Canada's past.[57] It is not an especially surprising result, since depth of historical knowledge and understanding is likely to result in a more nuanced and critical view of both the past and of history; but it does suggest that those who see history as a bulwark of national identity and national unity might need to think again.

## NOTES

1 See Ken Osborne, "'Our History Syllabus Has Us Gasping': History in Canadian Schools – Past, Present, and Future," *Canadian Historical Review* 81 (2000): 404-35; and Penney Clark, "The Historical Context of Social Studies in English Canada," in *Challenges and Prospects for Canadian Social Studies*, ed. Alan Sears and Ian Wright (Vancouver: Pacific Educational Press, 2004), 17-37.
2 George J. Reeve, *Canada: Its History and Progress* (Toronto: Oxford University Press, 1926), iii.
3 Joseph Katz, *The Teaching of Canadian History in Canada: A Survey Study of the Teaching of Canadian History in Junior and Senior High Schools* (Winnipeg: University of Manitoba Press, 1953), 1, 13-14. Morton's comments can be found in the introduction to the report.
4 Kenneth N. Bell, "History Teaching in Schools," *University Monthly* 10 (1910): 381-82.
5 National Council of Education, *Observations on the Teaching of History and Civics in Primary and Secondary Schools of Canada* (Winnipeg: National Council of Education, 1923), 10.
6 *Report of the Royal Commission of Inquiry on Education in the Province of Quebec*, vol. 3, Part 2B: "The Programmes of Study and the Educational Services" (Quebec: Government of Quebec, 1965), 142. More generally known, after its chairperson, as the Parent Report.
7 Dominion Education Association, *Dominion Education Association, Minutes and Proceedings, 1892* (Toronto: Dominion Education Association, 1892), 50.
8 Ibid., 52.
9 On the textbook contest, see Geneviève Laloux-Jain, *Les manuels d'histoire du Canada au Québec et en Ontario de 1867 à 1914* (Quebec: Les Presses de l'Université Laval, 1974), 80ff.

10. Simon Roy, Clermont Gauthier, and Maurice Tardif, *Évolution des programmes d'histoire de 1861 à nos jours* (Quebec: Université Laval, les cahiers de recherche en administration et politiques scolaires, 1992); Stéphane Lévesque, "History and Social Studies in Quebec: An Historical Perspective" in *Challenges and Prospects in Canadian Social Studies*, ed. Alan Sears and Ian Wright (Vancouver: Pacific Educational Press, 2004), 55-72.

11. Daniel Moreau, "Les réformes de l'enseignement de l'histoire nationale, du rapport Parent au rapport Lacoursière," *Bulletin d'histoire politique* 14 (2006): 31-52.

12. Paul Cornell, Jean Hamelin, Fernand Ouellet, and Marcel Trudel, *Canada: Unity in Diversity* (Toronto: Holt, Rinehart, and Winston, 1967).

13. Isabel Skelton, *The Backwoodswoman: A Chronicle of Pioneer Home Life in Upper and Lower Canada* (Toronto: Ryerson, 1924), 7.

14. Cited in Carl Berger, ed., *Approaches to Canadian History* (Toronto: University of Toronto Press, 1967), 47.

15. Mary B. McCallum, "Embryo Citizenship," *Western School Journal* 14 (June 1919): 234-39.

16. Roscoe Fillmore, in *The Steelworker*, 24 November 1934, cited in Nicholas Fillmore, *Maritime Radical: The Life and Times of Roscoe Fillmore* (Toronto: Between the Lines, 1992), 174.

17. H.G. Wells, *Phoenix: A Summary of the Inescapable Conditions of World Reorganisation* (London: Secker and Warburg, 1942), 11. The "poison called history" is from Wells's *Travels of a Republican Radical in Search of Hot Water* (Harmondsworth: Penguin, 1939), 89-121.

18. Arthur Maheux, *Pourquoi sommes-nous divisés?* (Montreal: Beauchemin, 1943); André Laurendeau, *Nos écoles enseignent-elles la haine de l'anglais?* (Montreal: Éditions de l'Action nationale, 1941); Charles Bilodeau, "L'histoire nationale," in *Royal Commission Studies: A Selection of Essays Prepared for the Royal Commission on National Development in the Arts, Letters, and Sciences* (Ottawa: King's Printer, 1951), 217-30; Arthur Godbout, "Enquête sur l'enseignement de l'histoire au Canada français," *Culture: Sciences religieuses et profanes au Canada* 5 (1944): 156-68.

19. I have explored the 1944 Senate debate in "The Senate Textbook Debate of 1944," *Canadian Social Studies* 37 (2002), http://www.quasar.ualberta.ca/css. For the CNEA model curriculum, see "Report of the Committee for the Study of Canadian History Textbooks," *Canadian Education* 1 (October 1945): 3-35. See also my "Canadian Historians and National History: A 1950 Survey," *Canadian Social Studies* 36 (2002), http://www.quasar.ualberta.ca/css; and André Laurendeau, "Pour ou contre le manuel unique d'histoire du Canada?" *L'action nationale* 35 (1950): 337-95. The 1968 comment is in A.B. Hodgetts, *What Culture? What Heritage?* (Toronto: OISE, 1968), 13.

20. Ken Osborne, "Fred Morrow Fling and the Source-Method of Teaching History," *Theory and Research in Social Education* 31 (2003): 466-501 at 471.

21. For Alberta's embrace of social studies, see Amy von Heyking, *Creating Citizens: History and Identity in Alberta's Schools, 1905 to 1980* (Calgary: University of Calgary Press, 2006); and her "Selling Progressive Education to Albertans," *Historical Studies in Education* 1 and 2 (1998): 67-84. On the enterprise method, see Donalda

Dickie, *The Enterprise in Theory and Practice* (Toronto: Gage, 1940). More generally, see David W. Saxe, *Social Studies in Schools: A History of the Early Years* (Albany: SUNY Press, 1991).

22 S.E. Lang, "History," *Educational Journal of Western Canada* 3 (1904): 69-74; Fred Clarke, *The Foundations of History Teaching* (London: Oxford University Press, 1929); Lorne Pierce, *New History for Old* (Toronto: Ryerson, 1931); William A. Deacon, *My Vision of Canada* (Toronto: Ontario Publishing Company, 1933).

23 National Council of Education, *Observations on the Teaching of History and Civics in Primary and Secondary Schools of Canada* (Winnipeg: National Council of Education, 1923); Walter N. Sage, "The Teaching of History in the Elementary Schools of Canada," *Canadian Historical Association Annual Report 1930* (Ottawa: Canadian Historical Association, 1930), 55-63; Women's International League for Peace and Freedom, *Report of the Canadian School History Textbook Survey* (Toronto, 1933); André Laurendeau, *Nos écoles enseignent-elles la haine de l'anglais?* (Montreal: Éditions de l'Action nationale, 1941); Canada and Newfoundland Education Association, *A Report on the Text-books in Social Studies in the Dominion of Canada* (Toronto: 1941); Joseph Katz, *The Teaching of Canadian History in Canada: A Survey Study of the Teaching of Canadian History in Junior and Senior High Schools* (Winnipeg: University of Manitoba Press, 1953), 41; Northrop Frye, ed., *Design for Learning* (Toronto: University of Toronto Press, 1962), 111; Hodgetts, *What Culture?* 21.

24 Hilda Neatby, "Education for Democracy," *Dalhousie Review* 24 (1944): 49; National Council of Education, *Observations on the Teaching of History and Civics in Primary and Secondary Schools of Canada* (Winnipeg: 1923), 14.

25 See, for example, Mary Sheldon Barnes, *Studies in Historical Method* (Boston: Heath, 1896); American Historical Association, *The Study of History in Schools: Report to the American Historical Association by the Committee of Seven* (New York: Macmillan, 1899); Maurice W. Keatinge, *Studies in the Teaching of History* (London: A. and C. Black, 1910).

26 Cited in Robert Stamp, *The Schools of Ontario, 1876-1976* (Toronto: University of Toronto Press, 1982), 165.

27 Hodgetts, *What Culture?* 44ff.

28 Robert Martineau, *L'histoire à l'école: Matière à penser ...* (Montreal: L'Harmattan, 1998).

29 George W. Brown, *Readings in Canadian History* (Toronto: Dent, 1940); Guy Frégault and Marcel Trudel, *Histoire du Canada par les textes* (Montreal: Fides, 1952).

30 "The Teaching of Canadian History," *Report of the Royal Commission on Bilingualism and Biculturalism*, vol. 2 (Ottawa: Queen's Printer, 1968), 269-85; Manoly R. Lupul, *The Politics of Multiculturalism: A Ukrainian-Canadian Memoir* (Edmonton: Canadian Institute of Ukrainian Studies, 2005).

31 George Grant, *Lament for a Nation: The Defeat of Canadian Nationalism* (Toronto: McClelland and Stewart, 1965); Donald Creighton, *Canada's First Century* (Toronto: Macmillan, 1970).

32 Garnet McDiarmid and David Pratt, *Teaching Prejudice: A Content Analysis of Social Studies Textbooks Authorized for Use in Ontario* (Toronto: OISE, 1971). See also

Sylvie Vincent and Bernard Arcand, *L'image de l'Amérindien dans les manuels scolaires du Québec* (Montreal: Hurtubise, 1979); and Denis Blondin, *L'apprentissage de racisme dans les manuels scolaires* (Montreal: Editions Agence d'ARC, 1990).

33 Solange and Michel Chalvin, *Comment on abrutit nos enfants: La bêtise en 23 manuels scolaires* (Montreal: Les Éditions du Jour, 1962), 108.

34 Hodgetts, *What Culture?* 20, 24.

35 Robert Bothwell and J.L. Granatstein, *Our Century: The Canadian Journey in the Twentieth Century* (Toronto: McArthur, 2000), 250. More generally, see J.L. Granatstein, *Who Killed Canadian History?* (Toronto: HarperCollins, 1998).

36 Ken Osborne, "Some Psychological Concerns for the Teaching of History," *History and Social Science Teacher* 11 (1975): 15-25; Sam Wineburg, *Historical Thinking and Other Unnatural Acts* (Philadelphia: Temple University Press, 2001), 28-60; Edwin A. Peel, "Some Problems in the Psychology of History Teaching," in *Studies in the Nature and Teaching of History*, ed. William H. Burston and D. Thompson (London: Methuen, 1967), 159-90. For dissenters from the Piagetian orthodoxy, see Kieran Egan, *Educational Development* (New York: Oxford University Press, 1979); and Martin Booth, "Ages and Concepts: A Critique of the Piagetian Approach to History Teaching," in *The History Curriculum for Teachers*, ed. C. Portal (Lewes: Falmer Press, 1987), 22-38.

37 Jerome S. Bruner, *The Process of Education* (Cambridge, MA: Harvard University Press, 1960); Paul Hirst, *Knowledge and the Curriculum* (London: Routledge and Kegan Paul, 1975). More generally, see Ken Osborne, "'To the Schools We Must Look for the Good Canadian': Developments in the Teaching of History since 1960," *Journal of Canadian Studies* 23 (1987): 104-26.

38 Edwin Fenton, *The New Social Studies* (New York: Holt, Rinehart and Winston, 1968); Van R. Halsey, Jr., "American History: A New High School Course," *Social Education* 27 (1963): 249-52, 271; Richard H. Brown, "Learning How to Learn: The Amherst Project in History Education in the Schools," *Social Studies* 87 (1996): 267-73.

39 Tony Boddington, "The Schools Council History 13-16 Project," *History and Social Science Teacher* 19 (1984): 129-37; Ian Dawson, "The Schools History Project: A Study in Curriculum Development," *History Teacher* 22 (1989): 221-38.

40 Bob Davis, *Whatever Happened to High School History? Burying the Political Memory of Youth, Ontario 1945-1995* (Toronto: Lorimer, 1995), 184-98.

41 Patricia Bourne and John Eisenberg, *Social Issues in the Curriculum: Theory, Practice, and Evaluation* (Toronto: OISE, 1978); Donald W. Oliver and James P. Shaver, *Teaching Public Issues in the High School* (Boston: Houghton Mifflin, 1966).

42 Mel Levin, "Analysis of Public Issues: An Interdisciplinary Focus for Canadian Studies," *Canadian Journal of History and Social Science* 5 (1969): 1. On values clarification, see Sidney B. Simon, Leland B. Howe, and Howard Kirschenbaum, *Values Clarification: A Handbook of Practical Strategies for Teachers and Students* (New York: Hart, 1972). On values analysis, see Fred M. Newmann, *Clarifying Public Controversy: An Approach to Teaching Social Studies* (Boston: Little Brown, 1970); and Lawrence Metcalf, ed., *Values Education: Rationale, Strategies, and Procedures* (Washington: National Council for the Social Studies, 1971). On moral reasoning,

see Lawrence Kohlberg, "Moral Development and the New Social Studies," *Social Education* 37 (1973): 369-75; Clive Beck, Brian S. Crittenden, and Edward V. Sullivan, eds., *Moral Education: Interdisciplinary Approaches* (Toronto: University of Toronto Press, 1971); Clive Beck, Norma Bradley, and Jane Bradley-Cameron, *Reflecting on Values: Learning Materials for Grades 1-6* (Toronto: OISE, 1980); and Clive Beck, *Values and Living: Learning Materials for Grades 7 and 8* (Toronto: OISE, 1983). More generally, see Edward V. Sullivan and Clive Beck, "Moral Education in a Canadian Setting," in *Moral Education ... It Comes with the Territory*, ed. David Purpel and Kevin Ryan (Berkeley: McCutchan, 1976), 221-34; and John Meyer, Brian Burnham, and John Cholvat, ed., *Values Education: Theory/Practice/Problems/Prospects* (Waterloo: Wilfrid Laurier University Press, 1975).

43  Joe Clark, A *Nation Too Good to Lose: Renewing the Purpose of Canada* (Toronto: Key Porter, 1994), 194-98; Keith Spicer, "Canada: Values in Search of a Vision," in *Identities in North America: The Search for Community*, ed. Robert I. Earle and John D. Wirth (Stanford: Stanford University Press, 1995), 18.

44  Michael Bliss, "Privatizing the Mind: The Sundering of Canadian History, the Sundering of Canada," *Journal of Canadian Studies* 26 (1991-92): 5-17; Granatstein, *Who Killed Canadian History?*

45  For more on this, see Ken Osborne, "Teaching History in Schools: A Canadian Debate," *Journal of Curriculum Studies* 35 (2003): 585-626.

46  Patricia Shields and Doug Ramsay, *Teaching and Learning about Canadian History across Canada* (Toronto: Historica Foundation, 2002); Jean-Pierre Charland and Sabrina Moisan, *L'enseignement de l'histoire dans les écoles françaises du Canada* (Toronto: Historica Foundation, 2003); Ken Osborne, *Canadian History in the Schools* (Toronto: Historica Foundation, 2004).

47  *Social Studies Kindergarten to Grade 12 Validation Draft May 2003* (Edmonton: Alberta Learning, 2003), 1.

48  For the flavour of this research, see Ola Hallden, Gaea Leinhardt, Isabel Beck, and Catherine Stainton, ed., *Teaching and Learning in History* (Hillsdale: Erlbaum, 1994); Peter Lee, Alaric Dickinson, and John Slater, eds., *International Yearbook of History Education*, vol. 2 (London: Woburn Press, 1999); Peter Stearns, Peter Seixas, and Sam Wineburg, eds., *Knowing, Teaching, and Learning History* (New York: New York University Press, 2000); Wineburg, *Historical Thinking and Other Unnatural Acts*; S.G. Grant, *History Lessons: Teaching, Learning, and Testing in US High School Classrooms* (Mahwah: Erlbaum, 2003); and M. Suzanne Donovan and John D. Bransford, eds., *How Students Learn: History in the Classroom* (Washington: National Academies Press, 2005).

49  On this, see Stéphane Lévesque, *Thinking Historically: Educating Students for the Twenty-First Century* (Toronto: University of Toronto Press, 2008).

50  Mary Sheldon Barnes, *Studies in Historical Method* (Boston: Heath, 1896); American Historical Association, *The Study of History in Schools*; James Harvey Robinson, *The New History* (New York: Macmillan, 1912).

51  Quebec Ministry of Education, *Learning from the Past: Report of the Task Force on the Teaching of History* (Quebec: Ministry of Education, 1996), 4. Also known, after its chairperson, as the Lacoursière Report.

52 For criticisms of Quebec's new history curriculum, see Félix Bouvier and Michel Sara-Bournet, eds., *L'enseignement de l'histoire au début du XXIe siècle au Québec* (Quebec: Septentrion, 2008). For its defence, see Christian Laville, "La crise du programme d'histoire au Québec: Quelles leçons à tirer?" *Canadian Issues* (Fall 2006): 80-85; and his "L'enseignement de l'histoire à travers des lunettes noires de la question identitaire," *MENS: Revue d'histoire intellectuelle de l'Amérique française* 9 (2009): 243-63; and Michèle Dagenais and Christian Laville, "Le naufrage du projet de programme d'histoire 'nationale': Retour sur une occasion manqué accompagné de considérations sur l'éducation historique," *Revue d'histoire de l'Amérique française* 60 (2007) : 517-50.

53 Granatstein, *Who Killed Canadian History?* 2nd ed. (Toronto: HarperCollins, 2007), 11.

54 Desmond Morton, "Is National History Possible?" *Canadian Issues* (October 2003): 54.

55 For some attempts to delineate what such a curriculum might contain, see Ruth Sandwell, "Creating a Model Curriculum for Canadian History" (2007), http://www.pageflakes.com; Ken Osborne, *In Defence of History: Teaching the Past and the Meaning of Democratic Citizenship* (Toronto: Our Schools Ourselves, 1995), 29-40; and Paul Bennett, *Rediscovering Canadian History* (Toronto: OISE, 1980).

56 Jocelyn Létourneau, "Mémoire et récit de l'aventure historique du Québec chez les jeunes Québécois d'héritage canadien-français: Coup de sonde, amorce d'analyse des résultats, questionnements," *Canadian Historical Review* 85 (2004): 325-56; and "Remembering Our Past: An Examination of the Historical Memory of Young Québécois," in Ruth M. Sandwell, ed., *To the Past: History Education, Public Memory, and Citizenship in Canada* (Toronto: University of Toronto Press, 2006), 70-88.

57 Jack Jedwab, *Teaching Canadian History in the Era of Diversity* (Montreal: Association for Canadian Studies, 2008), http://acs-aec.ca.

# The Debate on History Education in Quebec

JOCELYN LÉTOURNEAU

In a book that caused quite a stir when it first appeared, the French historian Marc Ferro said that history was under surveillance.[1] How better to characterize the critical activity that, since April 2006, has been unleashed against efforts by the Quebec Ministry of Education (MEQ) to transform the national history course previously offered to high school students into a history and citizenship education course. The term "unleashed" is not exaggerated here. It properly conveys the magnitude of the reaction provoked by the ministerial decision to have young Quebecers acquire a broader and more complex comprehension of the Quebec historical experience, with a view toward building the Quebec of tomorrow. As the opponents to the state's initiative see it, the contemplated reform of the national history course had a quite different and utterly reprehensible goal: undoing the existing corpus of historical references underlying young Quebecers' historical consciousness. Hence the need, felt by those protesting the new history curriculum, to represent the MEQ's decision as a Trojan horse leading to the possible dismantling of a collective identity. Such a curriculum, one critic noted, would lead to nothing less than the "tranquil denationalization of Quebec's identity."[2]

The purpose of this chapter is not so much to resurrect the polemics surrounding the implementation of the new history curriculum as to set forth the general context of this particular debate, a context that persists: an open conflict between the partisans of two major politico-ideological currents, with the "conservatists" on the one hand and the "reformists" on the other,[3] for the purpose of establishing the meaning of the story to be told about Quebec's historical experience and determining the pedagogical-educational approaches specific to the teaching of history and its methodology.

This chapter focuses on the evolution of this debate and offers an analysis of its consequences for the teaching of history in Quebec.

## History of a Reform

### Background

Until September 2007, the history education of young people in school consisted mainly of a history course on Quebec-Canada, the basics of which dated back to 1982.[4] A mandatory part of the education of students, and required for a high school diploma, this course – taught in fourth high school (equivalent to the tenth year in English Canada) – had been adjusted over time. Nevertheless, its main narrative thread had seen few changes. While not factually incorrect, the body of knowledge and skills around which it was structured seemed due for an update. At least, this was the conclusion reached by the Task Force on History Teaching, chaired by the historian Jacques Lacoursière.[5] This body had been established in the wake of the Estates General on Education, a colossal enterprise undertaken in April 1995 for reflection and consultation on the effectiveness of the educational system. One of its main objectives was to reform the school curriculum (both primary and secondary), updating it from the triple perspective of existing knowledge, innovatively rich pedagogical trends, and society's needs for development and progress.[6]

Established in October 1995, the Lacoursière Committee submitted its report in May 1996. It recommended, among other things, that the current history curriculum be reworked to open it to the study of non-Western societies and to ensure that Aboriginal people and cultural communities were given a place commensurate with the role they played in Quebec history. The committee also recommended increasing the number of hours devoted to the teaching of Quebec history to bring it up to 100 hours a year for two consecutive years (third and fourth high school). Lastly, the committee urged the MEQ to introduce, in the mandatory examination on the history of Quebec-Canada, questions asking students to express their thinking in writing, in order to evaluate their acquisition of the reflective and interpretative skills already targeted in the old 1982 curriculum, but not previously well evaluated.

Much of the reaction to the Lacoursière Report was positive, but it also drew considerable opposition, directed mainly against the committee's supposed goal of teaching a history of Quebec that focused less on the conflict between francophones and anglophones than on the multicultural nature of Quebec society.[7] According to several critics, the Quebec historical experience, based on the committee's recommendations, would now be told *outside* the narrative thread of a "victim people" – an ill-timed and even dangerous move. Some critics went even further, arguing that by pushing the idea of cultural pluralism in Quebec society, the committee was trying to limit Quebec's francophones to playing second fiddle in their own history and society – an intolerable strategy, not to mention politically suicidal.

Notwithstanding the harshness of the critics, several of the Lacoursière Committee's recommendations on the teaching of history were taken up, borne by the mood of a period open to the idea of conjugating Quebec's identity differently, this time based on its relationship to otherness and on a new appreciation of its historical experience.[8]

**The Current Situation**
The replacement of the History of Québec and Canada curriculum with the History and Citizenship Education curriculum in the autumn of 2007 brought criticisms that mirrored those following the publication of the Lacoursière Report, the Inchauspé Report, and the wording of educational policy in *L'école, tout un programme*.[9] In all of those documents, the government was being pressed toward three major reforms. The first was to turn school into a vehicle for social cohesion by vesting the curriculum with a socialization mission in a pluralistic world. The second was to focus on proactive learning exercises capable of helping students develop their world view, personal identity, and ability to act – in particular, by acquiring the historical method and its basic principles (reflective practices, interpretive competence, criticism of sources, problem solving). The third was to take into account the diversified reality of Quebec society by broadening the content of the History of Quebec course.

In one sense, the new history curriculum was a product of its time. The end of the 1990s coincided with the appearance in Quebec's public space of new structuring concepts – a shared public culture, inclusive citizenship, social integration, interculturalism, Quebec nationhood, otherness – concepts that have permeated the speech, projects, expectations, and initiatives of many individual and institutional players. According to several advocates, such as Gérard Bouchard, a prominent historian and public intellectual, Quebec's historical experience urgently needed to be re-examined in view of these concepts, which would open a new area of scientific inquiry for understanding both Quebec and its political horizon so that it could achieve full emancipation.

It was not Bouchard, of course, who created the new history curriculum, which was designed by a team of specialists well versed in such exercises. But it was he, as a historian, who offered to a society awaiting new collective representations a different concept of its condition over time. It is clear that aspects of this seductive historical view, adapted to the present situation, resonated with the curriculum designers, who also had to meet the government's call to make the history course a means of preparing students to "participate responsibly in discussion, social choices, and living together in a democratic and pluralistic society, open to a complex world."[10] Hence the strong bond in the new history curriculum between acquiring historical knowledge and exercising citizenship. Simply put, the new history curriculum would encourage students to question the realities of their time in light of facts about the past, and offer ways for them to increase their awareness of the idea of change over time and of their role as change agents in their own society.

### *In the Heart of the New Curriculum*

The History and Citizenship Education program led to significant changes in educational content, educational approaches, and learning evaluation. I will now discuss the main characteristics of the ministry's initiative. This will suggest the degree of the change and allow us to evaluate the matter.

The new curriculum is spread over two cycles, from the first to the fourth years of high school. Covering Western history at the first level (first and second high school), and then the history of Quebec (third and fourth high school), it goes beyond event-based, chronological history. It pushes students to reflect on their own society as well as societies from other periods and places. It fosters their assimilation of historical knowledge as well as the acquisition of skills such as critical thinking and reflection.

The curriculum's educational objectives are as follows: (a) to lead students to understand the present in light of the past; and (b) to prepare them for enlightened participation in community life. These objectives are applicable to both the first and second cycles. Together, they assign a double purpose to the study of history: the past must bring about a comprehension of the present, and it must train a well-informed citizenry. The majority of students will not be pursuing studies in the social sciences, so this curriculum amounts to their final contact with the discipline of history, the objective of which is to train tomorrow's citizens at the same time as it equips them with the skills they need to understand history.

These educational objectives are reflected in the curriculum's three competencies, or skills, which are similar in the first and second cycles: integrate social realities into a historical perspective (skill 1); interpret social realities using the historical method (skill 2); and build (first cycle) and then consolidate (second cycle) their civic consciousness through history (skill 3). During the second cycle, however, the three skills become more complex: students are encouraged to pursue their reflection by seeking to understand history from within, evaluating the multiple causes of events, and considering changes over a long period of time.

Regarding educational content, the first history cycle is different from the second. As noted, the first-cycle history course mainly covers the history of the Western world, with a focus on those major events whose impact continues to be felt today. The second-cycle curriculum covers a series of social realities in order to provide an overview of Quebec's social history. The first year of this cycle (third high school) covers the history of Quebec chronologically; the second year (fourth high school) takes a thematic approach over time.

The first year of the second cycle covers the following periods: first occupiers; emerging society in New France; change of empire; claims and struggles in the British colony; forming the Canadian federation; modernizing Quebec society; and challenges facing Quebec society since 1980.[11] The second year allows for the exploration of four main topics: population and populating; economy and development; culture and intellectual movements; and power and authority. The final reality, a present-day challenge to society, arises from these four social realities, which can be studied in any given order. This final reality has students take stock of the knowledge and skills acquired in the course of the two cycles of the history curriculum.

To examine and understand these identified social realities, a study focus is proposed for each topic; a list of the concepts linked to the topic is drawn up; and the subject of inquiry (skill 1), subject of interpretation (skill 2), and subject of conscientization (skill 3) – that is, the subject of citizenship – are presented. Added to this is a list of the historical knowledge related to the subjects being interpreted as well as suggestions for how to go about viewing other societies. However, in fourth high school, the list of historical knowledge is much more developed than that for the previous year.[12]

What stands out from this summary description of the new history curriculum?

As its designers see it, the curriculum's objective is the acquisition of the skills and knowledge needed for understanding present-day society. A consideration of societies encourages students to compare their society with other societies and put them into perspective. To guide them when analyzing past and present social realities, students are provided with several tools, such as "cultural and chronological markers." Also, they are required to select and interpret a range of historical documents throughout the curriculum. The historical method allows students to apply horizontal skills such as information and communication technologies, effective work practices, language mastery, and so on; it also enables them to be more reflective and knowledgeable about the past, as well as about the present in relation to the past. This puts students in a position to question and interpret past and present social realities so that they can act as enlightened citizens in the society in which they are maturing.

## Disputing the Reform

### Initial Context of the Controversy

At a minimum, one can say that the new program, while closely related to other history curricula in the Western world for some time now, does not enjoy unanimous approval.[13] At present, it is difficult to determine how this curriculum has been received by the parties directly concerned – that is, by teachers and students. It is true that one of the two recognized groups of high school history teachers, the Société des professeurs d'histoire du Québec (SPHQ), opposes the curriculum and has denounced it vociferously.[14] But it should be added that the SPHQ's indictment has led to unease within the organization and does not have the consensus backing of the teachers.[15]

After a sharply critical article on the front page of *Le Devoir* on 26 April 2006, the controversy over the new history curriculum ignited.[16] Within days, the supposed flaws of this curriculum became a hotly debated subject in Quebec society. That debate generated a frenzy of commentary, much of which was ill informed. Indeed, many of the debaters – including editorial writers and columnists with no expertise in the field or experience with the challenges of teaching history – muddled the facts and saw a conspiracy just about everywhere.[17] Setting aside their confusion,[18] the critics focused on three main points: the curriculum had introduced a concept of Quebec history that was "less political," not "national," and "more plural"; the teaching focused on acquiring intellectual skills (historical method) rather than on the assimilation of factual knowledge (narrative of history); and the learning of history was geared toward revisiting the past in order to build a more cohesive Quebec society in the present.

In other words, and to be perfectly clear about the critics' position (as I understand it),[19] the history of Quebec is no longer presented on the basis of the canon of a francophone nation struggling for political recognition and resisting outside domination. And therein lies the first danger of the new curriculum: memories of survival and, therefore, a shared cultural heritage are fading away. Students are being taught that history is a mere presentation of the past, that there are several possible accounts of the past, and that the past can be built using a method that leaves room for interpretational relativity and that brings established accounts into question. Here lies another danger: that of going off course in the education of the young, who are for the most part ignorant of Quebec history, yet who are being allowed to play with the *form* of the past before mastering its substance. The past is no longer approached or studied in and of itself, but in conjunction with the present, with a view toward building an inclusive society in the future, and here, the danger is double: first, of submitting the past to the designs of present-day social correctness; and second, of sanitizing history by skirting around anything in it deemed to be overly political, with the risk of mortgaging a socially cohesive future.

Let us review each of these "dangers" by elucidating the supporting argument.

**A Transmission Crisis**

The critics of the new curriculum find an organic relationship between identity and history; it follows that altering or revising history means modifying or changing identity. It is dangerous for a small, fragile, and vulnerable nation such as Quebec, which is in a constant state of tension with Itself and with the Other, to challenge or even re-examine the answers to its fundamental questions (Where do we come from? Who are we? Where are we going?), for doing so would reopen the question of collective identity. By proposing another history of Quebec's experience over time, "a history finessing the politico-national framework familiar to most Quebecers,"[20] the ministry is opening the door to a risky reworking of the collective identity. In no longer telling the story of the Quebec people through a painful narrative of its condition – "the essential key of its identity" – the ministry is jeopardizing the transmission of Quebec culture to the younger generation. How can a culture be reproduced if, instead of regenerating it in the great chambers of its history, where its national "We" was formed, it should become lost either in the labyrinths of its past, where multiple identities were asserted and unleashed,[21] or in the vast expanses of modernity, where abstract generalities and other disembodied processes hold sway against entrenched, historicized, and politicized communities?[22]

**Taking Education Off Course**
According to its critics, the new history curriculum is also culpable with regard to its emphasis on skills acquisition rather than knowledge. Taking their inspiration from the socio-constructivist current, the curriculum designers have indeed, in the name of blind pedagogical progressivism, put the cart before the horse by trying to turn students into competent builders of knowledge rather than apprentice students of knowledge. Changing the status of students in this way, thus enabling them to discover and apply interpretive skills, constitutes a major risk: they will believe they can reflect on and debate history even though they have neither the factual nor the conceptual knowledge to elaborate on and assert a point of view.

Given the age and intellectual rawness of high school students, there cannot be any question of pursuing any other educational goal than instilling facts – and yet more facts – in them, thereby filling them with the raw material they must know before beginning to think about the past or to entertain it. This is the perspective brought to the debate by the journalist Christian Rioux,[23] who bases his point of view on the opinions of eminent French historians, including Alain Corbin and Pierre Nora.

According to Rioux, who is passionately concerned about the new curriculum and sharply critical of its focus, the learning of history should indeed centre on chronological facts – a tried and true approach to combating the amnesia affecting today's youth, whom the new teaching methodology refuses to subject to a "memorization effort" on the pretext that "teaching history in school is not for memorizing a simplified version of the learned knowledge constructed by historians or for assimilating encyclopedic-type factual knowledge."[24] For Rioux, the substitution by educational experts of abstract issues and thematic approaches for concrete dates and places of (national) life can only consolidate the chronological amnesia of youth, who no longer know how to organize knowledge hierarchically around a "temporal grammar" – a grammar that is the bearer of the sense of history that today's students lack. Rioux implicitly asks: What is the point of learning history if not to acquire a comprehensive, general sense of the world – and of concrete societies? The new teaching methodology – the value of which remains to be proven – is challenging, even undoing, that sense of the world in the name of fashionable socio-constructivist theories, interpretive pluralism, and neocognitivism.

**A Distortion of History**

The same critics point to a third danger of the new curriculum: its pervasive "presentism." Given its objectives for citizenship education, the curriculum is attuned to society's present-day need to rebuild its civic space, but the approach it takes involves laying out this task in the form of retrospective teleology – a kind of narration of the deliberative, consensual Nation, from yesteryear to tomorrow. But in the recitation of this historic process, besides emptying the past of everything it contains in terms of enduring or deadlocked disputes – as present social cohesion requires! – modern citizenship ethics require a highly skewed reading of what has come before. So it is that the new curriculum, directed toward what is presumed to be the diktat of citizenship, is depoliticizing, denationalizing, and desubjectivizing the history of Quebec. It is no longer a matter of studying the record of a historically nameable *people*, colonized and minoritized, that has developed a special relationship with modernity and that remains fragile as a political community. Rather, it is a matter of being aware, in a tediously functionalist way, of the historical roots of present-day Quebec *society*, a society that is also perceived in terms of (its) universal and normative figures rather than through its specific, unique historicity. In terms of raising young Quebecers' consciousness of their identity, it goes without saying that such a narrative of the past disrupts or atrophies their relationship to their culture and memory. The historian Jacques Rouillard expressed in no uncertain terms the fear – in terms of identity and memory – of such a split between the generations: "The focus of the new curriculum," the University of Montreal professor wrote, "will mold the memory of future generations of Quebecers. [Yet] it is through its perception of the past that a people gives meaning to its evolution, an important ingredient that helps shape the choices of a society."[25] To that, the Collectif pour une éducation de qualité (CÉQ) adds:

> In the same fashion that poor teaching of French undermines the vitality of our common language and hinders the integration of immigrant children,

the incomplete, ideologized, teaching of history deprives them, as it does all young Quebecers, of the keys to reading they need to comprehend our contemporary debates, all of which have their roots in the history of our community. As it becomes more and more exposed to the diversity of beliefs and cultural backgrounds within it, Quebec will have trouble finding any unifying language or shared reference, if it neglects the very foundations of that language, and will risk condemning part of its youth to poor teaching.[26]

## The Controversy at the Present Time

It seems odd that the CÉQ, a "conservatist" lobby with a strong presence in the debate on the teaching of history, would insist so much on finding common historical points of reference for Quebec society as a means of coalescing that society's diversity around a shared narrative. Odd, because it was precisely this compulsion to propose a narrative of the past relevant to Quebec's diversity that motivated the "reformists" to produce a different history of Quebec.

In this context, the Bouchard-Taylor Report was a crucial event in the ideological struggle between the two sides. While the report, when it was published, was rather poorly received in political circles, the document's content may well influence future thinking on a large number of delicate questions, including what history will be produced and taught to young Quebecers.[27]

In this regard, the report contains some absolutely critical passages that partially confirm the reformists' positions and consequently trouble the conservatists. Two principles underpin the commission's positions regarding the building of a conciliatory future for Quebec society.[28] The first is that in order to build the Quebec of tomorrow, all of Quebec's inhabitants – including new Quebecers – *must* be able to recognize themselves in the idea of a (Quebec) nation conceived as a civic and historic project and find (their) shared values therein. The second is that school serves as one of the instruments and places where social cohesion – a sense of belonging to Quebec society – can be developed in all Quebecers.

The commission built its argument about what relationship to establish with the past on the basis of these two principles. This argument's logic is structured around a few key concepts, including the following:

- *The past is not a closed book, written once and forever; it can be reinterpreted.* A nation is a historic project within which everyone tries to live according to certain values – values that, however, change over time. There is no historical determinism: every generation has its own way of redefining and appropriating tradition and projecting it forward. At any given moment, several frames in the past can be perceived. History is never linear, which renders complex the issue of faithfulness to history. Indeed, the "future of the past" remains an open question; and here, democratic debate is the only possible arbiter. In this way, we can view the past from an angle leading into the present. This approach is acceptable to the extent that the past is an infinitely complex breeding ground. The past can give rise to several interpretations that are not incompatible with the meanings it bears and that are to be (re)discovered or brought into being, in light of what is presently useful to society.

- Quebec's collective experience encompasses strong values that must be identified. A collective experience is defined, first, by the values that it allows to flourish within it – values that over time become referential and that constitute a cultural heritage, a living-togetherness. Among the values central to the Quebec experience, strongly asserted at present, are pluralism, equality, solidarity, secularity, non-discrimination, non-violence, education, and the concept of community. These, of course, are universal values, so one might well wonder how they could feed a unique identity, how they could have taken on a specific meaning in a given community. The answer lies in what we shall call "historicization." This is a process by which a universal value acquires a particular meaning or connotation for a given society owing to its association with a past or memorable collective experience: struggles, traumas, wounds, achievements, founding acts, and so on. Such intensely lived experiences mark the collective memory and imagination profoundly. When such universal values within a history are appropriated, they become founding values. Moreover, there is a process to be initiated for recognizing and gathering the values borne by the ethnocultural traditions present in Quebec's territory.

- Quebec's experience should be told through historicized values. Building a national memory and history that takes increasing ethnocultural diversity into account and that renders the French Canadian past significant and accessible to citizens whatever their origin, without emptying it of its substance, is one of the main ways to consolidate a growing collective identity in Quebec. In this regard, members of ethnic minorities could be valuable interlocutors when new questions to ask of Quebec's past are being sought. They could also enrich Quebec's memory and history substantially by adding their own accounts. Finally, building and disseminating that memory and history could contribute greatly toward making known and promoting the shared values specific to that Quebec society/nationhood, as the product of historicizations leading to as many contemporary appropriations.

At first glance, it is understandable that the "conservatists" would have had trouble embracing the commission's perspective, which bluntly suggests that Quebec's history be rewritten by building a new narrative around current themes (the value and ideal of equality, for example, or of diversity), "historicized" in Quebec's experience. Similarly, the report's contention that it is possible to make something of the past other than what the past appears to have made of us seems to have disturbed several conservatists, who see in the historiographical process the possibility of a new, sneakier "conquest" than the first – a conquest that would be carried out in the name of collective happiness by absorbing a people into a big abstract We that would be empty of historic substance and that would reinterpret the meaning of Quebec's destiny on the basis of the present-day needs of the civic nation.

While some of the commission's proposals for a new historiography are bold, it has never attempted to break radically with the central narrative thread of Quebecers' great collective narrative, which in its customary version speaks of struggles and resistance, subordination and survival, failures and hard-earned successes.[29] For the commission, it would indeed appear that it is within the narrative of shared oppressions lived by a majority of French Canadian origin – as well as by many of those who, individually or as members of ethnic minorities, settled in Quebec over time – that the possibility of a new history of Quebec nationhood can be found, a history consequently focusing on painful memories of the sufferings shared by its inhabitants, as well as on the values they developed as a result of their experience of this difficult condition.

According to the commission, the history of Quebec is to be built around the traces of coercion, dependency, servitude, subjugation, and humiliation suffered by the majority of those who made Quebec in the past, a narrative of oppression to be transmitted to Quebec's youth so that they can shape their sense of belonging to today's Quebec nation, a nation resisting the Other since time immemorial and confident in itself, now and forever. This is the process that, for those who currently make up Quebec, could build the bridges favouring encounters among the multiple identities constituting the Quebec political community.

## Conclusion

It is difficult to "forecast" Quebec's history. The coming years will surely be marked by a continuing dispute between the conservatists and the reformists over which history of Quebec to tell and teach. This controversy indicates a wider social debate touching on renewal of the symbolic foundations of Quebec society/nationhood. This renewal finds part of its conditions, not to say its obligation, in the fact that Quebec, by transforming itself demographically (fairly high levels of immigration) and sociologically (settling a new generation in the heart of the society), is having trouble recognizing itself in the accounts on which it has founded its collective identity up to now. On the one hand, new Quebecers are not familiar with the history of Quebec, and this relative ignorance – which is no more profound than it is among Quebecers who have been rooted in the province for a longer time – does not appear to worry them. Indeed, it is in the present that new Quebecers want to build the Quebec of tomorrow, and it appears that the "old stories" that made this society/nation leave them rather cold. In contrast, the younger generation, the one calmly carving out a place for itself in society, appears to want to establish a relationship with Quebec's past that is free of the four mythico-histories on which Quebec's identity and imagination have been based until now: the unfinished quest of Self, destiny gone awry, the Other blamed, the uncompleted nation.[30]

Where its symbolic representations are concerned, Quebec is presently living through a transitional, transitory period – that is, a period of tension and ambiguity between its ancient founding myths, which have not disappeared and continue to structure its memory and collective identity, and the new myths, which have not fully emerged and have yet to find their legitimate place in the public space. For the past several years, Gérard Bouchard has devoted his intellectual undertaking to this effort to invent new refounding myths of Quebec nationhood. He is not alone in pursuing this goal, and his approach has been contested. But that same approach points to what he and others perceive as decisive in Quebec's program for the future: changing the collective grand narrative to pave the way for better social integration, which will be the cornerstone of tomorrow's Quebec.

Basically, the debate concerning the new history curriculum first and foremost involves the issue of reproducing a society in its known or modified historic and mnemonic figures, and the renewal of its heirs within the identity space opened up by those old or new figures. Like many other societies throughout the world, Quebec is trying to enter the future while avoiding committing cultural and identity hara-kiri. The problem is simple: Quebec society only has a future to the extent that it updates its ancestral figures. And here lies the rub: How do you regenerate a culture and identity without having its heirs become alien to that culture and identity in the process of transformation? This is where history comes into play as the link or connection between both "old" and "new" Quebecers and the past/present.

What kind of history does the future of Quebec hold – and for whom, and created with what aim and what collective meaning? This is the essential question underlying the debate on the nature of the past to be presented, taught, and transmitted to young Quebecers.

## NOTES

This is a shortened and translated version of an article published in *Revue française de pédagogie* 165 (October-November-December 2008): 43-54. This chapter was translated from French by Yolanda Stern Broad.

1 Marc Ferro, *L'histoire sous surveillance* (Paris: Calmann-Lévy, 1985).
2 Mathieu Bock-Côté, *La dénationalisation tranquille* (Montreal: Boréal, 2007).
3 In my view, "conservatist" and "reformist" are the least pejorative terms. They simply designate, in the case of the "conservatists," those who are opposed to the new curriculum and who want to return to the more traditional teaching of the history of Quebec as a nation. The reformists are those who support the new curriculum and who endorse the idea of updating the learning content and instructional approaches specific to teaching the history of Quebec.
4 Daniel Moreau, "Les réformes de l'enseignement de l'histoire nationale, du Rapport Parent au Rapport Lacoursière," *Bulletin d'histoire politique* 14, 2 (Spring 2006): 31-52.
5 Comité Lacoursière, *Learning from the Past: Report of the Task Force on History Teaching* (Quebec City: Ministry of Education, 1996).
6 Paul Inchauspé, *Réaffirmer l'école, prendre le virage du succès: Rapport du Groupe de travail sur la réforme du curriculum* (Quebec: Ministère de l'Éducation, 1997), http://www.mels.gouv.qc.ca.
7 Josée Legault, "Histoire d'exister," *Le Devoir*, 17 July 1996; Béatrice Richard, "Se souvenir et devenir, ou oublier et disparaître?" *Le Devoir*, 25 August 1996; Louis Cornellier, "Comment peut-on être Québécois pure laine?" *Le Devoir*, 7-8 September 1996; Jean-Marc Léger, "L'histoire nationale révisée à l'aune du multiculturalisme," *Bulletin d'histoire politique* 5, 1 (Fall 1996): 59-63; Marc-Aimé Guérin, *La faillite de l'enseignement de l'histoire au Québec* (Montreal: Guérin, 1996).
8 Robert Martineau, "Le Rapport Lacoursière: Une relecture dix ans après," *Bulletin d'histoire politique* 14, 3 (2006): 13-29.
9 Ministère de l'Éducation, *"L'école, tout un programme"* (1997), http://www.mels.gouv.qc.ca.

10 This goal appears in the first introductory paragraph of the curriculum, *Histoire et éducation à la citoyenneté*. See *Programme de formation de l'école québécoise: Enseignement secondaire, deuxième cycle* (Quebec: Ministère de l'Éducation, 2006).
11 In the initial version, dated 26 May 2005, which set off all the reaction, the curriculum focused more on the following periods: first occupiers; emerging Canadian society; achieving democracy in the British colony; forming the Canadian federation; modernizing Quebec society; and present-day Quebec.
12 This section reproduces *in extenso* certain items from the unpublished document "Analyse du nouveau programme d'histoire au secondaire," prepared by the Comité d'analyse (histoire) and submitted to the Comité-conseil du programme d'études préuniversitaires, sciences humaines, ministère de l'Éducation, du Loisir et du Sport, Québec.
13 Michèle Dagenais and Christian Laville, "Le naufrage du programme d'histoire nationale: Retour sur une occasion manquée, accompagné de considérations sur l'éducation historique," *Revue d'histoire de l'Amérique française* 60, 4 (2007): 517-50; Marc-André Éthier, "Apprendre à exercer sa citoyenneté à l'aide de l'histoire," *Bulletin d'histoire politique* 15, 2 (2007): 53-58.
14 Felix Bouvier and Laurent Lamontagne, "Quand l'histoire se fait outil de propagande," *Le Devoir*, 28 April 2006.
15 Note that a rival group to the SPHQ, l'Association québécoise pour l'enseignement en univers social (AQEUS), which includes a fair number of history teachers, along with high school geography and economics teachers, was formed in April 2007.
16 Antoine Robitaille, "Cours d'histoire épuré au secondaire," *Le Devoir*, 27 April 2006.
17 Franco Nuovo, "Drôle d'histoire," *Le Journal de Montreal*, 28 April 2006; Michel David, "La culture de l'oubli," *Le Devoir*, 29 April 2006; Denyse Bombardier, "Les belles histoires des pays d'en haut," *Le Devoir*, 29 April 2006; André Pratte, "L'histoire sans dates," *La Presse*, 28 April 2006; Josée Boileau, "Pas de chicane!" *Le Devoir*, 28 April 2006; Christian Rioux, "Suicide assisté," *Le Devoir*, 5 May 2006; Lysianne Gagnon, "L'histoire pour les nuls," *La Presse*, 5 May 2006.
18 Jean-Francois Cardin, "Les programmes d'histoire nationale: Une mise au point," *Le Devoir*, 30 April 2006.
19 For more evidence on the accuracy of my reading, see Michel Seymour, "L'impossible neutralité face à l'histoire: Remarques sur les documents de travail du MEQ 'Histoire et éducation à la citoyenneté (secondaire III et secondaire IV)," *Bulletin d'histoire politique* 15, 2 (2007): 19-38; Denis Vaugeois, "Les mérites de l'histoire," *Le Devoir*, 4 May 2006 ; Lucie Piché and Marc Vallières, *Avis sur le projet de réforme du programme Histoire et éducation à la citoyenneté du deuxième cycle du secondaire* (Montreal: Institut d'histoire de l'Amérique française, 2006); "L'état des lieux en éducation au Québec," special issue of *Argument* 9, 1 (2006-7); Chaire Hector-Fabre d'histoire du Québec, "Quelle histoire du Québec enseigner?" *Bulletin d'histoire politique* 15, 1 (2006): 183-90.
20 CÉQ (Collectif pour une éducation de qualité), *Transmettre adéquatement un patrimoine culturel et historique*, brief submitted to the Bouchard-Taylor Commission, Montreal, 19 October 2007, 6.

21 Jacques Beauchemin, *La société des identités: Éthique et politique dans le monde contemporain* (Montreal: Athéna, 2004); Jacques Beauchemin, *L'Histoire en trop: La mauvaise conscience des sourerainistes* (Montreal: VLB, 2002).
22 Joseph Yvon Thériault, *Critique de l'américanité: Mémoire et démocratie au Québec* (Montreal: Québec-Amérique, 2002).
23 Christian Rioux, "Une génération d'amnésiques," *Le Devoir*, 25 May 2006.
24 Christian Rioux, "La fin de l'histoire," *Le Devoir*, 30 June 2006.
25 Jacques Rouillard, "Le nouveau programme d'histoire a largué le 'nous' au profit du 'je,'" *Bulletin d'histoire politique* 15, 2 (2007): 85-88.
26 CÉQ, *Transmettre adéquatement*. This quote was translated by Yolanda Stern Broad.
27 Rapport Bouchard-Taylor (Commission de consultation sur les pratiques d'accommodement reliées aux différences culturelles), *Fonder l'avenir: Le temps de la conciliation* (Quebec: 2008), http://www.accommodements.qc.ca.
28 One is reminded of the title of the report, *Fonder l'avenir: Le temps de la conciliation* [Building the future: A time for reconciliation].
29 Jocelyn Létourneau, *A History for the Future: Rewriting Memory and Identity in Quebec* (Montreal and Kingston: McGill-Queen's University Press, 2004).
30 Jocelyn Létourneau, "Mythistoires de losers: Introduction au roman historial des Québécois d'héritage canadiens-français," *Histoire sociale/Social History* 39, 77 (2006): 157-80.

# Teaching History from an Indigenous Perspective
## Four Winding Paths up the Mountain

MICHAEL MARKER

For Aboriginal students, history courses in Canadian schools are probably the most difficult. The problems are not simply a matter of the lack of inclusion of Native content and that Aboriginal students must endure readings and discussions that still regard their ancestors as part of the conquest of a wilderness tamed in the making of a civilized nation. Rather, the deeper problem is that the categories of what counts as history do not often correspond with the ways that traditional indigenous communities make meaning out of the past. While revisionist and more inclusive histories have brought the experiences of indigenous peoples into a more public conversation about social justice and the consequences of "nation building" as colonization, the deeper perspectives of Aboriginal peoples in regard to their understandings of the processes of time and the principles of their knowledge systems are usually missing.

In this chapter, I discuss four themes of indigenous historical consciousness that travel outside of ways that history courses are constructed and taught. These themes reverberate around the ways that indigenous elders, traditional knowledge specialists, and Native scholars have referenced the past to communicate truths and identities that bind their worlds together. The predicament in the teaching of history from an indigenous perspective has not just been the application of the "selective tradition," as Raymond Williams puts it, which selects the facts and stories; it lies more in the ways that the stories are told and in the purposes of the stories. Cherokee author Thomas King has written that "the truth about stories is that that's all we are."[1] There is a deep and dangerous purpose in narrating the past, and indigenous people understood this well. A wrongly told story – and by this I do not mean strictly inaccurate – could have devastating consequences for a village, since people made important survival decisions based on their reading of the environment and on the oral traditions that referenced sacred relationships with the ecologies of the past.

Remembering the ways my grandfather talked about time, landscapes, and animals, and my work with Coast Salish communities in British Columbia and Washington State, has taught me a great deal about how the past is understood and experienced in indigenous communities. Four themes of indigenous ways of understanding the past that are difficult to integrate into the conventions of Western historiographies have to do with (1) the circular nature of time and the ways oral tradition is integrated with recurring events – notions of "progress" are problematic in this way of understanding history; (2) the often central theme of relationships with landscape and non-humans; (3) an emphasis on the local landscape as containing the meaning of both time and place rather than on analyses of global social and political change; and (4) indigenous narratives and perspectives on the histories of colonization that have attempted to displace and replace indigenous knowledge.

These concepts have been central concerns of the indigenous scholars who have emerged in the past twenty years to challenge the assumptions of Western epistemologies and interpretations of the past. The focus on decolonization and the assertion of indigenous meanings have been challenges for historians and history teachers wanting to find common ground with historiographies that seem to be worlds apart. The crisis in confidence that has plagued history, anthropology, and even the sciences, as a result of indigenous voices "writing back" to the empire, has not produced changes in the way history is understood and taught in schools outside of universities. These four themes of indigenous historiography are all integrated; but to use an indigenous metaphor, they can be thought of as intersecting paths up a mountain. Many indigenous peoples have sacred mountains and other revered sites within their traditional territories. These are places where important stories happened, many of them related to the creation of the world. In systems of place-based traditional knowledge, stories are located in these spots on the physical landscape. Elders often refer to the many paths that one takes to arrive at the top of the mountain. Each path constitutes a physical *and* metaphysical journey. Comprehending indigenous ways of seeing the past requires travelling these intellectual trails up an indigenous mountain and leaving behind some of the expectations about what constitutes "history" from a Western mindset.

In classrooms, Aboriginal students come up against an almost impenetrable wall of historical "facts," which teachers deliver in tightly sealed conceptual boxes. Aboriginal students who sometimes question these "facts" can be regarded as disruptive to educational processes. One of my Aboriginal graduate students told me how questioning historical "facts" in a public school history classroom was a "defining moment" in her educational experience. The teacher was explaining the early origins of Aboriginal peoples in Canada by telling the students that the Bering Land Bridge enabled the early "Aboriginal immigrants" to cross to North America. The graduate student remembered asking "if they had left footprints, or a note, or something. How do we really know this for sure?" She was questioning the "truth" of the official explanation: an explanation that contradicted the creation stories of human origins from her own Aboriginal community. The teacher insisted that the class had gone over the ways in which scientific evidence shows the reality of the past, but the Aboriginal student continued to be dissatisfied with an official history that placed her ancestors as part of someone else's story of the past – and as immigrants. The student told me: "I remember being punished by having to stand in the corner."

In many ways, this story of an Aboriginal student's "defining moment" in schooling reveals much about the problems of cross-cultural communication in the classroom as they relate to interpretations of history. Aboriginal children who are raised to respect the traditions of their communities grow up hearing elders tell creation stories of how the people were placed on the land by the Creator. These stories are not the same as religious traditions that clash with teleologies of modernist education. They are narratives that define the meaning of the *local* geography. These stories are told in ways that expose deep truths about the people's responsibilities and relationships to the land. There is a fundamental difference between a story that places people as coming *to* the land and a story that has people coming *from* the land. Vine Deloria is the scholar most recognized for his critiques of the Bering Land Bridge theories. While all indigenous academics are familiar with Deloria's work, social studies and history teachers in schools usually are not aware of iconoclastic Native scholarship. Too many teachers are seldom aware of writings that contradict accepted school-based knowledge about the past. Deloria has articulated what is often felt but not said by Aboriginal students in classrooms: "By making us immigrants to North

America they are able to deny the fact that we were the full, complete, and total owners of this continent. They are able to see us simply as earlier interlopers and therefore throw back at us the accusation that we had simply *found* North America a little earlier than they had."[2]

Deloria, like other indigenous writers and community leaders, understands the concrete consequences of how students are taught the history of Aboriginal peoples. The self-determination efforts of First Nations communities are part of a larger movement toward decolonization. When Aboriginal students are told that their cultural interpretation of history is not the correct one, the hegemony of this moment is often internalized. This deteriorates the ability of indigenous communities to organize around their own epistemologies. Mi'kmaq scholar Marie Battiste has called this "cognitive imperialism." She has pointed out that the processes of colonization through education have produced "cognitive prisons" for Aboriginal students.[3]

## Circular Time and Linear Time

Many indigenous scholars have referred to the contrasts and even contradictions between indigenous and Western understandings of time and reality. This is often discussed as the difference between circular and linear conceptions of time. Donald Fixico, an indigenous historian, has explained that "to understand Indian people and their ways of life, it is evident that the 'circle' occupies an integral role in the beliefs of American Indians."[4] He goes on to point out differences in "thinking" between Aboriginal and non-Aboriginal peoples: "From an opposing point of view, the linear way of thinking and perceiving the world is the non-Indian way that Native Americans have had to learn in schools and while working with other Americans ... Their philosophies, ideologies, logic, and world views proved distinctively different due to the separate evolutions of the human mind set in the Eastern Hemisphere and Western Hemisphere during the pre-Columbian era."[5]

Linguist Benjamin Whorf, in his work with the Hopi, is probably the best-known scholar for seeing the connections among cognition, language, and conceptions of time. Whorf wrote that for the Hopi, "time is not a motion but a 'getting later' of everything that has ever been done."[6] History, from an indigenous point of view, then, is not a linear progression of people and ideas in time, but rather a spiralling of events and themes that appear and reappear within circles of seasons and that are identified in oral traditions. Of course, this does not mean that indigenous historical thought has no way of accounting for changes over time; it is only that the changes in both human societies and landscapes include characters and contexts that circulate to merge eras together in a non-linear fashion.

As Whorf discovered indigenous conceptions of time through linguistics, Julie Cruikshank and other anthropologists doing work on oral history and oral tradition have described the contemporary presence and utility of the circular way of understanding the indigenous past. Cruikshank, drawing on the views of Canadian historian Harold Innis, points to ways that oral tradition has the "potential to counterbalance mechanical segmentation of time and space."[7] In her work with Aboriginal elders in Yukon, Cruikshank collected stories that shifted back and forth in time and that did not respond to Western categories of past, present, mythos,[8] and fact. Recognizing that the past is culturally constituted and culturally narrated, she listened to elders tell stories about the 1940s that included individuals from oral traditions hundreds of years before that era. The sense of linear time was folded and curved to account for the merging of events and characters; this created a circular and recurring moral universe within an indigenous epistemology. "These narratives erased any distinction between 'story' and 'history.'"[9]

Indigenous historiographies that emphasize the circular patterns of time are essential components of a decolonizing curriculum for Aboriginal students and schools. One of the central goals of First Nations communities is to "bring back" pre-contact knowledge and values that integrate these understandings of space and time into a contemporary curriculum that fortifies a sense of Aboriginal identity in the youth. Moving away from a linear version of time and toward an indigenous way of understanding the past reinforces the community's ways of thinking about social organization and identity. Indigenous world views tend to emphasize the moral and spiritual structure of events. These are immersed in recurring stories that circulate to bind reality together. The linear version of time, associated with Eurocentric values, as Leroy Littlebear points out, "manifests itself in terms of bigger, higher, newer, or faster being preferred over smaller, lower, older, or slower."[10] From an indigenous perspective, the assumptions of "progress" that are inextricable from both modernity and hierarchical categories that emerged from colonization are in collision with a circular cosmology that sees new shapes of reality as returning versions of both ancestors and ideas. History curricula for schools in Canada have emphasized notions of progress that tend to relegate First Nations to a primitive past on a timeline leading to a more progressive present era.

Indigenous language teachers have often explained to me how important the circular experience of time is in bringing the languages back into a contemporary context. To make the languages a vital part of the place-based identities of Aboriginal students, the stories, place names, and moral understandings from ancestors must be integrated into the contemporary experience that youth have with their present socio-economic conditions. The contemporary experience of Aboriginal youth includes the dominance of digital technology and media. Language revival, for Aboriginal communities, requires an engagement with the natural ecology such that the oral traditions and mental maps of the landscape are recycled from the past into the present consciousness. Indigenous elders understand the connection between landscapes and mindscapes for future generations. The language comes from the land, and learning the language builds a cognitive geography of the traditional territory. Indigenous languages are often referred to as "verb oriented" rather than "noun oriented." This is related to the sense that words describe a universe in constant motion, a "doing" rather than a "being" in the world. This is also connected to the concept of circular time such that reality moves in and out of present and past and the language captures the dynamism of this revolving motion.

## Relationships with Landscape and Non-Humans

While Canadian history textbooks and courses usually include some discussion of plants and animals, this inquiry is usually limited to considerations of the socio-economic effects of certain plants and animals as resources for human exploitation. For example, histories of the fur trade era would probably include a discussion of the importance of the beaver, and the history of British Columbia would include information about the value of the salmon fishery to both Aboriginal and non-Aboriginal societies. Indigenous systems of knowledge and understandings of the past are different from these approaches in that they place animals as unsegmented from human beings. Many indigenous traditions recognize the animals as having been created first and therefore as being older and wiser than humans. From an indigenous perspective, much of the knowledge of the past *came* from the relationships that human beings developed with animals. The histories of tribal people are filled with stories of how particular animals sacrificed and taught the human communities. In these narratives, the sacred ecology of animals and humans and the sustaining cycles of life are explained. Many of these stories demonstrate the reasons for particular seasonal ceremonies. Among

Coast Salish peoples, for instance, the First Salmon Ceremony is conducted each year to honour the Salmon People who sacrifice themselves to feed the villages. The stories of how the people originally came to have the fish are told, and the respectful relationship between salmon and humans is affirmed in the stories and ceremonies. The salmon are not just a resource that can be traced historically; they are integrated into all aspects of the past, present, and future for the Coast Salish people. Relationships between animals and humans are central to indigenous approaches to history.

These ways of understanding relationships to animals are more than simply metaphorical frames of reference about cultures in the past. They are essential concepts for understanding treaty negotiations and present-day land claims – concepts predicated on the ways people used and took care of their land. A history text that explains Aboriginal starvation and dislocation as a result of the extermination of the bison on the Plains does not usually account for the loss of a deep spiritual webbing between humans and the buffalo. The physical and metaphysical materials for an entire way of life were lost when the buffalo were exterminated by Western "progress." Moreover, it is difficult to explain, within Eurocentric frames of reference, the deeper goals and purposes of indigenous communities that are trying to reclaim ancient relationships to culturally important animals through a combination of modern and pre-modern means. Inuit seal hunts and efforts to return to hunting whales for groups like the Nuu-chah-nulth and Makah are often misunderstood by the public.[11] These self-determination moves on the part of First Nations are based on understandings of how their own histories are inextricably linked to particular animals. Indigenous leaders see the prospects of healing the social and economic woes of their communities by reconnecting the links to relationships with animals that sustained the people in the past.

Approaches to history that show indigenous peoples' relationships to plants and animals are some first steps toward recognizing a deeper sense of how, as traditional people often put it, "the land knows you're there." Julie Cruikshank has used the term "sentient landscape" to refer to the ways in which human beings in pre-contact times formed relationships with geographic and geologic entities that recognized the presence and conduct of people. Discussing the problems of Eurocentric binaries such as *mythos* and history, Cruikshank writes that the Aboriginal women who explained aspects of Yukon's past to her did not make rigid distinctions between historical truth and moral and cultural truth: "The stories these women tell summon up a moral system that includes relationships with non-humans – animals and also features of landscape, like glaciers – that share characteristics of personhood."[12] It is clear that narrating the past is a selective and creative process that calls upon the cultural conventions of maintaining particular boundaries of thought. It is not that indigenous approaches to the past do not have categories of explanation for events and meanings; it is that these categories do not necessarily correspond to Western intellectual frameworks and purposes. Indigenous historical narratives place human beings in a landscape that is understood to have mythic forms converging with everyday forms of experience. Many Aboriginal communities are familiar with hearing the past narrated in this seamless fashion, which places mythic and moral understandings alongside genealogies that include animals and culturally important places on the landscape. Histories include moral teachings from encounters with animals such as Owl, Raven, Wolf, and Bear. For a number of indigenous groups in Canada, these animals have important spiritual connections to families and clans. Thus, a history that ignores animals is, to a certain extent, a disrespectful and incomplete telling of the past.

An indigenous perspective on animals and the "sentient landscape" could be included in a history text, but the hegemony of modernity in historiography tends to marginalize these narratives as myth, legend, or "alternative" ways of thinking; as a consequence, they end up being treated as "subalternate" ways of seeing the world. At the same time, indigenous historical narratives that combine oral traditions with ecological knowledge have informed environmental scientists about ways of seeing reciprocity among animals, humans, and changing landscapes. Indigenous elders have told stories about the past with the goal of connecting human experience to the ecologies of places. This way of narrating the past is vital for helping youth understand their responsibility for maintaining the place-based traditions that have sustained their communities. In the 1997 *Delgamuukw* decision, the Supreme Court of Canada recognized this use of oral tradition for chronicling the past as an ancient yet also emergent form of legal discourse – one having equivalent power with documentary evidence to demonstrate historic truth. In that decision, oral tradition was given the same weight as written evidence. The Gitxsan and Wet'suwet'en Nations were thereby able to demonstrate their occupancy and ownership of their land – 58,000 square kilometres of northern British Columbia – by resorting to their *adaawks*, traditional creation stories.[13] Those creation stories revealed to the Court how the land and the resources had been maintained through practices and protocols emphasizing responsibilities to animals, plants, and culturally important sites on the landscape.

By examining indigenous categories that merge human and animal histories, we might rethink the ways in which major events and accomplishments, such as the building of railways and industries, are framed around discourses of "advances" in human society. A history that includes the ways in which the natural ecology was altered and degraded by industrialization is illuminating; but First Nations also focus on how the conditions of "relationship" between humans and animals are affected by the actions of human society. Historians such as William Cronon have made inquiries in this environmental direction, pointing out that the history of colonization in North America was "as much an ecological as a cultural revolution and the human side of that revolution cannot be fully understood until it is embedded in the ecological one. Doing so requires a history not only of human actors, conflicts, and economies, but of ecosystems as well."[14] Having said that, one of the key differences between an environmental emphasis in historiography and an Aboriginal approach to the histories of humans, animals, and landscapes relates to the blurring of time divisions between the mythic era and the present one. The animals are immersed in a landscape that is at once physical and metaphysical. It is, as Vine Deloria has said, a sacred ecology. The relationships between humans and animals frame this sacred ecology.

## Place and Indigenous Understandings of the Local

For indigenous communities, the past is located in the local and traditional territory. Scholars such as Eric R. Wolf have shown how events in Europe intertwined with the events that shaped local indigenous experience through colonization and eventually globalization; by contrast, the indigenous vision of the past is sublimely local.[15] Because history is always a selective telling of the past, indigenous peoples often select the events and meanings of the past from their home territories as the most important stories to tell. This does not mean that Aboriginal communities are unaware of the international forces that have driven colonization; rather, elders and community leaders are more focused on local understandings of political, historical, and cultural processes than on events occurring globally. As one Lummi elder told me: "We have to take care of this place, we won't be moving to some other place. We are the people from here and we must concern ourselves with protecting our land." For indigenous people, the local history that frames the community's relationship to the traditional territory is the most important knowledge to be passed on to the youth.

A significant example of how indigenous communities are focusing on local knowledge of the past is the publication of the Sto:lo Atlas, which is a collaborative effort between the Sto:lo Aboriginal Rights and Title department (AR&T) and a selected group of anthropologists and historians. That atlas provides important information on Sto:lo history, place names, traditional knowledge, identity themes, environmental issues, social structure, and sacred sites. It is replete with photographs, maps, and elaborate graphics. The Sto:lo have decided to carefully publish aspects of their traditional knowledge in order to educate the dominant Canadian society. Editor Keith Thor Carlson's preface explains that the atlas is "a powerful educational tool with application to ongoing Sto:lo Nation treaty negotiations."[16] Such works produced by First Nations can be contentious in Aboriginal *and* non-Aboriginal communities. In British Columbia, versions of regional history that present indigenous interpretations of land occupancy are often rejected by non-Natives in a backlash environment in which there is opposition to the return of stolen land and resources. At the same time, indigenous communities often view the publication of their local traditional knowledge as a kind of Faustian bargain, in the sense that intricate understandings that have been kept within a small circle become public knowledge for the sake of greater social acceptance of Aboriginal values and social justice perspectives. While the goal of the atlas is to educate Aboriginal and non-Aboriginal audiences alike about S'ólh Téméxw (Sto:lo territory), it is a problem for Coast Salish communities to publish information about sacred sites and traditional knowledge. In the case of the atlas, elders were consulted and the text was carefully chosen so as to not reveal knowledge protected by community protocols. It is especially a problem to publish information about ceremonies and personal understandings regarding such things as winter spirit dancing. Spiritual danger is associated with speaking publicly about personal knowledge and sacred rituals. Coast Salish families who participate in private longhouse ceremonies are taught not to discuss what goes on during these rituals.

In many respects, presenting local history from an indigenous perspective is one of the most politically difficult educational moves to be made in developing culturally responsive curricula. Elizabeth Furniss has explained the ways that, especially in rural communities, the "frontier myth" emphasizing progress is resistant to more diverse and inclusive approaches to the past. She discusses how, in British Columbia, a course on First Nations history and culture has been created to provide secondary students with a less ethnocentric view of Aboriginal people and the history of colonization. With its strong emphasis on critical thinking, colonialism's legacy, and the role of land claims in the province's economic future, the course can seem somewhat iconoclastic: indigenous people are not simply a feature of the past; they are a pivotal group both within and apart from Canadian society. Placing history in the role of challenging the assumptions about the present-day identity stories of a nation or a region is particularly contentious in high school settings, where youth are approaching adulthood directed by values and beliefs that have been cemented throughout childhood. Furniss explains both the imperative and the tension: "That such a curriculum was deemed necessary for British Columbia is undoubtedly a reflection of the growing prominence of First Nations issues in the media and in the courts, and the rising tension between Aboriginal and non-Aboriginal peoples over impending treaty settlements."[17] Furniss has shown how local historical interpretations are dominated by the social and economic hegemony of discourses around commerce and tourism. In British Columbia, towns celebrate their colourful pasts and the important families that contributed to the development of modern community life. A local history that includes First Nations voices has the potential to challenge old assumptions about the community's identity. For local indigenous people, the narratives of progress that are celebrated in chronicles of the development of industries and the economic benefits generated by local natural resources contain "inaudible" stories of the displacement and marginalization of Aboriginal life.

One reason that a local telling of the past is so controversial in places like British Columbia is that the stage play of history is so personal and intimate in this local context. First Nations communities and settler immigrant communities are living these histories in the present controversies about ethics and identities. Aboriginal communities on the fringes of these towns raise questions about the conduct of the newcomers and about how the world became so divided – and degraded. The past in such places is not remote; it is being challenged and struggled for locally as the names of rivers, mountains, and culturally important sites are renamed in indigenous languages. These stories of the local collide with Eurocentric assumptions about the conduct of pioneer ancestors. In examining the use of local histories to supplement nationalist histories, Furniss has pointed to how seamless the historiographical approach is in both kinds of texts. In local *and* national narratives, the role of the Native is subordinated and shaped by the need to narrate a selective story that silences dissenting indigenous voices:

These books are united by their common situation within the frontier myth. They focus almost exclusively on the challenges and triumphs of pioneers and colonial systems. Natives are either invisible in these histories or are scripted as supporting characters in images that are negative, quaint, childlike, and/or passive. These books, by their sheer volume, constitute a dominant historical discourse that cannot but pervade the consciousness of the general population.[18]

Aboriginal storytellers have often wanted their local narratives of the past to inform the settler societies about dangerous ecological conditions and the consequences of bad choices in industrialization and development. I attended a conference held in Seattle on salmon and environmental problems where a Yakima elder told the traditional story of Coyote and the Swallow Sisters as a way to explain how his people came to know that dams on rivers were ecologically and morally wrong. In the story, Coyote must help the starving human beings by destroying a dam that has been built by two greedy sisters who wish to keep all the salmon for themselves. Coyote undergoes a number of transformations in order to accomplish this. In the end, he changes the sisters into swallows and leaves the presence of the birds and the story as a kind of text written on the landscape to inform future generations of the consequences of bad ecological and ethical choices.

In her work with Okanagan elder Harry Robinson, Wendy Wickwire gives us another example of how local traditional knowledge, from an indigenous perspective, is not supplementary, but rather a central core of history. The stories perform a teaching task that illuminates culture conflict themes in Aboriginal–non-Aboriginal relations:

> Harry told his nature power stories to set straight the historical record so that everyone, Native and non-Native alike, would know why Whites and Indians are different. He was concerned that the deep knowledge of the past was disappearing ... Harry also believed his stories would help people, both Native and White, to understand where they came from and why their interactions have been so antagonistic.[19]

For indigenous communities, local history and traditional ecological knowledge provide the template for their expressions of identity and self-determination. Local and regional histories often provide the detail and complexity that can break down the persistent stereotyping of the "Native other."

## Colonization and the House of Murky Mirrors

The stereotypes of the "drunken Indian" and the "lazy Indian" are part of the legacy of colonization. Unravelling some of the complexities of the collision of world views is one of the most difficult yet also essential tasks in efforts to present indigenous ways of making meaning from the past. Too often the history of Aboriginal–white relations in Canada is presented as a melodramatic morality play casting the Native people as victims of progress and as unwilling to adapt to the social transformations of the nineteenth century. More recent attempts to show some previously neglected aspects of nation building and colonization, such as residential schooling and racism, are too often oversimplifications of a story filled with ironies and paradoxes. Historian John Lutz has shown that the Coast Salish people of British Columbia responded to the conditions of nineteenth- and twentieth-century colonization by using wage labour opportunities provided by the logging and fishing industries to develop their own culturally structured economies.[20] Aboriginal people were not lazy; rather, they used money from employment toward economic goals connected with the "prestige economies" of the potlatch. Their cultural goals were different from those of white society; their choices about making and spending money reflected a world view that the dominant society could neither understand nor accept. Missionaries and government agents tried to promote individual acquisition of wealth among Aboriginal communities as a necessary step toward assimilation. Colonization involved more than taking away Native space; it was a complex struggle to redefine the goals and purposes of life. Indigenous people responded, not by refusing to participate, but by participating in the new forms of economic life within the cultural sensibilities of their own collectivist cultures.

To white observers, it often seemed as if Aboriginal peoples were eager to abandon their traditional ways of life and become crude versions of Euro-Canadians. So it is often difficult for students to understand how quickly indigenous communities adopted Christianity. What is often ignored is how indigenous cultures sometimes resisted but at other times adapted new ideas and new forms that could supplement traditional religious practices without replacing them. Many First Nations amalgamated Christianity into traditional spiritual beliefs, creating new religious practices that often frustrated missionaries but that worked well in the context of the new and complex realities of colonization. This is an example of the labyrinthine history of indigenous community responses to overwhelming forces of assimilation and transformation. Clearly, indigenous peoples never responded to colonization in one-dimensional ways.

For indigenous communities and indigenous scholars, the legacy of colonization is an important point of reference not just for understanding the sources of confusing present social conditions, but for framing the ideological divide that must be navigated in the course of decolonization. Reinterpreting this history has been a central goal of many indigenous scholars, who understand how deeply the past is implicated in the unresolved issues of identity and injustice. Linda Smith has written about the messy business of struggling for an alternative, indigenized history:

> Our colonial experience traps us in the project of modernity. There can be no "postmodern" for us until we have settled some business of the modern. This does not mean that we do not understand or employ multiple discourses, or act in incredibly contradictory ways, or exercise power ourselves in multiple ways. It means that there is unfinished business, that we are still being colonized (and know it), and that we are still searching for justice ... Transforming our colonized views of our own history (as written by the West), however, requires us to revisit, site by site, our history under Western eyes.[21]

For indigenous peoples, a history of Canada as a nation-state is a colonizing way of thinking about people, relationships, and land. This situation is amplified for Aboriginal groups such as the Coast Salish, whose traditional territory was divided by the border between Canada and the United States. Elders and Coast Salish leaders see the need to reimplant a cognitive geography in the minds of youth to help them see the pre-contact world of connected villages across imposed borders. Some community leaders are encouraging youth to think of themselves as Coast Salish rather than Canadians or Americans. People are intermarrying across the border, and many have lived on both sides of the line and are affiliated with two or more communities. Paige Raibmon has explained that "when the Canada–U.S. boundary sliced intervillage communities in two, many of the required journeys became border crossings. Coast Salish, who travelled from British Columbia to Washington, re-entered a familiar orbit of extended kin more than they entered a foreign country."[22]

For these indigenous communities, a history of their own "borderless" territory from the perspective of their own traditional way of seeing space is a more decolonizing approach to understanding the past than a telling of how nation-states fought with each other over how to divide Coast Salish land. It will be more than difficult to reconcile a history curriculum that seeks to inculcate national identity and citizenship with indigenous desires to assert sovereignty and reclaim pre-contact understandings of time and space.

History will likely continue to be one of the most difficult subjects for Aboriginal students because of its embedded assumptions about progress and modernity. For history teachers who want to include indigenous perspectives, the metaphor of the four winding paths up the mountain may contain some practical hints about what is needed to change things. A common principle among indigenous peoples is that when one approaches a sacred site, such as a mountain, knowledge acquisition requires some form of sacrifice. Teachers who want to be more inclusive toward indigenous perspectives will have to acquire the time-space in classrooms for considering the four themes of an indigenous historical consciousness; this will necessarily entail sacrificing some conventional ways of teaching Canadian history. Including indigenous principles in history curricula could inspire students to imagine alternative ways to structure the societies of the future as a result of learning about indigenous ways of experiencing time and space. Indigenous historical consciousness is a holistic and interdisciplinary way of understanding reality. The four themes in this endeavour – (1) circular time, (2) relationships with land and animals, (3) local knowledge, and (4) the complexities of colonization and decolonization – have been core concerns for Aboriginal communities and scholars. Including these considerations in Canadian history texts and courses will require a shift in the goals and purposes of studying history. If we can begin to see the land and the flow of stories from the land as part of a past that carries us on a common journey, the way indigenous people view history may help schools reconfigure our relationships to the ecologies of our communities and revise our thinking about how to live sustainably in the future.

## NOTES

1. Thomas King, *The Truth about Stories: A Native Narrative*, CBC Massey Lectures Series (Toronto: House of Anansi Press, 2003), 2.
2. Vine Deloria, *Red Earth, White Lies: Native Americans and the Myth of Scientific Fact* (New York: Scribner's, 1995), 84.
3. Marie Battiste, Introduction to *Reclaiming Indigenous Voice and Vision* (Vancouver: UBC Press, 2000), xvii.
4. Donald Fixico, *The American Indian Mind in a Linear World: American Indian Studies and Traditional Knowledge* (London: Routledge, 2003), 42.
5. Ibid., 45.

6 Benjamin Whorf, "The Relation of Habitual Thought and Behavior to Language," in *Language, Culture, and Personality: Essays in Memory of Edward Sapir*, ed. Leslie Spier (Menasha: Sapir Memorial Publication Fund, 1941), 209. http://sloan.stanford.edu.
7 Julie Cruikshank, "Oral History, Narrative Strategies, and Native American Historiography: Perspectives from the Yukon Territory, Canada," in *Clearing a Path: Theorizing the Past in Native American Studies*, ed. Nancy Shoemaker (London: Routledge, 2002), 7.
8 *Mythos*, in this sense, refers to the stories that define the interrelations among spirits, landscapes, animals, and humans.
9 Ibid., 13.
10 Leroy Littlebear, "Jagged Worldviews Colliding," in *Reclaiming Indigenous Voice and Vision* (Vancouver: UBC Press, 2000), 82.
11 See Michael Marker, "After the Makah Whalehunt: Indigenous Knowledge and Limits to Multicultural Discourse," *Urban Education* 41, 5 (September 2006): 1-24.
12 Julie Cruikshank, *Do Glaciers Listen? Local Knowledge, Colonial Encounters, and Social Imagination* (Vancouver: UBC Press, 2005), 60.
13 See Patrick Macklem, *Indigenous Difference and the Constitution of Canada* (Toronto: University of Toronto Press, 2002).
14 William Cronon, *Changes in the Land: Indians, Colonists, and the Ecology of New England* (New York: Hill and Wang, 1983), 6.
15 Eric Wolf, *Europe and the People without History* (Berkeley: University of California Press, 1982).
16 Keith T. Carlson and Sonny McHalsie, *A Sto:lo Coast Salish Historical Atlas* (Vancouver: Douglas and McIntyre, 2001), xv.
17 Elizabeth Furniss, "Pioneers, Progress, and the Myth of the Frontier," *BC Studies* 115-16 (1997-98): 20.
18 Ibid., 33.
19 Wendy Wickwire, *Nature Power: In the Spirit of an Okanagan Storyteller* (Vancouver: Douglas and McIntyre, 1992), 14-15.
20 John Lutz, *Makuk: A New History of Aboriginal-White Relations* (Vancouver: UBC Press, 2008).
21 Linda Smith, *Decolonizing Methodologies: Research and Indigenous Peoples* (London: Zed Books, 1999), 34.
22 Paige Raibmon, *Authentic Indians: Episodes of Encounter from the Late-Nineteenth-Century Northwest Coast* (Durham: Duke University Press, 2005), 109.

PART 2

# ORIENTATIONS TOWARD HISTORICAL THINKING

# 5

## What It Means to Think Historically

STÉPHANE LÉVESQUE

> *The chief object of every experienced teacher is to get pupils to think properly after the method adopted in his particular line of work; not an accumulation of information, but the habit of correct thinking, is the supreme result of good teaching in every branch of instruction.*
>
> *– American Historical Association*

The notion of "historical thinking" is far from new or revolutionary. It has been part of the conversation in history education for over a century, as evidenced above in the 1899 report of the American Historical Association on history in the schools. Yet it is equally fair to claim that historical thinking has, until recently, remained marginal and undocumented compared to the tradition based on the memorization of factual knowledge. These days, this domain-specific way of knowing the past is *en vogue* in educational discourse. But it has often been reclaimed in various jurisdictions for a multiplicity of purposes, many having more to do with patriotic allegiance and heritage practices than with sophisticated thinking in history. "The odds of achieving mature historical understanding," as Sam Wineburg rightly observes, "are stacked against us in a world in which Disney and MTV call the shots." "But it is precisely the uses to which the past is put," he goes on, "that endow these other aims with even greater importance."[1]

In "Schweigen! Die Kinder!" Peter Seixas contends that the problem of knowing history is "both difficult and contentious."[2] It is difficult because the past is a useful and even necessary resource in our everyday life. From popular historical movies to heritage fairs and battlefield tours, people are exposed to and engaged in a variety of historical activities. Yet we cannot understand how history is constructed and narrated without some sophisticated forms of knowing the past. Shared narratives are important in the shaping of identities and in providing a sense of direction. But they cannot make informed citizens in a pluralistic society precisely *because* they offer no alternative mode of analysis of competing versions of the past. Knowing history is also contentious because history is no longer accepted as an exact science based on universal principles. As postmodernists insist, historical narratives, historians, and the tools of historiography are all in themselves "historically contingent and positioned."[3] They are cultural artifacts emerging from particular social systems. At the school level, this question of relativism is further complicated by "pedagogical considerations of what students are capable of understanding and philosophical disputes over the purposes of public education, and lacks the complexity of the arguments historians pursue among themselves."[4]

Clearly, there is a lot at stake in history education. As Bruce VanSledright observes, it is increasingly of concern to "shed some light on how it could more successfully be taught."[5] This chapter offers some clarifications on the nature of historical thinking and presents a set of interrelated key concepts to help foster this domain-specific process through which people master – and ultimately appropriate – the knowledge and concepts of history and critically apply them to resolve contemporary and historical issues.[6] A key feature of my argument is Jerome Bruner's notion of disciplines as dynamic and self-regulated scholarly ways of knowing; another is the related conception of sophisticated understanding as a disciplinary mode of thinking and reasoning about complex questions and issues using "methods of inquiry, networks of concepts, theoretical frameworks, techniques for acquiring and verifying findings, appropriate images, symbols systems, vocabularies, and mental models."[7]

## Substantive and Procedural Knowledge of History

Historical thinking requires competence and ultimately a high degree of expertise in doing history. For Howard Gardner and Veronica Boix-Mansilla, "experts may be thought of as individuals who really do succeed in replacing their earlier, imperfect notions with more serviceable ones."[8] From this perspective, historians and their works can serve as "benchmarks in relationship to which we can understand what the less sophisticated historical thinkers do."[9] In trying to make sense of the process of doing history and understanding how students can gradually acquire the "rules of the game," Gaffield's analogy from sports can help. "In the history courses I took in school," he observes, "we read about history, talked about history and wrote about history; we never actually did history." He goes on, "If I had learned basketball in this way, I would have spent years reading the interpretations and viewpoints of great players, watching them play games, and analysing the results of various techniques and strategies. Instead, though, I was soon dribbling a basketball and trying to shoot into the hoop after just a few instructions."[10]

Students today are still very much taught what the sport (history) is about, which is, the stories of political leaders, military generals, social activists, statistics on their successes and failures, viewpoints and remarks from historians, and so on. These stories delivered to students typically represent the content of the "sport." They surely help novices know more about what happened in the past from the interpretative viewpoints of others. However, they do not make intelligent "players." What they need as well is to gradually appropriate the concepts, methods, and rules to ultimately play the game themselves. This sports analogy shows all the challenges involved in considering a complex and intellectually demanding discipline such as history. Without sophisticated thinking, students are left passively absorbing the stories of authorities, too puzzled or indifferent to use the tools and mechanisms for making sense of the past. Students cannot practise history, or even think critically about its content, if they have no understanding of how one constructs and shares historical knowledge.

In an attempt to conceptualize historians' ways of doing historical scholarship, Lee has laid out an extremely helpful model of historical knowledge development, based on two types of interdependent knowledge: substantive and procedural.[11] The first type of historical knowledge focuses on the substance of the past. It is what historical knowledge is *about* – the "content" of history.[12] This type of knowledge focuses on certain historical themes and actors and has traditionally been framed in story form. Forms of substantive knowledge include textbooks, movies, and oral histories. It is substantive knowledge that has been the subject of lively debate in various curricular reforms because it is highly political and contentious and often justified by competing groups for a variety of collective purposes such as identity, memory, and patriotism.

The second type of historical knowledge, referred to as procedural, concentrates on the concepts and vocabulary that provide "the structural basis for the discipline."[13] These key concepts (evidence, empathy, progress, decline, etc.) are not what history is *about* – that is, they are not the *substance*. They are, rather, conceptual tools needed for the study of the past as a discipline and for the construction of historical knowledge. Without these concepts, it would be impossible to make sense of the substance of the past, for "they shape the way we go about doing history."[14] Because these concepts are rarely apparent in use, they are often left hidden in historians' investigations and even more so in school textbooks, which leads to the assumption that they are unworthy of study.

It is important not to misconstrue the distinction between, and transition from, substantive to procedural knowledge as a simplistic dichotomy of content versus skills. It is impossible for students to understand or use procedural knowledge if they have no knowledge of the substance of the past. To claim, for example, that there has been remarkable progress in human rights over the past century makes no sense unless one knows some content (key dates, events, declarations, charters) relating to the history of human rights. To understand the various claims made about the past, therefore, students need to be introduced to the disciplinary concepts and procedures that led to the crafting of these historical claims. "The acquisition of more powerful procedural or second-order ideas," Peter Lee and Rosalyn Ashby contend, "is one way – perhaps the best – of giving sense to the notion of progression in history."[15]

Equally important to this conceptualization is the *progression* in historical thinking. There has been a misleading tendency to view knowledge as a binary, "all or nothing" mode of acquisition. Learning outcomes are typically designed for teachers to assess whether students have mastered the prescribed expectations. Yet as the sports analogy makes clear, players do not all of a sudden become experts after some exposure to the game. They gradually become skilled, and not necessarily at an equal pace, as they engage in various drills, practices, and games suited for their own development. The same holds true for history (see Figure 5.1). Novices, whether they are junior students or mature adults, do not magically turn into sophisticated thinkers because of their age or exposure to history. Intuitive and common-sense ideas often remain durable even after repeated learning activities and life experiences. To achieve expertise, people require "ample doses of discipline in the alternative sense of the term: regular practice, with feedback, in applying those habits of mind that yield understanding."[16]

*What It Means to Think Historically*

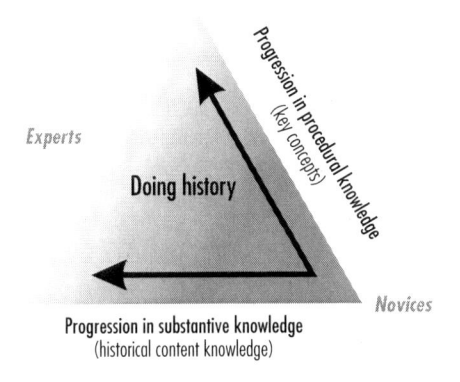

**Figure 5.1** Conceptual framework for progression in doing history

(Figure shows a triangle with "Experts" at top-left, "Novices" at bottom-right, "Doing history" in the center. Axes labeled: "Progression in procedural knowledge (key concepts)" along the hypotenuse, and "Progression in substantive knowledge (historical content knowledge)" along the bottom.)

At a different but equally problematic level is the placement of substantive and procedural knowledge on a linear scale of historical reasoning. This vision of historical development tends to suggest that progress in historical thinking should be from the former to the latter – that is, from lower- to higher-order thinking. But this understanding is highly misleading. Progression in historical thinking ought to be developed *simultaneously* within each of these domains of knowledge and not from one to the other, as displayed in Figure 5.1. School history can help with this type of progression in historical thinking. But how?

**Progression in Historical Thinking**

Historians and philosophers of history have employed procedural knowledge in their works for a long time. The problem has been the absence in the literature of a coherent articulation of these key concepts for history education purposes. As a result of a drastic change in British history education from content acquisition to historical thinking, scholars in the United Kingdom have engaged in the study and dissemination of ideas about historical thinking in general, and procedural concepts in particular. However, the ideas developed across the Atlantic have not always been disseminated to the North American context. Notably because of the progressive education movement, which stressed teaching interdisciplinary subjects as part of the new social studies, the focus in history education has traditionally been on citizenship education, republican democracy, and the "common good."[17]

The recent debates over the teaching of American history in schools and the subsequent National Standards for history perhaps offer some indications of a rapprochement between the two school-history traditions. But as Bruce VanSledright recently claimed in light of his experience with teaching history, "the British example may help us understand that, in order to learn to think historically, an obsession with asking children to commit a nationalist narrative to memory is a misguided approach."[18] In Canada, where the provinces have followed various and sometimes divergent traditions, it is difficult to point to the systematic and influential role of the British history education movement. Even if some progressive ideas and authors have made their way into some Canadian schools, history education reforms have traditionally focused on "fears for the future of the country, rather than on concerns for the purpose and nature of school history."[19]

Perhaps the most significant contribution to the field in the past few decades has been made by Peter Seixas, the first scholar to conceptualize the notion of historical thinking in Canadian education. It was Seixas who offered Canadians a creative conceptualization of growth in historical understanding centred on a set of related elements initially developed in Western historiography: significance, epistemology and evidence, continuity and change, progress and decline, empathy and moral judgments, and historical agency. These elements are, for him, "closely related core issues that must be confronted in order to foster growth in historical thinking."[20] He is careful to note that these concepts should not be viewed as fixed or given but rather as developing, always problematic and incomplete, contingent on and limited by people's own historiographical culture. Like any other discipline, history has meaning and justification in "the context of the questions, procedures, and debates in which it develops."[21] Perhaps more important, because history is a dynamic discipline, new discoveries or methods in the discipline gradually challenge and ultimately undermine current tenets.

For the purpose of this chapter, I will focus on the inquiry process of turning the residues of the past into historical narratives and show how that process can be understood in terms of progression in historical thinking using key concepts. Historians have developed a time-honoured process of investigating the past that goes back to Leopold von Ranke's principles of scientific history.[22] This investigation process more or less resembles the following: Historians approach the past with some personal interests, areas of significance, and questions in mind. These interests and questions are typically informed by historians' positionalities and knowledge (or lack of knowledge) of certain historical subjects – often in terms of prior knowledge and stories. Implicit in the questions that historians initially consider significant are their own historical narratives, hypotheses, and evaluative judgments about these events as signifying continuity and change or progress and decline in history. Then begins, for historians, a complex research process of gathering, selecting, and making sense of the evidence they think worth collecting and analyzing. When they believe they have gone as far as possible into the subject and that they possess a good understanding of it, they offer some interpretative answers to their initial questions; this in turn may prompt them to investigate some other related aspects of the past.

Of course, this simplified model of inquiry does not do justice to the practice of historical research and writing. That being said, separating this process into a number of conceptually distinct steps and elements provides a didactically useful and convenient sequence. Perhaps more important, it enables us to uncover the analytic processes involved in investigating the past and can establish attainment targets for what might be considered levels of sophisticated thinking. Unlike common-sense theories, the discipline of history is not based primarily on acts of intuitive thinking, the intention of which is to arrive at a given answer, with little awareness of the process of reaching that answer.[23] Historical investigation involves a deep understanding of both the power and limits of history as well as the steps and procedures necessary for crafting a defensible response to a given problem. Intuitive thinking, in contrast, is more instinctive and unconscious, based on prior perceptions and a sense of familiarity with the domain of inquiry.

So if one considers the analytic model above, a number of procedural steps and concepts can be identified. First, historians investigate aspects of the past because they think they are worth studying and uncovering. Why would historians question, research, or think about certain historical events or personages unless they strongly believe they are *historically significant*? Second, historians approach the significant past with some *judgments* and understanding of past events as part of a larger narrative that provides meaning and direction. This understanding implicitly rests on a process of perceiving events as signifying the complementary concepts of *continuity* and *change* and those of *progress* and *decline*. Because historians' interpretations must rely on supporting evidence, the third step of an inquiry is the research. It is at this point that the *evidence* must be selected and analyzed with a deep sense of *historical empathy* to avoid contemporary judgments of past actors' decisions. This whole process finally brings historians back to their initial questions, which they then attempt to answer, usually in writing.

Building on this simplified inquiry process, next I will briefly address how to make progressions in using these procedural concepts, resorting to various studies in the field, including my own recent work and the recent

*Benchmarks of Historical Thinking* (www.historybenchmarks.ca). I recognize that other concepts (e.g., agency) have been developed in the discipline, but space limitations force me to focus more explicitly on these.

**Historical Significance: What Is Important in History?**
Ranke's original principle of scientific history was grounded in the belief that historians had to "show what actually happened."[24] Yet this task is conceivable only if historians first make a decision on *what it is* that they want to show and provide justifications for wanting to do so. Historians cannot simply study everything from the past. Their initial interests, research questions, and selection of relics are inevitably influenced by how they ascribe significance to past events. The historian's ability to create historical interpretations is necessarily tied to what he or she sees as significant. For Seixas, a historical event or character does not become significant simply because of its place or importance in the past itself, or because of someone's special interest in it. "Standards of significance," he argues, "apparently inhere not only in the past itself, but in the interpretative frames and values of those who study it – ourselves."[25] Historical significance is thus a quality determined by historians in response to the past. Drawing on the influential works of Robert Phillips, Geoffrey Partington, and Martin Hunt, certain criteria of significance have been developed to inform the initial questions, interests, and selection and organization of events by historians.[26]

- *Importance.* One way to appreciate the significance of a historical event is to contextualize the past and consider what was perceived as important to those who lived then. Was the past in question important to predecessors? Why? In what ways? From this view, importance might be understood as what affected predecessors – that is, the actions that had an influence on their thinking or behaviours of the time. Attempting to consider other historical periods or events not only as different from ours but also as having their own importance for those who lived then may offer historians a means to counter presentism – that is, the imposing of present-day values on the past – and to realize that every present can have its own meaning, salience, and prominence.
- *Profundity.* The notion of profundity offers an evaluative component to the factor of importance. In trying to contextualize the importance of the past for those who lived then, it might be valuable to consider how deeply people were affected by an event. Was the event superficial or deeply affecting? How were people's lives affected? Partington argues

that in selecting a topic for study, historians and educators must "ensure that the hopes, fears, and other concerns of all the interested individuals or groups must be adequately investigated."[27]

- *Quantity.* One of the most common ways of ascribing significance to the past is to look at the number of people affected by an event: How many victims? How many survivors? How many more were affected by this event than by another one? As long as history was primarily focused on the "great men," numbers were hardly necessary. But once historians became interested in issues of economic growth, social change, or histories of workers, questions of numbers had to assume greater importance. "History by numbers" has thus redirected historians to elements, relics, and phenomena once perceived as insignificant from the point of view of the study of great men. Yet the focus on numbers must be taken up extremely carefully in history, as it may lead historians to ascribe significance only to events affecting masses of people or to those that lend themselves to quantification.

- *Durability.* Related to the factor of numbers is that of the durability of an event. How long does an event have to endure to be considered significant? Should it be lasting, or may it be ephemeral? At first glance, it is not always easy to draw a line between the beginning and the end of an event. But even when historians agree on the exact length of an event, the notion of durability can lead people to believe incorrectly that the longer the event lasts in history, the more significant it becomes. Both the historical context and historians' relationships with the past are necessary to making that evaluative judgment. The individual terrorist attacks of 11 September 2001 lasted only a few minutes, yet the historical significance and legacy of the event is uncontested.

- *Relevance.* Should relevance inform historians' selection and study of past events? The idea that what is significant in history must be relevant to current interests has been the subject of lively debate in history. For Herbert Butterfield, the study of the past with one eye on the present "is the source of all sins and sophistries in history."[28] Michael Oakeshott presented a similar charge by drawing a sharp distinction between the "practical" and the "historical" past. Only the latter – that is, the study of history with complete detachment – was, for him, the proper subject for historians. "Whenever the significance of the past lies in the fact that it has been influential in deciding the present and future fortunes of man," he claimed, "the past involved is a practical, and not an historical past."[29] Yet other historians, notably Carl Becker, E.H. Carr, and Pierre Nora, have insisted that those who study history cannot divorce themselves from the present in which they work and live.[30] Historians are social actors influenced by the forces and concerns of their own time.

- *Intimate interests.* Another way people ascribe significance to the past is through their intimate interest in aspects of the past: Is the event important to me personally? My family? My ancestors? Family history, ancestral obligation and belonging, and personal experience of events are some of the factors (or even motives) for people to connect with the past. These connections, and the interpretations they ultimately generate, not only seem highly authentic to many but also, and more problematically, seem more reliable and legitimate, regardless of the internal or external validity of such connections and interpretations.[31]

- *Symbolic significance.* The use of particular historical events for collective or patriotic justification is of an entirely different order of significance. Here it is not the intimate connectedness to the past but the symbolic nature of the event that matters most. Is the event emblematically important? Does it represent something significant in the collective consciousness? In this case, the line between the "personal" (or intimate) and the "national" (or collective) past often becomes blurred. Events are selected because they reflect the importance of certain aspects of the past in defining a community of identity. Yet the notion of symbolic significance has serious political implications, particularly in terms of how individuals in the community conceive of the first-person plural (i.e., "we" and "our"). Who is included or excluded from the community? On what grounds? In taking for granted the experience of the collective "we," people may naively invoke the past to legitimate social order, bind past and contemporary peoples in a collective venture, and – more dangerously – exclude disparate or ethnically different peoples from the nation's past and envisioned future.

- *Contemporary lessons.* A different approach is taken by people who conceptualize the present by using past events for simple historical analogies: What lessons should we learn from the past? The use of past events for contemporary lessons is often regarded by historians as the sin of history. Novices in all spheres of society often misuse the past by drawing simplistic lessons from it to guide them in the present, without acknowledging the historicity of the actors and the context of events. As Lee argues, "there are clearly summative generalizations in history, which are explanatory in an everyday sense, but they make a weak basis for prediction."[32] Perhaps the best that historians can do is supply what Lee calls "vicarious experience" – that is, offer knowledge of what might be expected, knowing that what is expected is rarely exactly what happens.[33] In this sense, history can be useful for historical analogies.

Whether people use the past for academic research or contemporary meaning making, whether they are professional historians or history students, they cannot escape the concept of significance. To be meaningful, the past must somehow be coherently organized. And this implies distinguishing and selecting "significant" history, in contrast to "trivial" history. The key problem in education today is the absence of this terminology, which leaves teachers and students with their own bricolage of criteria of historical significance. The results can sometimes be astonishing and leave students highly vulnerable to constructions that fall far short of enhancing historical thinking.[34] Educators who are aware of their own and the provincial authority's selection are in a better position to help students reconsider their initial interpretations of the collective past and to advance the learning of other, equally significant events. In other words, clarifying the concept of historical significance – with regard to both concepts and topics – can help to identify and question those aspects of the past that the authorities see as significant for study, as well as to help compare these with teachers' and students' approaches to significance.

**Continuity and Change: What Is the Shape of Continuity and Change Over Time?**
The interaction between continuity and change has serious implications for historians. Though historical events are, by definition, changes perceived as significant in a given state of affairs, changes are possible, and perceptible, only if historians posit a certain continuity in human affairs, often by employing transhistorical colligatory concepts to illuminate the phenomena they wish to describe (e.g., war or technology). Historians may legitimately write about circumscribed events in time and space, yet the events selected are always set and understood as part of a sequence. "It is at least in part a claim," Louis Mink argues, "that for the historical understanding of an event one must know its consequences as well as its antecedents."[35] The problem, for Mink, lies in the difficulty of establishing a causal relation between events within a larger narrative explanation. As historians well know, events in history often have many causes, some more important than others, which must be evaluated carefully. "The historian," as Carr confesses, "is simultaneously compelled, like the scientist, to simplify the multiplicity of his answers, to

subordinate one answer to another, and to introduce some order and unity into the chaos of happenings and the chaos of specific causes."[36] With this state of affairs, the sequence of events constructed by historians should be understood as one of "causal possibilities" as opposed to definite "logical possibilities."[37] In this sense, probability rather than certainty is what governs the crafting of historical explanations. Thus, it is historical perspective and detachment that allows historians to make judgments of probability.

This advantageous point of view, which allows historians to create coherent historical narratives retrospectively, would also require what Walsh refers to as "colligation" – that is, the tracing of the *intrinsic* relations of one event to others in a series.[38] In his view, explaining and ultimately understanding the past by means of colligation is possible because historians select past events not only as occurring in chronological order but also as parts of a larger phenomenon or movement. "If an historian is asked to explain a particular historical event," Walsh insists, "he is often inclined to begin his explanation by saying that the event in question is to be seen as part of a general movement which was going on at the time."[39] If Walsh is correct, historians need some transhistorical categories as backdrops for their construction of narrative explanations. "Without such a transhistorical category," as Seixas observes, "it becomes difficult or impossible to understand change within that category."[40] Following Walsh, one could argue that the whole notion of change in historical studies only makes sense if historians can study the past with a set of tools allowing them to see things at once and together – a "big picture" of the past.[41] The recent redefinition of historical studies has led historians to consider aspects of the past that were previously ignored or deemed insignificant (e.g., gender, the body, ethnicity). This redefinition has resulted not only in a richer and more complex understanding of continuity and change in human affairs but also in the creation of colligatory concepts formerly ignored (e.g., masculinity, human rights, multiculturalism). In many ways, these concepts now illuminate significant aspects of the past that had previously lacked the terms or ideas needed to make them intelligible.

Curriculum guidelines and content standards now acknowledge the need for concepts such as these in structuring courses and, to a certain degree, in introducing students to perceived changes and continuities in historical affairs.[42] Yet like the concept of historical significance, those of continuity and change are rarely presented to students as key concepts; rather, they are offered as implicit elements for structuring the content of textbooks or curriculum guidelines. It is no surprise, then, that the limited number of studies conducted on these concepts suggest that "change is a historical concept that adolescents initially find difficult to entertain in any but everyday use."[43] In England, for example, Shemilt found that teachers often take continuity and change for granted in their course planning. History is typically presented as an overcrowded list of disconnected events falling under a variety of subject titles (e.g., revolutions, reforms, battles, bills, inventions). The result is that students largely see change "as an episodic not a continuous process, and one change (event) is not constructed in any way connected with changes (events) preceding it in time."[44] "The fabric of History," as he eloquently puts it, "is like a volcano occasionally convulsed by random explosions. Recorded History is seen as a chronicle of disruptions within the crater of the volcano."[45] The difficulty for students may well come from a weak ability to imagine and create a big picture – a colligatory picture – of the larger sequence in which the event is situated.

**Progress and Decline: Did Things Change for Better or Worse?**
Historians make sense of the past by creating sequences of significant events, using colligatory concepts to structure and give coherence to their narrative interpretations. As useful as they might be, these features do not provide historians with a clear evaluation of the direction of change. As historical actors and events have changed, have they improved? In what ways? For whom? To address these critical questions, a third element is required: an evaluative judgment to assess these changes as being for better or for worse. Historians may find common ground on the first two elements (continuity and change); the third one is more contentious in the discipline, for it requires the acceptance of a certain value judgment regarding the direction of change. It necessitates a shared belief in a particular direction of progress or decline for a series of perceived changes set by historians.

Clearly, imposing value judgments on the past raises a host of questions about historical interpretation. At every step of their inquiry, historians must make decisions in response to research questions, selection of evidence, acceptance or rejection of past moral beliefs, and so forth. The principle of evaluation of progress and decline adds to the contested nature of this process because historians do not all judge the direction of change in the same ways. In an attempt to grasp the relational meaning of progress and decline, two contrasting stances should be considered to foster historical thinking: oppositional, and successional.[46]

The first stance – oppositional – starts from the premise that, like the concepts of continuity and change, progress and decline are not only relational but also indispensable to each other – like two sides of a coin. In talking about advances in certain human affairs (e.g., technology), the oppositional stance suggests that one necessarily assumes that changes signifying progress in some aspects of human affairs imply decline in other aspects (e.g., the environment). "What seems for one group a period of decline," Carr contends, "may seem to another the birth of a new advance."[47] In this sense, one concept would exist only by virtue of the other. The advance of diesel trains in the twentieth century, for example, necessarily brought with it the decline of steam trains as a mode of transportation. All human advances in certain aspects of life, be they in human rights or biotechnology, inevitably led to decline in some other aspects. Progress and decline are thus not only relational but also mutually compatible, in that they can exist or occur at the same time in history.

The second stance concerning progress and decline – successional – is precisely the opposite. An instance of one of these concepts *cannot* occur at the same time as an instance of the other. Faith in humanity, from this standpoint, means that one concept (progress) must inevitably be perceived as superior to the other (decline). This revolutionary idea emerged during the Enlightenment. When philosophers conceptualized the modern idea of the progress of humanity, they also enthusiastically spread the belief that progress is not only general but also continuous and desirable. For them, regression or decline ceases to be equal, or oppositional, to progress. Nowadays, rapid developments in science and technology often lead naive thinkers to accept overall progress of modernity; these people do not realize that some societies or aspects of their own society can be subjected to decline or even collapse.

Clearly, there is no simple approach to understanding the direction of change in history. People in general, and students in particular, are exposed to a variety of sources about the past that use the nation, technology, or even civilization for specific moral claims. Presenting collective history as stories of inevitable freedom and progress – as is often the case in textbooks – seriously limits people's ability to evaluate critically the direction of historical change. One way of addressing these questions would be to have teachers engage their students in the use of evaluative criteria to allow for a critical analysis of change in history. This approach would include an analysis of a sequence of events based on supporting evidence; an awareness of progress and decline as oppositional stances (and not necessarily successional); and the use of relevant standards or concepts to evaluate the past so as to prevent presentist judgments. This might well provide an entry point into a critical analysis of master narratives and "official" stories of national progress of the sort that characterize many textbooks and curriculum guidelines.

**Evidence: How Do We Make Sense of the Traces of the Past?**
A critical approach to evidence of the past was Ranke's first principle of scientific history. To this day, it continues to be evidence that allows for warranted statements and credible narratives in history. But the traces left behind by human actors have their own intricacies. They appear in various forms, shapes, and locations. In many ways, everything resulting from human action could be considered a trace or evidence of the past. A distinction between evidence-as-relic and evidence-as-record might be useful here. On the one hand, relics such as pottery shards and arrowheads are traces that have survived into the present and that wait to be questioned and analyzed by historians. It is only when historians select and question them that such traces become historical evidence. Records, on the other hand, are pieces of information such as letters, photographs, books, and films that provide historians with some evidential arguments about the past. Like relics, they may also originate at the time of the event, but they are less mute because they do provide historians with first-hand information in visual or print form. As useful as records might be, they must nonetheless be selected and analyzed carefully because they do not always expressly reveal what happened.

Typically, naive thinkers see the past in terms of factual stories to be mastered, whereas historians develop accounts based on prior knowledge, interests, and careful analysis of conflicting records and relics from the past. As Wineburg concludes from his empirical studies, "for students, reading history was not a process of puzzling about author's intentions or situating texts in a social world but of gathering information." He goes on to say that "to historians, a document's attribution was not the end of the document but its beginning; sources were viewed as people, not objects, as social exchanges, not sets of propositions."[48] For students, historical sources and accounts provide factual information. The authority, from this perspective, resides in the texts they use. The more accessible those texts are, the more credible they appear. For historians, on the contrary, sources and accounts are speech acts. The locus of authority emanates from the questions historians ask and from the answers those questions generate.

Clearly, questioning and assessing accounts and traces from the past is a complex task requiring various cognitive acts. These "sourcing heuristics" in evaluating selected evidence are at least fourfold: (1) identification of the source (What type of source is it?); (2) attribution of the source to its author (Who created it? For what purpose?); (3) contextualization of the source in time and space (Where is this source from? What was the context of the time?); and (4) corroboration of the source with other sources (Is the information in the source supported or contradicted by other sources?).

The use of evidence to answer research questions and ultimately engage in reconstructing the past is a long and demanding process. Students are not being educated in a school environment that places them in an inquiry situation to select sources and struggle with issues of historical interpretation. The result is that many do not understand that knowledge of the past is the result of human constructs based on the critical use of evidence. Rather, they understand history as the straightforward acceptance or rejection of authoritative stories, which are presented to them as self-evident. Students, as Barton reminds us, "[act] as though knowledge of the past [exists] independently of evidence."[49] Yet it would be unrealistic and ill advised to assume that historical thinking inevitably engages students in disciplinary activities as performed by professional historians. Disciplinary inquiries, as embedded in a community of experts, cannot be transplanted to the world of school history. For that reason, the place of evidence in the classroom must be different from its place in the craft of historians. "Unlike historians," Husbands argues, "school pupils will not claim to generate 'new' public knowledge from the study of (selected) historical evidence; they will generate new *private understanding*."[50] From this perspective, evidence should be included in classroom instruction not because it will lead novices to become mini-historians but because of its great potential for fostering historical understanding. "Without an understanding of what makes an account historical," Lee concludes, "there is nothing to distinguish such an ability from the ability to recite sagas, legends, myths or poems."[51]

**Historical Empathy: How Can We Make Sense of Predecessors?**
The past, as Lowenthal so eloquently puts it, is "a foreign country."[52] People lived under very different circumstances and moralities that often appear alien to we who live in the present. More problematic, we can no longer revisit the actors of the time and experience how they lived, thought, and acted. Historians' re-creations of past actions and events are shaped not

only by the relics and records they select but also by careful consideration of the perspectives and beliefs of predecessors.[53] But how do historians get to re-enact, or rethink, the states of mind of past actors? What kind of machinery or sorcery would be necessary to do so? Naive historical thinkers typically assume greater continuity between past and present than is historically warranted. The result is a presentist imposition of present-day values, norms, and attitudes on past actors and their actions. The inquiry into the thinking of historical actors, though logically impossible, can be rendered more or less feasible through historical empathy. Far from an affective achievement, empathy is a way of knowing that requires at least three conceptual tools: imagination, contextualization, and moral judgment.

*Imagining* the past implies knowing what someone (or some group) believed, valued, felt, and intended to do. It is being in a position to mentally entertain these beliefs and to "consider the impact of these emotions (not necessarily to feel them)."[54] Because historians are not in direct contact with the people they study, it is impossible to know for sure what they believed, thought, or intended to do. The only possible way to understand more about past actors is to mentally recreate – to *imagine* – what it was like to be in their position from the evidence they left. As Collingwood put it, using the helpful analogy of a ship,

> if we look out over the sea and perceive a ship, and five minutes later look again and perceive it in a different place, we find ourselves obliged to imagine it as having occupied intermediate positions when we were not looking. That is already an example of historical thinking; and it is not otherwise that we find ourselves obliged to imagine Caesar as having travelled from Rome to Gaul when we are told that he was in these different places at these successive times."[55]

In this sense, imagination in history is not about entertaining fantasy feelings of people in the past; rather, it is about a key disposition – an "achievement" in Lee's term – for making sense of historical actions, events, and evidence.[56] It requires two somewhat complementary but incongruent elements: (1) an appreciation for different perspectives on human activities and beliefs; and (2) an acknowledgment of a shared humanity that transcends time, space, and culture. Indeed, historians cannot imagine predecessors' actions and behaviours unless they attempt to understand their fundamentally different positionalities. Barton and Levstik refer to this as a "sense of otherness." "Empathetic understanding," they contend, "requires the obvious: recognizing the fundamental otherness of people beyond oneself. Without some sense of how other people think and feel, there is little chance of making sense of their actions."[57] But historians can only imagine what it was like for predecessors if they can conceive of themselves as living inside that historical period or culture, even if it is fundamentally different from their own. People cannot entertain the possibility of empathizing with others if they do not see some transhistorical commonalities or forms of life between now and then. The struggle against the plagues of the human condition (scarcity of resources, natural disasters, existence of disease, aging, the inevitability of death, etc.) is an example of transhistorical commonalities across time and cultures.

*Contextualizing* the past is essential for empathy because historians must take into account at least three contexts to make sense of predecessors' actions, feelings, and beliefs: the personal (inner), the socio-cultural (outer), and the contemporary (present-day). The personal context refers to the inner beliefs, perspectives, and environment of the author of the source. Relics and records, I argue, are traces left behind by predecessors. To grasp their particular meaning, it is necessary to attribute them to their authors in light of their own set of *mentalités*. This consideration for personal contextualization should be complemented by the outer (socio-cultural) context in which the author lived. Indeed, historical actors were not living and thinking in a vacuum; they had their positionalities "deeply imbued with sociocultural, racial, ethnic, class, and gendered components."[58] But contextualization could not be adequate without thoughtful consideration of those who study the past – that is, ourselves. Indeed, the ever changing milieux in which historians find themselves shape the way they imagine and contextualize the past. Because history is an "unending dialogue" between the past and the present, contextualization is only possible if contemporary actors can differentiate the past from the present and thereby contextualize their own positionalities in light of those of their predecessors.

*Judging* the past and predecessors is a tricky but necessary step in understanding the past to the present. "We make judgments," Seixas argues, "by understanding historical actors as agents who faced decisions, sometimes individually, sometimes collectively, which had ethical consequences."[59] Because historians' interpretations are contextually situated in the present, these necessarily involve contemporary judgments on the meaning and significance of the selected past actions and actors. In this sense, historians would not, as Partington contends, "simply investigate facts and leave the moral judgements to others, but must perforce often make moral judgements themselves."[60] But imposing contemporary moral judgments on past actors is an extremely risky business.[61] As Oakeshott claimed, to draw moral lessons from the past is to turn history into "a field in which we exercise our moral and political opinions, like whippets in a meadow on a Sunday afternoon."[62] The challenge is thus to develop a sense of "prudential judgment" that involves the ability to understand "the codes of behavior which inform his subjects' actions."[63] It implies the ability to recognize the historicity of predecessors and their actions, knowing that their decisions had moral consequences for the future of history.

People in the past not only had different forms of life but also experienced, interpreted, and acted according to different norms, values, and belief systems. In trying to make sense of the ways these people felt, thought, and acted, historians must recreate and imagine the situation through empathetic understanding. More important, they must contextualize the past according to their own contemporary assumptions and moral judgments while remaining aware of all the problems that empathy generates when historical knowledge is being produced. With the recent focus of school history on issues of imagination, perspective taking, and morality, it becomes imperative for students to be introduced to empathy in the study of history. Only with such a sophisticated approach to the past will it become possible to teach students how to empathize with predecessors and use moral judgments appropriately in history.

## Conclusion

People in general, and students in particular, are exposed to masses of conflicting stories; and to various degrees, they are engaged in a variety of forms of historical practice. The family stories they share at home, the historical movies they take pleasure in watching, the visits they make to museums, the headlines they read in magazines, the virtual discussions they have about terrorism or Afghanistan, and the lessons they learn (and too quickly forget) in class are, to varying degrees, forms of historical knowledge and practice. It is true, as Barton and Levstik critically observe, that most students will never grow into professional historians.[64] But it is equally fair to maintain that they cannot understand or ultimately use *any* history if they have no exposure to, or experience of, the discipline. Knowing what historians do in terms of cognitive acts offers some targets of what expertise looks like and how we can make progress in thinking historically about the past – keeping in mind that such progress is always relative and never set in locksteps. As

Bruner makes clear with reference to learning, intellectual activity is the same anywhere, whether at the frontier of knowledge or in a history classroom. The difference, he notes, is in *degree,* not in kind.

Returning to my introductory analogy, for a kid, the goal of learning to play a sport is rarely to become a professional player. Expertise in playing the game does not provide an end itself, but rather a benchmark in relation to what players can do to improve the quality of their experience. The same holds true for history. Students will become more critical in their understanding of the past – and the present – if they replace their naive conceptions and theories with better and more serviceable ones. Historically, the assumption has been that knowing history implies gradually accumulating more content knowledge. Yet I hope to have made it clear in this chapter that without the intervention of a formal and critical sense of how historical knowledge is developed, manipulated, or conveyed, students are left naively apprehending what is presented to them by authorities, be they political leaders, movie producers, parents, or teachers. The history profession has developed useful concepts, procedures, and ways of thinking about the past that are quite pertinent to the concerns of contemporary students. Outlining history as both substantive and procedural knowledge can help students make sense of the analytic process of constructing the past. Growing research now indicates that students can learn, even at an early age, to engage in disciplinary thinking, provided that they are introduced gradually and repetitively to doing history.[65] What history educators urgently need is a theory of progression in historical learning. We know what experts do and how they do it, but we need a clearer, scaffolded vision of what it is to progressively develop expertise, in both substantive and procedural knowledge of history, with realistic attainable targets. Innovative projects, such as the *Benchmarks of Historical Thinking* (see Seixas, Chapter 6, and Morton, Chapter 9, in this volume), offer hope for a more robust theory of history learning for the twenty-first century.

## NOTES

1  Sam Wineburg, *Historical Thinking and Other Unnatural Acts: Charting the Future of Teaching the Past* (Philadelphia: Temple University Press, 2001), 7.
2  Peter Seixas, "Schweigen! Die Kinder! Or, Does Postmodern History Have a Place in the Schools?" in *Knowing, Teaching, and Learning History: National and International Perspectives,* ed. Peter Stearns, Peter Seixas, and Sam Wineburg (New York: New York University Press, 2000), 33.
3  Ibid.

4 Ken Osborne, "Teaching History in the Schools: A Canadian Debate," *Journal of Curriculum Studies* 35, 5 (2003): 586.
5 Bruce VanSledright, "What Does It Mean to Think Historically ... and How Do You Teach It?" *Social Education* 68, 3 (2004): 230.
6 This conception of disciplinary thinking is discussed in further detail in Stéphane Lévesque, *Thinking Historically: Educating Students for the 21st Century* (Toronto: University of Toronto Press, 2008), Chap. 1.
7 See Jerome Bruner, *The Process of Education*, 2nd ed. (Cambridge, MA: Harvard University Press, 1977); and Howard Gardner and Veronica Boix-Mansilla, "Teaching for Understanding in the Disciplines – and Beyond," in *The Development and Education of the Mind: The Selected Works of Howard Gardner*, ed. Howard Gardner (New York: Routledge, 2006), 147.
8 Ibid.
9 VanSledright, "What Does It Mean to Think Historically?" 230.
10 Chad Gaffield, "Toward the Coach in the History Classroom," *Canadian Issues* (October-November 2001): 12.
11 Peter Lee, "History Teaching and Philosophy of History," *History and Theory* 22 (1983): 21-28.
12 Peter Lee and Rosalyn Ashby, "Progression in Historical Understanding," in *Knowing, Teaching, and Learning History*, 199.
13 Lee, "History Teaching and Philosophy of History," 25.
14 Lee and Ashby, "Progression in Historical Understanding," 199.
15 Ibid., 200.
16 Gardner and Boix-Mansilla, "Teaching for Understanding in the Disciplines," 147.
17 See Hazel Hertzberg, "History and Progressivism: A Century of Reform Proposals," in *Historical Literacy: The Case for History in American Education*, ed. Paul Gagnon (New York: Macmillan, 1989), 80-89. Keith C. Barton and Linda S. Levstik's most recent book, *Teaching History for the Common Good* (Mahwah: Lawrence Erlbaum, 2004) typifies this interdisciplinary emphasis.
18 Bruce VanSledright, *In Search of America's Past: Learning to Read History in Elementary School* (New York: Teachers College Press, 2002), 141.
19 Ken Osborne, "To the Past: Why We Need to Teach and Study History," in *To the Past: History Education, Public Memory, and Citizenship in Canada*, ed. Ruth Sandwell (Toronto: University of Toronto Press, 2006), 117-18. Recent findings suggest, however, a common trend in Canadian curricular reforms. Most provinces are adopting history and social studies programs with similar constructivist approaches to past and human realities, with focus on skills acquisition and education for democratic citizenship. See Ken Osborne, *Canadian History in the Schools* (report prepared for the Historica Foundation, 2004); and Jean-Pierre Charland et Sabrina Moisan, *L'enseignement de l'histoire dans les écoles françaises du Canada* (report prepared for the Historica Foundation, 2003); both articles available at http://www.histori.ca.
20 Peter Seixas, "Conceptualizing the Growth of Historical Understanding," in *The Handbook of Education and Human Development*, ed. David Olson and Nancy Torrance (Oxford: Blackwell, 1996), 32. Similar ideas on historical understanding

have been advanced in French Canada by Christian Laville and Robert Martineau, "L'histoire, voie royale vers la citoyenneté?" *Éducation* 16 (octobre 1998): 33-37; Robert Martineau, *L'histoire à l'école, matière à penser* (Montreal: L'Harmattan, 1999); Jean-Pierre Charland, *Les élèves, l'histoire et la citoyenneté: Enquête auprès d'élèves des régions de Montréal et Toronto* (Quebec: Presses de l'Université Laval, 2003); and Christian Laville, "Pour une éducation historique critique, qu'attendre du courant de la conscience historique?" in *Identités, mémoires, conscience historique*, ed., Nicole Tutiaux-Guillon et Didier Nourrison (Saint-Étienne: Publications de l'Université de Saint-Étienne, 2003).

21 Linda S. Levstik and Keith C. Barton, *Doing History: Investigating with Children in Elementary and Middle Schools* (Mahwah: Lawrence Erlbaum, 2001), 13.

22 Leopold von Ranke, "The Ideal of Universal History," in *The Varieties of History: From Voltaire to the Present*, ed. Fritz Stern (London: Macmillan, 1956), 55. Editor's translation.

23 Jerome Bruner, *The Process of Education*, 2nd ed. (Cambridge, MA: Harvard University Press, 1977): 58.

24 In Stern, ed., *The Varieties of History*, 57.

25 Peter Seixas, "Mapping the Terrain of Historical Significance," *Social Education* 61, 1 (1997): 22.

26 Robert Phillips, "Historical Significance: The Forgotten 'Key Concept,'" *Teaching History* 106 (2002): 14-19. See also the recent work of Lis Cercadillo, "Significance in History: Students' Ideas in England and Spain," in *Raising Standards in History Education: International Review of History Education* 3, ed. Alaric Dickinson, Peter Gordon, and Peter Lee (London: Woburn Press, 2001).

27 Geoffrey Partington, *The Idea of an Historical Education* (Windsor: NFER, 1980), 112.

28 Herbert Butterfield, *The Whig Interpretation of History* (London: G. Bell and Sons, 1931), 31.

29 Michael Oakeshott, *Experience and Its Modes* (Cambridge: Cambridge University Press, 1933), 103.

30 Carl Becker, "Everyman His Own Historian," *American Historical Review* 37, 2 (1932): 221-26; Pierre Nora, "Between Memory and History," in *Realms of Memory: The Construction of the French Past*, trans. Arthur Goldhammer (New York: Columbia University Press, 1996), 1-20.

31 On the relationship between people and the intimate past, see Roy Rosenzweig and David Thelen, *The Presence of the Past: Popular Uses of History in American Life* (New York: Columbia University Press, 1998). Specific tables on the American survey can be found at http://chnm.gmu.edu/survey. A comparable study was recently conducted with Canadians; for preliminary results, see Margaret Conrad, Jocelyn Létourneau, and David Northrup, "Canadians and Their Pasts: An Exploration in Historical Consciousness," *Public Historian* 31, 1 (February 2009): 15-34. The Canadian online survey can be found at http://www.isr.yorku.ca.

32 Peter Lee, "Why Learn History?" in *Learning History*, ed. Alaric Dickinson, Peter Lee, and Peter Rogers (London: Heinemann, 1984), 6.

33 Ibid., 10.

34  VanSledright, *In Search of America's Past*, 140.
35  Louis Mink, "The Autonomy of Historical Understanding," *History and Theory* 5, 1 (1996): 33.
36  E.H. Carr, *What Is History?* (London: Macmillan, 1962), 85.
37  Denis Shemilt, "The Caliph's Coin," in *Knowing, Teaching, and Learning History*, 91.
38  William Walsh, *An Introduction to Philosophy of History* (London: Hutchinson's University Library, 1961), 59.
39  Ibid.
40  Seixas, "Conceptualizing," 771.
41  Shemilt makes a similar claim where he writes that "the historian must not be false to the chronicle of events but must also construct meaningful accounts that impute narrative significance to events by means of quantitative and colligatory generalizations, analysis of trends and turning points, and intentional and causal explanations." See Shemilt, "Caliph's Coin," 95.
42  See Ontario Ministry of Education, *Canadian and World Studies, Grades 11 and 12* (Toronto: Queen's Printer, 2000): 114.
43  Terry Haydn, James Arthur, and Martin Hunt, *Learning to Teach History in Secondary School: A Companion to School Experience* (New York: Routledge, 1997), 106.
44  Denis Shemilt, *History 13-16: Evaluation Study* (Edinburgh: Holmes McDougall, 1980), 35.
45  Ibid.
46  Reinhart Koselleck, *The Practice of Conceptual History: Timing History, Spacing Concepts* (Stanford: Stanford University Press, 2002), 219.
47  Carr, *What Is History?* 111.
48  Wineburg, *Historical Thinking and Other Unnatural Acts*, 76.
49  Keith Barton, "'I Just Kinda Know': Elementary Students' Ideas about Historical Evidence," *Theory and Research in Social Education* 25, 4 (1997): 420.
50  Chris Husbands, *What Is History Teaching? Language, Ideas, and Meaning in Learning about the Past* (Buckingham: Open University Press, 1993), 26 (my emphasis).
51  Peter Lee, "Historical Knowledge and the National Curriculum," in *History in the National Curriculum*, ed. R. Aldrich (London: Kogan Page, 1991), 45.
52  David Lowenthal, *The Past Is a Foreign Country* (New York: Cambridge University Press, 1985).
53  R.G. Collingwood, *The Idea of History* (New York: Oxford University Press, 1956), 218.
54  Peter Lee, "Historical Imagination," in *Learning History*, 89.
55  Collingwood, *Idea of History*, 241.
56  Lee, "Historical Imagination," 89.
57  Levstik and Barton, *Doing History*, 211.
58  Bruce VanSledright, "From Empathic Regard to Self-Understanding: Im/Positionality, Empathy, and Historical Contextualization," in *Historical Empathy and Perspective Taking in the Social Studies*, ed. O.L. Davis, Elizabeth Yeager, and Stuart Foster (Lanham: Rowman and Littlefield, 2001), 57.
59  Seixas, "Conceptualizing," 777.
60  Partington, *Idea of an Historical Education*, 74.

61 See Bernard Sheehan, "Problems of Moral Judgments in History," *South Atlantic Quarterly* 84, 1 (1985): 37-50.
62 Michael Oakeshott, *Rationalism in Politics, and Other Essays* (London: Methuen, 1962), 165.
63 Adrian Oldfield, "Moral Judgments in History," *History and Theory* 20, 3 (1981): 269.
64 Barton and Levstik, *Teaching History for the Common Good*, x.
65 For a recent and detailed overview on students' historical learning, see Bruce VanSledright and Margarita Limon, "Learning and Teaching Social Studies: A Review of Cognitive Research in History and Geography," in *Handbook of Educational Psychology*, ed. Patricia Alexander and Philip Winne (Mahwah: Lawrence Erlbaum, 2006), 545-57.

# Assessment of Historical Thinking

PETER SEIXAS

Research on assessment is often conceptualized as divided between assessment for accountability and assessment dedicated toward student learning. This chapter starts from the premise that, rather than being two entirely different entities, these represent two ends of a continuum.[1] Both ends are present in the classroom context: "summative" assessment, for assigning grades, is largely congruent with accountability functions; whereas the main function of "formative" assessment is more immediately to support and enhance opportunities for learning.

Considerable advances have been made recently to define both how students learn and how educators can know what students know. This work has been conducted and articulated mainly through a series of committees under the auspices of the US National Research Council (NRC).[2] The NRC Committee on the Foundations of Assessment has set out three components that ground all assessments: a model of cognition and learning; assumptions about tasks that are "most likely to elicit demonstrations" of that cognition; and assumptions about how to interpret the evidence drawn from those demonstrations.[3] To these, I would add a prior component: implicit in all assessments are assumptions about educational goals. That is, assessments measure progress in development *toward* some end, however openly defined.

While these components are widely recognized in educational research communities, only sporadically have they been articulated in practice. This chapter outlines how each of these components applies to the problem of assessment in history education – specifically, assessment of historical thinking.

## Goals and Assessment in History Education

Goals and assessment are intimately linked.[4] Implicit or poorly articulated goals have had somewhat differing consequences at the elementary, secondary, and post-secondary levels. In colleges and universities, historians' goals for their students include deep understanding of particular eras and themes, in a way that is not in any way conveyed by the flattened and misleading term "content" as a list of names and dates to be memorized.[5] In elementary and secondary schools, this notion of "content" may indeed constitute the goal in too many history classes, especially in those taught by teachers with little formal history training. In recent years, many high school curriculum documents have made a cursory nod toward the goal of "historical thinking"; but beyond allusions to "using primary sources," the term is rarely defined further for teachers.[6]

Implicit or poorly articulated goals bear serious consequences for assessment. Some university students, when faced with the task of writing research essays and examination answers, divine what counts as a demonstration of deep historical understanding – but many do not. In high schools, assessment too often takes the form of multiple-choice testing, which fails to measure the kinds of understanding that make history worth studying in the first place. Clearly articulated goals for history education at both these levels, then, constitute the first step in developing more sensitive assessments that will help make the ends of doing history more transparent to students.

Though factual knowledge is a building block for students' understanding of the past, the memorization of a catalogue of facts is clearly inadequate, by any standards, as a meaningful goal for history education. What, then, are the ends toward which history education aims? At the post-secondary level, goals are far less likely to be clearly articulated than at the high school level. In any case, I know of no study of goals as they appear in individual history professors' syllabuses. At the secondary level, goals are articulated in provincial curriculum documents. In these, it is remarkable how general the goals for history classrooms have become. There are general research and literacy goals: how to find information using library and digital resources, and how to use information in writing a well-organized essay. At a slightly more specific level, there are goals that might be classified as "social studies" objectives: how to detect bias, read a document critically, and communicate a reasoned opinion about an issue. Up to this point, however, there has been nothing specifically *historical* about the goals. In other words, these are all important goals, but there is no reason to use history, as opposed to literature (for general literacy objectives) or a social science (for social studies objectives), to achieve them.

To define those understandings that are specific to history education – understandings that reside at the heart of the discipline – one must move beyond these generic goals, toward the components of historical consciousness. These have been articulated in a variety of ways, but they include the following: (1) an understanding of the present in terms of developments and crisis points in the past; (2) an awareness of the vast differences between ways of life and ways of thinking in the present and those in the past, the profound challenges posed by transcendence of those differences, and the historical mutability of "human nature"; and (3) an understanding of the interplay between intentional human agency and the unintended consequences of human action, as well as the constraints imposed on human actors by structures inherited from the past. They also include modes of investigating the past: (4) understanding history as an interpretive discipline that requires criteria for inclusion and omission; (5) the ethical dimension: that crimes from the past, notwithstanding their historical distance, may impose demands for action in the present; and (6) a critical stance toward tradition and myth, enabled by the analysis of traces (or primary sources) from the past.[7]

In the Canada-wide Benchmarks of Historical Thinking Project, these aspects of historical consciousness have been codified into a form that is fairly easy to communicate.[8] The Benchmarks project defines the goals of history education in the service of more refined assessments. According to the project, students should be able to do the following:

- Establish historical *significance:* understand why we care, today, about certain events, trends, and issues in history. Without significance, history becomes antiquarianism.
- Use primary source *evidence:* know how to find, select, contextualize, and interpret sources for a historical argument. Without evidence, there is no basis for our accounts and explanations, and history becomes myth.
- Identify *continuity and change:* assess what has changed and what has remained the same over time. Without the idea that some things remain the same while others change, history turns into a mere list of events. Evaluation of change involves the related ideas of *progress* and *decline*.

- Analyze *cause and consequence:* weigh how and why certain conditions and actions led to others. This enables explanation; it also calls forth the related concept of historical *agency,* or the role played by human intention and action in historical change.
- Take *historical perspectives:* understand the past as a "foreign country" in which people's lives and actions were shaped by sometimes vastly different social, cultural, intellectual, and even emotional contexts. Otherwise, people of the past are seen simply as earlier, stupider versions of ourselves.
- Understand the *ethical dimension* of historical interpretations: understand how we, in the present, judge actors in different circumstances in the past; how various interpretations of the past reflect different moral stances today; and when and how crimes of the past bear consequences today. Tricky and problematic as it is, without an ethical dimension, history has no consequences.[9]

Acknowledging that "historical thinking" must be tied to substantive historical topics in any history curriculum, we have much less experience in articulating and assessing competence in historical thinking. Moreover, each of these six aspects of historical consciousness comprises multiple levels of complexity: reasonable expectations for performance in a ten-year-old will differ from those expected from a sixteen-year-old.

## A Model of Cognition and Learning

A "model of cognition and learning" refers to our ideas about how students confront problems that are central to the discipline of history, and the multiple paths by which they learn more sophisticated ways to confront those problems.[10] These models are generally based on empirical studies of students' thinking and learning.

To explore what such a model is and is not in history education, consider the model of learning that would be demanded by a historical epistemology that saw the central problem in history as the memorization of increasing numbers of pieces of information: the "catalogue of facts" approach to history education, or what has been called a "sedimentary" approach to learning, where each layer is deposited on top of previously learned layers. Students who memorized more facts would be judged as having a more sophisticated historical understanding. Assessment designed in accordance with such a model would be relatively straightforward. Indeed, despite widespread recognition that historical understanding demands a decidedly more complex model of cognition and learning, this model is sufficiently convenient that much assessment at the classroom and systemic levels is designed in accordance with this model.

A model of cognition and learning that is more in line with contemporary learning research takes account of three premises. First, new understandings are constructed on the foundations of existing knowledge and experience. Second, there can be *progression* in various aspects of students' historical thinking as they develop increasingly sophisticated and powerful concepts and procedures for developing their understandings. But there is no single linear path of progression: different students may take different routes toward more sophisticated understandings. Third and finally, progression, while potentially subject to age-related limits, can be actively promoted and enhanced by teaching in the *zone of proximal development* – that is, not so far away from students' current understanding that it leaves them behind, but far enough away that it stimulates growth.

For this general model to inform the assessment of history learning, a dialectical process is required in order to articulate a hierarchy of levels of understanding. Part of this involves empirical investigation of students' work in response to history problems; and part of it involves a research-based but a priori definition of more and less sophisticated stances, drawn from current thinking about historical practice.

Ercikan summarizes the characteristics of a developmental perspective on cognition, drawn from the literature on assessment for learning:

> A developmental perspective that describes a typical progression of learning and development, identifies performances that differentiate between different competence levels and notes landmark performances for each level of competence ... This developmental perspective needs to provide information about how students think and learn in the domain and allow for a variety of learning styles and progression models for children. The description of the progression should be specific enough to lend itself to provide fine-grained diagnostic information as well as coarser-grained summary information.[11]

On the basis of work that has already been done, we might sketch out levels for each of the historical thinking concepts defined above. Initially, these must rely heavily on typologies of historical thinking derived from disciplinary practices; but given sufficient research, they can be supplemented and revised based on empirical work with students.[12] For the purposes of this chapter, one of the historical thinking concepts – historical perspective taking – will be used to explore a developmental approach to assessment. In the course of this explication, it will become apparent how the six concepts are fundamentally interrelated.

## A Developmental Model of Perspective Taking

The past is a "foreign country" and thus difficult to understand.[13] At the same time, understanding the foreignness of the past provides a sense of the range of human behaviour and social organization, alternatives to taken-for-granted conventional wisdom, and a wider perspective for our present preoccupations. Historical perspective taking can be defined as the cognitive act of understanding the different social, cultural, intellectual, and even emotional contexts that shaped people's lives and actions in the past. Though it is sometimes called "historical empathy," it is very different from the common-sense notion of deep emotional feeling for and identification with another person. When taking the perspective of historical actors, we rely upon evidence for inferences about how people felt and thought. Empathetic leaps – a "feeling" of the presence of the past – must be based on the evidentiary record; and it is the depth of evidence, not the depth of feeling, that counts.[14] Understanding the perspective of a historical actor does not mean *identifying with* that actor. Any particular historical event or situation may involve historical actors who differ in their perspectives on it even though they share the same historical moment. For understanding the event, it is crucial to untangle what they have in common (owing to their shared historical moment) from what makes them different (because of their different social positions).

There are two common-sense (what Sam Wineburg might call "natural") approaches to dealing with the differences in life, thought, and experience that we confront when observing people in the distant past.[15] One is the "error of dismissal": the thought that people who operate in ways different from us are irrational, ignorant, stupid, racist, or sexist, without further questions or investigations into the totality of their historical circumstances. In other words: "If they aren't like us, we can ignore them." The other is the "error of presentism": the assumption that historical people are more like us than they actually were, which leads us to impose our own assumptions, ideas, and concepts on people to whom these would have been very foreign. The result is what some have called "Flintstones history," that is, history in which actors believe and behave just like us, except that they wear strange costumes. Much historical fiction and film embodies this kind of presentism. Both kinds of errors limit historical understanding of the people and events being investigated.

Yet these are not *simply* errors: each in its own way provides the basis for learning more sophisticated approaches to the past, which must involve a negotiation between similarity and difference, between proximity and distance. The problem of dismissal contains the seeds of recognition of difference across time. Starting from their recognition of the foreignness of the past, students can be brought toward historical questions: What circumstances contributed to people thinking and acting this way? What were the social, cultural, and material conditions to which they were responding? Ironically, to make hypotheses about the experience – across difference – of historical peoples, students will in some respects be forced to invoke common-sense, transhistorical notions of pain, pleasure, desire, agency, and so on – in other words, the components of "human nature."

Students who make presentist errors constitute a different problem in terms of the path their learning needs to take in order for them to reach more powerful understandings of people in the past. They need to be led beyond their assumptions of commonality, to appreciate strangeness and difference that they do not initially recognize. Immersion in rich, appropriately selected primary sources, along with well-targeted questions and critically examined secondary sources (e.g., historical film and fiction), can help these students understand the foreignness of the past and even, to some degree, its ineffability.

As students come to more sophisticated understandings of the thoughts and consciousness of historical characters, they will increasingly come to grips with the paradoxical nature of the problem: to understand others, we need to assume commonality at a certain level; but every time we do so, we risk misunderstanding them precisely because we inappropriately superimpose our own specific and peculiar frames of mind on them. At the most sophisticated level, students will be able to articulate what is known, what is not known, what additional evidence might shed more light, and, possibly, what is simply unknowable.

## Tasks Likely to Elicit Demonstrations of Historical Cognition[16]

Awareness of genres and media is helpful in designing tasks to elicit demonstrations of historical cognition. By continuing with the example of historical perspective taking, we should be able to illustrate the range of choices facing those who design assessment tasks. Tasks shaped around three different genres provide a sense of the different levels at which assessment tasks can be pitched.

At the most basic level, a common classroom practice involves asking students to write a letter, journal entry, or diary from the perspective of a historical character – a simulated autobiographical recount, to use the language of Caroline Coffin.[17] This kind of exercise has been lampooned by Keith Jenkins, for whom the uncertainties of bridging difference lead to skepticism about taking historical perspectives at all – a skepticism supported in the school context by teachers asking students to "pretend to be a fox, a snowflake, an angry king."[18]

At an intermediate level, students might be given an instance of a practice very different from our own (e.g., the Salem witch trials or trials by ordeal) and asked to analyze documentary sources in order to explain the actions and beliefs of the historical actors in terms of the conditions of their lives.[19] At the most advanced level, students might be asked to develop an argument that includes an explanatory hypothesis, weighs alternative explanations, and defends the proposed hypothesis as the one best supported by the available evidence.

It is important to think about what kinds of modelling and teaching students have for each of these kinds of tasks. Textbooks generally supply very little in the way of practice or modelling in any of these three genres. The writing of imaginary letters or journals is a genre with no currency except in historical fiction. Textbooks rarely explore in any depth the relationship between primary sources and historical actors' perspectives. And even more rarely do they acknowledge competing historical interpretations in the course of providing arguments for a particular one. Instead they offer an authoritative historical recount or account. So if models of successful performances are going to provide students with guidance toward competence and sophistication in constructing these responses, they will have to come from other kinds of materials or from the teacher.

It is interesting to speculate whether there is a post-secondary equivalent to these secondary school assessment tasks. When he assigns a book-length memoir, autobiography, or biography, Gerald Friesen (Chapter 10, this volume) wants his university students to "situate themselves in the past, accompany the central actor along a path not entirely unlike their own, and reflect on an individual's historical context, on how choices were made, and what were the implications of those choices." The essay he expects students to write runs parallel to our basic and intermediate levels: it is to be, on the one hand, from *within* the life, "accompanying" the actor (thus parallel to the basic level); and on the other hand, a retrospective "reflection on the individual's historical context" (which bears more in common with the intermediate level). Such closely related tasks offer some indication of the benefits of thinking of the development of historical thinking as operating on the same continuum as the tasks that elicit that thinking.

Increasing access to innovative technologies has opened the possibility of its uses in assessment tasks for students. Student-created documentaries using archival photos and films – either to tell a story or to make a persuasive argument – can be a powerful alternative to the written essay.[20] "Perspective taking" is an especially appropriate historical thinking concept whose mastery students can develop through these exercises: they assemble visual evidentiary sources that offer a prima facie sense of the times in which they were created; then they make sense of those times with narrative voice-overs. Such exercises test students' ability to enter into conditions very different from their own, while making sense of the images to contemporary audiences: negotiation, again, between proximity and distance.

### Interpreting the Evidence of Historical Cognition[21]

The final challenge of assessment involves interpreting students' performances as evidence of historical cognition. I will do no more here than suggest the kind of challenge this poses, again, using our example of historical perspective taking. As Lee has noted, students' sophistication on any measure of historical thinking is not independent of their knowledge of the substantive history.[22] A student who knows and understands more about the build-up to the First World War will stand a much better chance of completing a task requiring that he or she take the perspective of historical actors in 1914, than one who has little contextual knowledge. The two are bound together. Even so, it remains possible to assess student work on 1914 using criteria based on historical perspective taking.

The following essay was written by a student responding to a task set for the Benchmarks Project by Vancouver teachers Chas Desjarlais, Damian Wilmann, and Scott Anderson. Titled "Canada's Reaction to the Outbreak of War," this exercise provided grade eleven (age 16-17) students with a few visual and textual sources on Canadians' responses to the declaration of the First World War in 1914 and to the invasion of Afghanistan in 2001. After a well-structured sequence of scaffolding techniques, students wrote an essay comparing Canadian responses to the two international crises. The following excerpts from student work were from an essay that the teachers rated at the highest level. It offers a rich exemplar of historical perspective taking: students were confronted with the potentially "odd" spectacle of young men enthusiastically greeting the announcement of the onset of war, a war in which many enlisted eagerly and – students now know in retrospect – went off to suffer agonizing trauma and death. "Were they stupid?" would be a natural response from a twenty-first-century teenager. Most did better than that in entering the world of the young recruits. The passages are reproduced here (not in their entirety) in the order in which they appear in the student's essay.

> Two different perspectives emerge if Canada's response to the outbreak of war in 1914 is compared to its reaction to the outbreak of war in 2001. There is a dramatic difference between the two reactions, and this difference is mainly due to several factors which may have contributed to the people's opinions and affected their views in 1914 and in 2001.

By setting up the exercise as a comparison between 1914 and 2001, the teachers gave the students a head start on historical perspective taking. They were not quite comparing now and then, but rather two historical moments, one more familiar, the other less so. This helped students see the close-to-the-present as another historical moment and to enter the more distant moment respectfully.

> When Britain declared war on Germany in 1914, Canada was automatically at war since it was a British colony. During that time, the people's enthusiasm and excitement about the war were shown. Based on an article from Toronto *Mail and Empire*, 1914, the people were "cheering" and it was evident that they show patriotism towards Great Britain. It was indicated that they "greeted the news" that Britain, their "Mother Country" had declared war on Germany. In the article, it was noted that groups of men sang "Rule Britannia," "God save the King," and "Onward Christian Soldiers." These songs that they sang show that they are patriotic and religious people – primarily Christian people. Based on a visual source from *Queens' University Archives*, a photo taken in 1914, the pro-war crowd were mostly young, Caucasian males.

In this paragraph, the student uses some contextual knowledge ("automatically at war"), but the major argument comes from the sources provided in the exercise (they are patriotic and religious people – primarily Christian people). There is no judgment here, just a statement of fact.

> On the other hand, during the outbreak of war in 2001, a totally different perspective was shown. The people illustrated an anti-war stance. No enthusiasm or excitement was evident. Based on an article from *Vancouver Sun*, 2001, the people protested against the war and shouted for peace ... People were of different ethnicities, gender and religions. Diversity is very evident.

The contrasts between the two photographs chosen by the teachers are striking: not only is one prowar and one antiwar, but the homogeneity of the 1914 prowar crowd is even more striking when seen next to the 2001 antiwar demonstration. Here the student describes the differences without analyzing them. But the description of the contrast leads the student astray in the next paragraph:

> Analysing the primary sources from 1914, one could see bias. Both written and visual sources presented the perspective of a single majority group – young, white males. In the photo, one could hardly see females, and in the article it was indicated "groups of men." The primary sources from 1914 only contain a perspective from a single majority group, whereas in the primary sources from 2001, one could see multiple groups, and diverse crowd. Not only males were present, but also females. Ethnicities, ages, and religion also vary, so perspectives of different kinds of people were presented.

"Bias," identified by the student in the first line, is not really an issue in primary sources, as it is, for example, in textbooks. If the photographer were "biased" in trying to take, for instance, only one segment of the crowd, that would be of interest, for we would then try to analyze the reasons and consequences of this choice. But this kind of "bias" would not lead us to discount the evidence; rather, it would make it even more interesting. Here, however, the student is not pointing to the photographer's bias, but somehow to the "bias" of the crowd itself, which is a clear error.

In the final two paragraphs, the student analyses the differences, skilfully invoking historical perspective taking in both instances:

> Several factors played an important role in the response of the people to the outbreak of war in 1914 and in 2001. In 1914, Christianity (Anglican or Protestant) was the main religion of the people. Religion united the country, and it played a role in prompting the people to feel the sense of duty, and to feel obligated that they should protect and serve their families and country. Some Canadians of British origin also felt the "patriotic urge" to participate in the war. Also, due to some financial hardships, the people see the war as a source of income and jobs. Another factor is gender expectation, and in 1914, males were deemed by the society to be brave, and strong, and were heavily expected to participate in the war and serve.

Here, the student avoids entirely any negative judgment of the young men who greeted the war with enthusiasm; rather, this student is examining a variety of material and ideological conditions that set the young men up for the response they made. A final paragraph introduces another important set of factors, as well as a new set of problems:

> The media factor and technology contributed a lot to the people's views and opinions. Since in 1914, technology was not that advanced, there was a lack of media. Canadians would hardly see the negative effects of war. Due to a lack of media in 1914, Canadians were not educated nor informed about the destructiveness of war and how violent it could be. However, in 2001, technology and media were already advanced and people were aware of the violence of war. Canadians have seen the consequences of war through media, and this may have contributed to the development of their anti-war stance.

This is the only point where the student views the historical period as having a deficit in relation to the present: "due to a lack of media," in contrast to 2001, when "media were already advanced" (well, perhaps not quite like today, but "already," surprisingly, well on their way to the Facebook/YouTube-saturated present). The student is correct to point to media and technology as key factors in shaping people's ideas; but here, in the ultimate paragraph, a too-simple notion of historical progress in technology has got slightly in the way of the clearest perspective taking.

Now consider excerpts from this contrasting essay, judged by the team of teachers to be at the most basic level of historical perspective taking. Even here we can see the benefits of useful sources and contextual scaffolding provided by the teachers, but the lack of attention to details in the sources and the readiness to make an absolute, black-and-white contrast distinguish this essay from the last.

> These men [in 1914] were not sad or worried at all about going to war. Instead, their reaction toward war was very cheerful and exciting ... They didn't really understand much about war and the impact that would have caused on their lives because the newspapers didn't discuss it ...
>
> People in 2001 know how bad war can be and they understand the consequences in war and don't want to lose lives and money on war and equipments ... The community was diverse and by declaring war on one country, it would be singling out one part of society that didn't want to be discriminated against because of what was going on in their home country.

This essay (both in these excerpts and in the remainder of its two paragraphs) includes no direct reference to the documentary sources to anchor its claims about the perspectives of the people at the two historical moments. The central contrast revolves around historical ignorance versus contemporary knowledge – a tempting trap, given the particular circumstances, but one that students might be specifically cautioned against.

## Final Thoughts

Analysis of this assessment exercise allows us to circle back to some of the key findings of assessment theorists and researchers. First, the learning that students must undertake in order to complete this task – one that was designed around an aspect of "historical thinking" – necessarily involves students working with a considerable body of contextual (i.e., factual) material. The more conversant students are with the circumstances in Canada – social, political, economic, and cultural – at the outbreak of the First World War and the invasion of Afghanistan, the better a basis they will have for articulating the perspectives of Canadians facing those events and the logic of their actions. Second, the assessment exercise is intrinsically bound up with student learning: students in this history class have learned about the wars and about perspective taking in order to complete the task; but the assessment task contributes just as much to the process of learning as other classroom exercises that preceded it. Third, by articulating increased competence in "historical perspective taking" as one of its objectives, the course potentially achieves a through line for students, as they see a procedural consistency in their approaches to historical perspective taking in subsequent lessons on, for instance, the Co-operative Commonwealth Federation (CCF), the Union Nationale, unemployed workers during the Depression, and the War Measures Act in 1970. This should enable them to become increasingly comfortable with more complex aspects of perspective taking over the course of a year or more. Finally, not only is students' learning enriched and enhanced by such assessments, but teachers also have opportunities to enrich their own understandings of the qualities of historical perspective taking as they analyze students' work, articulate what makes the good essays good, and refine their scoring rubrics. This enables them to build the fruits of assessment back into their teaching, both for individual students and for the class as a whole.

It is, of course, fun as a researcher to be able to pore over a single student essay for an evening, trying to articulate where it does well, and where it goes awry, with respect to a single fundamental historical thinking concept. Suppose, however, I were faced, as a teacher, with a stack of two hundred student essays, exhausted from my full day of teaching, and facing all of those students in the next couple of days, most of them eager to read my comments and grades and know how they did: a different story indeed. Next time around, I might seriously consider a multiple-choice, machine-scorable exercise. A key challenge in assessing historical thinking, then – an unfinished piece of the history assessment puzzle – is to work with teachers to design tasks and interpretive strategies that are practicable for the classroom, without losing the focus on what really matters in the teaching and learning of history. This is only the beginning.

## NOTES

1 For an exploration of the relationships in the context of the classroom, see Paul Black, Christine Harrison, Clare Lee, Bethan Marshall, and Dylan Wiliam, "Working inside the Black Box: Assessment for Learning in the Classroom," *Phi Delta Kappan* 86, 1 (2004): 8-21.
2 National Research Council, *How People Learn: Brain, Mind, Experience, and School*, ed. John D. Bransford, Ann L. Brown, and Rodney R. Cocking (Washington: National Academy Press, 2000); James W. Pellegrino, Nancy Chudowsky, and Robert Glaser, eds., *Knowing What Students Know: The Science and Design of Educational Assessment* (Washington: National Academy Press, 2001); M. Suzanne Donovan and John D. Bransford, ed., *How Students Learn: History, Mathematics, and Science in*

*the Classroom, Committee on How People Learn – a Targeted Report for Teachers* (Washington: National Academy Press, 2005).
3   National Research Council, *Knowing What Students Know*, 20.
4   Education literature makes distinctions between large-scale goals and more tightly defined objectives, and similarly between evaluation and assessment. Neither distinction is particularly important for my purposes here.
5   For a discussion of the destructive consequences for history education of the use of the term "content," see Peter Seixas, "Beyond Content and Pedagogy: In Search of a Way to Talk about History Education," *Journal of Curriculum Studies* 31, 3 (1999): 317-37.
6   A major exception to this general case is the Quebec program of study (2004), which provides a well-articulated scheme for the development of three student competencies, fundamentally linking history and citizenship education. See http://www.meq.gouv.qc.ca.
7   Arie Wilschut, "History Teaching at the Mercy of Politicians and Ideologues," *Journal of Curriculum Studies* 42, 5 (2010): 693-723.
8   See Carla Peck and Peter Seixas, "Benchmarks of Historical Thinking: First Steps," *Canadian Journal of Education* 31, 4 (2008): http://www.csse-scee.ca/CJE.
9   See http://www.historybenchmarks.ca.
10  This is referred to as "the student model" in Kadriye Ercikan, "Developments in Assessment of Student Learning," in *Handbook of Educational Psychology*, ed. Patricia A. Alexander and Philip H. Winne (Mahwah: Lawrence Erlbaum, 2006): 929-53.
11  Ercikan, "Developments in Assessment," 11.
12  The work of the Benchmarks of Historical Thinking Project is based on the idea that teachers' work will accumulate data to inform such assessment exercises.
13  The phrase comes from David Lowenthal, *The Past Is a Foreign Country* (Cambridge: Cambridge University Press, 1985). Lowenthal, xvi, takes his title from L.P. Hartley, *The Go-Between*.
14  See Frank Ankersmit, *Sublime Historical Experience* (Stanford: Stanford University Press, 2005); and Eelco Runia, "Presence," *History and Theory* 45, 1 (2006): 1-29, for counterarguments aimed at historians that I believe are dangerous in the context of history education.
15  Sam Wineburg, *Historical Thinking and Other Unnatural Acts: Charting the Future of Teaching the Past* (Philadelphia: Temple University Press, 2001).
16  In Ercikan's evidence-centred design, this is the "task model." Ercikan, "Developments in Assessment."
17  Caroline Coffin, *Historical Discourse* (London: Continuum, 2006).
18  Keith Jenkins, *Rethinking History* (London: Routledge, 1991), 42.
19  Rosalyn Ashby and Peter Lee, "Children's Concepts of Empathy and Understanding in History," in *The History Curriculum for Teachers*, ed. Christopher Portal (London: Falmer Press, 1987), 62-88.
20  See Fiona MacKellar, "Editing Traces of the Past to Support Historical Thinking," master's thesis, Simon Fraser University, 2009.
21  In Ercikan, "Developments in Assessment," this is the "assessment model."
22  Peter Lee, "Understanding History," in *Theorizing Historical Consciousness*, ed. Peter Seixas (Toronto: University of Toronto Press, 2004), 139.

# 7

## History Education as a Disciplined "Ethic of Truths"

KENT DEN HEYER

> *We might as well face the fact, that if we're going to start talking about social action and, hence ethics, at all, its place is right in the center of the social studies.*
>
> – Michael Scriven

Writing in 1964, Michael Scriven provided a disciplinary reading of social studies subject matter, reflecting the "structure of the disciplines" trend of the time, most notably articulated by Jerome Bruner in *The Process of Education*. As Ken Osborne details, this trend was a return to Fred Morrow Fling's advocacy for disciplinary-based historical instruction in public schools during the decades before and after the turn of the twentieth century.[1] According to Osborne, Fling anticipated the academic vocationalism of Scriven and Bruner that has returned to us today in the form of calls to organize history education in accordance with disciplinary "second-order concepts" or "procedures."[2] (See Osborne, Chapter 2, this volume.) As I explore in this chapter, then as now, this particular disciplinary interpretation of historical thinking offers an inadequate model for a history education that has ethics and social action at its core.

An American historian of European history, Fling trained in the methodology of "scientific history" in Germany in the late 1880s. Returning to the United States to teach European history at the University of Nebraska, Fling energetically advocated what he called the "source method" in public schools. Fling's source method was concerned "not to provide information, but to examine the nature of historical proof and argument."[3] His program and its justifications "anticipated both the new social studies of the 1960s with its interest in the structure of the disciplines ... and more recent developments in history education [in which] the nature of historical evidence and interpretation [are] fundamental elements of any worthwhile history curriculum."[4] In contemporary terms, the "fundamental elements" are referred to as historical "second-order concepts" or "procedures" or "problems."[5]

Fling and recent advocates share a vision of what history as a discipline offers its students. For Fling, student skepticism constitutes the most valuable result of historical study:[6] "The student must be taught that 'historical work is critical work *par excellence*,' and that he is sure to fail if he undertakes it without having been previously put on his guard against his natural instinct to accept without examination anonymous information and to utilize good, bad, and indifferent documents without distinction."[7] In its more recent formulation, students working with historical concepts will learn "how to question historical accounts and understand the evidentiary base upon which they rest."[8] Historical second-order concepts provide "a rational way, on the basis of evidence and argument, to discuss the differing accounts that jostle with or contradict each other."[9] In each case, advocates claim that students' use of disciplinary thinking to investigate a problem from or about the past better prepares them to deliberate about competing public claims in the present: "Every hour in the day ... we are forced to pass judgments upon the truth or falsity of historical events, to apply the tests of historical method. The work is done, as a rule, unconsciously and crudely. Why not make it conscious and scientific?"[10]

This is a reasonable argument. The logic of this appeal, however, fails to place a sufficiently robust interpretation of ethics and social action at the centre of study. Rather, educators are expected to work for a hoped-for *deferred benefit* to democratic life in lieu of actually engaging what students' imaginative capacities might offer at this time in relation to pressing issues of personal and social concern.

In this chapter, I explore several shortcomings with this disciplinarian approach to history education.[11] In short, this approach ignores students' inventive capacities to use knowledge from or about the past when they explore possible, probable, and preferable futures with regard to present situations that are deemed inadequate – that is, it does not put ethics and social action at the centre of the curriculum. In a related move, disciplinarians justify their program with appeals to "deficit reasoning" – that the young deserve to be the objects of our disciplinary treatments because they lack knowledge or reason ineffectively (a rather self-serving formulation of the problem; after all, when does anyone know or reason well enough?).[12] We need a more affirmative and humanizing premise for our work with young people. Finally, even on its own terms, a disciplinary approach lacks disciplinarity when advocates exclude questions about an economy of historical distribution in which some interpretations of the past encountered in and outside schools are common and others are marginalized. Thus, while dedicated to elevating students' "reasoned judgments," these judgments are to take place within an unexamined social and political context of influence as to what is considered valid historical investigation, relevant topics, and worthy of wide public distribution. I illustrate these shortcomings by examining that for which the disciplinary school does not advocate.

### Historical Reasoning as Lab Work

As James Marsh asks, "is a single set of criteria for judging historical skills any more possible [or desirable?] than a single narrative?"[13] Working out of a "critical postmodern" perspective, Avner Segall argues that, rather than practice with criteria, history students require opportunities to question the changing epistemological basis of what it means to do history.[14] Forgoing a preoccupation with adherence to a particular contemporary interpretation of a set of historical procedures, Segall asks teachers to deconstruct with students the political-epistemological authority behind such interpretations:

> Disputing the notion that history rests upon sources and facts, and that changes in our vision and understanding of the past will result from advances in research and the unearthing of new facts, a critical perspective maintains that what governs the production of history are disciplinary and discursive conventions and that those are the actual sources of historical work ... It is interested in how and why particular pasts are constructed, legitimated, and disseminated by various discursive communities.[15]

Beverley Southgate provides an example of the historical and political contexts in which "disciplinary conventions" come to shape historical work.[16] Southgate studies the uneasy relationship of historians to their contemporary social and political situations. These relations have produced historical scholarship ranging from nationalistic histories in time of war (she studies European historical scholarship in the First World War) to calls for "affected disengagement" from partisan concerns in the name of pursuing the historical Truth about the past: "So 'Omnia veritas' wrote Geoffrey Elton[,] 'truth is everything' ... [Historians] must never again submit to 'lay' external pressures, or deviate from the central disciplinary tenet that 'the past must be studied for its own sake.'"[17] As Southgate details, Elton's lament expressed the despair of many in a generation that witnessed European pretensions to scientific history wash away in a tide of atavistic scholarship in support of the superiority of one's national tribe and its political status quo.

Of course, it may be objected that Southgate is documenting a failure of particular people at a particular time, not the general ideal of what should be achieved by following the procedures of "scientific" history more faithfully. What Elton witnessed, however, was neither the first nor the last time that such a thin interpretation of disciplinary thinking failed to transfer into the shadowy emotive, psychodynamic, and political relationships of historians to present issues. We should not be surprised; instead, we should ask ourselves why we continue with this faith in the democratic benefits of such a narrow "best practices" interpretation of what it is to do history. Training for a "scientific" or "procedural" interpretation of history omits a crucial subject: people's subjective relationship to the social and political influences that affect what is seen as relevant and valid work. Postmodernists interpret such influences in terms of "discursive conventions."

The political-disciplinary shifts detailed by Southgate, from scientific to nationalist and then again to objective history, exemplify a social politics of historical investigation. Such politics – as manifested in what comes to be recognized as epistemologically valid and reasonable within the discipline, and manifested as well in widely distributed historical interpretations beyond it – require student analysis if they are to offer any degree of refined interpretation of the histories encountered in textbooks, memorials, museums, and other sites of community imaginings. Of course, these issues have been taken up by historians themselves.[18] For reasons insufficiently explained, however, disciplinarians do not judge subjectivity or the social and political context of professional achievement to be important enough for students to take up as part of *what* historians do, or *why* they do what they do.

It is as if the historical procedures identified as relevant for student study have been extracted in labs from historians who lack hopes, fantasies, or racialized, gendered, classed, and desiring bodies and who also lack political intelligence. Given this level of abstraction, students have little opportunity to consider the complex reasons behind the distribution of some but not other histories (to cite but two widely circulated works articulating the Canadian nation-state's status quo story, see Pierre Berton's *The National Dream* and *The Last Spike* and CBC/Radio-Canada's *Canada: A People's History*). So we must ask: Which contextual forces make such an ahistorical and rather conservative view of the discipline appear reasonable to practise today as history education?

## Historical Thinking with an Ethical Point of Departure

In this section, I provide another example of what a disciplinary approach to history education excludes; offer one illustration of historical engagement grounded in ethical concern; and challenge the very common assertion (found in most educational authorities' mission statements) that we today in Canada live in a multicultural country containing diverse historical claims that require disciplinary forms of critical thinking to negotiate.

Historian and history educator Timothy Stanley argues that "the claim that society is growing more diverse makes sense only from within narratives of European settlement and from the points of view of socially dominant groups":

> A little more than one hundred years earlier [roughly around 1881 in British Columbia], English was spoken by a tiny minority making up less than 15 percent of the population. An aboriginal majority spoke over two dozen languages and lived in societies whose economics ranged from hunter-gathering to commercial ranching ... Not so long ago, many distinct cultural groups existed without any single one being dominant. Nor, given the homogenizing pressures of global capitalism, is it likely that the claim of unprecedented diversity is true on a global scale. The world as a whole is not growing more diverse culturally. If anything ... it would seem to be growing less diverse.[19]

If, as Stanley suggests, Canada is actually becoming less, not more, diverse, we need to question the assertion that multicultural distinctions constitute a diversity of historical claims.[20] To illustrate why this may be an important question, I briefly review English Canada's "grand narrative" (GN).

Building from the work of Daniel Francis and Timothy Stanley, we can identify several elements constituting English Canada's GN.[21] Allowing that regional emphasis on content varies for historical and constitutional reasons, this GN is reflected in the categories that divide textbook chapters (e.g., "the settling of the West" implying a lack thereof previous to the European arrival) as well as in the temporal organization of scholarship in university history departments across the country (e.g., pre- and post-Confederation university courses). Like those of other countries conceived in the forceful appropriation of land and culture, this Canadian GN tells a story of Canada as if the story were the past itself, unencumbered by interpretation or selective amnesia.[22] Rather, the past conveyed through this GN assumes an inevitable evolution of the nation-state through largely peaceful – if occasionally bumpy – progress. Other groups (defined most commonly by gender, race, ethnicity, religion, and – less often – political philosophy) enter the narrative only when they come into contact with – though without disrupting – the privileged story line, which involves a progressive overcoming of the implied limitations of what existed before.[23] Setting aside the questionable existence of diverse historical claims *outside* schools (supposedly by virtue of an "increasingly diverse" population, according to those who read the past and present through this GN perspective), this GN provides the relatively unchallenged frame *within* schools.

When I examined this narrative with my senior university social studies teacher education students (most of whom had a strong background in history), almost all were shocked that they had never heard of – let alone considered – the ways in which the GN had framed their historical understanding. As one student wrote, reflecting on the challenges of an assignment to produce historical narratives that differ from the GN, "we found it difficult to fully circumvent the clutches (in terms of both perspectives and assumptions) of an all-encompassing, intrinsically colonial and intensely reductionist grand narrative." Another wrote that "from kindergarten to graduation, we are constantly bombarded (and completely unaware) of the grand narrative. We learn how white men *civilized* the aboriginals, settled North America and created *Canada*." These are representative statements from almost all (forty-eight) students.[24]

As Stanley details, English Canada's GN is a racist narrative. It assumes white (i.e., male, British, of a certain class, or a classless settler of good capitalist intentions to put the land to proper use) to be the shading of those at the centre of the imagined community of Canada, with non-white "others" outside. Stanley reminds us that the word for this marginalization is racism. He grounds his work in a concern for justice, and I summarize his argument as follows: No refined historical reading of Canada as a nation-state or society can exist without interrogating the ways in which race and racism have been foundational to that nation-state's existence (e.g., in terms of who may and may not vote) and continue to support a racialized Canadian imaginary today, as reflected in whose Canadian-ness needs to be explained (e.g., "Where is your family *really* from?") and whose does not.

The racist framing of English Canada's GN, and its racializing effects today, lie beyond the disciplinarians' self-defined scope as a worthy object of student analysis. This is a choice to ignore Stanley's quite reasonable argument for making this GN visible so as to provide a more reasonably accurate history of Canada – one that also better informs ethical social action today by answering a call that does not come from the past at all but from a concern with present and future justice.[25]

The concepts identified by the disciplinary school have instigated thought-provoking research into the ways in which various populations presently reason about particular aspects of their experiences in relation to the past. (See Peck, Chapter 15, this volume.) This research greatly assists teachers who wish to think about the complexities of both their students and their own tasks. And we now have many classroom resources for teachers wishing to work with the concepts identified as relevant. I have already argued why the relevance of these concepts needs to be rethought.

I turn now to explore possibilities for a disciplinary commitment to work with students' reasoning (however defined) to serve more ethical ends than a questionable "deferred benefit." I do so in response to two questions guiding my recent scholarship: How might educators concerned with democratic options diversify the issues at stake about which historical claims are made? And what is a curricular example of a history/social studies program that has been organized with ethics at its core?

For the remainder of this chapter, I explore the following argument in response to these questions: The past – and reasoned judgments about its events and meanings to those of us present – should be positioned as warrants for our "affirmative inventions" of possible, probable, and preferable futures.[26] This would invite our creativity as citizens and our "desirous imaginations" as people rather than just our abilities to reason as teachers and students about the past.[27] Only by taking a deliberately ahistorical stance can any educator think that disciplinary thinking defined in narrow, rational terms offers even a deferred benefit in regard to the political and emotionally loaded judgments that historians and students make (or should make) about present issues. Unless we explicitly study the historical conditioning of our lives – of the ways we make sense of ourselves, our purposes, our shared present and future – we will impoverish students as historical thinkers, and they will likely and rightly interpret any proposed disciplinary program (regardless of concepts or procedures in vogue) as just another school assignment put before them without anything at stake – as a puzzle to figure out in the interest of completing a task (e.g., passing the grade, winning a scholarship, never having to take this course again). Teachers can devise richer engagements for their students if they use subject matter to explore alternatives to those aspects of our present social arrangements that are deemed inadequate. Such arrangements are, however, an issue of curriculum theory as much as any specific discipline.

## Becoming Subjects to a Disciplined Ethic of Truths

In this section, I outline an alternative orientation to history education organized around a "disciplined ethic of truths." I begin with a presumption articulated by Zongyi Deng and Allan Luke that "the formation of a school subject requires addressing an array of fundamental curriculum – not disciplinary questions."[28] Curriculum theory is that area of scholarship that seeks to understand diverse interpretations of the education subject as well as the educated subjectivity that teachers presume to teach and the ends to which they teach. Using the work of the philosopher Alain Badiou, I propose a guiding curricular question for history and social studies education: How best can we arrange knowledge so as to increase the likelihood that a teacher and student can engage in "truth-processes"? While he does not address education in any systemic manner, Badiou proposes that "'education' ... has never meant anything but this: to arrange the forms of knowledge in such a way that some truth may come to pierce a hole in them."[29] Let me provide some intellectual context for this claim.

Badiou's first philosophical assertion is that "truth" ought to be the primary category of philosophy and that ethics, in contrast to its concern with "abstract categories (Man or Human, Right or Law, the Other ...), should be referred back to particular *situations*."[30] Against any postmodern project, Badiou argues that when contemporary philosophy abandoned truth and elevated language as the object of its inquiry, it could no longer name or support an agent in the world to militate for justice.[31] In a supporting role, the "best practices" that exemplify the modernist education project finally dropped Truth in favour of an uninspiring and self-justifying stance of procedural neutrality that can never even reasonably be the case as long as – as with history education – the nation-state's grand narrative is assumed rather than questioned. Furthermore, neither disciplinary nor postmodern scholars adequately account for people's adventurous subjectivity and our capacity to affirmatively invent new realities for ourselves and our social situations: the first group chooses to ignore the creative energies of a subject's emotional and imaginative fluidity; for the second, the subject is a shadowy effect of language games ruled by interlocking regimes of pre-existing power. Each is a mirror image of the other. Their arguments rest on a mutually supporting logic of student deficit on the one hand and the philosophical abandonment of human inventive creativity on the other.

Against these positions, Badiou argues that truths are not achievements arrived at through predetermined techniques of reasoning, properties of interlocking social regimes, or facts temporally imprisoned by any dialectic.[32] His interpretation is that truth – or, rather, a generic truth process – lacks pre-specified content (as with a "scientific" Marxist interpretation of history), form (as in appeals to procedural reasoning), and destination (as articulated by any number of religious orders). Rather, truths consist of the material traces (e.g., in speech, art, and social movements) that a "becoming subject" produces through a singular truth-process instigated by an "event." Badiou argues that it is to these situated truth-processes instigated by an event that ethics and philosophy (and, I assert, history and social studies education) must lend support.

The status of an *event* is a matter of much philosophical debate. Mariam Fraser writes that "as a philosophical concept," an *event* "exists in relation to a specific set of problems, including the problem of how to conceive of modes of individuation that pertain not to being, or to essences and representation, but to becoming and effectivity."[33] For Badiou, at its most basic level, an event renders insufficient the "opinions" that previously provided the taken-for-granted coordinates of our daily lives: a disturbance that creates the possibility of a truth-process that implicates us in that "which cannot be calculated, predicted or managed."[34] Readers will be familiar with this interpretation of event and truth-process as speaking to those moments of "falling" in love or beginning intellectual lives in encounters with some "event" that pierced a hole in "all previous fictional assemblages through which [we] organized [a] self-representation."[35]

Encountering this event, we are confronted with the question and task of "fidelity," which is where, for Badiou, *the* question of ethics begins: "A crisis of fidelity is always what puts to the test, following the collapse of an image, the sole maxim of consistency (and thus ethics): Keep going!"[36] Badiou writes,

> I cannot, within the fidelity to fidelity that defines ethical consistency take an interest in myself, and thus pursue my own interests. All my capacity for interest, which is my own perseverance in being, has *poured out* into the future consequences of the solution to this scientific problem, into the examination of the world in the light of love's being-two, into what I will make of my encounter, one night, with the eternal Hamlet, or into the next stage of the political process, once the gathering in front of the factory has dispersed. There is always only one question in the ethic of truths: how will I, as some-one, continue to exceed my own being? How will I link the things I know, in a consistent fashion, via the effects of being seized by the not-known?[37]

In this sense, the proper verb tense with Badiou's use of an event and truth-process is neither the present nor the past, but rather the future anterior. In essence, a "becoming subject" – as one faithful to speaking and living in fidelity to an event – declares "this will have been true," pursuing exactly "what it will be absurd *not* to have believed."[38]

Encouraging this ethical maxim, Badiou also warns against the "Evil" (translated from his term in French, "le Mal") made simultaneously possible only because of the human potential to engage in the "Good" of truth-processes.[39] For Badiou, le Mal/Evil comes in three forms: *simulacrum* (of an event and truth-process)/*terror*, or embracing a teleological fantasy of an existing situation's promised fulfillment; *betrayal,* which is to either give up on a truth-process or to mistake one's truth-process for Truth; and *disaster,* when, mistaking the content produced by a singular truth-process for the Truth, Truth justifies the destruction of the material conditions that people require to potentially enact their truth-processes. Obviously, history is full of examples of truth inventions being distorted into "disaster."[40] For Badiou, the relevant conclusion is not to deny the affirmative Good that is a truth-process, but the necessity for vigilance against the distortion of the Good that is the Evil. Why should we not work with students to recognize these "Goods" and "Evils" both in the past and in the present? What historical and present-day social and political influences might make this question and these concepts appear to readers as unreasonable or irrelevant?

Those occurrences that may constitute events for students and teachers are, of course, as innumerable in possibility as they are particular in actuality. These events will share, however, a quality of "affirmative invention" of new situated possibilities. In this reading, the subjects of curriculum and education are not, for example, history, language arts, or mathematics.

Rather, the proper subject of teachers' work is a "becoming subject" whose fidelity and discipline are called forth by an event that renders previous and inherited knowledge insufficient.

I leave unaddressed here a host of philosophical issues related to Badiou's work. I direct interested readers elsewhere for fuller explorations of these as they relate to education.[41] For example, in contrast to what may be reasonably assumed by my limited depiction, for Badiou the "becoming subject" is a collective subjectivity entirely dependent on the encounter with an event. His is not a philosophical argument for enlightened "free will" or for a heroic individualism that is fully in charge or in possession of itself. There are also questions as to what qualities characterize an event. Again, these issues are explored in detail elsewhere. What I wish to emphasize here is the curricular question that emerges as a hopeful implication of Badiou's articulation of ethical subjectivity: How best are we to arrange knowledge so as to increase the likelihood that teachers and students will encounter an event and thus an opportunity to pursue a truth-process? Let me now provide a specific curricular example.

## Engaging Ethical Futures

Case and Wright each define critical thinking as both the means toward and the achievement of "reasoned judgments."[42] Recent work in this vein arranges historical questions as "critical challenges" through which – so it is hoped – students will gain facility with the knowledge, skills, and attitudes believed to describe historical thinking by deliberating on a question about the past or a problem located in the past.[43] As with the work of Fling noted earlier, this work connects critical thinking with a particular interpretation of historical work and convincingly argues that engaging with the latter promotes the former. I propose altering this temporal frame for historical thinking so as to open its ethical potential. To do so, I turn to the work of David Staley.

Staley argues that instead of directing students toward the past, teachers could develop students' critical/historical reasoning equally well by directing them toward the articulation of future "scenarios."[44] As Staley demonstrates, scenarios differ from predictions: "Where a prediction is a definitive statement about what will be, scenarios are heuristic narratives that explore alternative plausibilities of what might be."[45] Scenarios, which extend critical thought about an important question into the future, constitute one among many potential responses to Badiou's call to arrange knowledge for a certain "truth" to break through.

Having students think about future scenarios calls upon their historical reasoning both in terms of subject content and in terms of what is commonly referred to as historical thinking skills as articulated by the US National Standards for History: "to raise questions and to marshal solid evidence in support of their answers"; to "create historical narratives and arguments of their own"; and to "examine the interpretive nature of history."[46] Staley invites us to consider the ways that critical/historical thinking skills need not be applied solely to past incidents or narratives; they can also be aimed toward developing arguments about future probabilities that extend beyond mere reasonableness (however variously defined and policed) to include creativity and desirous imaginings.

Like any disciplined work, scenarios begin with clearly articulated questions. Here teacher and students design questions that emerge out of their pressing issues of concern. I refer to such questions as "throughlines."[47] We must distinguish throughlines from "essential questions."[48] Grant Wiggins and Jay McTighe define an "essential question" as "a question that lies at the heart of a subject or a curriculum … and promotes inquiry and uncoverage of a subject."[49] Rather than questions at the heart of a subject, throughlines are provocative questions that forefront the need for ethical responses requiring multidisciplinary perspectives or frames of analysis. These might range from the more local to the more general: from "To what extent, if at all, will bullying continue in our school?" to "What is the future of the Arctic and the Inuit people with regard to land claims, hunting rights, and sovereignty?"

After identifying their throughline questions, teachers and students scan the environment, looking for "driving forces" – that is, for "key factors that will determine (or 'drive') the outcome of the scenario."[50] Here "evidence" is identified in much the same way that historians work with artifacts from the past to explain events: "Like evidence from the past, evidence for the future is not intrinsically evident. It is made evidence by the historian's mind acting upon it."[51] Resources for such scanning include all aspects of news and media that may suggest a driving force that must be taken into account when thinking through scenarios. Here the past might become meaningful both as an indicator of past experiences and influences of driving forces, and in terms of the differing ways that such influences might be interpreted as meaningful (or not) in relation to a pressing issue. Of course, the unpredictable influences on the issue played by human agency and chance must also be considered.[52]

Once a question has been identified, the present environment has been scanned for driving forces, and historical content has been introduced by

*Scenarios in Response to a Question*

*Question:* What is the future of the Arctic and the Inuit people with regard to land claims, hunting rights, and Arctic sovereignty? Here are three examples of brief scenarios:

*Scenario #1: Probable*
The Federal Government makes no new amendments to the Nunavut Land Claim Act, deciding that monetary compensation is the only means of reconciling differences. Declining whale and seal populations cause the Canadian government to put a moratorium on all hunting until populations have recovered. Additionally, increasing toxicity levels in seals, polar bears, and fish cause Health Canada to warn that these animals are no longer safe to eat. The fate of the Inuit civilization is in the balance.

*Scenario #2: Possible*
Inuit peoples are included, as consultants, in deliberations concerning the fate of the Arctic. They have no direct influence in the process. Land claims are bogged down in legal deliberations between the government's lawyers and those of various Inuit peoples. There are insufficient guidelines to help reconcile the environment with traditional Inuit hunting practices.

*Scenario #3: Preferable*
Acknowledging the Inuit peoples' history and presence in the Arctic and the benefit to the Canadian nation this represents, Ottawa negotiates provincial status with their leaders for traditional Inuit territory. The resulting funding ensures the implementation of an educational system and cultural support that protects and promotes Inuit culture and identity. The new Inuit Province works closely with Ottawa's leading climate change specialists and biologists to make locally informed decisions about hunting quotas and resource extraction. These changes and initiatives work to sustain the Inuit traditional way of life, while ensuring viability of their culture within the context of contemporary Canada.

the teacher for its potential analogies, students then write the story of each scenario. (Staley, in his review of the literature on scenario writing, suggests a minimum of three – "possible, probable, preferable" – to emphasize the future's malleability). Each scenario has a plot that articulates a different but equally plausible logic playing out in the future: "The narrative of each scenario does not describe a linear procession of events ('this will happen on this date, then this will happen'). Rather, the scenario is a description of the context within which those events may occur."[53] As with the future anterior of truth-processes, scenarios describe a context as if one were there in the future looking around at a present already formed through identified driving forces.

Once articulated, scenarios – and the historical interpretations utilized to support their possibility – provide opportunities for students to distinguish between probable and preferable futures. Discussion may revolve around articulation of what makes one or another scenario more preferable; this provides students with practice at articulating their ethical commitments as agents of present/future social life. Furthermore, scenario reasoning can be part of other, related school projects.

One such project is "multiple historical narratives."[54] In this assignment, students identify a "historical perspective" (e.g., feminist, antiracist) with which to connect through "emplotment" a minimum of any three Canadian events they choose. Once one narrative is completed, students then tell another story of Canada from another historical perspective, weaving the second through at least one shared event with the first narrative. One rule of this assignment is that students cannot use the GN or its characteristics as a story. Through this assignment, students (a) confront – most often for the first time – and study the GN's framing of their historical understanding of themselves as nationalized, gendered, racialized, and classed beings; (b) consider alternative historical frames; and (c) extend those into the future in the form of scenarios, distinguishing between probable and preferable outcomes according to a particular historical perspective they choose.

These practices constitute examples of an explicit arrangement of knowledge in support of students' potential for "affirmative inventions." They open up spaces for the possibility of a "truth-process" as students potentially encounter the insufficiency of present opinions to express their hopes, desires, imagination, and reasoning. By doing so, teachers and students work through history education to augment the present lack of inspiring and democratically diverse claims. In this manner, history education may realize its ethical potential as a discipline.

## Summary

Badiou's articulation of an "ethic of truths" finds resonance with those seeking to affirm the emancipatory potential of historical work that lies beyond the regulative parameters of the disciplinary school. Historical work, with ethics at its core, positions knowledge and ways of knowing from or about the past as a warrant for claims centrally concerned with questions of justice grounded in particular situations. In this organization, teachers ask students to consider the ways in which they are personally and differently "implicated" in such questions.[55] History serves students when it helps them make sense of possible and preferable relationships to these questions as manifested in their present desires, sense of self and other, and hopes for the future.

In addition to its potential individual benefit, a curriculum organized around questions of justice and truth-processes best distinguishes democratic education from forms of indoctrination (as is, for example, likely found in historical education that employs a GN).[56] Yet even an education organized around justice themes or issues potentially suffers from overdetermined ideology.[57] Badiou's "ethic of truths" works against such a tendency. Applying his work to education, we might envision the potential of something more to serve than merely transmitting information (as is conveyed in the GN) or technique (at the heart of the disciplinary school) from one who is presumed to know to one who is presumed to be lacking. Where the disciplinary approach is premised on deficit reasoning (i.e., students do not possess either sufficient quality or quantity of information or refined reasoning capacities about the past), an ethical approach is affirmative. Put another way, skills are refined, made meaningful, and become influential to emerging selves and societies when teachers access students' existing capacities to imagine a situation differently.

"Events" and "truth-processes" could happen in schools regardless of curriculum organization. Institutionalized education is, after all, a game of percentages. We should, however, be inspired by "the truth of human aspiration and dreaming" and debate which organization of historical/social studies curricula best opens and supports an institutional space for truths to emerge from such creative and inventive potential.[58] This is a hope that our collective discussions might take up the possibility of "better" ends than the teaching of procedures or problems without historical context and absent of the opportunity for students to investigate the messiness of social power as it manifests itself in their daily lives and in the histories and futures that they constitute. Absent this type of historical engagement, we should not be surprised, despite appeals to the contrary, that students encounter dangerously few competing historical claims worth their time either in or outside schools.

## NOTES

I would like to thank David Scott, a University of Alberta graduate student, for his insightful feedback on earlier drafts of this manuscript and for helping improve the arguments contained within.

1. Ken Osborne, "Fred Morrow Fling and the Source-Method of Teaching History," *Theory and Research in Social Education* 31, 4 (2003): 466-501.
2. See, for example, Peter Lee, "History Teaching and the Philosophy of History," *History and Theory* 22, 4 (1983): 19-49; Peter Seixas, "Conceptualizing the Growth of Historical Understanding," in *Handbook of Education and Human Development: New Models of Learning, Teaching, and Schooling*, ed. David Olson and Nancy Torrance (Oxford: Blackwell, 1996), 765-83.
3. Osborne, "Fred Morrow Fling," 468.
4. Ibid., 466-67.
5. Differing slightly from previous lists, for Seixas these concepts are (1) historical significance, (2) evidence, (3) continuity and change, (4) cause and consequence, (5) historical perspectives, and (6) the moral dimensions of historical interpretations. See http://www.histori.ca/benchmarks. I should note that, in personal discussion, Seixas sees the issue of historical education in terms not of procedures but of "problems" related to historical thinking.
6. Osborne, "Fred Morrow Fling," 472.
7. Fred Morrow Fling, *Outline of Historical Method* (New York: Lenox Hill, 1971 [1899]), 11.
8. Peter Seixas, "Schweigen! die Kinder! Or, Does Postmodern History Have a Place in the Schools?" in *Knowing, Teaching, and Learning History*, ed. Peter N. Stearns, Peter Seixas, and Sam Wineburg (New York: New York University Press, 2000), 19-37, 24.
9. Peter Seixas, "The Purposes of Teaching Canadian History," *Canadian Social Studies* 36, 2 (2002), http://www.quasar.ualberta.ca/css.
10. Fred Morrow Fling, *The Writing of History* (New Haven: Yale University Press, 1920), 26. For another thoughtful explication of this position, see Stéphane Levesque, *Thinking Historically: Educating Students for the Twenty-First Century* (Toronto: University of Toronto Press, 2008).
11. I recognize that my usage of "disciplinarian" is perhaps contentious as a descriptor of the perspectives of many scholars I place under this rubric, given the impossibility for any word to entirely capture all the nuances of any particular body of work so associated.
12. Readers can check for themselves the reasonableness of my claim about deficit reasoning by examining other chapters in this collection.
13. James Marsh, "The State of History," http://www.histori.ca.

14 Avner Segall, "Critical History: Implications for History/Social Studies Education," *Theory and Research in Social Education* 27, 3 (1999): 358-74. See also Avner Segall, "What's the Purpose of Teaching a Discipline Anyway? The Case of History," in *Social Studies: The Next Generation*, ed. Avner Segall, Elizabeth Heilman, and Cleo Cherryholmes (New York: Peter Lang, 2006): 125-39.
15 Segall, "Critical History," 129.
16 Beverly Southgate, "'A Pair of White Gloves': Historians and Ethics," *Rethinking History* 10, 1 (2006): 49-61.
17 Ibid., 52.
18 See, for example, John Gaddis, *The Landscape of History: How Historians Map the Past* (Oxford: Oxford University Press, 2002).
19 Timothy Stanley, "The Struggle for History: Historical Narrative and Anti-Racist Pedagogy," *Discourse: Studies in the Cultural Politics of Education* 19, 1 (1998): 41-51, 48. Stanley's claims here are based on work done by Galois and Harris, who cross-referenced the nominal census of 1881 with other data sources to "fill in" the census' inadequate categories: "As this is done, intricate population geographies hidden within the broad regional categories of the published census begin to be discerned, and as they are teased out elements of British Columbia society begin to come into focus. So manipulated, the nominal census of 1881 is a revealing body of data; however deficient and warped" (38). See Robert Galois and Cole Harris, "Recalibrating Society: The Population Geography of British Columbia in 1881," *Canadian Geographer* 38, 1 (Spring 1994): 37.
20 I emphasize that I use the word "multicultural" to reference non-Aboriginal identifications. Certainly, there are competing claims between Aboriginal and non-Aboriginal Canadians – claims that have nothing to do with multiculturalism or increasing or decreasing diversity in this regard.
21 Daniel Francis, *National Dreams: Myth, Memory, and Canadian History* (Vancouver: Arsenal Pulp Press, 1997). Stanley, "The Struggle for History"; Timothy Stanley, "Whose Public? Whose Memory? Racisms, Grand Narratives, and Canadian History," in *To the Past: History Education, Public Memory, and Citizenship in Canada*, ed. Ruth Sandwell (Toronto: University of Toronto Press, 2006), 32-49.
22 For an exploration of the colonial context from which this story emerged, see Kent den Heyer, "R. Buckminster Fuller's 'Great Pirates': An Investigation into Narrative Coherency and Analysis in World History Courses," *World History Connected* 3, 1 (2005), http://worldhistoryconnected.press.illinois.edu.
23 For a resonate explication of a distinct GN particular to Quebec, see Jocelyn Létourneau, "Remembering Our Past: An Examination of the Historical Memory of Young Quebecois," in *To the Past*, 70-87.
24 For a fuller treatment of the study supporting this claim, see Kent den Heyer and Laurence Abbott, "Reverberating Echoes: Challenging Teacher Candidates to Tell and Learn from Entwined Narrations of Canadian History," *Curriculum Inquiry* (2011) (in press).
25 Keith Jenkins, "Ethical Responsibility and the Historian: On the Possible End of a History 'of a Certain Kind,'" *History and Theory* 43 (2004): 43-60.

26 Alain Badiou, *Ethics: An Essay on the Understanding of Evil*, trans. Peter Hallward (London: Verso Books, 2001), 3.
27 Alfred Schutz, *The Phenomenology of the Social world*, trans. George G. Walsh and Frederick. Lehnert (Evanston: Northwestern University Press, 1967).
28 Zongyi Deng and Allan Luke, "Subject Matter: Defining and Theorizing School Subjects," in *The Sage Handbook of Curriculum and Instruction*, ed. F. Michael Connelly, Ming Fang He, and JoAnn I. Phillion (Thousand Oaks: Sage Publications, 2008), 66-89, 73.
29 Alain Badiou, *Handbook of Inaesthetics*, trans. Alberto Toscano (Stanford: Stanford University Press, 2005), 9.
30 Badiou, *Ethics*, 3.
31 Alain Badiou, *St. Paul: The Foundation of Universalism*, trans. Ray Brassier (Stanford: Stanford University Press, 2003).
32 Etienne Balibar, "The History of Truth: Alain Badiou in French Philosophy," in *Think Again: Alain Badiou and the Future of Philosophy*, ed. Peter Hallward (London: Continuum, 2004), 21-88, 24.
33 Mariam Fraser, "Event," *Theory, Culture, and Society* 23, 2-3 (2006): 129-32, 129.
34 Badiou, *Ethics*, 122.
35 Ibid., 55. Tangentially, I read this line as a wonderfully accurate definition of curriculum qua curriculum.
36 Ibid., 79.
37 Ibid., 50.
38 Andrew Gibson, *Beckett and Badiou: The Pathos of Intermittency* (Oxford: Oxford University Press, 2006), 88.
39 It is important to note that Badiou's French translated into 'Evil' is "le Mal," which also connotes sickness in addition to something *very bad* and thus invokes shades of Lacanian and Foucauldian analyses into human situations. Evil, however, is a tactically useful translation in that it secularizes the term as a question of ethics and human situations.
40 Badiou, *Ethics*.
41 Kent den Heyer, "Education as an Affirmative Invention: Alain Badiou and the Purpose of Teaching and Curriculum," *Educational Theory* 59, 4 (2009): 441-63; "What If Curriculum (of a Certain Kind) Doesn't Matter," *Curriculum Inquiry* 39, 1 (2009): 27-40.
42 Roland Case, "Beyond Inert Facts: Teaching for Understanding in Secondary Social Studies," in *The Anthology of Social Studies: Issues and Strategies for Secondary Teachers*, ed. Roland Case and Penney Clark (Vancouver: Pacific Educational Press, 2008), 41-53; Ian Wright, "Taking Seriously the Teaching of Critical Thinking," *Canadian Social Studies* 32, 1 (1997): 12-19.
43 See Mike Denos and Roland Case, *Teaching about Historical Thinking* (Vancouver: Critical Thinking Consortium, 2006).
44 David J. Staley, "A History of the Future," *History and Theory* 41 (2002): 72-89; *History and Future: Using Historical Thinking to Imagine the Future* (Lanham: Lexington Books, 2007).

45 Stanley, *A History*, 78.
46 Available at http://www.ncss.org.
47 For more on throughlines, see Kent den Heyer, "Implicated and Called Upon: Challenging an Educated Position of Self, Others, Knowledge, and Knowing as Things to Acquire," *Critical Literacy: Theories and Practices* 3, 1 (2009): 26-36.
48 Grant Wiggins and Jay McTighe, *Understanding by Design* (Alexandria: Association for Supervision and Curriculum Development, 2005).
49 Ibid., 342.
50 Schartz, in Staley, "A History of the Future," 79.
51 Staley, "A History of the Future," 84.
52 Readers interested in the question of human agency related to historical education may wish to access Kent den Heyer and Alexandra Fidyk, "Configuring Historical Facts through Historical Fiction: Agency, Art-in-Fact, and Imagination as Stepping Stones between Then and Now," *Educational Theory* 57, 2 (2007): 441-57; and Kent den Heyer, "The Historical Agency of Ted. T. Aoki in Scholarly Fugues, Communities, and Change," *Educational Insights* 8, 2 (2003), http://www.ccfi.educ.ubc.ca.
53 Ibid., 80.
54 Den Heyer and Abbott, "Reverberating Echoes."
55 Den Heyer, "Implicated and Called Upon," 2009.
56 Consequently, the common absence of such curricular organization and purpose in North American schools should raise serious reflection about the accuracy of the adjective "democratic" to describe our contemporary political, social, and economic situation.
57 For example, see Ellsworth's critique of an overdetermined and supposedly progressive education in Elizabeth Ellsworth, "Why Doesn't This Feel Empowering? Working Through the Repressive Myths of Critical Pedagogy," in *Feminisms and Critical Pedagogy*, ed. Carmen Luke and Jennifer Gore (New York: Routledge, 1992): 90-119.
58 David G. Smith, "The Specific Challenges of Globalization for Teaching and Vice Versa," *Alberta Journal of Educational Research* 46, 1 (2000): 7-25, esp. 18.

PART 3

# CLASSROOM CONTEXTS FOR HISTORICAL THINKING

# 8
# Historical Thinking in Elementary Education
## A Review of Research

AMY VON HEYKING

Two nine-year-old children hunch over to peer closely at a photograph taken of a grade four class in their city one hundred years ago. They comment on how crowded the classroom is, how dingy it looks, and how uncomfortable the children's clothing is. They tell me that the teacher is mean and that the children do not have books to use, even though books are clearly visible on the desk at the front of the photograph. They tell me how much the children struggled with the ink pens they used. They know this because they practised using ink pens at a historic site on a field trip and stress how difficult and frustrating they found them. When I ask them whether the children in the photograph, children who had never used ballpoint pens, would have found them as frustrating as they did, both children look puzzled.

A ten-year-old child is assigned the task of writing a letter from the perspective of someone involved in a significant event in Canada's past that her class has examined. She persuades her teacher that she should be allowed to complete her assignment from the perspective of a child who is a victim of the 1919 influenza epidemic. She explains that she read extensively about the epidemic after reading a compelling fictional account. In making her case, she recalls information about the epidemic included in the "historical notes" at the end of the novel and then gleaned from relevant websites she sought out. Arguing that "Spanish flu" killed more people worldwide than the First World War, that two million Canadians contracted it, and that important lessons were learned that could apply to present-day pandemics, the grade five student persuades her teacher that she can write convincingly about this event, drawing on historical evidence to support her character's perspective.

My research with elementary school children has offered many opportunities to see children struggle to make sense of the historical accounts they have read, and like the first pair of children above, express pity for the people of the past because, as they see it, life is so much better now. I have also seen children like the grade five student, actively engaged in learning about Canada's past, fascinated by the experiences of people long ago and full of wonder and enthusiasm to investigate further.

This chapter will describe the requirements for history instruction in Canadian elementary schools, review research into the nature of children's historical thinking, and consider the implications of that research for teaching and learning in Canadian classrooms. The research summarized here has largely been conducted with elementary school children in the United States and the United Kingdom. My own preliminary studies with children in Alberta classrooms, however, confirm that there is little reason to doubt that many of the conclusions apply to Canadian children.[1]

## History in Elementary Social Studies

Across Canada, history is taught in the context of the school subject of social studies from grades one to six (children ages six to eleven), the grades generally categorized as "elementary education." Since education is a provincial responsibility, each provincial ministry of education determines school curricula and authorizes basic resources for use in delivering the programs it has designed. While there are variations in the specific topics of study in elementary school social studies across the country, there are general trends in the content and nature of instruction. Most provinces approach social studies as an interdisciplinary subject in which information and inquiry skills associated with a range of social science disciplines are applied in order to answer questions or explore issues relevant in the development of active citizens. Units of study in the elementary school program are typically historical or geographical in nature, or they involve studies of specific cultural groups, or they address roles and responsibilities of citizenship and government structures. So for example, students in grade one (children age six) examine their responsibilities as members of a classroom and school community and of a family. Western Canadian provinces (British Columbia, Alberta, Saskatchewan, and Manitoba) include an examination of personal changes and families in the past and present, thereby introducing historical concepts at a very early age. In grade two, most provinces include studies of students' local communities, including changes over time and the cultural groups that contributed to their development. This is most children's introduction to the study of history, but in a very localized and familiar context. Grade three children typically continue a more detailed study of their community's early history. Many provinces include in grade four a detailed study of their region's Aboriginal communities and their early history of contact with European explorers and traders. Grade five consists of an introduction to Canada's national history, typically focusing on the period before Confederation and emphasizing the stories of immigrants and settlers. (A notable exception to this pattern is in Ontario, where grade four students spend half the year studying Europe in the medieval period, while grade five students study several early civilizations.) There is considerable variation in content in grade six, with students in British Columbia focusing on issues of citizenship and governance and the role of Canada in the global community, and students in most of Atlantic Canada examining world cultures. By the end of grade six, most Canadian children have had opportunities to study their family's history, their community's and region's pasts, the early history of Canada's Aboriginal communities, and some variation of a national story. Many have also had opportunities to explore an ancient culture such as Egypt, Greece, or the Maya or Inca civilizations.

In addition to increasing the historical content in elementary school social studies, most provinces have recently reshaped their curricula to reflect an understanding of history as an interpretive discipline rather than *the* story of the past. They have incorporated curricular outcomes that reflect an understanding of history as a form of inquiry that requires specific ways of thinking. For example, the Province of Alberta's 2005 program of studies describes historical thinking as "a process whereby students are challenged to rethink assumptions about the past and re-imagine both the present and the future ... Historical thinking skills involve the sequencing of events, the analysis of patterns, and the placement of events in context to assist in the construction of meaning and understanding."[2] Since 2004, Ontario elementary school children have been required to consider "various forms of historical evidence" and then "apply these skills to develop an understanding of Canadian identity and democratic values, to evaluate different points of view, and to examine information critically in order to solve problems and make decisions on issues that are relevant to their lives."[3] *The Foundation for the Atlantic Canada Social Studies Curriculum,* which provides a framework for the development of provincial programs of study, states that through a study of history, "students learn to recognize and evaluate different perspectives and biases in historical writing." It also articulates specific outcomes so that by the end of grade three, students should be able to "identify and use primary and secondary sources to learn and communicate about the past." By the end of grade six, the students will "research and describe historical events and ideas from different perspectives."[4] The expectation is that children will engage in historical inquiries in order to develop the structural or disciplinary concepts that are the basis of historical thinking.

Social studies programs across Canada provide opportunities for children to study past eras and to think historically. Two points, however, must be made to clarify the challenges associated with developing the historical understandings of children in Canadian elementary schools. First, because history units are taught in the context of social studies, they represent only a portion of the year's required work. For example, while students in Alberta study the early history of Canada in grade five, they are also required to complete an examination of Canada's physical geography and explore issues surrounding natural resource development the same year. This makes it extremely difficult for teachers to spend the extended time needed for deep historical inquiries, given the range of social studies content they must cover in any year. Second, most elementary school teachers are subject generalists. They have no specific training in the discipline of history and none in history pedagogy. Researchers have often found that teachers without sufficient pedagogical content knowledge in history lack the background to facilitate children's growth in historical thinking or to anticipate and address the problems that children will have in making sense of history texts.[5] So while the provincial curricula may require extensive historical studies and the development of historical thinking skills, teachers often lack the time and the strategies to engage their students in investigations that would enhance their growth in historical thinking. That said, the recent curriculum revisions have sparked changes in pre-service teacher education and have also increased professional development opportunities for teachers. These opportunities have focused on familiarizing them with insights gleaned from the past two decades of work done by history education researchers as well as those engaged in reading and social science research with children. This research suggests that there are some challenges and many possibilities in helping children make sense of history.

## Research on Children's Historical Thinking

Reading researchers have identified one important reason that children in grades four to six often find history confusing: most students learn history by reading textbooks of doubtful quality. Researchers Isabel Beck and Margaret McKeown have indicated that textbooks typically overestimate the amount of specific content knowledge children are bringing to the reading; that they are not sufficiently explicit about the relevance of the information they present; and that they fail to address the causes and consequences of the events they recount.[6] As a result, children read "bits and pieces" of information without any organizing conceptual framework in which to place that information. The texts list names and dates, or describe events, but do not explain them. When researchers revised sections of a textbook in order to address these deficiencies, some (but not most) of the children improved their comprehension and retention of information.[7] Not even a livelier style and more explicit "voice" in the text improved the information retention and accuracy of the majority of students studied, though they did enjoy reading the material.[8] It is not surprising, then, that students interviewed before and after instruction in American history in grade five and grade eight demonstrated some familiarity with events associated with the Revolutionary War, but "instruction seems to have failed to help students construct the significance of that outcome and how the struggle with Britain laid the roots for the kind of nation the United States became."[9] The students may have remembered some of the facts, but they did not grasp the conceptual framework that gave those facts meaning.

Moreover, reading in the context of history instruction offers unique challenges when children are required to read primary documents and to make sense of varying secondary accounts about the past. These tasks require critical literacy skills, such as reading for subtext, that are extremely challenging for elementary school students. History education researchers Bruce VanSledright and Christine Kelly, for example, found that students without sufficient content background or contextual information assessed the validity of a primary source by the amount of information it provided.[10] They concluded that this criterion was not unreasonable, given that this is often how sources are used in elementary classrooms. VanSledright also points out that research collaborations between reading and history education researchers may yield important insights into the unique demands that reading history texts makes on young readers, given that "the work on expertise in the history domain suggests that expert readers employ particular kinds of strategies and knowledge that require an array of complex reading methods and a peculiar epistemology of text."[11]

Social science research in the United States, the United Kingdom, and Europe indicates the extent to which elementary school children struggle with many abstract concepts that form the content of their history instruction – that is, with the "substantive concepts" of the discipline. History instruction often addresses political concepts such as colony, nation, and government, as well as economic concepts such as trade. Even familiar social and cultural concepts such as family and community may mean something very different in a distant historical period than in the present day. This is not to say that children cannot or should not grapple with these concepts; research simply clarifies how explicit and attentive teachers must be in developing these concepts with young learners, as well as how realistic we should be in terms of children's understandings.[12]

Researchers have discovered that children bring considerable prior knowledge to the learning of history. Peter Seixas stresses that children from a very young age encounter traces of the past in the natural and human-made landscape, in the relics of the past, in the language they use, and in the cultural institutions of which they are a part. Moreover, children experience many accounts of the past on television and film, in books, in family stories, and in commemorations.[13] British researcher Hilary Cooper likewise argues:

> The past is a dimension of children's social and physical environment and they interact with it from birth. They hear and use the vocabulary of time and change: old, new, yesterday, tomorrow, last year, before you were born, when mummy was little, a long time ago, once upon a time. They ask questions about the sequence and causes of events: when did we move here? Why? What happened in the story next? ... They encounter historical sources: old photographs, a baby book, an ornament, a statue, a church, maybe a closed-down factory or a derelict cinema being replaced by new roads and flats ... Before children start school there are many contexts in which they are implicitly aware of the past.[14]

Research projects designed to determine children's prior understandings of history support the contention that while students may have limited understandings of the concepts that are the content of school history, they often have well-constructed narratives about their personal history, particularly their families' history.[15] The students in my investigations, for example, made reference to family connections when struggling to make sense of historical evidence, indicating that a grandfather drove a trolley like the one pictured in an archival photo, or that a grandmother rode to her one-room school on a horse like the character in a picture book we had read together.[16] Moreover, many children have some conception of history as the study of significant events in the past and even possess specific understandings of particular historical events as early as the second grade.[17] Children in these studies made reference to films, television shows, and the historical fiction they had read when explaining how they knew about life in the past. Clearly, history instruction in elementary school must begin with children's prior understandings of their own history as well as their understandings of "the past."

Studies also support the claim that elementary children can develop quite sophisticated historical thinking skills in an appropriate context of active engagement with source material, alternative accounts, and teaching that scaffolds their emerging understandings and skills. In other words, elementary school children can "do" history. The historical thinking concepts (see Lévesque, Chapter 5, and Seixas, Chapter 6, this volume) have largely framed these studies into children's historical thinking as researchers have sought to define children's ideas about these concepts and to describe how they progress to more sophisticated understandings. British researchers Peter Lee and Rosalyn Ashby stress that these procedural concepts – which they generally identify as evidence, explanation, empathy, change, and accounts – "are not what history is 'about,' but they shape the way we go about doing history."[18] Therefore, examining the nature of children's thinking about these concepts helps us understand how they might "do" history and how they might understand and appreciate the nature of historical knowledge. Researchers working with elementary school-age children have generally limited their studies to children's ability to understand the role of – and use – primary source evidence in creating historical narratives; and to children's understanding of continuity and change over time. Their studies have, however, provided some insights into other elements of historical thinking that were not actually the focus of their studies, elements such as children's understandings of historical significance; their appreciation of the reasons for change (i.e., cause or agency); their ability to appreciate and articulate the perspectives of people in the past; and their tendency to judge the people of the past. The following summary will, therefore, concentrate on research findings regarding children's work with historical evidence and their understandings of continuity and change; but will also, where relevant, refer to findings regarding the other elements of historical thinking.

**Evidence**

If children are to think historically, they need to understand how we come to know about the past. Given the central importance of this insight for historical thinking, it is not surprising that many history education researchers have studied how children work with historical evidence, in an attempt to determine whether children are capable of understanding that history is a way of making sense of the past, not a report from the past. Researchers suggest that this element of historical thinking is difficult for children.

Perhaps the most important epistemological insight that teachers can nurture in elementary school is the understanding that there are many different sources of information about life in the past. Before children can work with evidence, they need to understand both the need for and the nature of historical evidence. In a comparison of how primary children in Northern Ireland and the United States understood historical evidence, Barton revealed the extent to which the American children thought information about the past was simply transmitted orally throughout generations and eventually recorded in books. As a result, they assumed that more recent accounts would be less accurate than older ones. Children in Northern Ireland, in contrast, emphasized the importance of physical remains and could identify inferences that archaeologists and historians might make by examining relics. Both groups of children pointed to the influence of family members in telling them stories about the past; but the influence of the Northern Irish curriculum, which stresses learning about sources of historical evidence, was evident even among these young children.[19]

Given the emphasis in the Canadian elementary school curriculum on Aboriginal culture and history before European contact, there are ample opportunities for teachers to help children understand the range of sources available to us about life in the distant past (see Conrad, Chapter 1, and Marker, Chapter 4, this volume). Making use of Aboriginal oral accounts, anthropological studies, and archaeological artifacts, as well as accounts written by Europeans would help children address the central epistemological issues of historical thinking explicitly and meaningfully.

Children can also begin to appreciate how historians might use the same information about the past but come to different conclusions about what that information means. British researcher Peter Lee and his colleagues on the Chata team confirmed earlier findings by Denis Shemilt when they found an age-related but not age-*determined* progression of ideas about the nature of historical accounts.[20] They presented children aged seven to fourteen with differing accounts of the same historical event. The youngest children were more likely to believe the accounts at face value: they maintained that the accounts were different less in content than in the vocabulary they used. When obvious contradictions were pointed out to them, they assumed that one narrator had more information or was mistaken. Older children were more likely to see the accounts as authored by people with particular biases, and some understood that accounts would differ according to the questions historians asked or the nature of their investigations.[21] While these understandings represent children's natural progression in ideas, the researchers stressed that children could be moved from simplistic or naive understandings to more powerful ones through teaching.

Many studies indicate that by upper elementary school, children are quite capable of sophisticated reasoning when appropriately supported through the analysis of historical evidence and accounts. When presented with a variety of primary sources that would help them answer historical questions, students in these studies could extract information, make inferences, and construct different viewpoints in order to answer those questions.[22] They began to appreciate the tentative and interpretive nature of historical knowledge. But researchers concede that challenges remain. A study by Bruce VanSledright and Peter Afflerbach demonstrated how difficult it was for grade four students to move beyond a simplistic or naive understanding of bias: once the students understood that they needed to read primary source documents to determine the writer's point of view, they assumed that all the documents were equally as valid because they all represented someone's opinion.[23] After spending four months guiding grade five students through the tasks of interpreting primary and secondary accounts of American history, VanSledright was frustrated that "many students still held fast to the belief that the answers to our historical questions ultimately could be arbitrated by the encyclopedias on the wall shelves below the windows."[24]

Barton was impressed with the ability of fourth- and fifth-grade students to identify historical sources, evaluate evidence, and reconcile contradictory accounts of the Battle of Lexington Green. But when students were asked to construct their own accounts of the battle, they completely ignored the evidence they had spent so much time and effort sifting through and analyzing.[25] He suggested several reasons for this curious failure – in particular, the tendency of elementary school teachers to make use of historical fiction in their teaching. Barton and other researchers argue that an overreliance on and uncritical use of historical fiction undermines students' emerging understanding that historical narratives are based on evidence; and that it also frustrates any attempt to engage in critical investigations of historical questions. Fictional accounts, because of their emotional impact, are simply more convincing to children than factual accounts. As a result, children in some studies responded to questions about the history they had learned with invented stories that seemed to satisfy their need for drama and a predictable plot structure, with little regard for the facts they had gleaned from their investigations.[26] Clearly, since students at this age are most familiar with narrative as a fictional form, they need explicit instruction in and opportunities to examine the evidence on which historical narratives are constructed.

## Continuity and Change

There are critical concepts that must be addressed with children if they are to come to a rich understanding of the nature of continuity and change over time. First, children must have a grasp of time concepts. Primary children can recite days, months, and seasons in order and can use terms like "tonight" or "tomorrow" to describe a point in time.[27] But researchers stress the importance of helping even very young children with time categories such as "past" and "present" or "then" and "now," though even these seemingly simple distinctions can be difficult for them. Cooper suggests that children examine archival and current photographs of familiar scenes as well as objects, and categorize them as past and present.[28] Shemilt, however, found that when children were asked to sort photographs, they identified the well-dressed nineteenth-century child as "from now" and the contemporary elderly man as "from long ago."[29] This should reinforce the importance of appropriate photo selections and of seeing these sorting tasks as opportunities for clarifying just such misconceptions. Well-illustrated picture books provide a chance for teachers to work with children to identify elements of the story or illustration that provide clues as to its setting in time.

Many studies indicate that when faced with pictures and photographs from various historical eras, young children can place them in the correct chronological sequence, indicating their understanding of change over time. Using clues from the material culture portrayed in the photographs, children could identify the sequence. Older children were more likely to identify historical eras, include references to political history; they were also less likely to rely on evidence of technological change when sequencing the pictures. They were sometimes able to identify pictures with specific dates, and they made obvious attempts to draw on their background knowledge of school history as well as media, family history, and trade fiction.[30] More recently, British researcher Alan Hodkinson has pointed out that while vague and extremely subjective references to time, such as "long ago," may be useful with very young children, older students require more specific understandings of time concepts (such as decade and century) and dating systems. He stressed that the development of historical time concepts does not emerge spontaneously or naturally among children; instructional strategies such as timelines and frequent references to chronological frameworks are needed for children to begin to understand the sweep of time and scale of events.[31]

Sequencing exercises, however, do not by themselves aid students' understanding of change and continuity. Carol Seefeldt stresses the importance of structuring opportunities for young children to observe and record changes in themselves, their school, and their community. Following the seasonal changes of a tree in the schoolyard, keeping records of the children's own growth, and tracking a construction project in the neighbourhood can all help children understand that "(1) change is continuous and always present; (2) change affects people in different ways; and (3) change can be recorded and become a record of the past."[32] But while young children should begin with, they should not be restricted to, an understanding of personal change. With appropriate support they can begin to think about changes over time in their families, schools, and communities as required by most social studies curricula from grades one to three.

Research suggests, however, that children have difficulty understanding change as a process rather than a series of events. They have difficulty grasping that change can happen in different ways, in different places, and at differing rates. In Barton's study, they seemed to assume, for example, that historical change follows a uniform and linear pattern: immigrants came to America, they lived in small cabins, they built cities. They were confused by evidence of "pioneer" life well after the establishment of cities on the eastern seaboard of the United States. They identified a photograph of a boat entering Ellis Island as the *Mayflower*. Typical teaching exercises like the construction of timelines tend to exacerbate these misconceptions, implying that one way of life replaces another. Barton emphasizes the importance of teachers providing opportunities for children to understand the wide range of lifestyles and experiences in any given historical period:

"whether studying Ancient Egypt, colonial America, or the 1960s, for example, students should constantly be comparing the experiences of men and women, urban and rural residents, and upper, middle, and lower socio-economic classes."[33]

Related to their notion of change as linear, students also see change as logical or intentional, the result of rational decisions made by individuals.[34] When Barton asked one child why the Salem witch trials ended, she explained: "When they accused like the mayor's wife or somebody's wife that they were a witch, and he said, 'This has gone too far, we've killed enough innocent people, I want you to let everyone go, my wife is not a witch, and this has just gone too far,' and then, just like that, everybody just forgot, and they didn't accuse people of witches anymore."[35]

This narrative structure that children tend to impose on the past also demonstrates the theme of progress that is typical of elementary school children. This is partly because school textbooks usually convey an underlying positive message of physical, intellectual, and social advancement over time. But many studies suggest that elementary students believe that history is the story of constant progress. Children in the United States and Northern Ireland used evidence of progress – improvements in technology or advancements in architecture, for example – as clues when placing historical photographs in chronological order. This occasionally led them to place photos incorrectly.[36] Challenging students with examples that encourage alternative readings might create the cognitive dissonance necessary for a more balanced understanding. When studying a particular era in history, it may be helpful to ask students to consider in what ways life has improved and in what ways life has gotten worse since the period being examined. If children are interviewing parents or elders about their childhoods, they could be directed to ask these adults whether life had improved or declined and in what ways. Such considerations would encourage a more complex understanding of change.

While history education researchers have generally studied children's ability to work with historical evidence and their understandings of continuity and change, their research has also generated some insights into children's understandings of the other historical thinking concepts: significance, cause, perspective, and moral judgment. This reflects the interconnectedness of the concepts. All are foundational to the work historians do. Students would not be able to make reasoned judgments about the significance of the Battle of the Plains of Abraham without understanding the causes and consequences of that event; students would be unable to articulate the perspective of an Irish immigrant to Upper Canada without a thorough understanding of relevant evidence. Just as teachers may emphasize only one or two historical concepts during instruction or for the sake of assessment, researchers have tended to focus on one when designing their research tasks; but these tasks, by virtue of being authentic historical tasks, result in insights regarding the other concepts also.

**Significance**
Research suggests that children as young as second grade can distinguish between "history" and "the past" by pointing out that history involves decisions about what is important; and that by grade six they are able to explain and support their definitions with examples, and also to suggest that historical events are often rooted in conflict and result in social change.[37] Research also suggests, however, that teachers could be much more deliberate in their discussions with children about historical significance, given their belief in progress. American students in Barton and Levstik's study avoided identifying events like the Great Depression as significant in history, because they did not "fit" the master narrative of America's continuous progress that is typically encountered in school textbooks.[38] Researchers stress that teachers should engage students in discussions about why some events, people, or ideas are included in school history curricula and texts while others are omitted.

**Cause, or Agency**
Research suggests that elementary children also have extremely simplistic notions of the reasons for historical change. They tend to see history as a record of the accomplishments of a few important people: for example, changes in the rights of African Americans were the achievement of Abraham Lincoln or Martin Luther King. They believe that great people "solve" social problems.[39] They often misunderstand the scale or numbers of people involved in historic events. After studying the American Revolutionary War, for example, grade five students "did not understand that there were many thousands of soldiers, engaged in many different conflicts throughout the colonies; they thought there were simply two bodies of troops who kept meeting each other in battle."[40]

Given their difficulty with many of the abstract, substantive concepts of history, it is not surprising that children have difficulty appreciating the social, economic, and political factors that lead to change. The biographical approach to history appeals to children, but researchers suggest that it should be taken with caution because it tends to reinforce children's tendency to "personalize" history. Because children so readily appreciate that history is about real people, history teaching at the elementary school level has the potential to encourage an inflated sense of personal efficacy because these students do not understand the institutional constraints on individual action. Fertig, however, suggests that biographies may actually be useful provided that they address these constraints and clarify the context of a historical figure's actions.[41] Moreover, reading several biographies on one theme (e.g., of Benjamin Banneker, Ruby Bridges, Martin Luther King Jr., Marion Anderson, and Satchel Paige) may help children appreciate the enduring nature of beliefs and attitudes that result in discrimination and that require the efforts of many people, and many groups of people, to change over time.

Lee indicates that children understand causes as "special kinds of events ... [that] can be thought of as piling up so that eventually there are enough causes to make something happen."[42] Obviously, the more important the event, the longer the list of causes must be. Younger students, however, miss the interactions or relationships among underlying conditions and events that are often characteristic of causal explanations in history. Grades four to six are probably not too early for teachers to start challenging these simplistic notions of agency and to make the distinction between underlying factors and causes of change.

## Historical Perspective and Judgment

One potential benefit arising from children's inclinations to personalize history and be drawn to the human drama of history is that it may incline them to empathize with the people of the past. But here again, the everyday sense of empathy runs generally counter to historians' notions of historical empathy, which do not include making emotional connections or sharing the feelings of the people of the past, but rather understanding their perspectives in order to explain ways of living and thinking in the past.[43]

Two things are clear from research at this time. Elementary school children initially bring a "presentist" perspective to their understanding of the past: they judge the people of the past according to present standards; they see the past and the people of the past as deficient in some way.[44] However, teacher modelling and explicit discussions about why people in the past thought and acted as they did are important in helping children begin to develop sensitivity to past ways of thinking. Students who engaged in such discussions, and who completed activities in which they were required to articulate the varied perspectives of people involved in the historical events, demonstrated their emerging ability to take those perspectives in an informed and credible way.[45]

## Conclusion

It must be stated that researchers are not expecting young children to be or become sophisticated or expert thinkers in history. One of the most important insights gleaned from the work of Lee and Ashby is that many of the structural concepts in history represent "counterintuitive" or "unnatural" ways of thinking that are contrary to children's everyday understandings.[46] For example, children naturally assume that if two historians offer differing accounts of the same historical event, then one must have made a mistake. When they are asked to articulate the perspective of someone in the past, they naturally project their own values and beliefs onto historical actors. Researchers' work, however, demonstrates that children progress in their understandings and that they can be supported in their development of more powerful ideas about the concepts that are foundational to historical inquiry. Students' progression to more sophisticated understandings is not necessarily related to age; rather, research indicates that "teaching changes pupil ideas."[47] A review of studies of children's understanding of some of the structural concepts of historical thinking not only helps us understand what we might reasonably expect from children in terms of their historical thinking, but also offers insights into the *kind* of teaching required to support children's growth toward more powerful understandings.

So what kind of history instruction do elementary children need? Children need breadth and depth in order to progress in their historical thinking. The narratives of events, the "bits and pieces" of information, that have typically been the focus of history in elementary school have not served children well. To acknowledge the importance of historical thinking is not to say that children need process rather than content. Children need information, but this information must be in a usable framework, in organizing themes that allow them to grapple with important substantive and procedural concepts. They need opportunities and the time to investigate questions in depth in order to build their understanding of history as a discipline.

Children need a range of resources in order to build their understandings. Textbook accounts alone do little to aid children's understanding of major concepts underpinning the historical content they are learning, nor do they help foster historical thinking skills. Children must use a range of primary sources of evidence and a variety of secondary accounts – both nonfiction and fiction – in order to gain the depth of knowledge required, confront problems of interpretation that must be solved, and begin to appreciate ways of thinking unlike their own – skills all essential to historical thinking. They must also engage in meaningful learning activities led by a knowledgeable teacher. All of the research summarized here acknowledges the fundamental importance of teachers' questions and interventions, as well as the impact of appropriate guided practice on the growth of children's historical thinking.

Historian Gerda Lerner said that meaningful historical study "demands imagination and empathy, so that we can fathom worlds unlike our own, contexts far from those we know, ways of thinking and feeling that are alien to us. We must enter past worlds with curiosity and respect."[48] This is why elementary school children must learn history and must grow in their historical understanding. This is also why history is given a prominent place in social studies. Children's active and thoughtful participation in a pluralistic democracy requires the knowledge, skills, and attitudes that only a meaningful study of history can provide. Thinking historically does not just mean thinking about the past; it involves seeing oneself in time, as an inheritor of the legacies of the past and as a maker of the future. Much research remains to be done, especially with elementary school children in Canada, if we are to better understand how best to cultivate children's historical thinking. What cannot be doubted, however, is the fundamental importance of the task.

## NOTES

1 Amy von Heyking, "Historical Understanding in the Elementary Years," paper presented at the biennial Conference on the Teaching and Learning of History, Association for Canadian Studies, Vancouver, 27-29 October 2006; "The Nature and Development of Children's Historical Empathy," unpublished paper.
2 Alberta Education, *Program of Studies: Social Studies, Kindergarten to Grade 12* (Edmonton: 2005), 9.
3 Ministry of Education, *The Ontario Curriculum: Social Studies, Grades 1 to 6, History and Geography, Grades 7 and 8, revised* (Toronto: 2004), 2.
4 Atlantic Canada Regional Social Studies Committee, *The Foundation for the Atlantic Canada Social Studies Curriculum* (Halifax: 1999), 26.
5 Isabel L. Beck and Margaret G. McKeown, "Outcomes of History Instruction: Paste-up Accounts," in *Cognitive and Instructional Processes in History and the Social Sciences*, ed. Mario Carretero and James F. Voss (Hillsdale: Lawrence Erlbaum, 1994), 254; Bruce VanSledright and Lisa Frankes, "Concept- and Strategic-Knowledge Development in Historical Study: A Comparative Exploration in Two Fourth-Grade Classrooms," *Cognition and Instruction* 18, 2 (2000): 281; Peter Lee and Rosalyn

Ashby, "Progression in Historical Understanding among Students Ages 7-14," in *Knowing, Teaching, and Learning History: National and International Perspectives*, ed. Peter N. Stearns, Peter Seixas, and Sam Wineburg (New York: New York University Press, 2000), 215.

6  Isabel L. Beck and Margaret G. McKeown, "Toward Meaningful Accounts in History Texts for Young Learners," *Educational Researcher* 17, 6 (August-September 1988): 38; Isabel L. Beck, Margaret G. McKeown, and Erika W. Gromoll, "Learning from Social Studies Texts," *Cognition and Instruction* 6, 2 (1989): 151-53; Beck and McKeown, "Outcomes of History Instruction," 238-40; Anthony Blake, Lynn Newton, Douglas Newton, and Kathleen Brown, "Do Primary History Books Show a Concern for Explanatory Understanding?" *Westminster Studies in Education* 26, 2 (October 2003): 156.

7  Isabel L. Beck, Margaret G. McKeown, Gale M. Sinatra, and Jane A. Loxterman, "Revising Social Studies Text from a Text-Processing Perspective: Evidence of Improved Comprehensibility," *Reading Research Quarterly* 26, 3 (Summer 1991): 272-73; Beck and McKeown, "Outcomes of History Instruction," 242-43.

8  Isabel L. Beck, Margaret G. McKeown, and Jo Worthy, "Giving a Text Voice Can Improve Students' Understanding," *Reading Research Quarterly* 30, 2 (April-June 1995): 233-34.

9  Beck and McKeown, "Outcomes of History Instruction," 253.

10  Bruce A. VanSledright and Christine Kelly, "Reading American History: The Influence of Multiple Sources on Six Fifth Graders," *Elementary School Journal* 98, 3 (January 1998): 261.

11  Bruce A. VanSledright, "What Does It Mean to Read History? Fertile Ground for Cross-Disciplinary Collaborations?" *Reading Research Quarterly* 39, 3 (July-September 2004), 345.

12  See Anna Emilia Berti, "Children's Understanding of the Concept of the State," in *Cognitive and Instructional Processes in History and the Social Studies*, ed. Mario Carretero and James F. Voss (Hillsdale: Lawrence Erlbaum, 1994), 73; Peter J. Lee, "Putting Principles into Practice: Understanding History," in *How Students Learn: History in the Classroom*, ed. M. Suzanne Donovan and John D. Bransford (Washington: National Academies Press, 2005): 61-65.

13  Peter Seixas, "Conceptualizing the Growth of Historical Understanding," in *The Handbook of Education and Human Development: New Models of Learning, Teaching, and Schooling*, ed. David R. Olson and Nancy Torrance (Cambridge, MA: Blackwell, 1996), 766.

14  Hilary Cooper, *History in the Early Years* (London: Routledge, 1995), 1-2.

15  Keith C. Barton, "'My Mom Taught Me': The Situated Nature of Historical Understanding," paper presented at the Annual Meeting of the American Educational Research Association, San Francisco, April 1995.

16  Von Heyking, "'The Nature and Development."

17  Linda S. Levstik and Christine C. Pappas, "Exploring the Development of Historical Understanding," *Journal of Research and Development in Education* 21, 1 (Fall 1987), 14.

18  Lee and Ashby, "Progression in Historical Understanding," 199.

19  Keith Barton, "Primary Children's Understanding of the Role of Historical Evidence: Comparisons between the United States and Northern Ireland," *International Journal of Historical Learning, Teaching, and Research* 1, 2 (June 2001), http://centres.exeter.ac.uk.
20  See Denis Shemilt, *History 13-16 Evaluation Study* (Edinburgh: Holmes, McDougall, 1980).
21  Peter Lee, "Making Sense of Historical Accounts," *Canadian Social Studies* 32, 2 (Winter 1998): 52-54; Lee and Ashby, "Progression in Historical Understanding"; Peter Lee and Denis Shemilt, "A Scaffold, Not a Cage: Progression and Progression Models in History," *Teaching History* 113 (December 2003): 13-23; "'I Just Wish We Could Go Back in the Past and Find Out What Really Happened': Progression in Understanding about Historical Accounts," *Teaching History* 117 (December 2004): 25-31.
22  Linda S. Levstik and Delia B. Smith, "'I've Never Done This Before': Building a Community of Inquiry in a Third-Grade Classroom," in *Advances in Research on Teaching, Vol. 6: Teaching and Learning in History*, ed. Jere Brophy (Greenwich: JAI Press, 1996): 85-114; Bruce VanSledright, "Confronting History's Interpretive Paradox While Teaching Fifth Graders to Investigate the Past," *American Educational Research Journal* 103, 2 (Winter 2002): 1089-115; "Fifth Graders Investigating History in the Classroom: Results from a Researcher-Practitioner Design Experiment," *Elementary School Journal* 103, 2 (November 2002): 131-60; *In Search of America's Past: Learning to Read History in Elementary School* (New York: Teachers College Press, 2002); Hilary Cooper and Dursun Dilek, "Children's Thinking in History: Analysis of a History Lesson Taught to 11 Year Olds at Ihsan Sungu School, Istanbul," *International Journal of Historical Learning, Teaching, and Research* 4, 2 (July 2004), http://centres.exeter.ac.uk; Kathleen Owings Swan, Mark Hofer, and David Locascio, "The Historical Scene Investigation (HSI) Project: Examining the Use of Case Based Historical Instruction in the Fifth Grade Social Studies Classroom," *International Journal of Social Education* 22, 2 (Fall 2007–Winter 2008): 70-100.
23  Bruce A. VanSledright and Peter Afflerbach, "Assessing the Status of Historical Sources: An Exploratory Study of Eight US Elementary Students Reading Documents," in *Understanding History: Recent Research in History Education*, ed. Rosalyn Ashby, Peter Gordon, and Peter Lee (London: RoutledgeFalmer, 2005), 15-16.
24  VanSledright, "What Does It Mean to Read History?" 345.
25  Keith C. Barton, "'I Just Kinda Know': Elementary Students' Ideas about Historical Evidence," *Theory and Research in Social Education* 25, 4 (Fall 1997): 418-19.
26  Barton, "'I Just Kinda Know,'" 421; Bruce VanSledright and Jere Brophy, "Storytelling, Imagination, and Fanciful Elaboration in Children's Historical Reconstructions," *American Educational Research Journal* 29, 4 (Winter 1992): 851-52.
27  Carol Seefeldt, "History for Young Children," *Theory and Research in Social Education* 21, 2 (Spring 1993): 145-46.
28  Cooper, *History in the Early Years*, 39-43.
29  Reported in Lee, "Putting Principles into Practice," 42.
30  Penelope Harnett, "Identifying Progression in Children's Understanding: The Use of Visual Materials to Assess Primary School Children's Learning in History," *Cambridge*

*Journal of Education* 23, 2 (June 1993): 137-55; Keith C. Barton and Linda S. Levstik, "'Back When God Was Around and Everything': Elementary Children's Understanding of Historical Time," *American Educational Research Journal* 33, 2 (Summer 1996): 419-54; Linda S. Levstik and Keith C. Barton, "'They Still Use Some of Their Past': Historical Salience in Elementary Children's Chronological Thinking," *Journal of Curriculum Studies* 28, 5 (September 1996): 531-76; Stuart J. Foster, John D. Hoge, and Richard H. Rosch, "Thinking Aloud about History: Children's and Adolescents' Responses to Historical Photographs," *Theory and Research in Social Education* 27, 2 (Spring 1999): 179-214; Keith C. Barton, "'Oh, That's a Tricky Piece!': Children, Mediated Action, and the Tools of Historical Time," *Elementary School Journal* 103, 2 (November 2002): 161-83.

31 Alan Hodkinson, "Does the English Curriculum for History and Its Schemes of Work Effectively Promote Primary-Aged Children's Assimilation of the Concepts of Historical Time? Some Observations Based on Current Research," *Educational Research* 46, 2 (Summer 2004): 99-117.

32 Seefeldt, "History for Young Children," 147.

33 Keith C. Barton, "Narrative Simplifications in Elementary Students' Historical Thinking," in *Advances in Research on Teaching*, vol. 6, ed. Jere Brophy (Greenwich: JAI Press, 1996), 74.

34 See Peter Lee and Rosalyn Ashby, "Empathy, Perspective Taking, and Rational Understanding," in *Historical Empathy and Perspective Taking in the Social Studies*, ed. O.L. Davis Jr., Elizabeth Anne Yeager, and Stuart J. Foster (Lanham: Rowman and Littlefield, 2001): 21-50.

35 Barton, "Narrative Simplifications," 67.

36 Keith C. Barton and Linda S. Levstik, "'It Wasn't a Good Part of History': National Identity and Students' Explanations of Historical Significance," *Teachers College Record* 99, 3 (Spring 1998): 478-513; Barton, "Narrative Simplifications"; Foster, Hoge, and Rosch, "Thinking Aloud about History"; Barton, "Oh, That's a Tricky Piece!'"

37 Linda S. Levstik and Christine C. Pappas, "Exploring the Development of Historical Understanding," *Journal of Research and Development in Education* 21, 1 (Fall 1987): 10-12.

38 Barton and Levstik, "It Wasn't a Good Part of History," 482.

39 Keith C. Barton, "History Is about People: Elementary Students' Understanding of History," paper presented at the annual meeting of the National Council for the Social Studies, Phoenix, November 1994; Barton, "Narrative Simplifications," 68; Keith C. Barton, "'Bossed Around by the Queen': Elementary Students' Understanding of Individuals and Institutions in History," *Journal of Curriculum and Supervision* 12, 4 (Summer 1997): 300.

40 Barton, "Narrative Simplification," 66-67.

41 Gary Fertig, "Using Biography to Help Young Learners Understand the Causes of Historical Change and Continuity," *Social Studies* 99, 4 (July-August 2008): 148.

42 Lee, "Putting Principles into Practice," 52.

43 Christopher Portal, "Empathy as an Objective for History Teaching," in *The History Curriculum for Teachers*, ed. Christopher Portal (London: Falmer Press, 1987): 89-99; Stuart J. Foster and Elizabeth A. Yeager, "The Role of Empathy in the

Development of Historical Understanding," *International Journal of Social Education* 13, 1 (Spring-Summer 1998): 1-7.
44  Keith C. Barton, "History Is More Than Story," paper presented to the annual meeting of the National Council for the Social Studies, Nashville, November 1993; "Did the Devil Just Run Out of Juice? Historical Perspective-Taking among Elementary Students," paper presented to the annual meeting of the American Education Research Association, New York, April 1996; VanSledright, *In Search of America's Past*, 147-48; Lee and Ashby, "Empathy, Perspective Taking, and Rational Understanding," 27; Lee, "Putting Principles into Practice," 47.
45  Barton, "History Is More Than Story," 8-12; Barton, "Did the Devil Just Run Out of Juice?" 23-26; VanSledright, *In Search of America's Past*, 148; von Heyking, "The Nature and Development of Children's Historical Empathy"; Nancy Dulberg, "Engaging in History: Empathy and Perspective-Taking in Children's Historical Thinking," paper presented to the annual meeting of the American Educational Research Association, New Orleans, April 2002.
46  See Lee, "Putting Principles into Practice," 33-36.
47  Lee and Ashby, "Progression in Historical Understanding," 214.
48  Gerda Lerner, *Why History Matters* (New York: Oxford University Press, 1997), 201.

# Historical Thinking in Secondary Schools
## Zones and Gardens

TOM MORTON

The Benchmarks of Historical Thinking Project is a multi-year, pan-Canadian program to reform history teaching through sustained professional development and the creation of curriculum and assessment tools. In the summer of 2006 at the University of British Columbia, Dr. Peter Seixas gathered together "lead teachers," chosen for their active involvement in professional development and history education, with several prominent university history educators to plan the implementation of Benchmarks. During that institute, in subsequent meetings during the school year, and through their own teaching, the lead teachers studied and applied the concepts of historical thinking. (See Seixas, Chapter 6, in this volume.) Subsequently, they led workshops for others in their local school districts. For three years, while I was teaching high school in Vancouver, I was one of the Benchmarks lead teachers.

A benchmark is a metaphor that compares teaching to mapping new terrain, to seeking new levels. This image of mapping or surveying reflects the importance for both teachers and students to find meaning in historical thinking, to understand the nature of the discipline. The metaphor also suggests adventures, risks, and uncertainty.

What follows is a description of some of my own adventures as I passed through "zones of uncertainty." The chapter also tells the tales of other teachers in diverse corners of the country and their promising "victory gardens" of exciting classes as well as their uncertainties.

## The Complexity of Teaching

There is a pernicious belief that teaching is only about practice. While this chapter is about the practice of teachers, it is worth remembering here Kurt Lewin's famous dictum: nothing is as practical as a good theory.[1] We cannot find meaning, we cannot teach, without some reflection on the complex elements of our craft.

Lee Shulman introduced the term *pedagogical content knowledge* to conceptualize the nature of teaching a subject area like history.[2] Teachers need to master both knowledge of the content of that subject area and knowledge of which teaching approaches best fit the content. This "craft knowledge" is different from that of a disciplinary expert and also from the general pedagogical knowledge shared by teachers across disciplines. According to Peter John, a history teacher's craft knowledge includes, among other things, knowledge of history, knowledge of ways to teach it, and knowledge of how children learn history.[3] This last element refers to the most appropriate teaching approaches to help students come to grips with history and its special procedures and standards for valid claims about the past – that is, to identify common student preconceptions and seek to modify and develop the mental tools students need to make sense of history.

Reflecting on the complexity of these various elements, Shulman put the teacher's situation this way: "Teaching is impossible. If we simply add together all that is expected of a typical teacher and take note of the circumstances under which those activities are carried out, the sum makes greater demands than any individual can possibly fulfil. Yet, teachers teach."[4]

Most of my colleagues manage this impossibility with some skill and flare. However, Shulman's hyperbole highlights the challenge of changing our practice. As complex and demanding as history teaching may be, there is a whole other layer of complexity and demands when a new approach is being implemented, such as a change in the teaching of historical thinking concepts. Innovations like Benchmarks involve more than the use of new rubrics or the use of new inquiry questions; they also involve a change in beliefs about the nature of history and progression in historical understanding. Reform involves more than putting concepts into practice; it also means changing the culture of the classroom, the school, the provincial ministry curriculum, and so on.[5]

When a culture of support for change is lacking, innovations come with large costs and few incentives. As Ernest House notes: "The personal costs [for a teacher] of trying new innovations are often high ... and seldom is there any indication that innovations are worth the investment. Innovations are acts of faith. They require that one believe that they will ultimately bear fruit and be worth the investment."[6]

Sharing is key to successful educational change. An innovation cannot be assimilated "until its meaning is shared."[7] In one-to-one and group settings, teachers need to receive and give help and, more simply, talk about the meaning of what can be slippery concepts such as historical significance. Efforts to establish a common meaning of disciplinary thinking about history were a feature of early meetings of Benchmarks organizers, and those efforts continue to be important for me as well as for the teachers with whom I work.[8] Understandably, the Benchmarks project has involved what Schön describes as "passing through zones of uncertainty ... the situation of being at sea, of being lost, of confronting more information than you can handle."[9]

## Through Zones of Uncertainty toward 11 November

What follows is an account of one of my Benchmarks explorations and the zones of uncertainty that my students and I encountered. The context here was the creation of videos about the historical significance of the First World War for our school's Remembrance Day ceremonies. My greatest uncertainty related to knowledge of how children conceived the historical concepts of both significance and evidence in their inquiry and how those concepts interacted with our collective meaning of Remembrance Day.

Remembrance Day is a remarkable day for a history teacher in English Canada. At no other time do English Canadian schools and communities honour the past to such an extent. Stories from as distant in time as the First World War fill the news media prior to 11 November, especially stories about Vimy Ridge, the celebrated Canadian victory.

Steeped in ritual, Remembrance Day has been called "history's Christmas Day."[10] Just as the non-religious still evince some regard for Christmas, so the "non-historians" have at least some sort of regard for Remembrance Day. As with the religious holiday, there are almost-sacred rituals: the parade of uniforms and poppies, the special music, the incantation of "In Flanders Fields," and the minute of silence.[11] Such reverence. Such an opportunity. My grade elevens (sixteen year olds) had a ready audience of younger students at school assemblies for their videos. Yet there would also be challenges when I asked my students to give some historical scrutiny to the ritual and reverence.

The idea for the video came when I discovered the National Film Board's (NFB) website *Images of a Forgotten War: Films of the Canadian Expeditionary Force in the Great War*. I dreamed of my students using the rich documentary footage on that site to construct their own accounts of the world war. But when I spoke with the NFB, I learned that their stock department sold the film commercially for $60 a second. I estimated that with my annual school stipend, I could buy 1.6 seconds. Yet as I spoke on the phone with the NFB manager, he warmed to the idea of student videos, and after some exchange of correspondence, five CDs arrived in the post.

I was twice lucky when Fiona MacKellar, a film instructor and graduate student, agreed to organize the instructional technology. The first of many tasks she performed was to choose relevant footage of the NFB material and organize it for students on a user-friendly CD. She also gave guidance to students in how to use the MovieMaker software and helped resolve many IT challenges. However, collaboration on the IT did not extend to collaboration in planning with other history teachers. As is common in the culture of Canadian schools, I prepared the unit on my own.

In the first month of term, though I felt limited by the need to "cover" the course for the provincial exam, my grade elevens did considerable work on the concept of evidence. To answer the essential questions, "Why did the Canadian government enter a war that was so far away and had so little to do with our national interests?" and "Why were Canadians in 1914 so willing to fight?" they interpreted a variety of visual and print texts.

I would have liked to have spent more time on the heuristics of sourcing, contextualizing and corroborating sources, but as 11 November approached, I was keen to explore the illusive "so what?" – historical significance – and more specifically to consider multiple narratives of the First World War.

First, we established criteria for historical significance: resulting in change, revealing and connected to a larger, meaningful narrative. (See Lévesque, Chapter 5, in this volume.) To these, I grafted philosopher Jörn Rüsen's four orientations to historical consciousness as a way of framing how Vimy might reveal something for us today.[12] On the opposite page is an excerpt from my handout to students that describes Rüsen's four orientations as related to Vimy and Remembrance Day.

I also posed the question of Vimy's significance in narrative form with this question: "Was Vimy Ridge the birth of a nation or the ruin of a nation?" We looked at Vimy as an important step on Canada's progress to autonomy. Here I quoted historian Desmond Morton: "Doing great things together ... is how nations are formed. Vimy was such a moment."[13]

*Four Orientations: Vimy and Remembrance Day*

Vimy is significant because it resulted in deep changes, but it also can reveal something for us today. Which of the following is your viewpoint on Vimy's relevance today?

*The past defines us:* We are clearly tied to our military past because it is this tradition that has made us who we are today. Vimy, for example, led to greater autonomy for Canada and a sense that we are one nation. On Remembrance Day we should pay tribute to this traditional story and to the sacrifice of our soldiers.

*The past is a source of lessons and models:* Vimy Ridge clearly showed what Canadians can do. It also showed the importance of a core of experienced military leaders, disciplined soldiers, and careful planning. In addition, many Canadians have been inspired by the sacrifice and bravery of our soldiers. Remembrance Day could be a time to teach these and other lessons to young people.

*The past is not relevant to us today:* This approach does not accept the traditional stories. For example, the many deaths at Vimy Ridge and subsequent battles led to Conscription, which divided the nation on ethnic lines. The story of Canada's increasing autonomy and national identity achieved on the battlefields of Europe may also have less importance for more recent Canadians whose war memories are from Asia, Africa or Latin America. Moreover, the war was a long time ago; Canada and the world have changed. (If you take this approach, be sure to be respectful, nonetheless, to the soldiers and civilians who sacrificed so much in the wars and to the many Canadians for whom Remembrance Day is a moving, powerful day.)

*The past is important but we need to consider modern circumstances:* For example, a Remembrance Day ceremony based on this approach might recognize the contribution of our veterans and the value of joining our allies to defeat Germany after it invaded Belgium, but argue that we should still be cautious in sending our troops to other foreign wars such as those in Iraq or Afghanistan. Likewise, Vimy Ridge may teach a lesson about Canadian leadership, discipline, and courage but maybe these qualities in today's world could be put to use for purposes other than war.

We then examined two alternative stories. First, we considered the view of Daniel Francis, who wrote that "there has always been a counter narrative, muted but persistent, that found the appalling slaughter pointless, and the people who sanctioned it incompetent, even evil."[14] Second, we studied the narrative that sees the casualties of Vimy as an important factor leading to Conscription and the division of the country between anglophone Canadians and francophone Quebecers.

**The Videos**

I taught the Remembrance Day project each year for three years, revising it each time. By many measures it was a success. The students and I were thrilled to see their videos at the school assembly. Surveys showed that overall, most students were able to use the criteria to explain significance, as illustrated in the narration below (all student quotations are from MacKellar):[15]

> There aren't many occasions where an event results in over 30,000 casualties, but this isn't the only reason why the battle was so significant. World War I was greatly affected by the Battle of Vimy Ridge. Many historians believe that this battle alone was the cause of the war ending two years prior to the expected date.[16]

Many students contrasted the traditional English Canadian narrative with the French Canadian one, as did the following student:

> After Vimy, there were very few volunteers to go help fight in the war and replace casualties. In 1917, Borden passed the Military Service Act, which allowed for conscription, forcing men to go overseas to fight in the war. French Canadians and Quebecers were highly against conscription, and marches were organized against Borden in protest. Many people think that conscription separated the country from the English and the French.[17]

Several others found a visual way to illustrate the same point.[18] However, I was uncertain as to the extent to which the students were actually reasoning about significance rather than merely following the prompts and scaffolding I had given them. Moreover, many students only repeated the theme of the traditional ceremony by constructing their videos almost exclusively as tributes to the fallen soldiers. These often included the traditional rhetoric of admonishments to seek lessons from the war.

Seeking lessons from the past is the habitual justification for studying history; often, though, these lessons are unwarranted. I still smile when I recall two bright boys whose movie about the Dieppe Raid (in the first year of the project, when it was broader than the focus on Vimy Ridge) concluded that the disastrous consequence of the late landing of the Canadian soldiers on Dieppe's beaches should teach students to arrive in class on time. More common for the Vimy project were more relevant but still superficial commentaries such as this one: "We at least owe the heroes of yesterday who died to end future wars not to make the same bloody mistakes as we did in the past, or else their deaths with outstanding bravery would be for nothing."[19]

MacKellar suggests that students may have been transferring practices to their history work that they had learned in English classes – that is, they may have been teasing out the "moral of the story" in history just as they might do with a fable or story in English class. She also suggests that the students may have assumed that they were *meant* to be drawing these lessons from the past, in the belief that the very purpose of studying history is to learn from it in order to avoid repeating mistakes of the past.[20] This orientation to the past – what Rüsen calls "exemplary historical consciousness" – is almost de rigueur with Remembrance Day ceremonies.

The uncertainty about what constitutes proficient reasoning about significance is also a likely consequence of my assessment practice – less about the criteria I gave to students than about how I used them. Assessment was intended to be a key "first step" of Benchmarks according to Siexas and Peck,[21] but in the workshops I led in the Vancouver School District this has been a trial-and-error process focused on creating and revising rubrics based on student work. We have not discussed how best to use these assessment tools. My rubric for the videos described the criterion for historical significance as "resulting in change, revealing or relevant today," while the highest standard of achievement was "clearly applies all appropriate criteria; events are connected to a larger narrative; considers modern situations; includes insightful ideas not discussed in class or the readings; rich in supporting details; sensitive to the audience." This language of assessment may have been clear to me and other history teachers, but for students, phrases like "connected to a larger narrative" and "considers modern situation" needed more explanation and examples than I provided.

Moreover, inasmuch as the Remembrance Day project emphasized the concept of significance, it spent less time on interpreting the video sources. The class did study the use of film as evidence, considering its reliability and limitations, using two excellent essays on the NFB's website.[22] However, on the assumption that the CD MacKellar had created would ensure that all images were at least accurate and relevant, I did not include a separate evaluation criterion for interpretation, except that the narrative be accurate. When students used images beyond what were supplied, several of these were anachronistic – for example, soldiers from the Second World War, the Boer War, and even the American Civil War.

Students progressed in their historical thinking on significance and evidence mainly when they wrote their scripts and responded to my feedback. Subsequent work on the movie was often overwhelmed by technical challenges or by the goal of entertainment. MacKellar concluded that "students made visual selections based on an image's communicative properties as opposed to its historical properties."[23] The tension between the discipline of history and video documentary and the shortness of the documentary also limited the depth of historical thinking relative to what an essay might have offered.

In reflecting on my pedagogical content knowledge of how students learn history, I believe I came up short in assessing how my students would evaluate evidence and be influenced by the collective rituals for Remembrance Day. Perhaps if the project had been organized more as an inquiry, with students generating their own questions, or if I had given more explicit scaffolding and requirements for the use of visual evidence, there might have been fewer anachronisms and a greater understanding of the process of interpreting sources in constructing narratives. This was my first unit to focus on reasoning about significance, and I felt that students made subsequent progress as the year went on; however, I did not have any formal means of measuring broad, age-specific progress. The creation of such assessment tools is, of course, one goal of the Benchmarks project.

The broader context of school and educational culture also influenced the project. At the school level, collaboration with teaching colleagues might have helped me revise the unit along the lines suggested above. At the provincial level, the pressure of a content-laden course with a final exam limited the amount of time that I felt I could give the project. Lack of time is often the enemy of in-depth understanding and was the students' main criticism in subsequent surveys. Though a success by many measures, the project clearly passed through several of Schön's "zones of uncertainty."

As stated earlier, at the same time as I was trying to develop my own pedagogical content knowledge for teaching historical thinking with units like the Remembrance Day project, I was also a lead teacher or coach for other teachers in Vancouver. For this chapter, I wanted also to explore their efforts and those of others across the country who have been part of Benchmarks and see how their experiences were similar to mine and how they might provide further direction to the project as it unfolds. What follows are their accounts of successes and uncertainties and a switch of metaphors.

**Victory Gardens**
"Victory Gardens" were private gardens where Canadians grew food as part of the war effort. In small backyards, people would lovingly raise carrots, potatoes, Brussels sprouts, and other vegetables to feed their families and support their country. The victory gardens in history education are small corners of schools and districts where unusually savvy, dedicated, and caring teachers have cultivated historical thinking.[24] The roots are not yet deep in Canadian schools, but there are many flourishing small efforts, some of which are described below.

In interviews, these teachers speak of student successes, notably with students who often struggle to achieve at school. Several speak of how teaching historical thinking has transformed their practice and that of others to the point that some have become "evangelical." Yet they also speak of uncertainties.

As I did for the Remembrance Day project, Jan Haskings-Winner of Toronto chose the concept of historical significance to teach to her grade tens (fifteen year olds):

> We were studying whether the 1920's "roared or not" and I used a jigsaw activity and divided them into four expert groups investigating First Nations (and residential schools), Chinese Immigrants (and the head tax), Workers and Black Canadians. They first ... record[ed] information on their topic and then shared it with their home groups. This was to help them differentiate the relevant from irrelevant. Then I had them determine the most significant event of the 1920's (from a long list that they had generated) and write a supported opinion paragraph with evidence.

Even though Haskings-Winner's students had struggled with attendance and punctuality, on a Friday last-period class "they did not want to leave until they 'finished' getting all the information they could from the jigsaw activity."[25]

One of the ways that students can demonstrate their reasoning about significance, according to Counsell, is for them to create and apply their own criteria. This is what Haskings-Winner's students did.[26] One of their criteria was "dismay over the event at the time" – an original blend of Benchmark's criterion for deciding on historical significance, "remarked upon by people at the time," and Welsh educator Robin Phillips's criterion – that an event can be significant if it is "terrifying."[27]

Kim Cooke, a "lead teacher" who participated in the first Benchmarks summer institute, teaches in the Selkirk School District, situated along both sides of the Red River north of Winnipeg. She takes pride in her grade five class, who also applied the concept of significance:

> It is amazing to see ten year olds discussing photos, timelines and artefacts with such in-depth conversations and opinions. Instead of a student just stating facts about Henry Hudson that they got off the internet or from a text book, they are able to talk about the impact Henry Hudson made on people from the 1600s and how that impact is "revealing" to us today. They can look deeper into the history and make it more meaningful to them. Still, my most noteworthy successes would be to see students who typically struggle in school feel successful and proud of their ability to participate successfully in history class and be able to state and back up their findings without ridicule or negative reactions from their peers.[28]

Graeme Stacey and Lindsay Gibson have been working with Peter Seixas in Kelowna, BC, where they organized a group of teachers from four high schools to develop a series of inquiries on the interwar period in Canada. These inquiries were framed around essential questions that emphasized historical thinking concepts such as the moral dimension in this question: "Were the actions of the federal government during the Winnipeg General Strike justified?" And historical significance in this question: "What was the most historically significant event that led to improved women's rights during the Interwar period?"

Stacey believes that one of the main benefits of the emphasis on historical concepts is that they offer the students purpose and clarity: "It moves them away from the right answer syndrome."[29] Lindsay Gibson agrees: "[The Benchmarks project] gives my units and lessons a focus other than pure historical content or disconnected skills and processes that I was previously trying to work on."[30]

Chas Desjarlais of Vancouver reflects on how teaching historical thinking concepts has transformed her pedagogical content knowledge. Her first

Benchmarks unit centred on the concepts of evidence and continuity and change. Students analyzed newspapers and political cartoons from 1914 and 2001 to compare Canada's initial enthusiasm for fighting in the First World War to its resistance to joining the Second Iraq War. She says that since her initial unit, she has kept trying to do "more and more and more ... The more I get involved the more I change my practice. My whole philosophy of teaching is changing to emphasize historical thinking ... I am still trying to get my brain around some of the concepts and I say that to the students."[31]

One Benchmarks lead teacher claims that once teachers learn about the concepts, "most become almost evangelical – they want to 'go tell it on the mountain!'"[32]

### Uncertainties

Yet there are challenges to teaching historical thinking concepts. Teachers commented, first, on the inevitable zones of uncertainty in implementing a new approach – in particular, in understanding the concepts and how to assess them. Also, as the Benchmarks project moves beyond victory gardens, some of the lead teachers have referred to the challenges of the education culture.

Several teachers found – as I did with the Remembrance Day project – that students had trouble identifying and applying the criteria for historical significance. They were readily able to recognize the criterion of change, but they found it hard to move beyond this. Alan Sears, a social studies researcher and pre-service teacher educator in New Brunswick, comments that "at one level, significance seems the easiest (of the historical thinking concepts) to communicate but when we explore the elements of significance it gets far more complex and teachers have difficulty thinking of activities that will push students to greater understanding of the elements or critical attributes of the concept."[33]

Kelowna's Lindsay Gibson's comments reflect a similar concern about defining the concepts and levels of student understanding:

> Assessment has been a huge issue. How do you assess the development of students' historical thinking abilities? Obviously these concepts are shifting away from "right" and "wrong" answers, but how do you implement these ideas with students who have been taught that in history there are clearly right and wrong answers. I tell students it is about developing historically plausible answers, but we have to spend considerable time understanding

what a historically plausible answer is. It is defensible, justifiable, based on accurate facts and evidence, and most importantly it uses thoughtful, considered reasoning. Students are sometime too quick to jump to a conclusion and then justify that conclusion as "right" just because they came up with it.[34]

Mark Perry of New Brunswick sees challenges in the culture of teaching:

Few teachers engage in practices in their own lives that reflect historical thinking – much to the same degree that we teachers do not think critically – we are institutionalized to a degree – we jump at the sound of a bell – we walk through the same doorframe at the same time every day. Our routines are often established for us. It is difficult to create another culture. One of the few times that we pretend to be applying the skills of reasoning is at the negotiation of a new contract."

Moreover, professional development is often focused on generic methodologies relating to classroom management. Rarely is it focused on pedagogical content knowledge.[35]

That history teachers focus mainly on covering content and on memorization is hardly a new finding. The empirical evidence is clear that principals, parents, and teachers see covering a curriculum as a teacher's duty. If primary sources and historical inquiries get in the way of that duty, coverage will win out.[36] As the earlier quotation from House reminds us, the costs for the busy teacher in terms of extra work and breaking group norms to teach an innovation are often too high.

## Conclusion

The experiences of teachers across Canada show the promise of using a coherent conceptual framework, such as the one delineated in the Benchmarks project, for helping students think historically. Students set foot on the firm ground of disciplinary understanding, rather than scramble on the scree and scrag of random facts in unrelated lessons. Teachers value the purpose that the concepts give their lessons and the excitement that historical thinking can generate. Kim Cooke's observation of "students who typically struggle in school [feeling] successful and proud of their ability to participate successfully in history class" argues persuasively for the value of Benchmarks.

Yet the comments of the teachers and my own experiences with tasks such as the Remembrance Day video also underline the primacy of support and time for teachers to find their own meaning of historical thinking in order to cross the inevitable zones of uncertainty. As Shulman maintains, teachers must understand the structure of their discipline – implementing inquiries, teaching multiple viewpoints, and the like – and know how to transform it in a way that will make sense to students. For complex concepts like historical significance, as history educators in the United Kingdom have also discovered, this can be hard.[37] The increasing number of new textbooks and other curricular resources that feature historical thinking concepts should make it easier.[38] However, as Bruce VanSledright concludes, "teaching children to think historically is a slow, arduous process."[39]

In addition, in the capricious world of teaching, one that Shulman labelled as "impossible," there is also the need to reform the culture. Perry's comments about professional development suggest that developing individual pedagogical content knowledge will not be enough to ensure the teaching of historical thinking. Knowledge of the concepts of the discipline and how to teach them are necessary conditions for teaching historical thinking, but implementing a deep and broad change in pedagogy will require addressing teachers' predominant value systems and cultural expectations.[40] There has been progress: bottom-up changes through teacher-led workshops and conferences[41] are now being complemented by top-down curriculum changes. Eight of the provinces and territories have recently revised their curricula to include at least some outcomes and teaching suggestions on historical thinking. Quebec has developed progressive levels of assessment for historical inquiries.[42] At the time of writing, the Benchmarks project is organizing its third meeting of ministry representatives and publishers to plan further initiatives. These are good beginnings, but whether they will be enough to turn the victory gardens of excellence into widespread practice is as yet unclear.

## NOTES

1 Kurt Lewin, "The Research Center for Group Dynamics at Massachusetts Institute of Technology," *Sociometry* 8 (1945): 126-35.
2 "Dr. Lee Shulman," 2008, http://www.leeshulman.net.
3 Peter John, "The Professional Craft Knowledge of Teachers," *Teaching History* 64 (1991): 8-12.
4 Lee Shulman, "Autonomy and Obligations: The Remote Control of Teaching," in *Handbook of Teaching and Policy*, ed. Lee Shulman and Gary Sykes (New York: Longman, 1983), 497.

5. Michael Fullan, *The New Meaning of Educational Change* (New York: Teachers College Press, 2007).
6. Ernest House, *The Politics of Educational Innovation* (Berkeley: Sage Publications, 1974), 73.
7. Peter Marris, *Loss and Change* (New York: Anchor/Doubleday, 1975), in Fullan, *The New Meaning of Educational Change*, 31.
8. Peter Seixas, *Draft Benchmarks Framework* (Vancouver: Centre for the Study of Historical Consciousness, University of British Columbia, 2006).
9. Donald Schön, *Beyond the Stable State* (New York: Norton, 1971), 12.
10. Geoff Lyon, "Is It Time to Forget Remembrance?" *Teaching History* 128 (2007): 45.
11. Ibid., 44-51.
12. Jörn Rüsen, "Historical Consciousness: Narrative Structure, Moral Functions, and Ontogenetic Development," in *Theorizing Historical Consciousness*, ed. Peter Seixas (Toronto: University of Toronto Press, 2004), 63-85.
13. Desmond Morton, *Understanding Canadian Defence* (Toronto: Penguin Canada, 2003), 49.
14. Daniel Frances, *National Dreams: Myth, Memory, and Canadian History* (Vancouver: Arsenal Pulp Press, 1997), 126.
15. Fiona MacKellar, "Editing Traces of the Past to Support Historical Thinking," master's thesis, Simon Fraser University, 2009.
16. Ibid., 180.
17. Ibid., 101.
18. Ibid., 195.
19. Ibid., 106.
20. Ibid., 117.
21. Carla Peck and Peter Seixas, "Benchmarks of Historical Thinking: First Steps," *Canadian Journal of Education* 31 (2008): 1018.
22. Catherine Saouter, "Filmmaking and the Great War: What to Film and How to Present It?" and Michael R. McNorgan and John Marteinson, "Some General Comments on Great War-Era Films," in *Images of a Forgotten War*, National Film Board, n.d., http://www3.nfb.ca.
23. MacKellar, "Editing Traces of the Past," iii.
24. I have taken the metaphor of victory gardens from David Perkins, *Smart Schools* (New York: Free Press, 1992), 183.
25. Jan Haskings-Winner, e-mail correspondence with author, 17 November 2008. Note that a jigsaw is a cooperative activity in which a student team divides the material that needs to be mastered into sections. Students study their part and then teach it to the others in the group. As Haskings-Winner uses it, there is an additional step: students meet in a "home group" to divide up the material, then meet with an "expert group" comprised of those who have the same content as they do to study together. Once they have mastered the material, they return to their home group to teach it.
26. Christine Counsell, *History and Literacy in Y7: Building the Lesson around the Text* (London: Hodder Murray, 2004), 79.
27. Robin Phillips, "Historical Significance: 'The Forgotten Key Element'?" *Teaching History* 106 (2002): 16.

28 Kim Cooke, e-mail correspondence with author, 7 January 2009.
29 Graeme Stacey, e-mail correspondence with author, 6 December 2008.
30 Lindsay Gibson, e-mail correspondence with author, 6 December 2008.
31 Chas Desjarlais, interview by author, Vancouver, 25 November 2008.
32 Mark Perry, "What Is the Shape and Place of Historical Thinking in High Schools?" paper presented at the Sixth Biennial Conference on the Teaching and Learning of History, Quebec City, 24-26 October 2008.
33 As cited in Peck and Seixas, "Benchmarks of Historical Thinking," 1025.
34 Gibson, e-mail correspondence.
35 Perry, "What Is the Shape and Place."
36 Joseph Onosko, "Barriers to the Promotion of Higher-Order Thinking in Social Studies," *Theory and Research in Social Education* 28 (1991): 347-51; Keith C. Barton and Linda S. Levstik, *Teaching History for the Common Good* (Mahwah: Lawrence Erlbaum, 2004), 252-58.
37 Christine Counsell, "Looking through a Josephine-Butler-Shaped Window: Focusing Pupils' Thinking on Historical Significance," *Teaching History* 114 (2004): 130; and Phillips, "Historical Significance," 14-19.
38 At least five publishers in English Canada – Pearson, McGraw-Hill Ryerson, Thomson Duval, Oxford University Press, and Emond Montgomery – have produced textbooks that have featured Benchmarks concepts. The Critical Thinking Consortium has produced three teaching guides featuring historical thinking concepts, which are distributed by McGraw-Hill.
39 As cited in Stéphane Lévesque, *Thinking Historically: Educating Students for the Twenty-First Century* (Toronto: University of Toronto Press, 2008), 130.
40 Barton and Levstik, *Teaching History for the Common Good*.
41 In addition to the Benchmarks working groups, in my province, British Columbia, the provincial social studies teachers' association has featured historical thinking as a theme in two of its recent annual conferences.
42 Quebec Ministry of Education, *History and Citizenship Education* (2008): 56.

# 10

## The Shape of Historical Thinking in a Canadian History Survey Course in University

### GERALD FRIESEN

Is there a gap between history as it is taught in the schools and history as discussed in university? What is "the shape of historical thinking" in the university survey course on Canadian history? To address these questions, I begin with the comments of two experienced professors on teaching introductory university classes. I then turn to the "historical thinking" movement that is developing in today's secondary schools, using the work of Ken Osborne and Peter Seixas as a guide. Finally, I sketch the reasoning behind my own introductory Canadian history class. This chapter represents an attempt to reflect on issues that one addresses in practice every day of a teaching career but that, at least in my case, do not often become the subjects of extended scrutiny.

### Contemplating University Survey Courses

Two successful teachers of university survey courses, Erich Vogt and Robert Young, have recently published their reflections on long careers in the classroom. Vogt is a co-founder of TRIUMF, Canada's national laboratory for particle and nuclear physics, as well as a lobbyist for the so-called KAON Factory and a legendary teacher of first-year physics at the University of British Columbia. In a recent issue of a physics journal, in describing the joys of those introductory physics classes, he writes: "The students enter the university with great expectations, they are not jaded and their sense of wonder is largely intact, they respond to good teaching, and their learning ability appears to be at a maximum ... In first year physics there are endless opportunities to excite wonder and to make the students' eyes light up." Vogt's enthusiasm matches that of his students and, one suspects, kindles an infectious delight in the classroom. Understanding the pleasure he finds in learning and teaching is a first step in identifying the atmosphere we are seeking to establish in classes.

Apart from joy and wonder, what did Vogt hope to communicate? His brief list would be recognizable to any teacher because it includes such items as "knowledge of the physics content" and "a challenge to the intellect." But in his description of course objectives, Vogt adds some other useful phrases. He explains that he wished "to develop the students' analytical skills," "to describe how science works," and to demonstrate "how effective mathematics is for this purpose."[1] Each of these phrases takes us deeper into a disciplinary approach to knowledge; each seems entirely plausible; each seems achievable at any number of levels from the first grade in elementary school to the introductory class in university; and each helps us articulate what we all hope to do in our classrooms. These phrases represent what Vogt means by "content" and provoke us to think about comparable language for describing our history courses.

Robert Young, a winner of the CASE Canadian Professor of the Year designation, taught European history at the University of Winnipeg for forty years. In his last year, he published a long essay on classroom practice intended for the beginning professor and the beginning student. Young emphasizes the differences between secondary school and university, arguing that age and maturity distinguish the two levels of student while the demands of their jobs distinguish the two levels of instructor. He notes that university professors have little formal training as teachers, which puts a greater burden on the students themselves to generate intellectual interest and to take responsibility for their own development; and that professors have less contact with individual students and their families than do their high school counterparts, in part because, *as professors,* they dedicate more time to their research programs. These are sensible observations, complements rather than contrasts to Vogt's discussion, and realistic in their thesis that university is not a "mere extension of an education system which began at nursery school."[2] The university class may have similar goals and similar outward appearances, but its denizens on both sides of the lectern have to adjust their aims and expectations to the different demands of an undergraduate program.

On the matter of course content, Young accepts the principles enunciated by Vogt while adding one important theme. In introductory courses such as his own History of Western Civilization, he writes, the instructor has "three principal functions: Skill Enhancement, Character Development, and Content Provision." The skills include listening, writing, reading, and thinking. Content provision embraces "the transmission of a body of data, at a level appropriate to the given audience." The juxtaposition of "body of data" and "appropriate level" presents concerns that I will address later but they do suggest that, as Vogt was saying, knowledge and conceptualization travel together.

Character, which Young agrees is an old-fashioned, angular label, receives by far the largest share of his attention. Another writer might prefer to choose another term such as work habits or deportment; but whatever the label, the notion is intended to designate "the development of discerning and responsible citizens." Young is suggesting that teachers must convey

> the importance of work, effort, application ... we should identify whatever is listless, cheap, or fraudulent and hold the student accountable for the quality of his or her work. It means that we should insist on them learning the difference between reason and excuse, understanding that making concessions to them as individuals could be unfair to others, accepting that their work is improvable, with effort, and acknowledging that criticism is meant to help not belittle. It means, as well, that we do our part to promote the development of social skills and social maturity – by means of our expectations in the classroom, and by our own behaviour outside of it. And above all else, it means that we inculcate a respect for learning and, with it, a lifetime of openness to ideas. Here is the intersection where 'ivory tower' meets the 'real world,' because what we, as teachers, expect is precisely what their community in general, and their future employers in particular, will also expect."[3]

Like Vogt, Young is concerned about skills and the provision of content. To Vogt's discussion of undergraduate instruction, which emphasized excitement and wonder, he adds a concern for teachers' influence over students' behaviour and outlook.

Vogt and Young have outlined the central concerns of every teacher at every level, including history teachers in secondary schools and universities. These concerns include the communication of pleasure and content as well as the development of skills and good work habits. Such goals require restating simply because they are so important.

## Osborne, Seixas, and "Historical Thinking"

The leaders of the Historical Thinking Movement, if such a label can be applied to this diverse school, believe that the discipline of history employs distinctive approaches that enable us, as students and citizens, to develop especially fruitful understandings of the world.[4] Scholars such as Sam Wineburg and Ruth Sandwell would not ignore the general principles discussed by Vogt and Young, but they prefer to focus on the challenges posed by what they view as an influential mode of thought, the study of history. Two commentators on these themes in Canadian scholarly circles, Ken Osborne and Peter Seixas, can be taken as illustrative of the broader movement.

The general meditations on teaching discussed above do not consider disciplinary specialties at any length. Vogt employs several deceptively simple phrases to sketch his objectives, suggesting that he aims "to describe how science works" and to demonstrate "how effective mathematics is for this purpose." Robert Young hopes to "maximize the possibility of interpretation ... and to constrain it – especially at the undergraduate level."[5] These thoughts raise intriguing questions but do not provide elaborate answers. Because they are so general, they illustrate precisely why scholars like Osborne and Seixas are seeking sharper analyses of disciplinary modes of thought. Their goal is to define more clearly, and to communicate to teachers more effectively, a precise approach to social comprehension through the study of history.

We have all heard the time-honoured criticism that school history classes are boring. A recent American survey concluded that most students "had little good to say about the actual classroom experience of studying history ... [Said one respondent]: 'It was just a giant data dump.'"[6] This is mainly because, as Ken Osborne has explained, school history lessons used to be "a dry recitation of dates and facts." To which Osborne responds that school history classes should not simply provide a list of items to be memorized. In the bad old days, he writes, good teachers used to rely on human interest stories and "the unusual" – John A. Macdonald's drinking, Mackenzie King's seances – to arouse students' interest and counteract "the bitter medicine of names and dates." He argues that such stories, which could be turned to good use by a thoughtful teacher, were too often merely desperate expedients.[7]

Together with many of his colleagues who are attempting to inject energy and purpose into history in schools, Osborne believes that today's teachers are ready to move beyond the memory-work approach and to tackle more ambitious goals: "We now realize that the best way to make history interesting is to help students see the past through the eyes of the people who lived it, facing problems to which they did not have an answer and whose results they could not foretell ... We need to teach history looking forward into an unknown future, not backwards looking to a past that textbooks portray as over and done with." One might describe this as the primary source-based approach to historical issues. It is far from a new idea but it is a sound one.

Osborne's concern has also been with the "big ideas" that tie historical details together. Each teaching unit should be seen as related to others, he says. The teacher's role is to ensure that students develop a sense of this context and appreciate the shape of forests as well as details about trees. And then, in the most favourable circumstances, a teacher could show students how these big ideas were themselves mere human constructions imposed on events in order to clarify their meaning. I take Osborne's work to be one version of the Historical Thinking agenda. As Osborne himself puts it: "learning to think historically is a crucial part of learning history."

Like all recent promoters of historical thinking, Osborne rejects the suggestion made by Piaget and his followers that adolescent students cannot understand history. Instead, he believes with Sam Wineburg that school students can indeed cope with concepts that had formerly not been part of the teacher's toolkit: "We now have a much clearer idea than ever before ... of just how students at various ages understand history. Not what facts they know but how they handle concepts such as change and continuity, cause and effect, time and sequence, evidence and interpretation and others that are fundamental to understanding of history."[8]

If Osborne parts company with his colleagues in the Historical Thinking Movement, it is on the two preoccupations raised by Vogt: content and wonder. He approaches the "cultural literacy" movement with caution. He does believe that a certain amount of knowledge of the past is an important objective of history teaching, and, to that degree, he accepts E.D. Hirsch's insistence that students at least be exposed to – even if they do not master – basic aspects of national and international history. In a recent note, he said that "to read history is (to use what is now a cliché) to visit a foreign country and, like most foreign travel, it broadens the mind and calls into question what we might otherwise take for granted so that we come home seeing the world and home and ourselves a little differently."[9] This is a matter of content.

As for wonder, Osborne often quotes from the work of an eloquent English historian of an earlier day, G.M. Trevelyan: "The poetry of history lies in the quasi-miraculous fact that once, on this earth, once, on this familiar spot of ground, walked other men and women, as actual as we are today, thinking their own thoughts, swayed by their own passions, but now all gone, one generation vanishing into another, gone as utterly as we ourselves shall shortly be gone, like ghosts at cockcrow."[10] The repetition of the words "once" and "gone," in association with thoughts of a miracle, constitutes a rhetorical strategy that will be found in the lectures of the most persuasive teachers. By such repetition, simple enough as a literary device, Trevelyan convinces us to believe in wonderment and the working of miracles.

Readers of this volume will recognize that Osborne's language and concerns reflect the ambitions of many contributors to the Historical Thinking enterprise. Seixas and his colleagues have developed the Benchmarks of Historical Thinking Project as a response to criticisms of history teaching in Canada's schools. Their ambitious agenda promotes the teaching of six concepts: significance, continuity and change, cause and consequence, historical perspective (vs. present-mindedness), the moral dimension in historical judgments, and primary source-based analysis.[11] Each of these categories has a parallel in Osborne's list of historical concepts, and each has elicited volumes of commentary and historiographical debate for more than a century. These categories raise questions and invoke structures within which discussions of the past can be organized, but they do not provide answers. Seixas and Osborne, along with their colleagues, are asking Canada's teachers of history to engage meaningfully with such intellectual challenges and to communicate this engagement to their students.

Seen from the perspective of a university history department, the reforms being advocated for elementary and secondary schools are in line with the teaching practices and intellectual preoccupations evident in university classes. For example, consider the category of "historical significance." These two innocent words have appeared on university history tests for decades, perhaps the entire previous century, often as part of a short question intended to establish the range of a student's reading and the depth of his or her comprehension. "Identify and discuss the historical significance of ..." the rubric asks, and a list of choices follows: Pierre Berton, one of the subjects in a lecture, might be one. The answer might establish that the journalist's career took place mainly in the second half of the twentieth century and that it illustrated such themes as the development of anglophone Canadian nationalism, the impact of the media on society, the emergence of celebrity as a social phenomenon, and perhaps changes in historical writing itself. This is no different from what appears in secondary school classes. A selected topic's currency, as well as the range of materials available for answers, will always depend on the teacher's own experience and outlook. The point here is that the rubric of "historical significance," in and of itself, is a common feature on a teacher's checklist of tasks and on a student's checklist of examination types.

One can discover a different lesson by considering the Benchmarks category of "cause and consequence." E.H. Carr, author of the influential *What Is History?* (1961), believed that identifying causes of historical change was the historian's main preoccupation. And it is true that a key question in the following decades was why particular events occurred. Historians asked why the Winnipeg General Strike took place when and where it did. And the North-West Uprising. And Confederation. And the Industrial Revolution. If this still seems a time-honoured and appropriate focus of historical research to some, there are many other historians who disagree. It is now argued that a shift in historians' perspectives in recent years has led to a revised historical agenda. David Cannadine, in *What Is History Now?* (2002), suggests that the past forty years have seen a "shift in interest from causes to meaning, from explanation to understanding." He concludes:

> Every generation, scholars have arisen proclaiming that they have found a new key which unlocks the essence of the past in a way that no previous historical approach has ever done. Our own generation is no exception to this rule – and it will probably be no exception to this fate. For these claims have never yet stood the test of time. Twenty years from now, scholars will probably be concerned with something very different, and they will look back with bemused amazement that our generation could believe so confidently that unravelling the "meaning" of the past was the historian's crucial and essential task.[12]

In other words, the basic approach of historians changes over time, and any attempt to crystallize the basic questions asked by them will probably be misleading within several decades. Such an observation will not surprise students of historiography or, indeed, of curriculum planning, but it does serve as a reminder that even "cause and consequence" is not a sacred articulation of a historical theme.

Another Benchmarks category is "the moral dimension of historical interpretations." Moral and ethical issues do lie behind many of the subjects addressed by historians. What constitutes a wise choice in fiscal policy? In deciding between peace and war? In dealing with a group of "strangers," be they of foreign or local origin, within a state? In distinguishing a terrorist from a freedom fighter? There is no single "right" answer. But the historian usually tries to understand the *context* of such decisions or events instead of judging them according to some disciplinary scale of values. If students then respond with questions about the moral and ethical implications of the choices, history teachers are free to reply. When they choose to do so, they speak as citizens, not as experts on morality and ethics. They might note, indeed, that there are disciplinary specialists who make these matters their special subject. But all teachers, whether in university or in the schools, must rely on their own resources in raising and responding to such questions.

The Benchmarks rubrics encapsulate central aspects of professional historians' preoccupations. But – always the *but* – these concerns rest on difficult and eternally changing concepts. Can the Historical Thinking project communicate effectively to thousands of teachers – and through them to tens of thousands of students – the uncertain, contingent, and provisional nature of history's answers? Will it lead teachers to believe they possess ready-made tools with which to solve such puzzles? I have reservations. Given such caveats, I have no doubt that teachers will respond positively to the challenges of history study just as university historians do. And the Benchmarks approach itself does crystallize some of today's most important approaches to historical work.

## A Canadian History Survey Course
My first-year course is supposed to serve as an introduction both to history as a discipline and to Canada as a nation-state. Unlike Robert Young, I'm not sure that, in practice or goals, I differ substantially from teachers in the schools. The course consists of reading assignments, essay writing, examinations, and lectures. Do schoolteachers employ the same tools? I expect they do. Is the historical thinking expected of my students different from that expected in secondary schools? I will leave it to teachers to decide, but I do hope that my students' expressions of their historical findings show an

increase in subtlety, a greater awareness of the range of motivations of historical actors, and a greater willingness to consider a wider range of arguments than had been the case in their previous year's work. I doubt that this differs much from the aspirations of teachers at other levels of the educational system.

Consider first the essays: I assign a single book-length memoir, autobiography, or biography as the topic of a first essay with the expectation that, in reading it, students will situate themselves in the past; accompany the central actor along a path not entirely unlike their own; and reflect on an individual's historical context, on how choices were made, and what the implications of those choices were. In the early Canada course, the source might be La Vérendrye's letters, Elizabeth Goudie's autobiography, John Tanner's memoir, or Mary Weekes's *The Last Buffalo Hunter*. In the post-1867 course, the source might be Robert MacNeil's *Wordstruck*, Charles Ritchie's diaries, John English on the young Trudeau, and, next year, perhaps Brian McKillop on the young Berton. In a second essay, which addresses broader social themes, the students employ both primary documents and secondary sources. The object is to ensure a close reading of a few selected documents and to enable students to establish an appropriate context for the documents with the help of a few works drawn from contemporary historical writing.[13] Biography, historical context, primary and secondary sources – it will sound familiar.

Second, the lectures: In each seventy-five-minute lecture in the first-year class, I employ a video of eight to ten minutes, often a chapter of CBC's *Canada: A People's History*. My aim is to introduce a range of sites and artifacts and costumes as well as personalities. The images supplement students' impressions of the past and (one hopes) ensure that the lecture itself will not be delivered in a complete vacuum. The video also impresses on students – few of whom have seen many products of the national film industry – that Canadian subjects are worthy of big-budget cultural production, given that the implied contrast is always with American television and Hollywood. Most of the students appreciate this use of film. I have lost count of the number who have declared in course evaluations that they are "visual learners." They seem to find it much easier to deal with the lectures and printed materials having had these injections of colour, music, and action.

Beyond the undeniable effectiveness of big-budget scene setting (one million dollars per hour represents higher production values than my speaking style can compete with), the film offers another version of primary and secondary sources. Riel stands in the dock, speaking the words recorded during his 1885 trial. Agnes Macdonald "speaks" the words she wrote to a correspondent upon receiving the news of Thomas D'Arcy McGee's assassination. In each case, actors communicate emotions with the authority that comes from the original text as well as from their command of the dramatic arts. Such short set pieces, often less than a minute in length, teach students about the drama contained in the documents from which historians work. And behind the visuals the narrator – "God's secretary," as Mark Starowicz described Maggie Huculak's role – reads the usual narrative, a secondary source always worthy of debate, as much for its omissions as for its content.

What the students make of these excerpts can be discovered by a brief quiz. One such quiz involves the use of this fine critique by Robert Fulford:

> The programs use quotes from historical figures effectively, but the words written at the CBC are less impressive. The tone is too solemn and portentous, as if all those people lived through four centuries or so without once cracking a joke; few even smile. The writers of the narration (read by Maggie Huculak) are helpless when tempted by a cliché. We hear at one point that "the sun is setting on the fur trader's West." Rebellion is brewing, the die is cast, cholera spreads like wildfire, something or other "will change the face of the continent" and a certain letter "will change the course of history." The words are always far inferior to the pictures. It's like having captions for Matisse written by Tom Clancy.
>
> But even raising such questions about the approach and the writing style of *Canada: A People's History* acknowledges how important it is. As one of the grandest events in the history of Canadian mass media, it deserves extensive discussion and detailed criticism. With this series the CBC has produced an amazing amount of first-class television for a moderate amount of money, and has done it by making every shot count. Once the directors win our confidence and pull us into their way of seeing, they use modest visual elements (a corner of a spike-fenced wooden fort, a pile of documents on a table) to illustrate affecting stories. A man on horseback, seen partially as he kills a buffalo, precisely suggests an environment and a historic moment. In one scene, a dozen lower torsos, with legs attached, rush across the screen, hands holding muskets. We don't see the tunics, we don't see the faces, we don't even see the ground they're running on, but we effortlessly fill in the picture.

It's hard to remember any television documentary that used imagery with more power, or more attention to telling historical detail: the tough little voyageurs stuffing themselves into those terrifyingly fragile canoes, a Red River homesteader prying a huge tree's roots from the ground, a lush pile of beaver skins shining like gold in the sun. All this takes place against a background depicted with exquisite skill. Has anyone since the Group of Seven paid such elaborate (and convincing) tribute to the Canadian landscape? From the first seven episodes you could put together a gorgeous montage of Great Canadian Sunsets, then do another of rapids and waterfalls.

As a view of the past, *Canada: A People's History* embodies the inevitably narrow biases of one period in time – our own. As TV documentary, it's superb, as good as we are ever likely to get. Given our indifferent treatment of the CBC, it's also probably better than we deserve.[14]

There are many angles from which to comment on Fulford's statement. The quiz question might read: "Evaluate Fulford's judgments about secondary narrative [or primary document, or visual elements, and/or the bias of our times] with reference to several episodes of *Canada: A People's History*." The purposes of such an exercise include reinforcing students' awareness of the distinction that must be drawn between a primary source and a judgment delivered by commentators removed from the event – secondary sources – and showing them how critical one might be of the messages written by Mark Starowicz and his film producers.

The lecture following the video must build on the place, time, and characters occupying the screen. But it should also establish a context for a third component of the course – the students' reading. This context develops in the student's mind with the elaboration of a series of generalizations about human action and social interaction. Like any teacher, I am trying to explain what Ken Osborne labelled a "big idea." These ideas often have a contemporary urgency: the meaning of gender, democracy, the state, the body. But they are also rooted in realities that have endured for centuries: the Aboriginal experience in northern North America, the French and British experiences, the experience of ethnicity among minority newcomers. Big ideas also surround specific institutions that require careful dissection: federalism, the Crown, political parties, unions, and so on.

The lectures and readings also constitute an introduction to advanced language: the big ideas that are to be explained in class include classic generalizations in the humanities and social sciences such as Innis's synthesis on staples and transportation routes, Marx's on class, and Turner's on the frontier. Though opinions differ on how much instruction in the relatively arcane field of Canadian historiography is too much, I choose to tell my introductory class in Canadian history about some of the changes in historical writing during the twentieth century, including the differences between French- and English-language approaches; and the shift in English-language historians' focus from responsible government as a central theme in the 1920s to economic forces in the 1930s to biography in the 1950s to social history in the 1970s to today's social constructivism and postcolonialism. UBC's Vogt writes that his physics class canvasses how science works and why mathematics is effective for depicting its operations. In the introductory class in Canadian history, I, too, attempt to explain how the discipline works. Its "big ideas," including concepts and themes and events, constitute the history teacher's "language." They express the manner in which the practitioners of the discipline have been able to grasp the past and communicate its meaning to their colleagues. This language is our equivalent of Vogt's math.

Each discipline employs a specialized vocabulary and set of principles. How specialized it is becomes evident when we listen to individuals who choose not to rely on such approaches. Pierre Berton, for example, articulated the meaning of the Canadian past with hardly any reference to scholarly writing. Nevertheless, he identified many of the same concerns and incidents in the past as professional historians do, for the obvious reason that such events and characters represent important aspects of the community's story. Professionals, who have been refining their language in concert with colleagues around the world, find such popular histories frustrating when the popular work's use of idiosyncratic terms or reasoning does not reflect the latest academic usage. As university teachers, we try to advance the conversation, to standardize the terms, to establish particular measures of change, and to follow strict rules for uses of and references to sources. These same conventions we communicate to our students. Where Vogt tries to describe how science works, we claim to be describing how history works.[15]

How do schoolteachers fit into this story of professional history and the introductory survey course? Like teachers at every level and in every discipline, they try to communicate enthusiasm and interest. If the advocates of "historical thinking" prevail, schoolteachers will focus more and more on the concepts employed in university classes as a means of disciplining their students' inquiry. If my introductory survey of Canadian history has any lesson to offer, it is that in questions, instructional tactics, and goals, primary and secondary school courses need differ very little from their university counterparts. Using primary sources, discussing historical context and historical significance, identifying decisive moments of change, debating evidence, uncovering uncertainty about meaning, considering morality and ethical choices will all endure. But so, too, will the teacher's obligation to inspire a sense of wonder.

## NOTES

I would like to thank Penney Clark for the invitation to consider these issues and three generous readers, Ken Osborne, Robert Young, and Peter Seixas, for their very helpful comments on this chapter.

1 Jess H. Brewer, "Erich H. Vogt: Four Decades of First Year Physics," in *UBC Trek* (Spring 2008): 41, quoting Vogt, "The Special Joy of Teaching First Year Physics" *American Journal of Physics* 75 (2007): 581.
2 Robert J. Young, *Forty Years Professing: Tips and Thoughts for Undergrads and Teachers* (Winnipeg: Yaleave Books, 2006), 26. The CASE Canadian Professor of the Year designation is awarded by the Canadian Council for the Advancement of Education, an arm of the Council for the Advancement and Support of Education (Washington).
3 Young, *Forty Years Professing*, 13, 16-17. Young's list occurs frequently in discussions of education. He notes that Tema Frank, a human resource officer in a Canadian bank, prepared a similar statement on "What Do Employers Want" for the journal *University Affairs*, and included in it initiative, perseverance, leadership, and time management.
4 Ruth Sandwell, ed., *To The Past: History Education, Public Memory, and Citizenship in Canada* (Toronto: University of Toronto Press, 2006); Sam Wineburg, *Historical Thinking and Other Unnatural Acts: Charting the Future of Teaching the Past* (Philadelphia: Temple University Press, 2001); Peter Stearns, Peter Seixas, and Sam Wineburg, eds., *Knowing, Teaching and Learning History: National and International Perspectives* (New York: New York University Press, 2000).
5 Brewer, "Erich H. Vogt"; Young, *Forty Years Professing*.
6 Roy Rosenzweig and David Thelen, *The Presence of the Past: Popular Uses of History in American Life* (New York: Columbia University Press, 1998), 111-12.
7 Margaret Conrad, Jocelyn Letourneau, and David Northrup, "Canadians and Their Pasts: An Exploration in Historical Consciousness," *Public Historian* 31, 1 (February 2009): 15-34; Ken Osborne, "History Is Back," *Winnipeg Free Press*, 28 September 2008, B4.
8 Osborne, "History Is Back."
9 E.D. Hirsch Jr., *Cultural Literacy: What Every American Needs to Know* (New York: Vintage, 1988); Osborne to Friesen, 8 January 2009 (letter in my possession).
10 G.M. Trevelyan, "Autobiography of an Historian," in *An Autobiography and Other Essays* (London: Longmans, Green, 1949).

11 Peter Seixas, "Benchmarks of Historical Thinking: A Framework for Assessment in Canada," *Manitoba Social Science Teachers Association Bulletin* 33, 3 (February 2007): 6-10; "'Scaling Up' the Benchmarks of Historical Thinking: A Report on the Vancouver Meetings, 14-15 February 2008," University of British Columbia Centre for the Study of Historical Consciousness, Vancouver, Appendix II.
12 David Cannadine, *What Is History Now?* (Basingstoke: Palgrave Macmillan, 2002), x, xii.
13 This assignment is linked to a library tour and a survey of collections of scholarly articles on the Web.
14 Robert Fulford, "Robert Fulford's Column about *Canada: A People's History* on CBC-TV," *National Post*, 16 January 2001, http://www.robertfulford.com/CanadaHistory.html.
15 An impressive illustration of the popular/academic history divide is offered by Jill Lepore in "Plymouth Rocked: Of Pilgrims, Puritans, and Professors," *The New Yorker*, 24 April 2006, http://www.newyorker.com. Also David Pace, "The Amateur in the Operating Room: History and the Scholarship of Teaching and Learning," *American Historical Review* 109, 4 (October 2004): 1171-91, http://www.historycooperative.org/ahrindex.html. I would like to thank Peter Seixas for these references.

# 11

## History Is a Verb
## Teaching Historical Practice to Teacher Education Students

RUTH SANDWELL

In the fall of 2002, I read an article in the collection *Knowing, Teaching, and Learning History* that particularly intrigued me. The chapter "A Catwalk across the Great Divide: Redesigning the History Teaching Methods Course" by G. Williamson McDiarmid and Peter Vinten-Johansen had a simple premise: for a variety of professional, cultural, disciplinary, institutional, and historical reasons, historians and history educators – even those working inside the same institution – are separated by a "great divide":

> History faculty typically regard history education courses with mild contempt ... Historians regard educationists not merely as academic *arrivists* but as intellectual mountebanks, purveying watery nostrums and commonsense as knowledge. For their part, educationists often view historians as pedantic fussbudgets, concerned more about their next book than their students. Left to thrash about in the divide between these two camps are those who command the least experience and power and the fewest resources in the teacher education enterprise – prospective history teachers.[1]

The authors point out that "as the two camps at best ignore and at worst snipe at each other, prospective teachers are usually left on their own to make connections between the substance of historical studies, and how best to help others to learn this substance."[2] The article goes on to describe how the authors – a historian and a history educator – developed an experimental and innovative course for student history teachers, designed to bring the substance and the teaching of history together to create what the authors agree was an important, albeit somewhat fragile, catwalk across that great divide.

I was intrigued by the article because it spoke so directly to the frustration (and occasional exhilaration) that both my students and I were experiencing as I was building my own "catwalk across the great divide" in the History Teaching Methods course that I was then teaching in the Initial Teacher Education Program at OISE/University of Toronto. Like the first attempt by McDiarmid and Vinten-Johansen, my course was not a resounding success.[3] As a trained historian teaching student teachers in a faculty of education for the first time, I had already been made acutely aware of the "great divide" between what I did as a historian – engaging in an active, ongoing, and reciprocal dialogue, usually in the form of print media, with other interested people about evidence left behind from the past – and what student teachers felt they needed to know as high school history teachers – how to maintain discipline in the classroom while trying to transmit to a typically bored and unresponsive audience the enormous number of discrete content-and-skills items mandated for history teachers by their provincial curriculum documents.[4]

McDiarmid and Vinten-Johansen's article was comforting in its clear articulation of the myriad factors (in addition to my inexperience as a teacher new to history education) that brought the work of historians into conflict with the work of history teachers and educators. They explained to me what I was experiencing: just why it is so difficult for history educators to transfer a sense of historical thinking, knowing, and learning in an appropriate, *usable* way to students in a teacher education program. Particularly important stumbling blocks, they argued, were the privileging of practice over disciplinary knowledge in university teacher education programs and the privileging of research over teaching in university history departments; both these factors serve to limit fruitful dialogue between historians and history educators. "A Catwalk across the Great Divide" not only comforted me during my first teacher education experience but also helped me clarify and articulate some of the institutional, structural, and cultural problems affecting history education – problems that have, in the Canadian context, provided a focus for the research and network building I have done since then as a history educator.[5]

This article provides a brief history of my attempt to construct a catwalk that could bring – albeit in a small and elective way – what I believe to be some of the key aspects of historical thinking to bear on the teaching of student teachers and, in turn, their teaching of secondary school students in history classes. This is not a study or research project on teaching; instead, like McDiarmid and Vinten-Johansen's original article, it seeks to question and reinvent as well as reassure. This chapter is rooted in the belief that change in history education can most easily emerge through grassroots movements, such as one elective course in a crowded teacher education curriculum, rather than through top-down, curriculum-mandated directives. As a microhistory, this chapter aims to stimulate reflection on the relationship between small practices and big ideas.

## The Background to "History Is a Verb"

From the outset, my task was easier than that of McDiarmid and Vinten-Johansen, for instead of designing the compulsory history methods course for everyone going on to teach history and social studies in the intermediate (seven and eight) and secondary (nine to twelve) grades as one of their two teachable subjects, I had the luxury of designing a course that students could choose to take as their only elective in the nine-month teacher education program. This decision to teach the elective rather than the compulsory course was prompted by the kinds of professional issues that McDiarmid and Vinten-Johansen describe: as a tenure track professor, I could not afford the time away from my research that a substantial reworking of the compulsory course would have demanded.[6] On the positive side, because students could select only one elective from a number of choices, I was pretty much ensured a group of dedicated, interested, and knowledgeable history students, and this proved to be the case. Freed from the obligation to teach all of the aspects of history education that I could squeeze into eighteen weeks of classes, I had the opportunity and the challenge in this elective course of narrowing my focus to concentrate on elements of history education that I thought were most important, that I was most qualified to teach, and that I could teach in the nine four-hour classes that comprised the course. I quickly decided to focus on teaching history using primary documents.

Let me provide a little more background to this decision. From the time I taught my first undergraduate history class, I had been intrigued, shocked, and dismayed at another Great Divide: between what I did as a practising historian – engage in an active and vibrant dialogue about the past with other historians – and what I was expected to do as a university undergraduate teacher – deliver lectures that provided a seamless, authorless account of What Really Happened that students would dutifully digest and regurgitate on command.[7] As a historian, I was actively engaged in creating history as a process of knowing; as a teacher, I dispensed history as a product to be passively consumed. As Shirley Engle put it:

> For reasons I have never fully understood, most history professors completely change their colors once they step out of their role as researcher scholars and take on the mantle of "herr" professor. As scholars they hold truth in great tenuousness; they are not all of one mind; their disciplines are hotbeds of controversy; they are forever correcting one another's errors. But once they have laid aside their research eyeshades and donned their teaching robes, they become authorities whose mission is considered to be the transmission of their superior knowledge to students.[8]

I believed that students' lack of engagement with sources of historical evidence and with broader discussions of how to interpret that evidence constituted a significant reduction in, or even an erasure of, what it means to *do* history. I came to believe that without knowledge of how to *do* history, it is practically impossible to think historically and that without the ability to think historically, it is practically impossible to understand what history is about, or indeed, why anyone should care about it.

As I later discovered, Peter Lee, Rosalyn Ashby, and Peter Seixas were already articulating, and in much clearer terms, just what exactly it means to think historically.[9] McDiarmid and Vinten-Johansen had discovered early on that their history majors "had little understanding of how historical accounts are written" and that, as a result, "few demonstrated the ability to develop a thesis and substantiate its development with appropriate evidence."[10] This lack of engagement with the process of constructing historical knowledge, and history's passive transmission and consumption as a product, not only missed the point of what historical thinking *is*, but also was probably a key factor in history classes often being labelled as boring. In trying to understand the cause of and work toward a solution to these problems, I began to include the study of primary documents in my undergraduate history teaching as at least a partial solution to the most significant problem facing my students: they did not understand the tentative, contingent, and above all *constructed* nature of historical explanations.[11]

Around the same time that I was teaching undergraduate history students, I began to work with other graduate students on an online educational project, *The Great Unsolved Mysteries in Canadian History*, which provided secondary and undergraduate students with real-life mysteries from Canada's past as well as the archival evidence needed to solve them. The same sites provided a model and a guide for teaching history as a process of reasoned, disciplined, lively, and meaningful engagement with primary documents.[12] When I moved from a history department to a history program in a faculty of education, I brought with me the firm belief that primary documents are important for the teaching of history, for they help teach the processes involved in historical thinking.

When I turned to reading the research in history education, I quickly discovered that I was not alone in noticing the disjuncture between historians and history teachers and in suggesting that primary documents be used to remedy this perceived problem. In 1991, Sam Wineburg, an American educational psychologist, had published an important study documenting the profound differences between what historians do and what students do when they think historically.[13] Shortly afterwards, Peter Seixas was discussing the importance of communities of inquiry for history education and, with English history education researcher Peter Lee, refining just what it means to think historically.[14] As Ken Osborne has documented, teaching history using primary documents is far from being a new idea: it has popped up in Canada and in other countries with some regularity for more than a century.[15] By the time I began thinking about a course in teaching history using primary documents, it had already been established as a major industry in educational circles. Extensive classroom materials were available, and a growing body of research had already emerged on theories and practices relating to the use of primary documents in classrooms. Indeed, by 2005 the use of primary documents was already being challenged as the orthodoxy in history and social studies education.[16]

There are some well-aired reasons that primary documents have been used so extensively to teach history and social studies in the past decade. Primary sources provide a broader range of learning materials – photographs, oral histories, and archaeological artifacts as well as written documentary sources. This makes possible more and different kinds of learning activities than are provided by traditional textbooks; it also appeals to "multiple intelligences" theories of effective learning. Primary documents also involve active learning or learning that effectively engages students in the generation of their own knowledge. Even more significant, perhaps, is the immediate connection with the past that students often seem to find when they use primary documents, particularly those personal sources created by people who seem to be just like them. For many students and teachers, primary sources personalize history in a way that brings the past to light. This helps explain why professionals and amateurs had worked to bring reproductions of key historical documents into classrooms. In Canada, generations of teachers and students spoke fondly of the "Jackdaws" that provided a miscellany of documents, from photographs to newspaper reports to diaries, about a particular theme, topic, or issue.[17]

If the popularity of primary sources for teaching history motivated teachers to use them in classrooms, by the late 1990s, the very practical problem of how to obtain a variety of primary documents for use in classrooms, and at a low enough cost, was being solved. Online sources were by then providing access to documents in a way, and on a scale, hitherto unimaginable. Before the 1990s, published collections of primary documents had been created, but they tended to be limited to the broad and general topics that accommodated publishers' needs for profitable print runs; the publication of extensive primary documents was not well suited to a small country like Canada, much less to the needs of even smaller provincially developed curricula. And it was difficult for individual teachers to find primary documents in archives, even if they had the time to travel to an archive or were equipped with the expertise to find and evaluate those documents. For there had traditionally been a tension between the two aspects of an archivist's role – to preserve original historical documents for posterity, and to make them accessible to those wanting to use them to understand the past. Making documents accessible on the Web removed this tension. The Web has made it possible to read or use primary documents without damaging them; it has also made it possible for anyone with a computer to access these documents across space and time.

The computer has made historical research easier and therefore more accessible in other ways as well. Before computers made keyword searches workable, a researcher wanting to explore, for example, the history of childhood had to rely on the expertise of archivists in each archive to explore the multitude of records from diverse sources that mentioned or related to children and childhood. Hundreds of finding aids could provide some hints, but if the archivist had not catalogued and indexed these, or did not personally know what they contained, researchers would probably not know to explore them. Searching for relevant documents typically took time and dedication that only professional historians or studious amateurs with a lot of time on their hands could afford. Thanks to the painstaking work of archivists, supported by substantial government grants, it is now possible to search by subject and keyword and to see (and even hear) reproductions of millions of historical sources, including photographs, oral histories, maps, films, newspapers, and public and private documents.

Unfortunately, as the use of primary documents in history classrooms mushroomed with pedagogical sanctions and increased variety and ease of access, so did problems associated with their use. Research has confirmed that simply providing students with access and opportunities to work with primary documents is not enough to promote their effective use.[18] There is the problem of definition: students are typically unclear about just what a primary document *is*. Especially at the elementary and secondary levels, students not only need assistance in finding out what a primary document is, but also typically need considerable help finding primary documents relevant to the questions they want answered. Without considerable guidance, students experience the vast number and variety of primary sources available on the Web on any given topic as simply overwhelming and confusing. They also need help using these documents as pieces of evidence as they build convincing and meaningful historical arguments.

Research has revealed more problems in the use of primary documents in classrooms. Even when students are taught how to use primary sources to build the evidence-based arguments that comprise historical practice, they are often reluctant to do so. Facing the complicated, arduous, and time-consuming process of building knowledge through the careful evaluation of evidence, some students prefer to follow the time-honoured practice of simply providing the answer they think the teacher wants. Others use search engines to find the right answer; still others abandon the attempt altogether. Keith Barton reports that after teaching students how to critically examine historical documents, he discovered

> one remarkable and unexpected problem. After three days of this [critical enquiry] activity, the teacher pulled students together to discuss their conclusions ... Each student had an opinion, and they were eager to share. *But none of the opinions had any relationship to the evidence that they had just spent three days evaluating.* Students did not use the evidence to reach conclusions; they were just making up what they thought must have happened.[19]

In other words, even when students learn to participate in the process of *doing* history by using primary documents, they continue to understand history as a dead, inert, and generally inaccessible set of facts about What Really Happened. For students who believe that history is "someone else's" statement of the facts, their own careful analysis of primary documents is essentially irrelevant:

> Even when students understand the process of evidence-based critical enquiry, their attempts to apply critical analysis to history are thwarted by deeply held and often contradictory philosophical beliefs about the nature of historical knowledge. Students tend to seesaw back and forth between believing in absolute truth, with its suggestion that students are simply required to find the "right" answer provided by some authority, and complete relativism, in which any interpretation is as good as any other, and all are equally meaningless.[20]

From the beginning, therefore, I worked from the principle that teaching history using primary documents rests not simply on teaching skills and content in a different and more interesting way; it involves a different understanding of what history *is*.

## Designing the Course

Armed with my own professional justification for using primary documents to teach history education students, supported by a scholarly literature cautiously celebrating their use, with an abundance of teaching materials, and inspired by McDiarmid and Vinten-Johansen's innovative course, I set out to design and get approval for my new course, titled History Is a Verb.[21] The course was designed around the idea that the study of primary documents works on a variety of levels to teach history and historical thinking. Designing a course teaching student teachers how to use primary documents in their history teaching would involve a delicate balance among three key objectives: *re-educating* student teachers to see history as an active engagement with the past; *reassuring* them that they could use this approach with their own high school students within a provincial curriculum that seemed to oblige them to adopt a traditional content-and-skills approach in their classrooms; and, finally, *showing* them how to teach this kind of history, or history in this kind of way.

One of my key concerns as I developed the course was my growing realization – supported by McDiarmid and Vinten-Johansen's experience with their first experimental course – that delivering a new way of thinking about and doing history was not going to be enough to keep my pragmatic and anxious student teachers interested or engaged.[22] I would have to demonstrate from the beginning that the course was going to give them something that worked well in their high school classrooms, something concrete to take away with them, and the sooner the better. Student teachers are under considerable pressure in their professional programs, not only from heavy workloads but also from the anxiety flowing from the urgent, pressing, and seemingly impossible demands that are placed on them in their practice teaching, especially in the first days and weeks. Those teaching in teacher training programs ignore this pressure at their peril.

I decided to use students' anxiety about their performance in their high school classrooms as the engine driving the course. Instead of trying to convince my student teachers to adopt a new way of thinking about history and then explaining how to teach it, I decided to show them how to teach history using primary documents, supported by the conviction that this method would, if it succeeded, inevitably and necessarily change the way they and their students understood history. Limiting what I was able to do in this single course was the inevitable time pressure: I could not ask my students to complete an entire unit plan in nine weeks. So instead, putting (almost) all my eggs in one basket, I built the course around the requirement that my students create one really good lesson plan, one that would be evaluated and reworked on several occasions throughout the course and that would use primary documents to teach history effectively. This was their only substantial assignment. Students agreed to present their lessons in the last class and to post their individual lesson plans online at the end of the course for all to use; this would expand the usability of the lesson plans in their classrooms. This was an effective strategy for meeting their needs for classroom-usable materials. It remained for me to ensure that their single lesson plan met the criteria I was busy establishing for the most effective history teaching.

## The Course

Fundamental to my approach was the difficult realization that it has been impossible for me to ever simply tell students about the nature of history; it was only by engaging them in the process that they would learn to think differently and to think about history as process. This is the first and most important point of teaching history using primary documents: it shows rather than tells students that history is an interpretive act. Since all of my students possessed at least one degree (the program is a post-baccalaureate professional program), I also provided plenty of space for intellectual reflection on their practice. And, as I will describe in more detail below, I was able to draw on some excellent conceptual tools relating to history education that were not easily available when McDiarmid and Vinten-Johansen were teaching their experimental courses in the early 1990s.

How did I begin? My course opened with a specific question that students considered on their own for a few minutes, then talked about in small groups, and then discussed with the entire class: What are the differences between history and the past? And what turns the past into history? This conversation, which we returned to several times during the remainder of the course, teased out key defining characteristics and principles: history is a narrative constructed around the evidence from the past about a significant issue or event, in a collaborative dialogue among professional historians and others. For reasons that I give my students, and that I have articulated elsewhere, the word "bias" is banned from almost all discussions.[23]

The second half of that first class consisted of an exercise asking students to speculate about what primary documents they had generated, or that had been generated about them, that a historian of the future might use in a historical investigation touching on their lives.[24] While students got the idea by the end of this first class that history is based on the reasoned and contextualized evaluation of evidence, it was an idea that kept slipping away from them throughout the course. In almost every class, in response to claims as varied as "that evidence is biased" to "we can't know the truth because we weren't there," we returned time and again to the first discussion: that history is the disciplined and collective interpretation of evidence (and a variety of often contradictory evidence created for a variety of reasons and with varying effects) from the past.[25] By the end of the course, most students were drawing on this definition themselves as they framed historical questions and worked through the lesson plans they had developed to answer them.

As I realized the first time I taught the course, part of the problem that students have with primary documents is related to their difficulty in understanding the concept itself. Speaking generally, most students assume that a primary document or source is simply one written or otherwise created by someone in the past. Some students go on to qualify this by noting that the person who created the document should be as close as possible in time or space to the event they are witnessing, or that the author should be as free from bias as possible. Their definitions should have alerted me immediately to some problems: to these naive history learners, a primary document is, in essence, a first-hand eyewitness account of an event by someone who was there to see what *really* happened.[26] Many go on to assume that a primary document, therefore, is a source that can tell them the truth about history, uncluttered by the historian's or textbook writer's interpretive framework. From this it follows that the key to good history is to accumulate as many of these eyewitness accounts as possible. Students typically falter when I ask them: How, exactly, do you sort through these accounts and deal with the inevitable differences, prejudices, and obvious inaccuracies, not to mention the lies and delusions? But the distinction between primary and secondary sources, as the difference between eyewitness accounts and history, was not clear to many.

These questions, of course, open the door for a more serious discussion about the nature of primary sources and indeed about the nature of history itself. One of the first steps in teaching students to use primary sources in history must be, therefore, to clarify that a primary source is not a thing, in spite of its (typically) empirical presence. Rather, the primary sources created in the past are primary because they provide a prospective partial answer to a meaningful question about the past framed by the researcher. For if history is a dialogue about evidence from the past, it is a dialogue relating both to a research question (albeit one that might shift in terms of the evidence that is found – or not found!) and to evidence from the past that illuminates it, bound up within an interpretive framework that the historian uses to knit question and evidence together. Primary sources, therefore, are a necessary but not sufficient part of historical inquiry.

This is a confusing but essential point about history and historical thinking that I often try to clarify with the following example: A textbook written in the 1980s about the Middle Ages would, if used by a historical researcher, seem at first glance to be a secondary or interpretive historical source, not a primary one. But that is because we assume that the question the researcher is asking is, "What happened in the Middle Ages?" However, if the researcher is instead asking the question, "What kind of binding was used in books in the 1980s" or even, "What did textbook writers in the 1980s think should be taught in history classes?" the textbook becomes a primary source, one that provides evidence created at the time and place on which the research question is focused, and within a relevant interpretive framework.

To conclude this discussion of my introductory class or two in the course, primary documents can be especially useful in showing students how to build reasoned, evidence-based arguments from documents created in the past. But they can only work if students understand that a primary source is a slippery and elusive life form. It is difficult to find, and not only because it is simply a fragment or trace left over from the past. Even worse, historians routinely have difficulty *recognizing* pieces of evidence relating to their research. A historian investigating inequality in nineteenth-century Toronto might look to the legislation relating to poverty in the House of Commons Debates, or to data compiled in Royal Commissions, but he or she may not think to look at incidents of mob activity reported in the daily newspaper as evidence of hunger-related popular protest, or to the incidence of premature births, though both may be excellent primary sources of evidence on the question. Turning a trace or fragment from the past into a primary document depends on the questions the historian is asking. For most students, this initial coaching about the nature of primary sources serves as an introduction to the most important reason for using primary documents to teach history: it shows students that history is an interpretive act, not a claim about absolute truth.

The course has also included a trip to the provincial archives, fortunately located close to the university. An archivist was on hand to give us a full tour (booked in advance) of both the reading room, where materials were researched and accessed by the public, and "behind the scenes," where students had the rare opportunity of seeing the vast range and organizational structure of a real archive. Students were able to follow a document from the finding aid through to the archival storage box. They were also fortunate to see a wide range of document types, including letters from nineteenth-century schoolteachers, beautiful hand-drawn maps, and early-twentieth-century training films for employees of Eaton's Department Store. Though time-consuming, this was, according to a number of students, one of the most valuable aspects of this course. As a follow-up to this tour, in the next class, students attended a workshop on finding and using online documents. Again, I was fortunate to have the services of a knowledgeable professional, Marian Press, the research librarian, who created for my students an excellent website that provided a point of entry for finding and using primary documents in the classroom. We debriefed each of these field trips by returning to our initial discussion about the relationship between primary documents and history – a process that provided me with important reassurance that this method was working.[27]

In the remaining classes, the framework I developed rested on three main pillars. The first was *to engage students in broad-ranging theoretical discussions around published research about how and why to teach and learn history.* Even though I knew from previous experience that student teachers have little patience with disembodied theorizing about their teaching, each class began very much as a graduate seminar, with discussions of at least three articles that were required reading. These articles were not about history; rather, they provided research and reflection on knowing, teaching, and learning history.[28] Keeping in mind that all my students had a university degree (most of them in history or classics), but recognizing their very heavy workloads, I asked them to sign up in advance for only one of the three articles assigned each week. They were required to write a one-page reading note on the article they had chosen, articulating the topic, thesis, and evidence presented and offering a brief assessment of the significance of the piece. The reading note, which I asked them to submit at the end of class, acted as their guide to class discussions. Students began each class by talking only with the other students (one-third of the class) who had read "their" article; then they broke into groups with two people who had not read it but who had read the other two articles assigned for the week. In this round robin format, students taught and learned from one another about these thematically connected articles. This component of the class, which typically lasted forty-five minutes to an hour, ended with a classroom-wide discussion of questions generated from the small groups. These discussions worked. While students initially grumbled about the readings, by the end of the course most of them (according to surveys they later completed) felt that the discussions and the reading note format had added an intellectual depth that would be useful in their professional roles, besides providing an important forum for discussing the relations between theory and practice in our class.

Discussions of academic articles relating to historical teaching and understanding usually opened each class, but a larger portion of the time thereafter was spent in a series of workshops, where I first *modelled, and then students explored, a variety of ways of teaching using primary documents*. I asked students for suggestions about what kinds of primary documents they would like to have specific workshops about. Their suggestions usually included these: strategies for interpreting primary documents; how to find course-specific online archival documents; how to use photographs; how to use film; how to use archaeological artifacts; and how to use inquests and other government documents. Students also requested a one-hour workshop that provided them with an "everything you need to know about teaching history using primary documents" overview, including principles for selecting and using primary documents while still meeting curriculum requirements, and the inevitable discussion of why it is important to do so.

Most of the time in the classroom was spent *establishing and exploring the criteria* for their only assignment for the course: the creation of a single lesson plan. In a number of short, workshop-style lessons throughout the course, I provided them with three clearly articulated sets of criteria for building a lesson plan using primary documents to teach "history as process":

- A very *particular method* of teaching, using the Critical Challenges created by the grassroots organization the Critical Thinking Consortium.
- A specific *conceptual framework,* the procedural or second-order concepts clarified for teachers by Peter Seixas.
- Close adherence to the "skills and content" articulated in their grade- and course-specific *curriculum documents.*

These three sets of criteria were formally articulated, modelled in almost every class, and worked out in a series of workshops during which students first applied and then evaluated their effectiveness in their own and in other students' lesson plans.

The Critical Challenge approach and the conceptual framework, developed by Roland Case and Peter Seixas respectively, have received extensive discussion elsewhere, so I will provide only a quick overview here.[29] The Critical Challenge method developed by Case and TC2 (The Critical Thinking Consortium) is a highly structured method of teaching that focuses on a key question or task that is completed as students explore the criteria for judgment that the activity obliges them to contemplate. Instead of students simply retrieving information on a question (e.g., "What did the Iroquois eat?") after reading a text or series of texts, a critical (i.e., criteria-based) question focuses students' attention on the evidence required to meet the criteria, which in turn are required to come to a reasoned conclusion or judgment. The criteria-based answer to a slightly different question "Did the Iroquois have a healthy diet?" obliges students to first define what criteria determine a healthy diet and then to find and critically evaluate evidence in their texts or elsewhere that leads them to a defensible answer. One of the great advantages of this method is that while students can come to different answers – which gives them ownership of their own historical interpretations – each answer must come from a reasoned, criteria-based interpretation of evidence. My experience of this method is that students find it liberating, invigorating, and empowering to have clearly established criteria for making meaningful knowledge claims.

Teaching the Critical Challenge method – teaching students how to frame a critical question, how to establish the criteria they would use in their answer, and how to structure the lesson in such a way as to address the question/task, and allowing students to adequately perform their critical understanding – took up a considerable amount of class time. In spite of their frustration as they tried to grasp the concept of criterial and evidence-based historical thinking, almost all of the students understood by the end of the course how to create critical challenges. And after many classroom discussions about "history as a process of understanding evidence," most understood why this kind of evidence-based thinking is so important to history education. Many students reported that this was, indeed, the most valuable part of the course: learning how to craft a lesson that really "works" at teaching their students the use of evidence and criteria for building a reasoned argument – in other words, how to teach critical thinking.

The second conceptual framework that students were required to manifest in their final assignment was provided by Peter Seixas's articulation of second-order or procedural concepts. As he explains, these concepts relate to what historians *do* – how and why historians carry out their work – as well as to their completed books and articles. The concepts include evidence, significance, continuity and change, progress and decline, empathy/perspective taking, moral judgment, and agency (see Lévesque, Chapter 5, Seixas, Chapter 6, and von Heyking, Chapter 8, in this volume). The articulation of these procedural concepts provided my students with a language with which to explore exactly what was going on as they used primary documents to teach the process of doing history. These second-order concepts provided an important conceptual thread to the course and to the final assignment. We used exercises from Mike Denos and Roland Case, *Teaching about Historical Thinking*,[30] to explore these concepts in general terms. Also, students were asked to situate their lesson plans in terms of which of these second-order concepts were explored therein.

Finally, students were required to create lesson plans that explicitly met the expectations for learning that were outlined in their provincial curriculum documents. This was a particularly important criterion for their assignment because so many teachers refrain from using primary documents precisely because they believe that it is impossible to "cover the content" while using primary-document materials, which typically relate to such a tiny issue, event, or topic. I provided students with some "tips and strategies" for using primary documents in the classroom, including these:

- Choose primary documents that illustrate more than one theme, issue, or event in the course you are teaching.
- Choose a document that represents a "big idea" with enduring value beyond the classroom.
- Choose a document that has the best potential for engaging students.
- Choose a document whose analysis requires real critical thinking and not just the recitation of facts.

As I explained to the students throughout the course, while the number of formal expectations they are obliged to meet as professional teachers in Ontario can at first seem daunting, these expectations are flexible and pliable; indeed, teachers throughout Canada generally have considerable freedom in what they teach and how they think. Curriculum requirements are often broad, and many history departments in secondary schools support a different approach to history education provided that teachers can demonstrate that it encourages both historical and critical thinking in the students while allowing teachers to meet curricular expectations.

## Conclusion

My goal here has been to discuss the ways in which I have tried to use one method of teaching history – through the use of primary documents – as a way of teaching student teachers how to teach history in a different way. This method also involves teaching a different kind of history, one that more closely resembles what historians do and that more closely reflects what history *is:* a dialogue about significant evidence from a meaningful past.

It is notoriously difficult to evaluate the success of teacher education, and this article has not ventured into that territory. Based on my unsystematic reading of the detailed course evaluation provided by my students, and the transformation in their historical thinking that I was sometimes able to see, I have reason to believe that the course has achieved some success. Like McDiarmid and Vinten-Johansen, however, I end with a plea for more research into courses like these, to see if they really do change – or have the potential to change – history teaching in Canada.

In lieu of such detailed research, here are some of my impressions. Most of my students left the course with a much clearer idea of what history is and how to teach it effectively as a process of historical understanding. While most will, I suspect, use primary documents, second-order concepts, and the Critical Challenge framework as strategies in their teaching, rather than as wholesale revisions of their practice, I must commend them for their openness to new ways of thinking about, doing, and teaching history. Given the structural problems confronting prospective history teachers – the dearth of real disciplinary knowledge among history majors graduating from most universities; the fact that my students need only three university history courses to enter into teacher education as secondary school history specialists; the very short duration of the teacher education program generally, and history teacher education in particular; the disdain for disciplinary knowledge, especially in the case of history, in the public school system; and the poor training in history education that too many students continue to receive throughout the country[31] – in spite of all these factors, I think there are reasons to celebrate the possibility of change at this point in time.

While most of my students were originally unfamiliar with the idea or the practice involved in doing history by using primary documents, they embraced this approach enthusiastically once they were assured they would be able to create a lesson plan usable in the classroom. Those who were able to use their draft lesson plans in their practice teaching classrooms were even more enthusiastic. Whether they simply saw the promise of primary documents in creating history lessons that were more interesting because of good materials that actively engaged their students, or whether they were interested in taking up my challenge to them to transform history education in Ontario by 2020, most of the students enthusiastically embraced the "history is a verb" approach, and some even took up my messianic fervour about the possibilities and promise of teaching history in a new way. As more research-based teaching practices are making their way into Canadian history classrooms, the future looks brighter than it has for some time for history education. It is my hope that the History Education Network/ Histoire et éducation en réseau (www.thenhier.ca), whose explicit mandate it is to bring more research-based teaching and more teacher-based research into history classrooms, will be able to work with history educators and education systems across the country to bring history as an active process of investigation and interpretation into Canadian history classrooms.

## NOTES

1 G. Williamson McDiarmid and Peter Vinten-Johansen, "A Catwalk across the Great Divide: Redesigning the History Teaching Methods Course," in *Knowing, Teaching, and Learning History: National and International Perspectives*, ed. Peter N. Stearns, Peter Seixas, and Sam Wineburg (New York: New York University Press, 2000), 156.
2 Ibid.

3   McDiarmid and Vinten-Johansen, "A Catwalk," 161-63.
4   Ruth Sandwell, "School History vs. the Historians," *International Journal of Social Education* 30, 1 (Spring 2005): 9-17. For a discussion of how these goals interfere on a broader level with meaningful history teaching, see the final chapter of Keith C. Barton and Linda S. Levstik, *Teaching History for the Common Good* (Mahwah: Lawrence Erlbaum, 2004).
5   See for example, Ruth Sandwell, ed. *To the Past: History Education, Public Memory, and Citizenship in Canada* (Toronto: University of Toronto Press, 2006). This problem was a prime motivator in the formation of the History Education Network/ Histoire et Éducation en Réseau, formed by a group of historians and history educators in 2005.
6   McDiarmid and Vinten-Johansen, "A Catwalk," 176.
7   See Ruth Sandwell, "The Internal Divide: Historians and Their Teaching," in *Bridging Theory and Practice in Teacher Education*, ed. Mordechai Gordon and Thomas V. O'Brien (Rotterdam: Sense Publishers, 2007), 17-30.
8   Shirley H. Engle, "Late Night Thoughts about the New Social Studies," *Social Education* 50, 1 (1986): 21. Thanks to Alan Sears for drawing this article to my attention.
9   Peter Lee and Rosalyn Ashby, "Progression in Historical Understanding in Students Ages 7-14," in *Knowing, Teaching, and Learning History*, 199-222; Peter Seixas, "Student Teachers Thinking Historically," *Theory and Research in Social Education* 26, 3 (1998): 310-41.
10  McDiarmid and Vinten-Johansen, "A Catwalk," 159.
11  For a fuller discussion of this point, see Ruth Sandwell, "Reading beyond Bias: Teaching Historical Practice to Secondary School Students," *McGill Journal of Education* 38, 1 (Winter 2003): 168-86.
12  "Great Unsolved Mysteries in Canadian History," http://www.canadianmysteries.ca; Ruth Sandwell, "The Great Unsolved Mysteries of Canadian History: Using a Web-Based Archive to Teach History," *Canadian Social Studies* 39, 2 (Winter 2005), http://www.quasar.ualberta.ca/css.
13  Sam Wineburg, "On the Reading of Historical Texts: Notes on the Breach between School and Academy," *American Educational Research Journal* 28, 3 (Fall 1991): 495-519.
14  Peter Seixas, "The Community of Inquiry as a Basis for Knowledge and Learning: The Case of History," *American Educational Research Journal* 30, 2 (Summer 1993): 305-24; "Student Teachers Thinking Historically," *Theory and Research in Social Education* 26, 3 (1998): 310-41; Peter Lee, "Putting Principles into Practice: Understanding History," in *How Students Learn: History in the Classroom*, ed. M. Suzanne Donovan and John D. Bransford (2005), http://www.nap.edu/openbook.
15  Ken K. Osborne, "Fred Morrow Fling and the Source Method of Teaching History," *Theory and Research in Social Education* 71 (2003): 466-501; "To the Past," in Sandwell, *To the Past*.
16  The seminal work of British history education researcher Dennis Shemilt was particularly important for stimulating the use of primary documents in history teaching. Dennis Shemilt, *Evaluation Study: Schools Council History 13-16 Project* (Edinburgh: Holmes McDougall, 1980). For a wide-ranging critique of their use, see

Keith Barton, "Primary Sources in History: Breaking through the Myths," *Phi Delta Kappan* 86, 10 (June 2005): 745-53.
17  To learn more about these thirty-year-old resources, see http://www.jackdaw.com.
18  These problems are nicely summarized in Barton, "Primary Sources in History;" See also Sandwell, "Reading beyond Bias," 2003.
19  Keith C. Barton, "'I Just Kinda Know': Elementary Students' Ideas about Historical Evidence," *Theory and Research in Social Education* 25 (1997): 407-30.
20  Sandwell, "Reading beyond Bias," 185.
21  The course was originally called "Teaching History Using Primary Documents." Near the end of the first version of this course, as I was struggling to find words to sum up what we had been doing, I was in the middle of saying that "history is an act of interpretation, not a fact, or a product, or a fixed thing," when a student jumped in and declared: "You are saying that history is not a noun; it is a verb."
22  McDiarmid and Vinten-Johansen, "A Catwalk," 160-64.
23  Sandwell, "Reading beyond Bias."
24  Both of these exercises can be found in the Teachers' Corner of "Great Unsolved Mysteries in Canadian History," http://www.canadianmysteries.ca.
25  Because of these discussions, students were particularly intrigued by the article by Peter Lee and Rosalyn Ashby, "Progression in Historical Understanding in Students."
26  Peter Lee does an excellent job of exploring this problem in history education in Peter J. Lee, "Putting Principles into Practice: Understanding History," in *How Students Learn: History in the Classroom*, Division of Behavioural and Social Sciences and Education, National Research Council, ed. M. Suzanne Donovan and John D. Bransford, (Washington, DC: National Academies Press, 2005), 31-78.
27  I have some reservations about students and researchers relying exclusively on online documents. I am concerned that students in particular miss something important about the nature of historical evidence and interpretation by side-stepping the historical research process and by relying exclusively on visual rather than tangible evidence. However, as noted above, until research demonstrates a significant problem in historical understanding resulting from online research, the benefits seem to far outweigh these possible problems.
28  A number of articles from Stearns, Seixas, and Wineburg, *Knowing, Teaching and Learning History*, were included in the course readings.
29  See, for example, Peter Seixas, "What Is Historical Consciousness," in Sandwell, *To the Past*; and Roland Case and LeRoi Daniels, "Teaching the Tools to Think Critically," in *The Anthology of Social Studies: Issues and Strategies for Secondary Teachers*, ed. Roland Case and Penney Clark (Vancouver: Pacific Educational Press, 2008).
30  Mike Denos and Roland Case, ed., *Teaching about Historical Thinking* (Vancouver: Critical Thinking Consortium, 2006).
31  See Linda Darling-Hammond and John Bransford, eds., *Preparing Teachers for a Changing World: What Teachers Should Learn and Be Able to Do* (San Francisco: Jossey-Bass, 2005).

PART 4

# OTHER CONTEXTS FOR HISTORICAL THINKING

## 12

# Historical Thinking in the Museum
## Open to Interpretation

VIVIANE GOSSELIN

> *It is our obligation to assist the public in drawing connections between the history of our sites and its contemporary implications. We view stimulating dialogues on pressing social issues and promoting humanitarian and democratic values as a primary function.*
>
> – International Coalition of Historic Sites
> and Museums of Conscience, 2001

The above statement evokes issues of social relevance and institutional responsibility, both of which are widely discussed in museum circles.[1] Many museum scholars and practitioners envision this responsibility as being to create opportunities for the public to make sense of the past in ways that are relevant to their lives. Fostering a dialogue between the interpreted past and contemporary reality is an inherently dynamic process requiring a thoughtful interpretive approach on the part of museum staff. History educators express similar concerns as they attempt to make history relevant to their students in ways that transcend the memorization of facts. For the past thirty years, academics and educators have been exploring ways to foster historical understanding. In doing so, they have learned to pay particular attention to how students and adults relate to the past.

In the museum field, on the other hand, little is known about the ways in which museum visitors' conceptions of history influence how they engage with exhibitions or historic sites. The same can be said of the exhibition as a learning environment: we do not have a strong grasp of how this medium nurtures historical thinking. These are important matters when we consider that museums are one of the few public institutions mandated to facilitate lifelong learning about the collective past.

My argument involves meaning making with historical exhibitions in history museums and at historic sites. Though historical meaning making can take place in all types of museal institutions, I am especially interested in exhibitions whose producers intend to convey historical knowledge and whose public intends – partly, at least – to learn about past events, people, and places. My motivation for exploring an interdisciplinary perspective (drawing from the work of history educators and museum theorists) stems from my professional experience in museums. Over fifteen years of developing exhibitions in British Columbia, I became increasingly fascinated and at times perplexed by the informal nature of the engagement associated with this medium. For this reason, I decided to focus my research on the potential and limitations of exhibition media in fostering historical meaning making. Formal education has different parameters with regard to content delivery, setting, audience, and performance expectations. It became obvious to me that research on historical learning and thinking could stimulate discussions about new forms of exhibition practice. To launch and contextualize my argument, I refer to current developments in the museum field and identify research gaps related to my area of research. I also point out how new questions about museums' educational projects emerge when considered in light of the discussion on historical thinking. The second part of the chapter demonstrates how experimenting with concepts of historical thinking can help develop innovative practice in both museum productions and research.

## Situating My Intervention

At first, I envisioned that my contribution would amount to an outlier in this collection – that it would be a peripheral discussion relative to the central one of history education in classrooms. As the writing progressed, however, I began to think of it as a manifestation of a community of practice, a term coined by anthropologist Etienne Wenger to describe "groups of people who share a concern or a passion for something they do and learn how to do it better as they interact."[2] As Wenger studied the dynamics of social learning, he identified three elements characterizing communities of practice: the domain (having a common interest), the community (members interacting and learning together), and a practice (shared experiences, tools, and resources). As a community of practice, The History Education Network (THEN/HiER) brings together practitioners and researchers with a common interest in nurturing historical understanding and literacy among people of all ages. Beyond the particulars of the many fields associated with history education, this chapter demonstrates that the sharing of intellectual tools can provoke new ways of thinking across disciplines to reimagine, in this case, aspects of the museum's educational task. It also signals the importance of considering the historical learning of individuals beyond the formal years of schooling.

## Brief Overview of Recent Museum Development

The redefinition of knowledge production and dissemination in the humanities and social sciences, referred to as the "cultural turn," has influenced museums over the past fifty years. The realization that knowledge is historically and culturally situated, and that until recently it favoured the world views of a few dominating voices, caused museums to revise the ways in which they collect, study, and display their collections.[3] Museums became aware that to fulfill an educational role, they would have to develop practices that were more inclusive, explicit, and self-conscious. Conversely, the realization that people do not absorb new knowledge but rather construct it by adjusting existing mental models to accommodate new experiences forced museums to reconsider what learning in the museum "means."[4]

Over the years, museums in the Western world conceived exhibitions that became more responsive to the audience's varied learning styles, ages, knowledge, and experience. I should state here that when referring to these recent museum developments, I do not imply the unanimous adoption of these recent perspectives. They do, however, constitute one important trend in current museum practice in a field characterized by a "cumulative diversification"[5] of philosophical positions. This self-conscious era saw the emergence of a museology that not only enhanced the professionalization of the museum field but also established an intellectual infrastructure from which to observe, analyze, and transform museum practice. My research program is situated within this disciplinary practice. Though it is positioned in a Canadian context, it draws extensively from the work of international museum scholars.

## Historical Meaning Making in the Museum: Research Gaps

Reviews of museum education literature have identified several important and interrelated gaps that impede our understanding of how people make sense of the historical content presented in museums. The first relates to the limited number of published visitor studies conducted in history museums and historic sites. Most visitor studies over the past twenty years have been conducted in science and children's museums.[6] Many of these studies have yielded useful and transferable information for other types of museums and have – among other things – demonstrated that visitors' agendas, prior knowledge, and predispositions toward certain topics and museums influence learning outcomes.[7] Hence the importance of capturing visitors' experiences in history museums and historic sites in order to develop a richer understanding of the learning that occurs at these sites.

The second gap involves the absence of a discipline-based theoretical framework for examining how people construct historical meaning.[8] Well-respected museum scholar Scott G. Paris recognizes this gap: "As visitors meander through recreated historical villages or homes, they are likely to discuss historical topics, the authenticity of primary sources, and the accuracy of the curators' interpretation. Appreciation of different intellectual domains, as well as discipline-based reasoning, can be nurtured in diverse contexts, and these issues, especially as they relate to children and education, are uncharted territory."[9]

A third area that begs for further research relates to investigating the exhibition or historic site environment's capacity (or lack of) to foster historical meaning making. Given that most visitors rely on the museum's physical environment alone and not on its staff to make sense of exhibitions, it seems fitting to consider how this medium supports historical learning. Exhibition design as an educational vehicle is an undertheorized facet of museum studies.

Another characteristic of museum studies literature is that many analyses of exhibitions tend to neglect the public's reception.[10] They are readings of the exhibition that take into account the curators' intent and the larger cultural and sociological context of production. In these analyses, the visitor is largely absent. It is striking that in anthologies such as *Thinking about Exhibitions*,[11] *Museum Frictions*,[12] and *A Companion to Museum Studies*[13] – all three of which are key museum literature references – most essays describe the public's response to exhibitions only in generic terms. The analyses tend to focus on conditions of production – that is, on the tensions and negotiations that influence the conceptualizing of exhibitions in particular socio-cultural contexts. The physical outcomes of the decisions thereby made (the exhibitions), and the public's reception, are discussed only superficially. Indeed, neither the individual visitor nor the public in general is credited with much agency in these essays. Little importance is placed on the individual's reflexivity and meaning making. The visitors are treated as a homogenous group that will be affected by a given exhibition in predictable ways related to gender, ethnicity, and class identity. These studies rarely include the perspectives of visitors or of front-line staff who are in direct contact with the public. Though an emerging trend in scholarly work is to consider both the broader context of production and the visitor as an important actor in the exhibition's "performance," the visitor in these more inclusive analyses continues, in most cases, to be an imaginary player.[14]

The fast-changing demographics of Western countries and the radical transformation of information technologies have together altered the ways in which people relate to time, space, and other people.[15] In considering these factors, it seems necessary to address concomitant research gaps. This examination will allow us to determine how today's visitors relate to time, space, and others through their encounters with historic sites and history museums. Central to my argument is a call for us to explore new analytical frameworks for thinking about exhibitions as environments that make historical meaning.

### Historical Thinking In and Outside the Museum

Discipline-based inquiries have made a decisive albeit still partial entry into history museums and historic sites through the development of school programs.[16] This partnership between schools and museums is not surprising, given the long-standing relationship between the two. I would argue, though, that this use of historical thinking concepts in museums is limited to serving the needs of school curricula. By this I mean that some museum educators are aware of the growing interest among schools in the historical thinking pedagogy and have started to offer school programs that apply these concepts. Even so, the development of exhibitions (themes, storylines, artifact selections) remains uninformed by this conceptual framework. I am calling for a more integrated and broader use of historical thinking concepts in museums, a use that would be reflected in the early phases of exhibition development.[17]

In the discourse of history education, much emphasis has been placed on the concept of "historical thinking," defined as making sense of the past in ways that are inspired by the work of historians.[18] In this context, thinking historically refers to considering history as a series of accounts that must be constructed, interpreted, and assessed. To do that, learners must become familiar not just with the "facts" of history, but with its organizing principles and modes of inquiry as well. Museum educator Christine Castle warns that, without this intellectual apparatus, people of all ages will be "vulnerable to the constraining forces of dogma, stereotype, and convention."[19]

A key aspect of this discussion, common in history education but not in museum studies, is the conceptualization of historical knowledge based on two interdependent forms of knowledge: *substantive history*, referring to historical data, events, actors, and places – the "facts of history"; and *procedural history*, or "metahistory," referring to the diverse processes involved in constructing historical interpretations.[20] To understand that history is not fixed but is always reconstructed by historians and other "consumers of history" requires familiarity with metahistorical or procedural concepts. These concepts, also referred to as *historical thinking concepts*, allow us, when involved in the act of *doing history*, to perceive the importance and value of specific events in time for a collective *(historical significance)*. They allow us to understand the use of a set of proofs to build a claim *(evidence)* and to differentiate what has changed from what has remained the same *(continuity and change)*. They also allow us to recognize how and why certain conditions and actions led to certain events *(causes and consequences)*. One historical concept requires us to consider the "foreignness" of the perspectives of historical individuals and collectives *(historical perspective)*, while another helps us draw conclusions about the actions of historical actors *(moral judgment)*. To some extent, everyone employs metahistory when relating to the past. The level of sophistication in the use of these procedural concepts ranges from novice to expert historians. The task at hand for educators is therefore to help students improve their use of these concepts. A historical thinking pedagogy favours the simultaneous acquisition of procedural and substantive historical knowledge. This is often referred to as the *discipline-based approach* to history education.[21] It opposes the many forms of *memory history*, or the grand narrative approach, which focuses on the acquisition of factual knowledge and proposes a unifying, unproblematic, uncontested version of history – an approach viewed by the promoter of historical thinking as undermining the interpretative and investigative nature of historical knowledge. Educators believe that by making students aware of how historical claims are crafted, learners both inside and outside school will take a more critical approach to competing historical accounts (see Lévesque, Chapter 5, Seixas, Chapter 6, and von Heyking, Chapter 8, in this volume).

From a museum practitioner's point of view, such pedagogical principles provoke new questions relating to how people connect with historical content in exhibitions. How do visitors think historically when visiting an exhibition? Do exhibitions ever explicitly address the "how" of history? Can museums be considered places of history education if they focus solely on the stories, the "what" of history?

To complicate the picture, many empirical studies conducted on young children and adolescents have concluded that students can understand historical thinking concepts, which enhance their ability to think historically, but that the process is long and arduous and requires multiple exposures.[22] Given the nature of the museum experience (short duration; sporadic visits; self-directed, leisurely group learning as opposed to formal instruction), to what extent is it possible for museums to foster a culture of historical thinking? How are museums to position themselves in relation to the procedural knowledge that is so critical to historical meaning making? If museums do not involve themselves in nurturing metahistorical concepts, are they not disengaging themselves from their educational responsibility?

Museums have always had an educational function.[23] The nature and substance of that function, however, has changed over time. As noted earlier in this chapter, today's museums are more inclined to see themselves less as providers of authoritative knowledge and more as facilitators or mediators of learning experiences. As Eilean Hooper-Greenhill noted: "Learning is a serious activity that needs to be fun."[24] This could not be truer for museums, which must create highly enjoyable learning experiences in order to maintain their existence. Museum going is not compulsory and is meant to be mainly a leisurely cultural activity enjoyed in a social context (i.e., a visit with a friend or family, a field trip, or a tourist activity). Visitors expect to learn something about their culture and their history and those of others.[25] It is noteworthy that studies have shown that people from various Western countries in general, and Canadians in particular, trust museums over other sources of historical information.[26] Keeping in mind the pressure for museums to propose "highly enjoyable learning moments" in a context in which they benefit from a huge capital of public trust, how should museums convey historical knowledge to the communities they serve? Should they provide updated stories that create common references? Or should museums provoke visitors to think about "the stories we tell ourselves about ourselves and others" and nurture a certain intellectual apparatus on the part of visitors? The aim would be to support visitors as they sift through information and pass informed judgments on historical accounts encountered both within and outside the museum. I would argue that it is possible for a museum to do both: tell the story, and provide clues about how the story has been crafted. To some extent, museums have already been attempting to do this. I believe that the appropriation of historical thinking concepts for exhibitionary practice may further this idea.

## Converging Exhibitionary Practice

The need to adopt a critical, inclusive approach to staging knowledge in history and ethnography museums has been a theme in museum studies for the past twenty-five years.[27] Indeed, many museum scholars and practitioners have called for exhibitionary practices to make apparent the subjectivity of the curatorial intent. They have supported multi-vocal, pluri-perspectival exhibitions to counteract nationalistic or colonialist history memory, and they have emphasized the constructed nature of history. But as mentioned earlier, very few studies have been conducted on how these new interpretive practices are understood by the public.

I would argue that most historical interpretations in museums and historic sites consist of updated story lines influenced by social history and, to some extent, by critical history. They emphasize, for example, the perspectives of historically marginalized individuals and groups, such as women's or Aboriginal and ethnic minorities' contributions to the development of Western nations. Yet the exhibition narrative is more often than not based on substantive knowledge (the facts) and provides very few clues about the processes used to construct these new historical narratives.[28] As a result, these accounts are innovative in substance rather than process, which serves to sustain the public's belief that museums' interpretations are about uncovering a *truer* picture of the past.

History museums could find more productive approaches to aligning historical knowledge (related to the academic discipline) with learning theories. Contemporary museums have largely embraced a visitor-centred approach. We recognize the influence of socio-constructivist theories when we see multi-age activities, multi-sensorial space, hands-on exhibits, object-based exploration, and texts referring to visitors' experiences. Yet these interpretive strategies would better serve the demands of historical inquiry if they were more attuned to the interplay between procedural and substantive knowledge.

## Experimenting with Historical Thinking Concepts in Exhibitionary Practice

The appropriation of the concept of historical thinking in exhibitionary practice can take multiple forms. This chapter now proposes a few avenues.

### Analytical Framework for Museum Researchers

If we subscribe to the notion that visitors *participate* in the exhibition performance and that by "taking part in" and "being part of," each person contributes to the shaping of the exhibition as a public event, then the social significance of an exhibition – and by extension, the museum – is enacted through its encounters with visitors. With this in mind, I wish to adopt a theoretical framework that examines the interplay between the exhibition team and the broader context of production, the exhibition space, and the visitors, instead of isolating these elements, which is the approach taken by so many current studies on exhibitions and visitors. Adopting this framework means that when visitors study an exhibition, the various historical thinking concepts can be used as *hinges* for analyzing both the museum staff's intentions and visitors' understandings. Researchers can examine how the concept of historical significance (in relation to a particular historical theme) is articulated by exhibition team members, represented in the exhibition space, and understood (or not) by visitors before and after they visit the exhibition. The visitors' responses from the "front end" as well as summative evaluations can be discussed with the exhibition team. This research design would emphasize the dialogical relationship between the museum and its audience. It would also propose an enlarged definition of the museum exhibition as a "meaning making" environment by exploring how it mobilizes the historical consciousness of multiple actors (visitors and exhibition makers).

Visitors, just like students, come with a range of abilities to engage with historical accounts. Visitor studies informed by the disciplinary frame can provide opportunities to explore how these various abilities are enacted in the museum. I recently undertook an empirical qualitative study to assess the historical meaning making involved in the production and reception of two exhibitions in history museums in Montreal and Vancouver.[29] Preliminary results converge with other studies that have demonstrated that visitors' assumptions about the nature of history, as well as their "entrance narratives" (individual and cultural ideas about specific historical narratives), inform their understandings of historical interpretations in the museum.[30] Perceptions of the museum's role (i.e., a place for the collective memory to be transmitted, not questioned) also influence visitors' engagement with exhibitions.[31] An analysis of the visitor interview transcripts indicates that concepts of historical thinking were activated as visitors explained how they made sense of the exhibitions. In most cases, these concepts were intertwined with information pertaining to the visitor's identity (ethnicity, family history, life experiences, profession, hobbies). The visit accordingly was very much an "identity-driven" learning activity rather than a "performance driven," school-like learning experience.[32] Visitors picked and chose portions of the exhibitions that spoke to them (often based on an initial emotive response) and from there constructed meaning using historical concepts. Stating that museum visitors thought historically in the exhibition does not necessarily imply that visitors took a critical approach toward the museum's interpretation of the past. Indeed, few visitors' responses were "critical"; that is, they did not question the museum's claim. Very few expected the museum to tell them how and why the historical account embodied in the exhibition consisted of a defensible claim. By examining how historical accounts are assessed by the public and how concepts of historical thinking are articulated by visitors on particular topics, it may be possible for researchers and practitioners to envision interpretive strategies that propose alternative perspectives relative to specific historical topics and historical epistemology. A greater awareness of visitors' historical meaning-making processes may not prevent public controversies over curatorial interpretations, but it may provide a basis for museums to better understand and respond to these situations.

### Analytical Framework for Exhibition Team: Shared Meaning about the Nature of History

Before confronting the assumptions of visitors about the nature of history in an exhibition, it is imperative to confront the assumptions of the exhibition team. This could involve examining the acquisition of a shared understanding of what "doing history" means for them and for the visitors engaging in the exhibition. This may seem surprising for people outside the field, but, except for history curators, most museum professionals involved in developing historical exhibitions do not have formal training in history. Conversely, except for museum educators, very few professionals have formal training in education. A typical exhibition team involved in a mid- to large-size exhibition project includes a curator, graphic and exhibit designers, a project manager, an exhibit fabricator, and an educator, along with numerous community members and consultants who help produce and validate various aspects of the exhibition from the research to the fabrication stage.

This means that more non-historians than historians are involved in the process of historical interpretation and that more non-educators than educators are involved in creating this learning space. Though the curator's authority is still prominent in most museums, significant decisions about graphic design, 3-D design, and educational strategies are still generated by other members whose understanding of history education will ultimately affect the final product. Discussing the exhibition themes and messages in terms of substantive and procedural historical knowledge with the team members renders tacit knowledge explicit and may facilitate a shared understanding of the interpretive and educational task of the exhibition team.

Robert Bain's thoughts on teaching students and history teachers are insightful in this regard.[33] He contends that it is not realistic to attempt to train students or teachers to become academic historians. In the same way, we cannot expect all museum staff (given their multidisciplinary academic and professional qualifications) to become professional historians or history educators. It is possible, however, to familiarize exhibition team members with the disciplinary perspective – this "other way of knowing," to use Samuel Wineburg's expression.[34] Through a consistent use of *history-specific tools* (procedural concepts such as historical significance or causes and consequences) and *vocabulary* (differentiating history from the past, memory from history), team members can acquire over time a *history-specific culture*. This shared lexicon among team members may increase coherence between the interpretive vision and the various physical attributes of the exhibitions to create *history-considerate exhibitions*. This new repertory can be used to bridge interdisciplinary concerns over issues of education, history, and design. This is not to suggest that any exhibition inspired by a historical-thinking theoretical framework will automatically generate a more critical engagement with the past. Nor is it fair to claim that a traditional museum exhibition (based on memory history and a transmission model of education) could not solicit an active and critical response on the part of visitors. Visitors create their own experience, and as such, they choose their own terms of engagement with the exhibition. Adopting such a framework would signal the museum's intention to create environments that support an investigative approach to historical content without imposing it. It would also indicate a new attentiveness to the visitor's capacity to make sense of the past.

An exhibition team sharing a common culture of history education may be able to experiment with a historical thinking pedagogy. For instance, historians and educators could work together to resolve questions around new ways to emphasize the notion of continuity in a particular story so that visitors do not get the impression that "everything has changed" between the present and the historical event. It is also possible to imagine designers recalibrating their design solutions to help visitors negotiate the tension between the familiar and the foreign past – which is, as Wineburg noted, "essential and irreducible" to history – so that visitors appreciate the striking differences between the historical frame of mind and their own while also appreciating a shared humanity with the historical actors.[35]

The idea of calibrating procedural knowledge in museographic terms (in this case, the concept of historical perspective) could be expressed through the example of a display at a war museum that I recently visited. In it, visitors enter a reconstituted First World War trench. Without any written texts, this form of display provides a sense of scale, as well as a level of detail rarely discussed in history textbooks, such as the holes carved by soldiers for extra protection. It envelops the visitor with its dim light, sound effects, and walls of artificial dirt. Visitors can pretend they are soldiers by peeking at the enemy through a periscope and crouching beside mannequin soldiers. In another gallery of the same museum, a discreet film display consists of a series of small screens showing vintage medical film footage of soldiers suffering from various post-traumatic syndromes, such as uncontrolled shaking and the inability to keep their balance. The screens are small, and flat on a wall. The film's topic alludes to a less than romanticized aspect of the war. There is a physical and psychological distance between the visitors and the sick soldiers. Now let us imagine a reversed emphasis: the life-sized trench becomes a small model contained in a display case; the sick soldiers appear on a series of large screens on multiple walls surrounding the visitors. The impression of proximity with the historical events and actors would change and would likely affect the meaning derived from the experience. The capacity of the exhibition design to emphasize *or de-emphasize* the "closeness" of the past with visitors is significant. In this sense, historical thinking concepts may help museum professionals articulate the learning experience they are creating, in this case, by manoeuvring between the dreadfulness of and fascination with war.

The idea is not to *teach* historical thinking concepts to visitors. Team members can discuss those concepts during the conceptual phase, such as in the example above. Those concepts can also become an explicit part of the exhibition narrative. If, for instance, an exhibition team wants to emphasize the polysemic nature of objects and the use of objects-as-evidence in making historical claims, a display could consist of a row of artifacts with short text panels for each object telling a different story on each side of the row. Each side would have a different interpretation using the same objects. In notifying the public that each side has competing but valid stories, the museum could stimulate visitors to think about what makes these two stories different.

I am not suggesting that historical thinking concepts become the driving force behind all exhibition concepts. I do think that once conversant with them, an exhibition team can generate new interplays between their public, the collections, and disciplinary knowledge. For example, in a historical storyline, one display could allude to the notion of selection inherent in the interpretive work. *Here are five objects that could have expressed and illustrated this event. We selected this one because of reasons x, y, z. Which one would you have chosen?* Such a display simultaneously conveys that history is open to interpretation, that it involves a selection process based on criteria. That process may slightly interrupt the flow of "the story," but it is not tangential.

Familiarity with what it means to think historically will enlarge the conceptual repertory of museum staff; this in turn may change the ways they tell stories in the exhibition space and ultimately influence the ways their audience considers history. This pedagogical approach would not prevent museums from providing enjoyable experiences. In fact, it would enhance the museum's ability to produce exhibitions that are compelling, poetic, and inspiring – and, when the topic allows, whimsical and playful.

**Museum's Motivation for Promoting Historical Thinking**
The degree to which such a framework would be of interest to museums has to do with how they envision their social and educational role. Though the focus of this text has been on the potential uses of historical thinking concepts in museums, I believe strongly that a museum's commitment to promoting intellectual curiosity through disciplinary knowledge is not an end in itself; rather, it is a means for museums to achieve social relevance. The museum's aim to communicate disciplinary knowledge – in this case, history – has to do with providing the public with a set of common references that help people adapt, understand, and critically engage with the dramatic social transformations shaping their lives. Historical knowledge is one means of contextualizing these transformations and envisioning our future.[36]

This chapter is part of an ongoing conversation in the museum field about the kind of *storyteller* museums ought to be and for whom. More often now, we are hearing that a museum should be a "house of critical thinking,"[37] a place that supports learning by "enabling the sifting and judging of useful material."[38] Museums say they want to "help individuals connect with generations, cultures and communities, inspiring them to become informed, open-minded and engaged citizens."[39] The act of connecting past and present means setting the stage not to determine history's relevance for visitors, but rather to create opportunities that enable them to establish relevance between the interpreted past and their own lives.

Along these lines, I will refer to the work of Jörn Rüsen, for whom a reference to future action is contained in the historical interpretation "because such [historical] interpretation must enable us to act. That is, it must facilitate the direction of our intentions within a temporal matrix."[40] In other words, historical interpretations provide an *orientation* for the present and the future, one that has moral implications. Our ability to understand the past affects our future actions. I want to connect this idea of orientation with the "wayfinding concept" used by exhibit designers. Wayfinders are strategic elements in the exhibition that orient visitors spatially during their visit. The following is a definition given by David Dean, the author of the much-cited book *Museum Exhibition, Theory, and Practice:* "Wayfinders are visual, tactile, auditory clues or devices that assist visitors in orienting themselves within museum facilities and surroundings, inform the audience of their options and help locate destinations."[41]

If museums are to deserve the public trust and their status as sites of history education, they should provide "conceptual historical wayfinders" to invite visitors with various levels of historical understanding to engage more critically with historical accounts. As in Dean's definition, these conceptual wayfinders could orient visitors about their surroundings *(right here, right now, with this exhibition team, this is our interpretation of what happened, based on this set of questions and criteria)*, inform them of their options *(you can engage with this historical account in many ways)*, and help locate destinations *(What are the implications of these past actions on our lives today? Do they still influence our decisions today, and do we wish to revise these decisions?)*.

## Conclusion

This essay acts as a research agenda: one that explores the heuristic potential of a historical thinking framework to study and experiment with exhibition production and reception. My forthcoming research will empirically address these questions while contributing to a body of museum literature concerned with the participation of history museums and historic sites in contemporary culture.

A shared understanding of what constitutes historical thinking means a new common language spoken within the exhibition team and within the broader history education community of practice. Shared language, anthropologist Wenger reminds us, leads communities of practice toward new actions.[42] We can conjecture that an exhibition team familiar with how people (including themselves) can engage more critically with historical accounts may lead to different ways of staging historical knowledge in exhibition spaces. Equally, such interdisciplinary conversations can provoke history educators to reconsider the potential of museums to nurture historical thinking. To begin with, museums can maintain a lifelong relationship with their audiences and in some respects can pursue the work being encouraged in schools. In addition, the fact that both knowledge dissemination and the production of historical research (or new knowledge generation) occur in the same institution may offer new opportunities for education scholars to explore.

My reflection is not a motion to eliminate the role of museums as sites of memory. Rather, it articulates a need, shared by many in the museum field, to make museums public spaces where visitors can posit and contemplate the tensions between history and memory, between the familiar and the foreign past, between previous and current ways of relating to time, space, and collectives.

## NOTES

An earlier version of this chapter was presented at *NaMU VI*, a museum research conference held at the University of Oslo, 17-21 November 2008.

1. Elaine Heumann Gurian, *Civilizing the Museum: Collected Writings by Elaine Heumann Gurian* (London: Routledge, 2006); Eilean Hooper-Greenhill, *Museum and Education* (London: Routledge, 2007); Stephen Weil, *Making Museums Matter* (Washington: Smithsonian Institution Press, 2002).
2. Etienne Wenger, *Communities of Practice* (Cambridge: Cambridge University, 1998), 4.
3. Tony Bennett, "Exhibition, Difference, and the Logic of Culture," in *Museum Frictions*, ed. Ivan Karp, Corinne A. Kratz, Lynn Szwaja, and Tomas Ybarra-Frausto (Oxford: Blackwell, 2006), 46-69; Bernard Deloche, *La Nouvelle Culture* (Paris: L'Harmattan, 2007); Eilean Hooper-Greenhill, *Museum and Education;* Suzanne McLeod, *Reshaping Museum Space: Architecture, Design, Exhibitions* (London: Routledge, 2005).

4 George Hein, *Learning in the Museum* (London: Routledge, 1998), 14-40; Hilda Hein, *The Museum in Transition, a Philosophical Perspective* (Washington: Smithsonian Institute Press, 2000), 108-26.
5 An expression coined by Simon J. Knell, *Museum in the Material World* (London: Routledge, 2007), 3.
6 Eilean Hooper-Greenhill and Theano Moussouni, *Researching Learning in Museums and Galleries 1990-1999: A Bibliographic Review* (Leicester: Research Centre for Museums and Galleries, Department of Museum Studies, Leicester University, 2002); Sharon MacDonald, *A Companion to Museum Studies* (Oxford: Blackwell, 2006), 12.
7 For a publication dedicated to the trend and synthesis of visitor studies findings, see John. H. Falk, Lynn D. Dierking, and Susan Foutz, eds., *In Principle, In Practice: Museums as Learning Institutions* (New York: Altamira, 2007).
8 How little we know about historical meaning making in the museum is also discussed in Bella Dick, "Encoding and Decoding the People: Circuits of Communication at a Local Heritage Museum," *European Journal of Communication* 15, 1 (2000): 61-78; Gordon Fyfe and Max Ross, "Rethinking the Visitor's Gaze," in *Theorizing Museums,* ed. Sharon Macdonald and Gordon Fyfe (Oxford: Blackwell, 2004), 127-51; Pascal Gielen, "Museumchronotopics: On the Representation of the Past in Museums," *Museum and Society* 2, 3 (2004): 147-60; and Kate Gregory and Andrea Witcomb, "Beyond Nostalgia," in *Museum Revolutions,* ed. Simon J. Knell, Suzanne MacLeod, and Sheila Watson (London: Routledge 2007), 263-75.
9 Scott G. Paris, *Perspectives on Object-Centered Learning in Museums* (London: Lawrence Erlbaum, 2002), xvii.
10 Richard Sandell, *Museums, Prejudice, and the Difference* (New York: Routledge, 2006), 4-11; Rhiannon Mason, "Cultural Theory and Museum Studies," in *A Companion to Museum Studies,* ed. Sharon MacDonald (Oxford: Blackwell, 2006), 17-20.
11 Reesa Greenberg, Bruce Ferguson, and Sandy Nairne, eds. *Thinking about Exhibitions* (London: Routledge, 1996).
12 Ivan Karp, Corinne A. Kratz, Lynn Szwaja, and Toma Ybarra-Frausto, eds., *Museum Frictions* (Oxford: Blackwell, 2006).
13 Sharon Macdonald, *A Companion to Museum Studies* (Oxford: Blackwell, 2006).
14 I am referring here to the work of Jem Fraser, "Museum, Drama, Ritual, and Power," in *Museum Revolutions,* 291-302; Sharon Macdonald and Paul Basu, *Exhibition Experiments* (Oxford: Blackwell, 2007); and Gaby Porter, "Seeing through Solidity: A Feminist Perspective on Museums," in *Theorizing Museums,* 105-26. See also Gregory and Witcomb, "Beyond Nostalgia."
15 For a detailed argument on the impact of new information technologies on museums, see Bernard Deloche, *La Nouvelle Culture* (Paris: L'Harmattan, 2007).
16 A number of studies have focused on enhancing the school/museum partnership through historical thinking. For a few examples, see Robert Bain and Kirsten M. Ellenbogen, "Placing Objects within Disciplinary Perspectives: Examples from History and Science," in *Perspectives on Object-Centered Learning in Museums,* 153-70; Christine Castle, "Teaching History in Museums," *Ontario History* 94, 1 (2002):

*Historical Thinking in the Museum*

29-47; and Irene Nakou, "Museum and History Education in our Contemporary Context," *International Journal of Historical Learning, Teaching, and Research* 3, 2 (2003): 83-93. See some museum applications at the Glenbow Museum school programs, http://www.glenbow.org.

17  I would like to note the substantial contribution to museum education research made by the Groupe de recherche sur l'éducation et les musées (GREM), based at the Université du Québec à Montréal. The research group, however, has not generated visitor studies or exhibition analyses using a disciplinary framework to assess the production of historical meaning making. See Anne-Marie Emond, ed., *L'Education Muséale Vue du Canada, des Etats-Unis et d'Europe: Recherche sur les Programmes et les Expositions* (Montreal: Editions MultiMondes, 2004); and Tamara Lemerise, Dany Lussier-Desrochers, and Vitor Matias, eds., *Courants Contemporains de Recherche en Éducation Muséale* (Montreal: Editions Multimondes, 2002).

18  For a concise explanation on the conditions informing this emphasis, see Peter Stearns, Peter Seixas, and Sam Wineburg, eds., *Knowing, Teaching, and Learning History: National and International Perspectives* (New York: New York University Press, 2000), 3-5; for a survey of historical and contemporary trends in history teaching, see Ken Osborne's chapter in this volume.

19  Christine Castle, "Teaching History in Museums," *Ontario History* 94, 1 (2002): 3.

20  Peter Lee and Rosalyn Ashby, "Progression in Historical Understanding Ages 7-14," in *Knowing, Teaching, and Learning* History, 199-222; Peter Seixas, "Conceptualizing the Growth of Historical Understanding," in *Handbook of Education and Human Development: New Models of Learning, Teaching, and Schooling*, ed. David Olson and Nancy Torrance (Oxford: Blackwell, 1996), 765-83; Stéphane Lévesque, *Thinking Historically: Educating Students for the Twenty-First Century* (Toronto: University of Toronto Press, 2008), 29-34.

21  Peter Lee, "Understanding History," in *Theorizing Historical Consciousness*, ed. Peter Seixas (Toronto: University of Toronto Press, 2004), 129-64; Stearns, Seixas, and Wineburg, eds., *Knowing, Teaching, and Learning History*.

22  Keith C. Barton and Linda S. Levstik, *Teaching History for the Common Good* (Mahwah: Lawrence Erlbaum, 2004); Jörn Rüsen, "Historical Consciousness: Narrative Structure, Moral Function, and Ontogenetic Development," in *Theorizing Historical Consciousness*, 63-85; Samuel Wineburg, *Historical Thinking and Other Unnatural Acts: Charting the Future of Teaching the Past* (Philadelphia: Temple University Press, 2001).

23  For concise histories of early museums, see Knell, *Museums in the Material World*, 1-29.

24  Hooper-Greenhill, *Museum and Education*, 67.

25  Linda Kelly, "Visitors and Learning," in *Museum Revolutions*, 276-91; John Falk, "Toward an Improved Understanding of Learning from Museums: Filmmaking as Metaphor," in *In Principle, In Practice*, 3-16.

26  American survey: Roy Rosenzweig and David Thelen, *Presence of the Past: Popular Uses of History in American Life* (New York: Columbia University Press, 1998). Australian survey: Paul I. Hamilton and Paula Ashton, "At Home with the Past:

Background and Initial Findings from the National Survey," *Australian Cultural History* 22 (2003): 5-30. Canadian survey as part of the "Canadians and Their Pasts" research project: see David Northrup, "Three-Part Harmony: The Presence of the Past in Canada, Australia, and the United States," paper presented at Association for Canadian Studies Conference, Quebec City, 24-26 October 2008.

27  Ivan Karp and Steven Levine, eds., *Exhibiting Cultures: The Poetics and Politics of Museum Display* (Washington: Smithsonian Institution Press, 1991); Eilean Hooper-Greenhill, "Education, Postmodernity, and the Museum," in *Museum Revolutions*, 367-77; Grisella Pollock and Joyce Zemans, *Museums after Modernism: Strategies of Engagement* (Oxford: Blackwell, 2007).

28  Christopher Clarke-Hazlett, "Communicating Critical Historical Scholarship through Museum Exhibition: A Museum Historian's View," in *Studies in History and Museums*, ed. Peter E. Rider (Hull, QC: Canadian Museum of Civilization, 1994), 57-76; Hooper-Greenhill, "Education, Postmodernity, and the Museum"; Gaynor Kavanagh, ed., *Making Histories in Museums* (London: Leicester University Press, 1996); Gregory and Witcomb, "Beyond Nostalgia."

29  The two temporary exhibitions used for this case study are "The Unnatural History of Stanley Park" (September 2008 to February 2009) at the Museum of Vancouver; and "Being Irish O'Quebec" (March 2009 to October 2010) at the McCord Museum of Canadian History in Montreal.

30  See Carla Peck's chapter in this volume for a discussion of the influence of ethnicity on understanding historical significance.

31  Discussed in John Falk and Lynn Dierking, *Learning from Museums: Visitor Experiences and the Making of Meaning* (Walnut Creek: Altamira, 2000), 37-52; Gaea Leinhardt and Karen Knutson, *Listening in on Museums* (Walnut Creek: Altamira, 2004), 158-61; Mieke Bal, "Exposing the Public," in *A Companion to Museum Studies*, ed. Sharon Macdonald (Oxford: Blackwell, 2006), 525-42; and Jocelyn Létourneau, "Museums and the (Un)building of Historical Consciousness," paper presented at the History Educators International Research Annual Conference (HERNET), London, 14-15 July 2005.

32  For a useful discussion of the "identity-driven" performance of museum visitors, see John H. Falk, *Identity and the Museum Visitor Experience* (Walnut Creek: Left Coast Press, 2009); and Jay Rounds, "Doing Identity Work," *Curator* 49, 2 (2006): 133-50.

33  Robert Bain, "They Thought the World Was Flat? Applying the Principles of How People Learn in Teaching High School History," in *How Students Learn: History, Mathematics, and Science in the Classroom*, ed. J. Bransford and S. Donovan (Washington: National Academies Press, 2005), 201-2.

34  Wineburg, *Historical Thinking*, 29.

35  Ibid., 1-28.

36  Keeping in mind the inherent tension between "usable" versus "critical past."

37  Pollock and Zemans, *Museums after Modernism*, 12.

38  Hooper-Greenhill, *Museum and Education*, 267.

39  Excerpt from the McCord Museum of Canadian History Mission Statement: http://www.mccord-museum.qc.ca.

40 Jörn Rüsen, "Historical Consciousness: Narrative Structure, Moral Function, and Ontogenetic Development," in *Theorizing Historical Consciousness*, 67.
41 David Dean, *Museum Exhibition: Theory and Practice* (London: Routledge, 1994), 166.
42 Wenger, *Communities of Practice*, 8-10.

# 13 Creating and Using Virtual Environments to Promote Historical Thinking

KEVIN KEE AND NICKI DARBYSON

How can historians and history teachers best use virtual environments (VEs) to support the teaching and learning of historical thinking? This question has received little attention from researchers. To most historians and history educators, "history" is expressed in words on paper. Yet in representing history through text alone, we turn the past into a sentence, in more ways than one – just ask a disengaged student in a traditional compulsory course. But the question deserves an answer for reasons beyond student engagement: VEs provide students with opportunities to encounter historical thinking in new and innovative ways.

This chapter outlines some of those opportunities. We begin by defining VEs and clarifying how these are a unique form of interactive media that require specific attention. We then acknowledge the larger academic interest in VEs for learning and the research this has spawned. Historians and history teachers have been slow to address the potential of history VEs: these environments are relatively new, as well as foreign to our experience of learning. To understand how VEs can be employed effectively, we need to understand how they function, which requires that we engage the work of game theorists. Drawing on the conclusions of these theorists, we couple their insights with research on historical thinking. As Peter Seixas points out, "'historical thinking' only becomes meaningful with substantive content,"[1] so we first address how VEs can be used to communicate the substance of history. But content gives only a partial understanding of historical thinking – we must also ensure that our students engage historical practices. We outline different genres of student engagement with history, the connections between these genres and concepts of historical thinking, and how these genres can be communicated in VEs. Several researchers and educators have begun to develop these applications for history, and their examples will serve to illustrate our conclusions. Our early experiments in building these forms of interactive media bode well for a future in which VEs will be used increasingly to enhance student knowledge of the content and practices of history.

## Virtual Environments Defined

According to Ralph Schroeder, a VE uses virtual reality technology to generate "a computer-generated display that allows or compels the user (or users) to have a sense of being present in an environment other than the one they are actually in, and to interact with that environment."[2] This definition, he points out, focuses on "sensory experience" – the "sensory element of experiencing a place or space." In essence, VEs are about "being there."[3]

VEs comprise technologies that support different kinds of user experiences, including single-player games, multiplayer games, and virtual worlds. One of the most popular subsets of VEs are games – environments built for the user's enjoyment. According to Edward Castranova, a game focuses "all thought and research on the user's subjectivity and well-being." The "being there" that Schroeder highlights – Castranova calls this "immersion" – is central to the enjoyment. And if the immersion is effective, the player will move beyond feeling "there," to investing her sense of self into the environment.[4]

As the term suggests, single-player games draw solitary players in, usually by squaring them off against computer-animated enemies.[5] In multiplayer games, and in massively multiplayer online role-playing games (MMORPGs), users invest themselves in relationships with other players.[6] Not all VEs are games, however; "virtual worlds," according to Schroeder, are "persistent virtual environments in which people experience others as being there *with them* [emphasis added] – and where they can interact with them." In short, these are online places for socializing.[7]

In the pages that follow, we examine how VEs can be used to support the teaching and learning of historical thinking, with a focus on the subsets of single-player games, multiplayer games, and virtual worlds. In each of these cases, a student engages the environment from a first-person perspective – she perceives herself to be inside the environment – through what game theorist Marie-Laure Ryan calls "internal interactivity."[8] We will deliberately leave out the following: (1) games that a user engages from the "outside," including environments seen from a bird's-eye view, a convention used in most computer strategy games (such as the blockbuster history franchise *Civilization*[9]); (2) "augmented reality games," where a user interacts with both the real and the virtual world (through a personal digital assistant [PDA], a mobile phone, or some other device);[10] and (3) "text games," where a user explores an environment solely through text (following instructions, for instance, to "open the door on the right and enter the parlour"). Each of these kinds of games holds considerable potential for historical thinking, but in ways that require specific attention. None of these uses virtual reality technology to create a feeling of "being there" in the same way as the VEs that are the focus of this study.

## VEs for Learning: The Perspective of Educators

While historians and history educators have for the most part ignored the potential of VEs for learning in school, scholars of education and psychology have given the subject significant attention. Indeed, research on VEs for learning has grown to the point that a new body of literature has emerged. Not all of the voices have been laudatory: some have questioned the appropriateness of "virtual" experiences for young people.[11] Early research suggested that there was no clear evidence that these environments added value to young people's education, pointing out that experience with other media did not demonstrate any significant effects on learning.[12]

More recent research, however, suggests the contrary – that VEs may provide useful applications for learners. There are several reasons for this. Virtual reality technologies[13] present opportunities "to experience environments which, for reasons of time, distance, scale, and safety, would not otherwise be available to many young children, especially those with disabilities."[14] In addition, games for learning appeal to twenty-first-century youth, "digital natives" who have grown up with and speak the language of computers.[15] A study of some two thousand children between the ages of eight and eighteen reported that eighty-three percent have at least one video game player in their home.[16]

Students who perform poorly in the classroom have been shown to benefit most from VE games, in part because they find these learning tools engaging.[17] Maria Roussos and her colleagues also point to evidence that immersion and presence can have a strong motivational impact.[18] Shazia Mumtaz has similarly shown that games and VEs can produce delight in learning.[19] While these games are marketed as entertainment, they can also be educational. A MediaWise report, summarizing the findings of a number of research studies, states: "Video games are natural teachers. Children find them highly motivating; by virtue of their interactive nature, children are actively engaged with them; they provide repeated practice; and they include rewards for skillful play. These facts make it likely that video games could have large effects, some of which are intended by game designers, and some of which may not be intended."[20]

Recent findings in brain research also point to the potential of VEs. Drawing on these developments, theorists led by Seymour Papert have advanced the notion of "constructionism,"[21] contending that knowledge is not deposited by the teacher into the student – what Paulo Freire (1970) termed "banking" – but rather is constructed in the mind of the learner. Tying insights into constructionism with conclusions drawn from other fields of study, literary theorist James Paul Gee has articulated a unifying theory of how games support learning, contending that these technologies enable students to experience new worlds where they can develop resources for problem solving and ultimately view the environment as a design space that can be engaged and changed. According to Gee, games for learning should be designed so that a student's thoughts, actions, and values are those of a professional.[22] A VE for physics learning, for example, should place the student in the role of a physicist.

But what about history learning, and historical thinking in particular?[23] Little research has been done on teaching and learning historical thinking in VEs. Most history games (and games that have been used to teach history) are strategy games that ask students to think like a political leader (such as President Franklin Roosevelt or Mohandas Ghandi). Kurt Squire has led research in this vein, with a specific focus on *Civilization*. That game allows the students to go back in time and "replay" history, making decisions to build empires and trade with other civilizations.[24] Squire has concluded that the students playing *Civilization* learn how to manage resources but make only limited advances in historical thinking in the game itself – such advances are achieved only *outside* of game play, in classroom discussions. As a result, the question remains: What is the best potential for teaching and learning historical thinking in VEs specifically?

## VEs and History Content

Research on the potential of VEs for history learning in schools must begin with a focus on the goals of that learning. We need to think about what it is we want to achieve as historians and teachers of history and look for ways that VEs might help us realize those goals. Fortunately for our purposes, the epistemology of history and history education has been the subject of public discussion for the past two decades in Canada, the United States, and western Europe. Much of the discourse has focused on content and on ways to transmit to students the substance of history. An understanding of names, dates, and events gained through secondary sources provides students with what history educators have called "first-order knowledge of history."

How can we best use VEs to support the teaching and learning of "first order" knowledge? Following Randy Bass, we need to ask: "Where are the critical and productive affinities between our methods and epistemology on the one hand, and the inherent structure and capabilities of interactive technologies, on the other?"[25] Here, too, we benefit from a substantive discussion among researchers – the inherent structure and capabilities of interactive technologies have also been the subject of a vociferous debate over the past decade.

On one side are the "narratologists," researchers with a background in narrative forms such as the novel, theatre, and film, who have heralded VEs and other forms of interactive digital media as new forms of storytelling.[26] In an attempt to work out the potential for these media, they have turned to modes of analysis concerned with these earlier, established narrative forms. The "ludologists" have countered that these media are not narratives, but rather a new form of entertainment that requires a new mode of analysis. Drawing on their backgrounds in computer science and design, they have argued for understanding their potential through a focus on the mechanics of play.[27]

The divisions between these two groups are clear in the abstract; however, when one analyzes the communication of content in VEs, the boundaries begin to soften. A VE is a hybrid medium that blends elements drawn from other narrative genres – text, image, sound – while providing the user with the opportunity to explore and play as she wishes. Problems arise when educators with little grounding in theories of effective engagement employ strategies to communicate content that were designed for older narrative forms: "telling" the user about the environment in long blocks of text or extended filmic sequences. Furthermore, as Georgia Leigh McGregor points out, VEs "are concerned with movement through space as a visceral experience."[28] Above all, users of VEs want to explore and play, not read and watch.

With this in mind, media theorist Henry Jenkins recommends that VE designers think of themselves as narrative architects who communicate content to users through the virtual space of the environment.[29] Jenkins takes inspiration from theme park designer Don Carson and his concept of "environmental storytelling." According to Carson, environmental storytellers build environments suffused with content that the user can explore and interact with to gain insight. Theme park design aims to fully immerse visitors in a ride experience by developing content in which the user is the central character. Every element of the space – lighting, architecture, contrasts, asymmetry, and characters – reinforces the ride's theme. For example, the Pirates of the Caribbean ride at Disney World immerses the visitor in a space in which all elements reinforce "pirates." Any object that is unrelated is removed, lest it ruin the sense of immersion.[30]

How do we apply these insights to the communication of content in VEs? In *A Journey to the Past: A Quebec Village in 1890/Un voyage dans le passé: Un village québécois à la fin du 19ième siècle,* my colleagues and I attempted to communicate first-order knowledge of history through environmental storytelling, making the space the medium of communication.[31] Instead of using a natural, "life-like" colour scheme, we adopted a sepia palette, thereby underscoring to our users that this was a "historic" environment. Following the "less is more" design mantra promoted by Jenkins, we populated the VE with buildings and artifacts that focused the user's attention on the goal of the experience: to determine the similarities and differences between the past and the present. And we developed non-player characters (NPCs) to support the appropriation of content. Gee has contended that games and VEs that support learning often employ "distributed authentic professionalism," providing the player with characters that help the player do her job more effectively.[32] Similarly, the NPCs in *Journey* provide information that helps the user fulfill her primary task of learning about life in late-nineteenth-century small-town Quebec and comparing it to the present. The entire environment, from the colours to the artifacts to the characters, has been assembled to facilitate this exercise.

## VEs and Historical Practice

While few would argue with the importance of content, it gives students only a partial understanding of the discipline of history. Scholarly research in the past two decades has focused on supplementing content with "second-order knowledge," which moves students beyond the who-what-where-when of history toward an understanding of the skills of historical practice – generating, corroborating, representing, and assessing interpretations of the past. This kind of history teaching and learning pays attention to the concepts, methods, and vocabulary required to do history and underscores the challenge of knowing the past.[33] The Benchmarks of Historical Thinking Project developed by Peter Seixas articulates "structural historical concepts [that can] guide and shape the practice of history."[34] Seixas suggests that students must be able to determine what constitutes *historical significance;* effectively use – including ask good questions of – primary source *evidence;* identify *continuity and change;* analyze *cause and consequence;* take *historical perspectives;* and understand the *ethical dimension* of history interpretations (see Lévesque, Chapter 5, and Seixas, Chapter 6, this volume, for a discussion of historical-thinking concepts).[35]

How can we use VEs to support the teaching and learning of historical practice as articulated in these benchmarks? We can begin by considering the different ways in which we have used media in the past, including text. As Caroline Coffin points out, historical literature comprises a repertoire of different types of text, or "genres," each of which enables different ways of thinking.[36] These text genres serve as useful organizational models for the multitude of ways that VEs can be employed.

**Biographical Recounts**

What Coffin calls "biographical recounts" revisit the events of a person's life, focusing on important moments or turning points and providing insight into the person and his time period. Biographical recounts in VE form take advantage of what Bass calls the "inherent structure and capabilities" of VEs.[37] These environments employ, as noted above, "just good enough" virtual reality[38] to immerse the user in a space she can explore in what feels like real time. The best way to think of this experience, according to Brenda Laurel, is in terms of theatre, because the user "participates in a representation that is not the same as real life but which has real-world effects or consequences."[39] Users "are like audience members who can march up onto the stage and become various characters, altering the action by what they say and do in their roles." They are not joining the actors on stage, but rather *becoming* actors by engaging in an act of role play.[40]

*Revolution,* a 3-D MMORPG prototyped at the Games to Teach lab at the Massachusetts Institute of Technology, is a biographical recount in VE form that allows a student to navigate the space of colonial Williamsburg, Virginia, in 1773, and act and react to events that preceded the American Revolution. This kind of game fits well within a unit in which the student is learning through other media (textbooks, films) and connected student activities about the events of this time and place. A student begins by assuming the role of the character she wants to play: a wealthy farmer loyal to the

Crown, a slave yearning for freedom, or a politician trying to negotiate a diplomatic minefield. When she enters the game, she is forced to respond, in concert with other students, to an event such as the escape of a slave from a nearby plantation. Some students play militia members canvassing the town for the runaway; others play slaves providing him shelter.

Students must engage a variety of historical practices while role-playing a VE like this. They encounter *continuity and change,* recognizing, in this case, that the race and class structure of eighteenth-century Virginia strictly delimited the manner in which members of society related to one another. At the same time, playing a role in *Revolution* helps students understand *cause and consequence* – that human beings actively bring about historical change. Historical role-playing games such as this are essentially simulations – playing these kinds of games involves a cyclical process of hypothesis formulation ("What happens if ... ?"), testing ("I'll try *this*"), and revision ("Well, that didn't work!"). This is what is called *cognitive disequilibrium,* the process whereby the learner readjusts her expectations in light of new information (resolution). Feedback is often immediate, allowing the cycle to begin again.[41] In taking on the identity of a historical character, a student becomes aware that her decisions shape the story – that her actions have consequences. In addition, assuming the role of a historical character in a VE requires that a student *take a historical perspective,* seeing events through the eyes of the character. As Seixas points out, this helps a student understand that studying the past is like visiting a foreign country.[42] It is a cognitive act of understanding the different social, cultural, intellectual, and even emotional contexts that shaped people's lives and actions in the past.

**Historical Recounts**
"Historical recounts," another genre, are narratives of past events, with a focus on the judgments that can be drawn about their historical significance. These are different from biographical recounts in that they are less concerned with the experiences of a person, but they are also similar, in that they focus on time as an organizing principle. *Journey,* referred to above, is a historical recount in VE form. It takes as its starting point two drawings of St. Hilaire, Quebec: "Road to the Church (St. Hilaire)" and "The Dance," by Ozias Leduc, one of Canada's leading artists in the late nineteenth and early twentieth centuries. The two drawings provide an entry point into this time and place: "The Road" is an idealized vision of the main village thoroughfare in May; "The Dance" is a scene during Mardi Gras, the feast that precedes the Lenten period of fasting and penance.

Entering the VE, the user finds herself in a twenty-first-century bookstore, where a young man and woman are debating the central question raised in the VE: "Was life one hundred years ago better or worse than today?" A guide approaches and shows them a "magic book" that may provide an answer. When the guide turns to a page showing "The Dance" and "Road to the Church," the student is pulled into a time tunnel that drops all of them into the chosen scene. In "Road to the Church," for instance, the user finds herself on the main road into St. Hilaire, beside an artist drawing his own picture of the scene – one significantly different from that of Leduc. Like all the NPCs she will encounter, he tells her a brief story of his own experience and then prompts her to find out more. Behind her lies a cottage where two farmers bicker about whether they should continue the farming practices of the past or adopt "newer" technologies and practices. Farther down the road, in the centre of the village, a priest dispenses advice on gender roles and job prospects for men and women. Inside the local inn, a maid and a cook – the cantankerous Madame Gauvin – are preparing a meal and demand the user's help.

In *Journey*, the student plays herself as time traveller, tasked with the work of a historian: she must determine how life in St. Hilaire was "better" or "worse" in 1890 than today and provide a report upon her return to the present. In this case, the historical practice of identifying and articulating *continuity and change* is central to the learning experience. Exercises built into the VE focus specific attention on the development of this historical practice. Madame Gauvin, for instance, demands help in cooking a chicken; if the user acquiesces, she must pick up a log, open the oven doors, place the log in the oven, light the log, close the doors before the kitchen fills with smoke, pick up a pitcher, fill it with water, pour the water into the pot on the stove, and finally pick up a plucked chicken and place it in the pot. It becomes clear in the course of this exercise that even the basics of "lighting" an oven have changed significantly since the late nineteenth century.

This VE also incorporates more sophisticated engagement with historical practices. The student's encounter with the concept of *taking an historical perspective*, for instance, requires that she move beyond seeing the past through a historical character's eyes, toward recognizing that any historical representation is a snapshot of an aspect of a vast and unfathomably complex reality.[43] Even at the elementary level, underscoring the "constructed" nature of history is an important aspect of history education. Seixas has suggested that the effective teaching of history might encourage users to approach the discipline from a postmodern orientation, providing them with opportunities to look behind constructed historical narratives to examine, for instance, what has been included or omitted, or the order in which the pieces of the story have been arranged.[44] In *Journey,* we tried to underscore the constructed nature of the VE in a variety of ways. As noted earlier, when the user arrives at "The Road," she finds herself facing an artist sitting at his easel. His drawing of 1890 St. Hilaire, he explains, looks fundamentally different from that of Leduc. Leduc had carefully excised all traces of the new technologies that were transforming his hometown at the end of the nineteenth century, but this artist includes the train, the railway track, and telephone poles. Even the environment the user is walking through, the artist points out, is a specific interpretation of the past.

**Factorial Explanations**
A "factorial explanation" differs from a historical recount and a biographical recount in its emphasis on the factors – typically multilayered – that contribute to a particular event or outcome. The focus here is not on a temporal sequence, but rather on answering a question with several explanations. In this kind of history narrative, the student is playing a role, but instead of playing a historian transported back in time, the student is a researcher in a present-day environment.

Jeffrey Clark and Brian Slator, at North Dakota State University, used text-based interactions among users in a 3-D space to create the *Virtual Archaeologist Educational Environment,*[45] in which students learn the methods of archaeology on a simulated excavation of the village of Like-a-Fishhook, North Dakota. In this VE, the student's job is to explain, with reference to various types of evidence, and multiple factors, the origins of these sites; in the process, she thinks like and uses the tools of an archaeologist.

Taking on the role of an archaeologist in a 3-D environment necessarily requires that the student engage several historical practices. The student must analyze various types of *primary source evidence* to determine who created it, when it was made, and what was going on at the time. For instance, the purposes of implements – pieces of which are uncovered in the ground – are far from obvious. As the student crafts her response, she comes to understand that her interpretation of the environment will determine her explanation of life in Like-a-Fishhook. In the process, she sees *cause and consequence* in historical interpretation. And drawing from the evidence she encounters, and reflecting on her own interpretation, can help her better understand what life was like in the past and the various *historical perspectives* that might be taken on people, places, and events in history.

**Expositions**

A factorial explanation explains the factors that contribute to an outcome; an *exposition* puts forward a point of view or argument. Historians and history teachers can use VEs to create an *exposition,* in the same way that we have previously used research papers, which require that students investigate primary and secondary sources and then assemble an essay to persuade the reader of a thesis. Instead of writing a paper, students can develop VEs (or parts of VEs), engaging sources and then building a place and experience to communicate a specific explanation of history.

As Ian Bogost has pointed out, the potential actions that a player can take in a computer game are controlled by the computer code. The code, therefore, determines the rules of the game – that is, the way a game operates. The rules promote a particular way of looking at the world – they make an argument in code for a specific world view. *Civilization,* to take the example of the most popular commercial history game franchise on the market, allows the player to guide a Stone Age tribe into the future, conquering the world as they go. The game has been programmed to make a case for American myths of benevolent capitalism and frontier expansion.[46]

Our students can create their own VEs and games, making their own arguments in code. Kevin Kee[47] teaches upper-level undergraduate courses in which students build historical VEs related to the War of 1812 in Niagara, using C++ (a general-purpose programming language) and Open GL (Open Graphics Library – a set of procedures enabling a computer's OS to produce 2-D and 3-D graphics). Other instructors assign the creation of game "mods" (modifications), which require that students use in-game editors to tweak, adapt, modify, or otherwise alter a game, resulting in the transformation of a commercial game into a history learning game.[48] Still others (Kee included) assign the development of historical places and artifacts in *Second Life* (SL). This environment was purpose-built for creation: any user can purchase all or part of an "island" and build a village, building, or artifact. Moreover, students can collectively build objects in the same space, at the same time, while working from different computers. For example, students in St. John could collaborate with students in Whitehorse to build a historical environment that would reflect the viewpoints inherent to their cities and cultures.

Whether building a historical VE "from scratch," as a mod, or in SL, students must determine which places and people are worthy of the act of creation. Seixas suggests that one way of determining historical significance is to ask which events and people have had the greatest impact over the longest period of time. Moreover, "significance is about a relationship not only among events and people of the past, but also about the relationship of those events and people to us, in the present, who are doing the historical thinking."[49] The construction of a historical VE inherently involves the act of building knowledge about what is and is not significant, from a student's vantage point.

The creation of historical VEs also requires that students engage primary source *evidence*. In a course taught by John Bonnett at Brock University, students are assigned a variety of sources related to the architecture of a historic building, such as streetscape sketches and fire insurance maps.[50] The students must use these to construct a 3-D virtual model of the building, analyzing the sources and selecting the relevant information from each. Moreover, they must critically analyze the strengths and weaknesses of each source and select appropriately from the available options. Inevitably, they encounter contradictory evidence and must justify privileging one source over another. In the process, they learn that the creation, or writing, of history is the result of a series of choices and that historians construct interpretations of the past using limited evidence.

Building a historical VE also compels students to engage *continuity and change*. The process of researching a specific place at a given time challenges students to consider what is different about the past – what has changed and why. Students involved in the development of *Découverte de la Nouvelle France,* a re-creation of a small village in New France, came face to face with the many ways in which their society had changed. Balancing a blend of online communication tools and offline research and role-playing tasks, the virtual villagers of New France began building lives, weaving their own stories, and linking their lives to local village history. As the volume of participants grew, so did the complexity of the lives of the villagers, their community interactions, and, later, the shape of the town.[51] In the same way, while constructing the environment for Kee's course on the War of 1812, students encountered the high ratio of churches to residences, the segregation of new immigrants from established ethnic groups, and the possibilities (and limitations) of nineteenth-century travel. The act of creation requires that students determine how the environment, and the characters inside it, are different from those of the present.

## Conclusion

In these ways, VEs can be used to teach students to think like historians. Historical thinking requires that students work with substantive content, and VEs provide multiple formalisms by which this can be communicated, including text, audio, and video. VEs are first and foremost environments that users explore and play in; and history educators who create VEs or who lead students in their creation must think of themselves as "narrative architects" communicating content to users through the virtual space of the environment. Historical thinking also requires that students engage historical practices; and in this regard the development of VEs as *expositions,* and the role playing in VEs as *biographical recounts, historical recounts,* and *factorial explanations,* encourages the acquisition of these skills.

Indeed, VEs may provide opportunities to develop these in ways that text cannot. Building a VE in the manner outlined above allows a student to literally build knowledge and understanding. As noted above, Papert called this constuctionism[52] – the construction of knowledge in the mind of the learner. In the field of computing, Papert drew on the research of Jean Piaget to develop the Logo programming language for students so that they could write and execute basic programming functions, including the programming of robots. In the field of history, students can use computer code or software to develop VEs. These projects can be ambitious (students can use programming languages and graphics libraries to develop VEs from scratch) or modest (students can use tools provided by a commercial VE and develop inside the VE space). Either way, as the research of Papert and his students has shown, they are likely to retain the knowledge and skills long after they are first acquired.

Also, students who play a role in historical VEs may learn historical practices in ways not possible through text. As James Gee points out, in the course of role playing in an established VE, the user develops an identity that is highly conducive to learning. Gee distinguishes among the three identities of a student in a game: (1) a virtual identity (the student's identity as a virtual character playing a role in a virtual environment); (2) a real-world identity (the student's identity in the real world); and (3) a "projective identity" (in which the student projects her values onto the virtual character and, in addition, views the virtual character as "a project in the making").[53]

While exploring inside a VE, a learner takes on a *virtual identity* (playing the role of a historical actor, such as a slave in colonial Williamsburg, Virginia, or a time-travelling historian) and views the environment through the eyes of that virtual identity. At the same time, she retains her *real-world identity*, often as someone with little interest in history. But because VEs are engaging, they draw learners in, offering them opportunities to try out virtual identities. As Gee points out, these provide what psychologist Eric Erickson has called a "psychosocial moratorium" – a learning space in which the student can take risks because the cost of failure is low. Because exploration and play in VEs is compelling, a student is enticed to put in a high degree of effort. Because VEs reward effort, they encourage and acknowledge success. As a result, a student can come to see that she can take on that identity – she can be an effective historical character or historian. In this way she develops a *projective identity*, viewing the development of her identity as a project she wants to continue. In the process, a student who might otherwise view history as "boring" may begin to see herself as that character, or as a time-travelling historian. And as a result of taking a historical perspective, and engaging the other skills of historical practice, she will be more likely to view history as historians do.

## NOTES

This research was made possible by funding from the Canada Research Chairs Program, the Social Sciences and Humanities Research Council, the Ontario Ministry of Research and Innovation, and Brock University.

1  Peter Seixas, "Benchmarks of Historical Thinking: A Framework for Assessment in Canada," unpublished paper, Centre for the Study of Historical Consciousness, University of British Columbia, Vancouver, 2006, 2.
2  Ralph Schroeder, *Possible Worlds: The Social Dynamic of Virtual Reality Technologies* (Boulder: Westview Press, 1996), 25.
3  Ralph Schroeder, "Defining Virtual Worlds and Virtual Environments," *Journal of Virtual Worlds Research* 1, 1 (2008), http://journals.tdl.org/jvwr.
4  Edward Castronova, *Synthetic Worlds: The Business and Culture of Online Games* (Chicago: University of Chicago Press, 2005), 291-92.
5  The most popular of these are "first-person shooter" role-playing games (RPGs) such as *Doom* (1993), which topped a 2004 industry insiders' list of the "Top 50 Games of All Time" (Gamespy.com, "GameSpy's Top 50 Games of All Time," 2004, http://archive.gamespy.com). In *Doom*, the player takes on the role of a space marine, stationed on Mars, who must destroy the monsters that have invaded his base.
6  In *World of Warcraft*, the most popular MMORPG today, with approximately 12 million monthly subscribers (Blizzard Entertainment, "World of Warcraft Subscriber Base Reaches 11.5 Million Worldwide" [2008], http://www.gamershell.com), a player takes on a character in the game world, then joins a guild of other player-characters, who then work together to complete quests.

7 Schroeder, "Defining Virtual Worlds." The most popular of these is *Second Life*, a commercially successful online virtual world that has been billed as "even better than the real thing." Anyone can join, create his or her own avatar (character), and build a life, engaging in social relationships and developing a lucrative career. Open to the public since 2003, in January 2009, it claimed 17 million residents (Linden Labs, *Second Life*, 2003, http://secondlife.com/whatis/economy_stats.php). The number of active participants in *Second Life* would be lower than the 17 million accounts that the creators of the environment publicize. There is nothing to "do" in *Second Life*, except what you want to do – a fact that sometimes drives new users away. Educators have been flocking to this world in droves, because this lack of restrictions allows them to create their own environments. Michael Rymaszewski, *Second Life: The Official Guide* (Hoboken: John Wiley and Sons, 2007), 318-24.
8 Marie-Laure Ryan, "Beyond Myth and Metaphor: Narrative in Digital Media," *Poetics Today* 24, 4 (2002): 595.
9 *Civilization IV*, the latest instalment of the franchise, lets the player guide any one of a number of cultures from the Stone Age to the Space Age. One of the highest grossing commercial-off-the-shelf computer games ever published, *Civilization IV* sold more than six million copies in the six months that followed its release in September 2005.
10 This technology is being used at the Tower of London, where the visitor, equipped with a mobile phone, must "help" famous (virtual) prisoners escape the tower. Along the way, the visitor is presented with historic materials traditionally delivered during a guided tour. But instead of listening to an interpreter, the user uncovers information through exploration and discovery, becoming immersed in the landscape of sixteenth-century politics, intrigue, and daily life. Aria Pearson, "Escape Old London's Most Feared Prison: Guided by GPS," *Wired Magazine* 15, 11 (23 October 2007), http://www.wired.com.
11 Frederick Brooks, "Virtual Reality in Education: Promise and Reality Panel Statement," proceedings of the IEEE Virtual Reality Annual International Symposium, Atlanta, 14-18 March 1998, http://ieeexplore.ieee.org; and Larry Cuban, *Teachers and Machines: The Classroom Use of Technology Since 1920* (New York: Teachers College Press, 1986).
12 H. Brody, "Video Games That Teach?" *Technology Review* (November-December 1993): 51-57; Richard Clark, "Media Will Never Influence Learning," *Educational Technology Research and Development* 42, 2 (1994): 21-29.
13 Schroeder does not differentiate between "virtual reality" technologies and "virtual environments" – a "virtual reality" technology supports the experience of a "virtual environment." Schroeder, "Defining Virtual Worlds."
14 Maria Roussos, Andrew Johnson, Thomas Moher, Jason Leigh, Christina Vasilakis, and Craig Barnes, "Learning and Building Together in an Immersive Virtual World," *Presence* 8 (1999): 247-63. See also Mike Scaife and Yvonne Rogers, "Informing the Design of a Virtual Environment to Support Learning in Children," *International Journal of Human-Computer Studies* 55 (1991): 115-43; M.R. Thompson, J.D. Maxwell, and P.M. Dew, "Interactive Virtual Prototyping," Eurographics UK 16th Annual Conference, *Eurographics* (1999): 107-20.

15  Marc Prensky, "Digital Natives, Digital Immigrants," *On the Horizon* 9, 5 (2001): 1-6.
16  Donald Roberts, Ulla G. Foeher, and Victoria Rideout, *Generation M: Media in the Lives of 8-18 Year Olds* (Washington: Kaiser Family Foundation, 2005), http://www.kff.org.
17  Maria Virvou, George Katsionis and Konstantinos Manos, "Combining Software Games with Education: Evaluation of Its Educational Effectiveness," *Educational Technology and Society* 8 (2005): 54-65; Sasha Barab and Kurt Squire, "Replaying History," *Proceedings of the 2004 International Conference of the Learning Sciences* (Los Angeles: UCLA Press, 2004).
18  See Meredith Bricken and Chris Byrne, "Summer Students in Virtual Reality: A Pilot Study," *Virtual Reality: Applications and Explorations* (New York: Academic Publications, 1993), 178-84.
19  Shazia Mumtaz, "Children's Enjoyment and Perception of Computer Use in the Home and the School," *Computers and Education* 36, (2001): 347-62; Tom Boyle, *Design for Multimedia Learning* (London: Prentice Hall, 1997).
20  David Walsh, Douglas Gentile, Jeremy Gieske, Monica Walsh, and Emily Chasco, *Ninth Annual MediWise Video Game Report Card* (2004), http://www.mediafamily.org.
21  "Constructionism" is a term coined by Seymour Papert in Idit Harel and Seymour Papert, *Constructionism* (New York: Ablex, 1991).
22  James Paul Gee, *What Games Have to Teach Us about Learning and Literacy* (New York: Palgrave Macmillan, 2003).
23  In contrast to the paucity of research on VEs, much work has addressed the potential of the World Wide Web. Through the development of websites such as the "Canadian History Portal" at http://www.canadianhistory.ca and "Projet Histoire-Hypermédia" at http://www.h-h.ca, José Igartua has illustrated the Internet's potential to teach historical thinking. For Igartua's insights into using the Web in an undergraduate context, see José Igartua, "Integrating Multimedia Technology into an Undergraduate History Curriculum: Pedagogical Considerations and Practical Examples," in *History.edu: Essays on Teaching with Technology*, ed. Dennis A. Trinkle and Scott A. Merriman (Armonk: M.E. Sharpe, 2001), 85-107. Igartua's colleague Luc Guay has researched how ICT, in general, can be used to teach history in Quebec schools. See Luc Guay, "Le Rapport Lacoursière: des nouvelles orientations aux nouvelles technologies de l'information (NTI)," *Bulletin d'Histoire Politique* 14, 3 (Spring 2006): 85-96.
24  Kurt Squire, "Replaying History: Learning World History through Playing *Civilization III*," PhD diss., School of Education, Indiana University, 2004.
25  Randy Bass, "The Garden in the Machine: The Impact of American Studies on New Technologies," 1997, http://www.georgetown.edu.
26  Brenda Laurel, *Computers as Theatre* (New York: Addison-Wesley, 1991); Lev Manovich, *The Language of New Media* (Cambridge, MA: MIT Press, 2001); Janet Murray, *Hamlet on the Holodeck: The Future of Narrative in Cyberspace* (New York: Simon and Schuster/Free Press, 1997).
27  For a discussion of ludology, see Gonzalo Frasca, "Ludology Meets Narratology: Similitude and Differences between (Video)Games and Narrative," originally published in

Finnish as "Ludologia kohtaa narratologian," *Parnasso* 3 (1999) (English version: http://www.ludology.org); Jesper Juul, *Half-Real: Video Games between Real Rules and Fictional Worlds* (Cambridge, MA: MIT Press, 2005); and Celia Pearce, "Towards a Game Theory of Game," in *First Person: New Media as Story, Performance, and Game*, ed. Noah Wardrip-Fruin and Pat Harrigan (Cambridge, MA: MIT Press, 2004).

28 Georgia Leigh McGregor, "Architecture, Space, and Gameplay in *World of Warcraft* and *Battle for Middle Earth*," Proceedings of the 2006 International Conference on Game Research and Development (Perth: 2006), 75-76.

29 Henry Jenkins, "Game Design as Narrative Architecture," in *First Person: New Media as Story, Performance, and Game*, ed. Noah Wardrip-Fruin and Pat Harrigan (Cambridge, MA: MIT Press, 2004), 118-30.

30 Don Carson, "Environmental Storytelling." *Gamasutra* (2001), http://www.gamasutra.com.

31 Kevin Kee, Jamshid Beheshti, and Andrew Large, *A Journey to the Past: A Quebec Village in the 1890s* (Montreal: Virtuel Age International, 2006).

32 James Paul Gee, *Why Video Games Are Good for Your Soul: Pleasure and Learning* (Altona: Common Ground, 2005).

33 Tom Holt, *Thinking Historically: Narrative, Imagination, and Understanding* (New York: College Entrance Examination Board, 1990); Samuel S. Wineburg, *Historical Thinking and Other Unnatural Acts: Charting the Future of Teaching the Past* (Philadelphia: Temple University Press, 2001).

34 Peter Seixas, *Benchmarks of Historical Thinking: A Framework for Assessment in Canada* (Vancouver: Centre for the Study of Historical Consciousness, University of British Columbia, 2006), 2.

35 Ibid., 3-11.

36 Caroline Coffin, *Historical Discourse* (London: Continuum, 2006), 10.

37 Bass, "The Garden in the Machine."

38 Castronova, *Synthetic Worlds*.

39 Laurel, *Computers as Theatre*, 112-13.

40 Ibid., 110.

41 Richard Van Eck, "Digital Game-Based Learning: It's Not Just the Digital Natives Who Are Restless ..." *EDUCAUSE Review* 41, 2 (2006): 20.

42 Seixas, *Benchmarks of Historical Thinking*.

43 Keith Jenkins, *Rethinking History* (New York: Routledge, 1991).

44 Peter Seixas, "Schweigen! die Kinder! Or, Does Postmodern History Have a Place in the Schools?" In *Knowing, Teaching, and Learning History: National and International Perspectives*, ed. Peter Stearns, Peter Seixas, and Sam Wineburg (New York: New York University Press, 2000), 19-37.

45 Brian M. Slator, Jeffrey T. Clark, James Landrum III, Aaron Bergstrom, Justin Hawley, Eunice Johnston, and Shawn Fisher, "Teaching with Immersive Virtual Archaeology," in *Proceedings of the 7th International Conference on Virtual Systems and Multimedia*, 25-27 October (Berkeley: VSMM, 2001), 253-62.

46 Ian Bogost, *Persuasive Games: The Expressive Power of Videogames* (Cambridge, MA: MIT Press, 2007), 28-44.

47 Kee leads the "Simulating History" project at Brock, which researches best practices for the design, development, and testing of computer simulations and serious games (including Virtual Environments) for history learning and public history (with funding from the Canada Research Chairs program, the Canada Foundation for Innovation, Heritage Canada, the Social Sciences and Humanities Research Council of Canada, the Ontario Ministry of Research and Innovation, Brock University, and other sources). See http://www.simulatinghistory.com/ and http://www.kevinkee.ca.

48 In the early days of computer gaming, this was often accomplished by exploiting bugs in the game's programming. Savvy game publishers soon realized that there were commercial benefits to this activity, and many now provide the in-game editors. The commercial rationale is straightforward: the more that players talk about the game, and provide additional content, the greater the "buzz" and the number of copies of the game sold. Some of these "mods" become so popular that they eclipse the original game. *Counterstrike*, to take the most notable example, was a "mod" that became more popular than its progenitor, *Half Life*.

49 Peter Seixas, "The Place of History within Social Studies," in *Trends and Issues in Canadian Social Studies*, ed. Ian Wright and Allan Sears (Vancouver: Pacific Educational Press, 1997), 116-29.

50 John Bonnett, "Following in Rabelais' Footsteps: Immersive History and the 3-D Virtual Buildings Project," History and Computing 13, 2 (2004): 107-50.

51 Offered to select schools only, "Découverte de la NouvelleFrance" was designed by Jean-Yves Frechette, a teacher and Les Technologies ÉVI founder. "Découverte de la Nouvelle France" was the first in a planned series that included the Manitoba Metis and the Acadiens, but none of these programs were ever commercialized.

52 Harel and Papert, *Constructionism*.

53 Gee, *What Games Have to Teach Us*, 45-70.

# 14

# Obsolete Icons and the Teaching of History

PETER SEIXAS AND PENNEY CLARK

## Symbols of Our Collective Past as Sites of Pedagogy

Around the world, people confront icons, symbols, and monuments that celebrate historical origins, movements, heroes, and triumphs that are no longer seen as worthy of celebration. The Voertrekker Monument in South Africa, the Canadian schools named for British admirals and generals, and statues of imperial conquerors pay homage, teach young people desirable character traits, and provide a positive sense of heritage and identity for a citizenry defined as excluding Aboriginal people, women, colonials, the poor, and the uneducated. What is to be done with these artifacts of earlier power configurations, outdated modes of understanding, bygone identities? Destroy them? Maintain them but strip them of their monumental status? Erect alternative monuments to celebrate those who were excluded or to tell a different version of the story?[1]

Public monuments, along with memorials, school history textbooks, museums, and commemorative holidays, occupy an arena in which modern societies define themselves most explicitly in relation to the past.[2] They are quintessential examples of what Pierre Nora has called *lieux de memoire*, sites of memory.[3] As such, they are also pedagogical sites whose messages are intended to convey values to the next generation.

Monuments are constructed to embody founders of the nation, heroes of the race. Extraordinary people whose deeds should be celebrated and whose character should be emulated (in the eyes of the monument builder) are the subject of grand edifices that have been constructed to last, presumably indefinitely, into the future. Moreover, the individuals celebrated in monuments are tightly linked to a collective historical trajectory – the founding and progress of the nation. Thus, where monuments do not celebrate individual heroes, they mark victories and other key events from the national past. And because monuments and their referents help define socially sanctioned virtues, they also foster solidarity and demarcate inclusion and exclusion in the social collectivity. To serve a monumental function, a *lieu de mémoire* occupies a public space. A hierarchy of public places articulated by urban planners, architects, and others helps confer greater or lesser status on particular monuments. Thus monuments are often located in central urban spaces and – even more crucially – at the seats of regional and national governments.

These sites become especially interesting at those moments when they inspire debate and contention. Such moments offer an opportunity to examine how people are thinking about their collective past and, it follows, how they are seeking to position themselves for the future. In those same moments, contemporary historical consciousness is uncovered, not so much through interpretations of the *lieu de mémoire* itself as through analyses of its reception. Controversies around a series of murals in the central rotunda of the British Columbia Legislature offer a prime example of these debates. An impulse to build monuments was what originally drove the painting of the legislature murals, in terms of both their content and their setting. They were meant to celebrate the arrival and progress of European civilization on the west coast of North America. They embody the laudatory qualities of justice, enterprise, labour, and courage, in the form of the European colonizers. This celebratory purpose, evident in the content of the murals, was reinforced by the public nature and political importance of their setting: the Legislative Building, the seat of the provincial government.

A crucial dimension of the study of historical consciousness relates to how cultural practices and tools for understanding the past are handed down to the next generation. While this handing down occurs most formally in textbooks and schools, recent research has also interrogated other sites of transmission and construction, including families, film, television, and commemorative celebrations.[4] Moments of debate offer a pedagogical opportunity: instead of seeking to resolve controversies before they make their way into classrooms and textbooks, the debates themselves might be mobilized to develop young people's capacities to construct meanings of the past in a conflict-ridden present.

The controversy around a four-panel series of murals in the BC Legislature's rotunda is a prime example of such debates. This particular one entered the schools in the form of a high school essay contest in which 553 students participated. Collectively, their essays are a rich source for investigating young people's ideas about contested communities.

## The Murals Controversy

In April 2001, controversy erupted in the BC press. The catalyst was the publication of a report by an advisory panel convened by the Speaker of the BC Legislature to consider the fate of four murals that had been on view in the building's rotunda for the past sixty-five years. The report had recommended that the murals be removed.

The panel had been established in the wake of concerns expressed by a First Nations group, whose objections centred on the mural called "Labour," which depicted bare-breasted Aboriginal women helping build Fort Victoria under the supervision of white men. In a letter to the province's attorney general, this group stated: "These paintings of bare-breasted Aboriginal women and of Aboriginal persons in subservient positions are, we are sure you will understand, highly offensive, demeaning and degrading to First Nations people in the province."[5]

Hemas Kla-Lee-Lee-Kla (Bill Wilson), one of the letter's authors, elaborated on this at a later date: "[These murals] may be reflective of attitudes of white people at the time [they were painted] but that doesn't make it right ... [They] depict a relationship with Aboriginal people that, if it ever existed, is over. The murals give the impression that the relationship still exists ... [They] are one of the most blatant examples of white superiority that exists in this province."[6]

The advisory panel delivered its report on 28 March 2001. The panel had considered five options: maintain the murals as they are; maintain the murals as they are with the addition of other materials; alter the murals; cover the murals; and remove the murals. Its recommendation was that the murals be removed from the rotunda. In support of this, it pointed to the overriding importance of the BC Legislature as a place where all British Columbians have a right to feel included. It also suggested an ongoing exhibition of contemporary art on the same site as a way of showcasing contemporary views. These displays would also serve to balance other statuary and decorations in the Legislature that, like the murals, "celebrate imperial expansion and proclaim the superiority of European civilization over the indigenous."[7]

The response to the panel's recommendations was divided. The province's premier at the time, Ujal Dosanjh, concurred with its findings: "It would be a fundamentally sound goodwill gesture of all British Columbians to accede to the request made by the First Nations."[8] But some members of the public objected vehemently. One letter writer compared the removal of the murals to a "Cromwellian rampage through Catholic churches."[9] Another facetiously suggested that the government "bring in the artillery and raze the legislature complex ... as it is the most blatant reminder of Vancouver Island's 'politically oppressive' colonial past."[10] A third offered as a solution that a new mural be added to balance the collection, this one depicting "white men, wearing no pants, building a First Nations village."[11]

We can only guess how quickly the New Democratic Party government would have responded to the report, because on 18 April 2001 an election was called, and in May the NDP was swept from power. Six years later, on 24 April 2007, the Honourable Michael de Jong, Liberal Minister of Aboriginal Relations and Reconciliation, proposed that the report be accepted for implementation and that its recommendation be adopted. The legislature voted 68 to 3 in favour, with the three dissenters arguing that to remove the murals would be to "rewrite history."[12] After a structural assessment, it became clear that removal would destroy the murals, since they had been painted directly onto the wall plaster. Accordingly, they were initially covered in black plastic to hide them from public view. On 3 June 2008, walls were constructed in front of them. As of this writing, each wall is adorned with a large archival photograph.

## The Murals in the BC Parliament Building

The four murals were commissioned in 1932 as a personal gift to the province by Provincial Secretary S.L. Howe and completed by BC artist George Southwell three years later. Howe asked the artist to illustrate "the historical qualities necessary for the establishment of a civilization."[13] According to the *Daily Colonist*, "the contribution that Colonel Howe is making towards the cultural advancement of the province and public appreciation of pioneer life will remain as a tribute to his ideals as long as the Parliament Buildings stand."[14]

In his history of the Parliament Buildings, Martin Segger described the murals as follows:

1 *Courage*. The meeting of Captains Vancouver and Quadra at Nootka Sound in 1792.

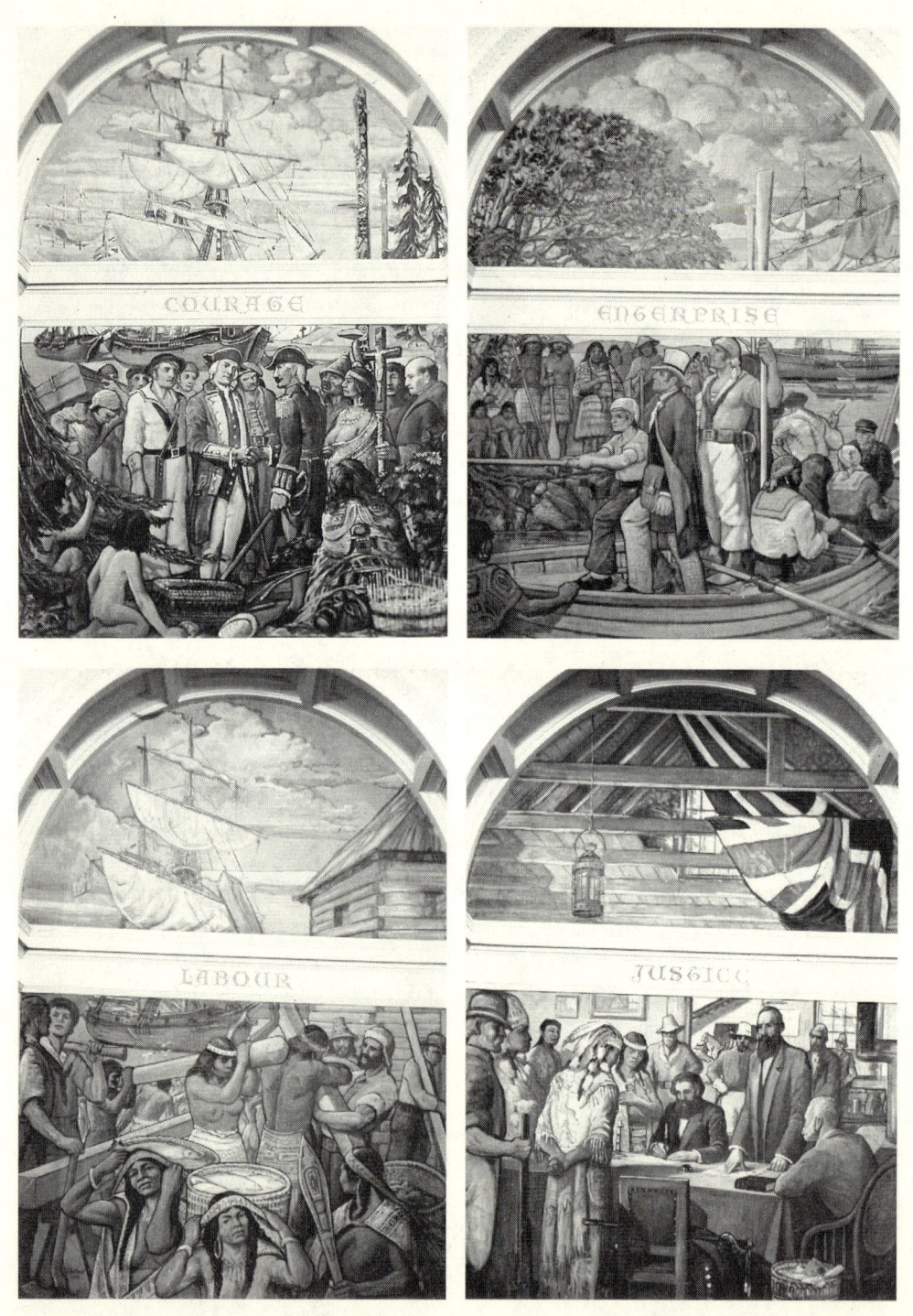

**Figure 14.1** Four murals, by George Southwell: "Courage" (B-06670), "Enterprise" (B-06675), "Labour" (B-0669), "Justice" (B-0668). All images courtesy Royal BC Museum, BC Archives, copyright Jane Munro.

2 *Enterprise*. Hudson's Bay Co. Chief Factor, James Douglas landing from the Cadboro at Clover Point to select the site for Fort Victoria [1843].
3 *Labour*. The building of Fort Victoria [1843] (alternately described as the building of Fort Langley [late 1820s]).
4 *Justice*. Colonial Chief Justice Sir Matthew Baillie Begbie holding Court in Clinton during the Cariboo gold rush [early 1860s].[15]

In a later letter to the Speaker's Advisory Panel on the Disposition of the Rotunda Murals by George Southwell, Segger states that "Justice" may depict British Columbia Indian Commissioner Lt. Dr. Israel Wood Powell's 1874 meeting with twelve Clinton area tribes.[16]

Each mural has two parts: a rectangular section below, which includes the human figures, and an upper section on the vault of the rotunda, which depicts the top part of each scene – the masts of a ship, the sky, and the ceiling of a room.[17] Originally, the title of each mural appeared on the strip of wall separating its two sections. Prior to 1977, the strips were painted over.

In this discussion, we will consider the murals as a pedagogical project. Indeed, in their origins they were explicitly pedagogical: artist George Southwell was asked to illustrate "the historical qualities necessary for the establishment of a civilization."[18]

## The Begbie Canadian History Contest as a Research Site

To understand young people's responses to the murals, we turned to the eighth holding (2001) of the Begbie Canadian History Contest, which is entered by grade eleven students.[19] Urban, suburban, and small-town schools, both public and private, in various regions of BC were represented. The test consisted of thirty multiple-choice questions, a paragraph question on the murals, and an extended essay question.

Accompanying a colour photocopy of the four murals, which included their titles, was this statement: "In the rotunda of the BC Legislative buildings in Victoria are four paintings intended to show the four qualities necessary for the establishment of a civilization: *Courage, Enterprise, Labour, and Justice*." The question on the murals – intended to be completed in about ten minutes – was as follows:

> There is currently a controversy about the way First Nations people are portrayed in four paintings found in the Legislative buildings in Victoria, BC. Consider the titles of the paintings and identify the elements that likely caused the controversy. Write a paragraph supporting either the retention

or the removal of the paintings, or suggesting some way to resolve the problem.[20]

In 2001, 553 students entered the contest, some because their teachers told them they had to, but many on a voluntary basis.

For this chapter, we read 53 test responses from the total of 553 and devised preliminary analytical categories. We then began coding individual sentences and phrases but quickly encountered ambiguities in the categories; this compelled us to twice revise the coding categories. After this, each of us coded the entire sample, selecting and recording key passages from every response that supported our categorization, along with annotations. We discussed discrepancies and reached a consensus in every case. We were left, however, with four students who spanned two categories each (so that the 53 entries became 57 records), and two students whose responses were impossible to categorize.

## Three Temporal Moments and Students' Reasoning

Analyzing the reasoning behind students' judgments of the murals was a complex task. We considered their statements in terms of three distinct but related temporal moments. The first temporal moment involved the colonial past, the time portrayed in the murals, between 1792 and the 1860s – the time when "civilization" was established in BC. The second temporal moment focused on the 1930s paintings themselves as pictorial representations of the past. The third temporal moment was the present. The contest question had asked about "some way to resolve the problem" – that is, it had asked explicitly for a judgment about action in the present. But in their arguments in support of these judgments, the students unavoidably included reasoning about the colonial past and pictorial representations of the past. Another part of the essay question asked for "elements of the paintings that likely caused the controversy"; in other words, students were explicitly required to analyze the pictorial representations of the past, even if they had not felt that they needed to do so to support their judgment about what should be done in the present. In the analysis that follows, we examine the reasoning that lay behind the judgments the students made about action in the present, based on a variety of configurations of statements about the colonial past and its pictorial representation in the murals. The reasoning regarding the colonial past and the pictorial representation of the past will allow us to examine systematically what lay behind students' judgments regarding what to do with the murals in the present. We arrived at this scheme

## TABLE 14.1
### Students' reasoning and judgments

| Moments | Reasoning |
|---|---|
| The colonial past (1792-1860s) | • The colonial relationship was unequal and involved domination of natives by whites, but this was ultimately for the benefit of civilization.<br>• The colonial relationship involved a meeting and sharing of cultures, to the benefit of both.<br>• The colonial relationship involved unjust and destructive domination of one people by another.<br>• The colonial relationship itself receives no comment; the students' entire analysis focuses on the 1930s pictorial representation. |
| Pictorial representation of the past (1930s) | • The murals present an unbiased, true, or accurate picture of the past: "It's what really happened."<br>• The murals present biased, unfair, or inaccurate representations of the past. |
| | *Judgments* |
| Monuments in the present (2001) | • Build the monument.<br>• Preserve the monument.<br>• Destroy the monument.<br>• Historicize the monument. |

through the recursive process described above: developing categories, coding some of the sample, revising the categories, recoding, and so on. (Note: all spelling and grammatical errors in the following sections' quotes are the students'.)

**Positive Colonial Past: Fair and Accurate Pictorial Representations (4)**
The small number of students – four – who expressed positive evaluations of the colonial past did so from two different positions. Student 48 saw, without any critique, a colonial relationship of unequal power. Thus s/he argued that domination was necessary and ultimately beneficial: "It is showing how we treat them like slaves, and that we have the power to do what we want with them." It is significant that this student used the first-person: "we." This student extended the circle of "we" to include George Vancouver, James Douglas, and Mathew Baillie Begbie. And not only are "we" powerful (in the

present tense, flattening historical time), but "we" also did what was necessary. As this student put it: "It shows what you need to establish a colony." Cecil Rhodes himself would not have seen the colonial relationship differently. The pictorial representation received no explicit comment from this student. It is no surprise that s/he recommended that the murals be preserved as monuments in their present setting: "I think that if these paintings are accurate then they should keep them up. If it shows that white men are stronger then the natives then let them stay. Just because it shows them at a lower level than us doesn't mean the paintings are wrong." This student was concerned about maintaining links with a past that s/he found quite acceptable and, therefore, worth preserving.

Three other students who saw colonial relations between whites and Aboriginal people as positive did so because they saw give-and-take in a mutually beneficial convergence of two civilizations. Thus, student 23 maintained that Canada had come into being "through much effort and comprimise": "In the painting, Courage, it represents the joining of two cultures. The handshake shows that they are willing to work together. In Labour, it shows the two cultures working equally and helping each other out."

Formally, these sentences read like discussions of the pictorial representation of the past; however, the student uses the representations transparently, to recount how two cultures came together in the colonial past. Indeed, these statements show just how tangled the reasoning is regarding the colonial past and its pictorial representation in the 1930s, despite our attempts to separate the two conceptually. In the following, again, we can read *through* the statement about the pictorial representation of the past to reasoning about the colonial past itself: "They should have named it 'Uniting' or something like that to show how whiteman and First Nations began to live together and work together" (39). Admittedly, the separation of the past from its later pictorial representation through statements such as these requires a high level of inference.

All four students recommended that the murals be preserved in their present location with no alterations. Accuracy of pictorial representation combined with a positive view of the colonial past supported a judgment of preservation of the murals as a link with the past.

**Negative Colonial Past: Fair and Accurate Pictorial Representations (11)**
Many students, though, understood the colonial situation negatively, as one of unjust domination. For these students, the murals were a fair or accurate

portrayal of an unjust chapter in history. Student 1: "Even though these paintings seem racist, it does show historical accuracy for the Europeans defeated the natives and took there land." Student 15: "There is the fact that this is history and it did happen, there is no denying the fact that First Nations people do get discriminated against often and more commonly through history the farther back you go." Student 32: "The courage is shown in Vancouver to actually shake the hand of his enemy, not to meet the natives. And that was how it was back then. The Europeans took over the land and fought amongst themselves for it, ignoring the natives that lived there." Student 38: "These paintings represent two very different cultures meeting, and because one culture was more civilized, that culture over powered the other."

In these statements there is an acceptance of the correspondence between an unequal and unjust representation in the paintings and the injustice that took place in the colonial past. The eleven students in this category were split about what to do with the murals in the present. The majority (six) took a preservationist position, recommending that the paintings be preserved unchanged so as to maintain links with the province's past. Student 25: "It is not a question of whether or not the paintings are racist and discriminatory but a question of history. These events took place and we cannot turn our backs on them."

Four students sought to destroy the murals' monumental status by severing the links with the past represented by their presence in the legislature. Student 38 thought the paintings should be removed and replaced with "new paintings of pride, progress, multiculturalism and the willingness to compensate and succeed in our province and its heritage." The problem for student 42 resided in the murals' titles: "The names are the most insulting because they inacceratly explain the paint." In this student's view, the titles provided a misleading textual interpretation of the content of the visual portrayal. For instance, "the title Courage suggests that Captin Vancouer has some threat on his life from the natives." If the "Labour" painting were to be renamed "'Salavery', it would then show the injustice of the settler's and suggest that the natives were being treated wrongly." This student concluded: "They are showing history, but they are suggesting the wrong theme in them." S/he seems to be saying that the titles reflect the European perspective on events. Perhaps this student would have appreciated the suggestion of student 39, which was to rename "Justice" with the title "We Get Our Way."

Finally, student 32, while recommending that the murals be saved, explicitly recognized our present distance from them and thus involved historicizing. This student deplored the colonial perspective: Europeans had "treated the people they met ... shabbily." However, s/he took the position that the murals form "part of our heritage, and we need to show the public what we did, so we do not make the same mistake. Learn from the past, so it does not repeat itself."

For six of the students, accuracy was sufficient grounds for a judgment of preservation, as it was for students in the previous category. However, the other five put more weight on their view of the past as morally corrupt. For them, accuracy could not provide sufficient support for a preservationist position.

## No Statements about the Colonial Past: Unfair and Inaccurate Pictorial Representations (30)

Over half the responses (30/57) avoided the question of correspondence between an unjust colonial past and an unjust representation of that past, by analyzing the paintings themselves without any explicit reference to the moral order of the colonial past they represented. For example, student 11: "The four paintings appearing in the BC legislative buildings depict First Nations People as unintelligent, violent people only useful for slave labour ... The Native peoples are shown gawking at the travelers. They are shown looking scared and unintelligent. The person who drew the piece was not around at the time and his interpretation of the event is unflattering and potentially inaccurate. It seems to say that Captain Vancouver was being courageous to step onto the shore where these 'barbarians' were and yet the Natives look more scared than anything else."

This strategy allowed for a detailed textual examination of the paintings, with scrutiny of their various elements: position of the characters; composition of the painting; colour, posture, and gesture; activities, clothing, and technology. These examinations were part of other students' paragraphs; but for students in this category, they formed the core of the argument. Hesitant, like student 11, to focus on historical inaccuracy in the details, these students concentrated on the kinds of messages they conveyed to the viewer. Thus, having considered the composition of "Courage," student 30 observed: "First Nations people are on the ground ... This positioning could be interpreted as a representation of the First Nations people as a base and backward people. As well, the positioning of the ships in the upper area while the art and technology of the First Nations remains on the very bottom further accentuates the feeling that the British Captains and their technology are 'courageous' and superior over the 'backward' First Nations people."

Students noted that the "qualities necessary for the establishment of civilization" were located solely among the white characters in the paintings. Student 8: "In the picture entitled 'Justice' the honourable Chief Justice Begbie is holding a native man on trial. This could be implying that the aboriginal people have a criminal nature and make the European settlers look good by giving them the position of keeping justice."

The reproductions of the murals in the contest reflected the lighting in the legislature dome, with the centre of each panel lit more brightly than the periphery. Since white figures occupy more of the central places, they tend to be more brightly lit. Student 18: "The First Nations appear to be relegated to the more shadowy parts of the picture." Students generally interpreted this literally highlighted Eurocentrism as having been painted into the murals. Student 2: "['Courage' portrayed] First Nations huddled into the background where the colours make them harder to see and Douglas bright and 'heroic.'"

These students saw posture, gesture, clothing, and technology contributing to unbalanced and unfair representations. Student 43: "[In 'Courage,' we] can see the white men standing proud and strong while the native peoples are shown sitting down." Student 9: "[In 'Enterprise,'] the way the natives are dressed and the awe and interest in which they seem to be looking at James Douglas (also the way he is arrogantly holding up his head) shows the natives as lesser people."

Student 29 sums up the problem: "Courage? Enterprise? Labour? Justice? Where the 'four qualities necessary for the establishment of a civilization' extended to all people over every descent? No! The First Nations people were portrayed unjustly, uncourageous, uninvolved and as a cheap work force."

Most of the students using this kind of reasoning (20/30) exhibited what Jörn Rüsen refers to as a critical historical consciousness, in that they were advocating the destruction of the murals' monumental status. Fourteen of them strongly recommended their removal. Student 9: "The four paintings found in the Legislative buildings in Victoria by George Southwell should be removed because of the degrading way they portray the First Nations people." The remaining six of this group called for the murals' monumental status to be erased through the provision of written explanations, by changing the titles, or by altering the paintings themselves. Student 40: "Perhaps a plaque describing the many wonderful things First Nations helped to accomplish would constitute as a supplement, or even a painting of 'Justice' with both a First nations and non-First-Nations man both being tried, rather than the singled out version currently used." Such additions would provide a *counternarrative*, in Rüsen's sense of this term – that is, a way to "unmask a given story as a betrayal, debunk it as misinformation."[21]

Given these students' recognition that the murals' portrayals were unfair, one might have expected them to recommend their destruction. Yet ten of the thirty made other suggestions. The recommendations of five of these students arose from a perspective of uncritical preservation. Two of these five recommended that the murals stay where they are, and three recommended that they be put on display in a museum or art gallery. (Student 41: "They are an artifact and deserve to be displayed"). The other five responses historicized the monument, incorporating a temporal dimension and emphasizing deconstruction of the latent messages in the murals' representations of the past. Student 12: "The paintings do represent the point of view of the times they were created in, and while these racist attitudes should by no means be endorsed, it is important that we remember they existed, and in many cases still exist." Student 11: "These four paintings are only useful to show the faults in Canadian history, the mistakes of the past. They should only be put up if this is their objective for they show nothing of the qualities necessary for the establishment of a civilization." Student 8: "Because the artist was brought up and lived during a period when native people did not have the same status as other Canadians, the paintings would not be controversial at the time they were first put up, but since 1961 when Native people were given the vote and considered 'people' the paintings should have been removed long ago."

Most students in this group recommended destruction of the monument, in one way or another, in the present.

**Negative Colonial Past: Unfair or Inaccurate Pictorial Representations (10)**

A substantial number of students (10/57) considered the paintings to be unfair and combined their observations with references to and reasoning about injustice in the past. Some among this group introduced questions of accuracy. Thus, student 22 examined "Enterprise" and doubted "the accuracy of the event." Similarly, s/he questioned a portrayal that showed that the "natives didn't mind having their land seized by Europeans." Other students in this group combined judgments of the pictorial representation with statements about fairness or justice in the past, but did so without making explicit statements about correspondence or accuracy. Student 6 objected to the interpretations conveyed in the titles. Regarding "Justice": "The scene is not a showing of justice, but a showing of the unjust treatment of natives, who, years after Douglas landed at Victoria, still treat natives as second-class people, inferior to white men." Here s/he was judging not only the historical representation but also the historical reality.

Many students using this strategy moved back and forth without much awareness that they were moving between judgments of the paintings and judgments of the past that the paintings portrayed. Student 7: "The uneducated native people were not accustomed to European style courts and had no way of defending themselves properly. The title 'Justice' is grossly misused and portrays Chief Justice Begbie as perhaps racist and cites native people as major contributors to crime."

Three of the ten responses in this category made a judgment to preserve the monument. Student 51: "Although [they] are biased, they are still a part of history." Student 7 advocated the preservation of "Courage" and "Enterprise" on the basis that they were "both arguably well intended and represent respectfully the bravery and ambition shown by European explorers and settlers in coming to an unknown land and dealing with a foreign civilization."

Five of the ten responses in this category advocated a destruction of the monumental status of the murals through removal. Student 28 suggested the addition of another painting that "displays the First Nations' triumph rather than manipulation by the British." Again, this additional painting would serve as a counternarrative, in Rüsen's sense.

Only two students whose assessment of the murals fell into this category recommended that they be historicized in some way. Student 53: "The public needs to recognize that these paintings are not only depicting four admirable elements of human nature; but also a time in our history. A time where the white man was the central theme because they were seen as superior. We cannot change these past ideas, but today we know better, we know that it was as much the Aboriginal people that made this country as the white people who came from overseas."

This student was judging not only the historical representation but also the historical reality.

## The Pedagogical Task of Monuments in a Historiographic Age

In assessing the responses, we must keep in mind that students wrote these paragraphs in a very short time: one ten-minute paragraph question as part of a larger, two-hour exercise. Nevertheless, they reveal something about how students use the resources they have at hand to reason about the past, its representation, and its uses in the present.

As we have seen, most of the paragraph responses considered the historical portrayal, the pictorial representation of the past, to be unfair or inaccurate, and made no direct reference to the moral order of the colonial past itself. Students used this reasoning as a basis for recommendations about what to do with the monument; the majority advocated its destruction. This line of reasoning was also the basis for many of the strong arguments to historicize the monument.

What can we learn about the pedagogical tasks posed by monuments and memorials in a post-colonial and historiographic age in which so many of our monuments are holdovers from the colonial era? Not only historians but also many members of the general public are ready to historicize the monuments themselves. The three different eras that framed the analysis of the students' responses to the monument now make possible a restatement of the pedagogical tasks of monuments in the present age.

**The Era of the Monument's Construction**

People need to be able to see the messages the monument attempts to convey in light of the historical context in which it was constructed. Most young people in this study understood the interpretive nature of the murals, and most were fairly comfortable with the idea of controversy over such historical representations. The textbooks they use are peppered with "issues": "Is today's government responsible for injustices of the past?" asks one of them.[22] Another elevates "issues" to an organizing framework for the text.[23] In the larger culture beyond schools, they have grown up on "fractured fairy tales" that undermine the morals of the old stories, and on popular films that challenge foundational myths.[24] If their history teachers have perhaps paid less attention to issues of historical interpretation and representation than they might, such ideas are at least circulating in literature for teachers.[25] So the students in this sample were at ease judging the murals on the basis of moral baggage that the pictures carried forward into the present. And most of them waded into the controversy using more or less close readings of the pictures themselves.

But the limitations of their arguments also point to some additional pedagogical goals that need to be addressed, if not regarding the monuments themselves, then regarding the schooling that prepares them to critically assess those monuments.

**The Colonial Moment**
People need to know what actually happened in the colonial era in order to be able to decide on the accuracy of the history represented in the monument. Though some of the students made claims about the "accuracy" of the paintings, they generally did not get far with these arguments, because they had only the most generic sense of the history of the colonial era that the paintings depicted. If the contest exercise had provided them not only with the murals, but also with transcripts of Begbie's court proceedings or the journals of George Vancouver's voyage, they might have gotten further. But this points to the kind of work that must be done in museums and schools, in preparation for the critical assessment of public monuments, and probably will not happen at the site of the monument at all.

**The Present**
People need to consider relevant factors in judging what should be done with the monument in the present. How does historical accuracy (or artistic value) matter? How does community response matter? And how should present-day values and considerations of human rights and respect shape the design, placement, and re-placement of monuments and memorials?

Despite recent calls for the creation of engaging narratives as staples of public and school history, our exercise points in a somewhat different direction.[26] When there is public controversy over the meaning of the past, with the definitions of the nation, civilization, and moral progress being contested, *lieux de mémoire* become central nodes in the debates. In this age, it will not serve us well to conceive of the central obligation of the older to the younger generation as the handing down of knowledge of the past in the form of memorial narratives. Rather, in an era during which the meaning of memory is openly debated, preparing students to engage in those debates assumes centre stage. Such preparation, moreover, requires students to be provided with texts that they can read analytically, as many of the students did the murals. But teachers, curators, and media artists, as creators of contemporary *lieux de mémoire*, should all be clear about which kinds of texts generate which kinds of readings. Examining a statue of Christopher Columbus or George Vancouver may generate a rich discussion about monuments. Viewing a play about 1776 in the United States or 1837 in Canada may generate a lively talk about theatre. And reading *Austerlitz* may stimulate important thinking about historical fiction. But additional texts are necessary in order to generate a similarly rich discussion of conquest and empire, the patriots and the *Patriotes,* or the Holocaust. These exercises require a variety of textual traces – those from the historical moment under discussion as well as historical representations constructed at various later times. With an array of traces from different moments in the past, teachers can lead young people to engage knowledgeably in debates about continuities and critical breaks in moral sensibilities over time (perhaps even more knowledgeably than some of the politicians who initiate them). And it is participation in these ongoing public debates – not inheritance of mythic, foundational narratives – that nurtures the identities that can help them sort through the moral dilemmas of our time.[27]

Representations of the past have uses in the present. The more that people are aware of the varieties of uses – and abuses – the more sensitive they can be to the historical references and images around them. The didactic nature of these murals was present at the outset. Their message was conveyed not only in how they depicted the colonial encounter, but also in their placement in the legislature's rotunda. A thorough understanding of these problems would allow people to avoid the errors of the three dissenters in the 2007 BC Legislature. They will help people understand the real differences between having murals painted in the 1930s in a museum and maintaining them in the central rotunda of the BC Legislature.

Even the removal of the murals themselves does not remove the colonial references from the BC Legislature, whose architecture is a monument to the colonial encounter, not to mention the city in which it sits – named "Victoria." Our best efforts will not erase the colonial past: there is no danger of that. So how should we think, in pedagogical terms, about its legacy?

### APPENDIX: A NOTE ON THE STUDENT SAMPLE

Our ability to use the Begbie Contest entries for the purposes of this research was serendipitous but came with certain limitations that restrict the kinds of claims we can make. The entire population of 553 contest entries does not comprise a scientific sample of the grade eleven school population of BC. Rather, it is composed of students from 43 BC schools where teachers chose to promote participation in the Begbie Contest. Moreover, schools are not equally represented. In some cases, teachers turned contest participation into an assignment for one or more classes. Thus, in the school with the highest participation, 112 students wrote the essay. In schools where participation was voluntary, fewer students wrote it – in three schools, only one student entered the contest. Finally, no individual demographic data were collected as a part of the contest. Thus any attempt to draw a scientific sample from among the 553 entries would be flawed from the outset. Faced with these limitations, we drew a sample from the 553 entries that would reflect (albeit roughly) the geographic regions of the province. We used all the entries from eight schools: two schools from the large metropolitan school districts of the Lower Mainland (9), two from midsize districts of Vancouver Island (14), three from midsize districts of the BC Interior (25), and one from a small northern district (5). We are confident that this number and range of responses has enabled us to construct a comprehensive and valid set of analytical categories. The sample we used does not support claims about proportions of students that might fall into these categories in a larger population, nor do we make such claims.

## NOTES

This chapter is adapted from a larger, published paper, Peter Seixas and Penney Clark, "Murals as Monuments: Students' Ideas about Origins of Civilization in British Columbia," *American Journal of Education* 110, 2 (2004): 146-71. © 2004 by University of Chicago. A shorter paper, with the title used here, was presented to the Canadian Historical Association, Vancouver, BC, 3 June 2008.

1 Annie Coombes, "The Struggle for History in the 'New' South Africa," paper presented at the World History Association International Conference, Victoria, 1999; John R. Gillis, "Memory and Identity: The History of a Relationship," in *Commemorations: The Politics of National Identity*, ed. John R. Gillis (Princeton: Princeton University Press, 1994), 3-24; Kerwin Lee Klein, "On the Emergence of Memory in Historical Discourse," *Representations* 69 (2000): 127-50; Ruth B. Phillips, "Settler Monuments, Indigenous Memory: Dis-membering and Re-membering Canadian Art History," paper presented at the conference Future of the Past: International Perspectives on the Relevance of History in the 21st Century, University of Western Ontario, London, 15-17 March 2002.
2 See Veronica Strong-Boag, "Experts on Our Own Lives: Commemorating Canada at the Beginning of the 21st Century," *Public Historian* 31, 1 (February 2009): 46-68, for a discussion of the Historic Sites and Monuments Board and the contested nature of public commemoration in Canada.
3 Pierre Nora, *Realms of Memory: The Construction of the French Past*, trans. Arthur Goldhammer (New York: Columbia University Press, 1996).
4 For examinations of textbook representations, see James Loewen, *Lies My Teacher Told Me: Everything Your American History Textbooks Got Wrong* (New York: Macmillan, 1995); Dan Porat, "A Contemporary Past: History Textbooks as Sites of National Memory," in *Raising Standards in History Education*, ed. Alaric Dickinson, Peter Gordon, and Peter Lee, International Review of History Education 3 (London: Woburn Press, 2001), 36-55; Jason Nicholls and Stuart Foster, "Interpreting the Past, Serving the Present: US and English Textbook Portrayals of the Soviet Union during the Second World War," in *Understanding History: Recent Research in History Education*, ed. Rosalyn Ashby, Peter Gordon, and Peter Lee, International Review of History Education 4 (London: RoutledgeFalmer, 2005), 173-87; Penney Clark, "Representations of Aboriginal People in English Canadian History Textbooks: Toward Reconciliation," in *Teaching the Violent Past: History Education and Reconciliation*, ed. Elizabeth A. Cole (Lanham: Rowman and Littlefield, 2007), 81-120. For national context, see Keith C. Barton, "'You'd be Wanting to Know about the Past':

Social Contexts of Children's Historical Understanding in Northern Ireland and the United States," *Comparative Education* 37 (2001): 89-106. For student responses to popular films, see Peter Seixas, "Confronting the Moral Frames of Popular Film: Young People Respond to Historical Revisionism," *American Journal of Education* 102 (1994): 261-85. For family and film, see Sam Wineburg, "Making (Historical) Sense in the New Millennium," in *Historical Thinking and Other Unnatural Acts: Charting the Future of Teaching the Past*, ed. Sam Wineburg (Philadelphia: Temple University Press, 2001): 232-55. For representations of nationhood on television, see Darren Bryant and Penney Clark, "Historical Empathy and *Canada: A People's History*," *Canadian Journal of Education* 29, 4 (2006): 1039-64; Lyle Dick, "'A New History for the New Millennium': *Canada: A People's History*," CHR Forum, *Canadian Historical Review* 85, 1 (March 2004): 85-109; "Nationalism and Visual Media in Canada: The Case of Thomas Scott's Execution," *Manitoba History* 48 (Fall-Winter 2004): 1-18; and "Representing National History on Television: The Case of *Canada: A People's History*," in *Programming Reality: Perspectives on English Canadian Television*, ed. Zöe Druick and Patsy Kotsopoulos (Waterloo: Wilfrid Laurier University Press, 2008), 31-49. For commemorations, see Gillis, *Commemorations*; and Jonathan Vance, *Death So Noble: Memory, Meaning, and the First World War* (Vancouver: UBC Press, 1997).

5  Jo-anne Archibald, Jean Barman, Martha Black, John Lutz, and Tsaqwasupp (Art Thompson), "A Review of the Depiction of Aboriginal Peoples in the Artworks of the Parliament Buildings," in *Report of the Speaker's Advisory Panel* (Victoria: Legislative Assembly of British Columbia, 2001), 7.
6  Ibid.
7  Ibid., 33.
8  "Premier Says Mural Must Be Removed," *Daily News* (Nanaimo), 10 April 2001, A4.
9  Jerry Blumenschein, "Victoria's Very Own Talibans," *Times Colonist* (Victoria), 11 April 2001, A11.
10 Christopher E. Spratt, "Leave Well Enough Alone," *Times Colonist* (Victoria), 11 April 2001, A15.
11 Joan O'Connor, "White Men without Pants," *Times Colonist* (Victoria), 19 April 2001, A15.
12 CBC News, "B.C. Legislature Murals Coming Down," 25 April 2007, http://www.cbc.ca.
13 Martin Segger, *The British Columbia Parliament Buildings*, quoted in Archibald et al., *Report*, 11.
14 *Daily Colonist*, 6 April 1933, quoted in Archibald et al., *Report*, 11.
15 Segger, quoted in Archibald et al., *Report*, 11-12.
16 As Segger further comments: "Indeed, it is almost certain that the seated man at the head of the table, as indicated by his red uniform, age and appearance, is British Columbia's first Dominion appointed British Columbia Indian Commissioner, Lt. Co. Dr. Israel Wood Powell (1836-1915). If this is so, the painting probably depicts the famous scene from the 1874 meeting of Powell with twelve Clinton area tribes. County Court Judge O'Reilly and interpreter/recorder Joe Bushey were in attendance as Powell listened to and discussed various issues with each of the chiefs, in

particular the lack of treaties and inadequate size of land grants. In the *Colonist* press account (July 14, 1874) of this event 'Fountain Chief Tsch-lo-ko-sultz' is described as 'tall and erect ... dressed in a white buckskin coat with fringes, panteloons of same, leggings and moccasins, his head adorned with a black fox-skin cap and a sword hanging by his side' ... Southwell knew Powell as he painted his portrait, and may have got the account of the event verbally from him many years later. 28 January, 2001." For further discussion of this issue, see: Stephen Hume, "'Justice Mural Likely Depicts the Opposite of What Critics Allege," *Vancouver Sun*, 17 March 2007, http://www.canada.com/vancouversun.

17 The Begbie Contest displayed photographs of the bottom portion of the murals only.
18 Segger, quoted in Archibald et al., *Report*, 11.
19 The Begbie Canadian History Contest, named after Matthew Baillie Begbie, the first judge in the colony of British Columbia, is an annual test originally available only to British Columbia students in grade eleven (and occasionally grades ten and twelve), but now offered in several other Canadian provinces. Developed by teacher Charles Hou and sponsored by the provincial Social Studies Teachers' Association, the test consists of multiple-choice and essay questions. Monetary prizes are awarded to the top three contestants.
20 Begbie Contest Society, *The Begbie Canadian History Contest: The First Ten Years* (Vancouver: 2003), 220.
21 Jörn Rüsen, "The Development of Narrative Competence in Historical Learning: An Ontogenetic Hypothesis Concerning Moral Consciousness," *History and Memory: Studies in Representation of the Past* 1 (1989): 47.
22 Michael Cranny and Garvin Moles, *Counterpoints: Exploring Canadian Issues* (Toronto: Prentice-Hall, 2001), 10.
23 Daniel Francis, Jennifer Hobson, Gordon Smith, Stan Garrod, and Jeff Smith, *Canadian Issues: A Contemporary Perspective* (Toronto: Oxford University Press, 1998).
24 Adam Gopnik, "Magic Kingdoms: What Is a Fairy Tale, Anyway?" *New Yorker*, 9 December 2002, 136-40; Seixas, "Confronting."
25 Thomas C. Holt, *Thinking Historically: Narrative, Imagination, and Understanding* (New York: College Entrance Examinations Board, 1990); Peter N. Stearns, *Meaning over Memory: Recasting the Teaching of Culture and History* (Chapel Hill: University of North Carolina Press, 1993); Walter Werner, "Reading Visual Texts," *Theory and Research in Social Education* 30 (2002): 401-28.
26 Gene Allen, James Cullingham, Adam Symansky, Bill Waiser, and Larry Hannant, "Canadian History in Film: A Roundtable Session," *Canadian Historical Review* 82 (2001): 331-46; Penney Clark, "Engaging the Field: A Conversation with Mark Starowicz," *Canadian Social Studies* 36 (Winter 2002), http://www.quasar.ualberta.ca; Alexander Stille, "The Betrayal of History," *New York Review of Books* 45 (11 June 1998): 15-20.
27 Nancy Wood, *Vectors of Memory: Legacies of Trauma in Postwar Europe* (Oxford: Berg, 1999).

PART 5

# PERSPECTIVES ON HISTORICAL THINKING

# 15 Ethnicity and Students' Historical Understandings

CARLA PECK

In the summer of 2002, Statistics Canada, in partnership with the Department of Canadian Heritage, embarked on an exploration of what it means to "be Canadian." The study, *The Ethnic Diversity Survey*, aimed to provide information on the ethnic and cultural backgrounds of the Canadian populace; it sought to understand in a more complicated way how Canadians of different ethnic backgrounds interpret and report their ethnicity.

Significant about this research is that for the first time, Statistics Canada was asking "an ethnic identity question" of its respondents.[1] The question was phrased as follows: "I would now like you to think about your own identity, in ethnic or cultural terms. This identity may be the same as that of your parents, grandparents or ancestors or it may be different. What is your ethnic or cultural identity?"[2]

Interviewers were not allowed to provide examples but were allowed to accept up to *six* responses from each participant. This survey question marks an important step in the Canadian government's recognition of the plurality of identity in general and of ethnic identity in particular. By reconceptualizing ethnicity as complex, fluid and ever developing, the Department of Canadian Heritage documented an important shift from past thinking that perceived ethnic identity as static, unchanging, and determined by birth.

In the past decade, many history education researchers have shown an interest in understanding the complex relationships that exist between students' ethnic identities and their conceptualizations of history. Their search for understanding was blunted because the nature of ethnicity has been inadequately theorized within the history education community. In this chapter, I explore how contemporary theorists employ the terms "ethnicity" and "ethnic identity"; provide an overview of research that has sought to explore the relationship between ethnic identity and students' historical understandings; argue that history educators interested in students' historical understandings must more explicitly investigate how identity – in particular, ethnic identity – can influence these understandings; identify and discuss a significant gap in the research on ethnic identity and students' historical understandings; and provide an example of a research study that was designed to fill this gap.

## Don't Box Me In

The Canadian government's recognition that some individuals needed to check more than one "identity" box on a census form is, in part, a reflection of the influence of critical and postmodern academic scholarship on society's thinking about ethnicity and identity that has emerged in the past two decades. This work has had important implications for our understanding of ethnic identity and related concepts such as ethnicity. In 1999, Rattansi called for a radical rethinking of ethnicity, wherein "the first 'postmodern' move must be to decentre and de-essentialize [our thinking on concepts like ethnicity], by postulating what is often glimpsed but rarely acknowledged and accepted with any degree of comfort: *there are no unambiguous, watertight definitions to be had of ethnicity, racism, and the myriad terms in between* ... Indeed, all these terms are permanently *in-between*, caught in the impossibility of fixity and essentialization."[3]

Rattansi's caution is an important one. Johnston, Gregory, Pratt, and Watts claim that ethnicity "is one of the most difficult concepts to define: researchers disagree on the meaning of the term; social groups differ in their expressions of ethnicity; and some theorists challenged the credibility of the concept in the first place."[4] These authors also articulate two major misconceptions about the term "ethnicity." The first concerns the use of the term only in reference to minority groups.[5] In North America, the dominant group is most often white and of European descent and rarely sees itself as "ethnic," even though it is commonly held that everyone is "ethnic." This inability, or refusal, of the dominant group to see itself as "ethnic" is due in large part to the privilege it wields in society.[6]

The second misconception arises "when the terms ethnicity and race are used interchangeably, or when they are seen as variants of the same classification system."[7] "Race" is a highly contested concept. It is widely held that the biological foundations of the term "race" have long been discredited. Nevertheless, racism and discrimination based on the idea of "race" continue to exist. McLaren and Torres posit that "it is racism as an ideology that produces the notion of 'race', not the existence of 'races' that produces racisms"; they argue for "a clear understanding of the *plurality* of racisms," including their historical evolution.[8] This view is widely contested. Scholars such as Dei, Karumanchery, and Karumanchery-Luik have theorized the salience of "race" in contemporary society and "question assertions that place race as an exclusively ideological construct."[9] They contend that "it is problematic to argue against the reality and utility of the race concept, based solely on the fact that pseudo-sciences backing *biological functionality* have no scientific grounding. To do so negates the practical applications and circumstances of race's social, political, economic and material impact on societies in general and on racialized bodies specifically."[10]

Johnston and colleagues argue that while racial identity is most often ascribed by others based on phenotype features, "the most basic difference between race and ethnicity is that ethnic affiliation arises from inside a group; ethnicity is a process of self-definition."[11] In other words, the development of a person's ethnic identity occurs through social interaction within a cultural group and personal reflection on what it means to belong to such a group. It is an ongoing process, and – as Rattansi argued above – it necessarily retains a certain level of ambiguity.[12]

Others suggest that the process of self-definition also occurs through interaction with people outside of self-identified ethnic groups. For instance, Nagel maintains that "ethnicity is constructed out of the material of language, religion, culture, appearance, ancestry, or regionality. The location and meaning of particular ethnic boundaries are continuously negotiated, revised, and revitalized, by both ethnic group members themselves as well as by outside observers."[13] Barker agrees that ethnicity is "centered on the sharing of norms, values, beliefs, cultural symbols and practices,"[14] but also argues that, because "ethnicity is a relational concept concerned with categories of self-identification and social ascription ... ethnicity is not best understood in terms of cultural characteristics *per se,* but as a process of *boundary* formation which is constructed and maintained under specific socio-historical conditions."[15] Similarly, Hall contends that it is important to conceptualize "identity as contradictory, as composed of more than one discourse, as composed always across the silences of the other."[16] Hall notes the importance of reflecting on the various aspects that make up one's identity and the ways in which identity is projected onto others or interpreted by them.

Though there are no clear-cut definitions of ethnicity or ethnic identity – indeed, Pryor and colleagues describe ethnicity as a "conceptual maze"[17] – all of these explanations of ethnicity carry similar characteristics. First, ethnicity is necessarily fluid and plural. The enunciation of one's ethnic identity may change depending on the social, political, and/or cultural context in which one finds oneself. Second, the development of ethnic identity is both a personal process and a social one and occurs through inter- and intra-group boundary formation. Individuals look not only within themselves but also within their group for clues to their ethnic identity. Individuals also take cues from the larger society – including people, institutions, and historical conditions – to define their identity. Finally, some of the markers associated with ethnic identity include language, religion, appearance, ancestry, regionality, non-verbal behaviour, values, beliefs, and cultural symbols and practices.[18]

Recognition by academia – and more recently by the state – of the complexity of ethnicity reinforces the idea that ethnic identity is both individually and socially constructed rather than determined a priori.[19] As Abu-Laban and Stasiulus note, this is especially true in the Canadian context: "Many Canadians, including those of second and further generations, have developed a hybrid sense of identity. While they are of Canadian *nationality*, their ethnicity is not simply that of being of English-Canadian *ethnic* identity."[20] In short, the consensus among researchers is that ethnicity and ethnic identity are complicated concepts.

In addition to underscoring the complicated nature of ethnicity and ethnic identity, researchers have insisted on recognizing "that we all speak from a particular place, out of a particular history, out of a particular experience, a particular culture, without being contained by that position … We are all, in that sense, *ethnically* located and our ethnic identities are crucial to our subjective sense of who we are."[21]

Like many Western societies, Canada relies heavily on immigration to maintain its population levels. In the past, immigrants to Canada originated primarily from the United Kingdom and Europe. More recently, immigrants are arriving from places such as Asia, Africa, and the Middle East.[22] Schools and teachers need to respond to this changing demography, particularly as educational systems across Canada move away from a British-oriented approach to education, where the end goal was the creation of "'good Canadian citizens' in the image of British loyalists,"[23] toward a more multicultural approach to education that responds to the needs of diverse students, embraces multiple perspectives, and advocates for social cohesion.[24]

## Research on Socio-Cultural Identity and Students' Historical Understandings

Research into various facets of children's historical thinking has demonstrated that socio-cultural positionality, including ethnic identity, can influence the ways in which students understand and interpret the past.[25] Though interest is growing, there remains limited research on this topic. Indeed, Barton argues that "much more research is needed to illustrate the specific ways in which students of given backgrounds [including gender and class] learn history both in and out of school."[26] In the remainder of this chapter, I will focus on the relationship between students' ethnic identities and their ascription of significance to moments in Canada's past. Historical significance is a central question in historical inquiry and is concerned with decisions regarding which people, events, and developments from the past should be remembered, commemorated, and taught. I begin by tracing the development of this line of research in the history education community.

One of the first studies to demonstrate that students' understandings of historical significance can be influenced by ethnic identity was conducted by Seixas.[27] He interviewed students about a school project on family oral histories. For most of the students, family experiences were important not only as sources of information but also in shaping "the students' underlying approaches to history."[28] Students relied on family histories and experiences to help them process historical information; thus, these "had a profound impact on how many of these students understood history."[29] For example, one student found that the family oral history project enriched the knowledge she had acquired in school; as a consequence, she felt "more confident vis-à-vis her own ethnic community."[30] In contrast, another student "found it difficult to make any connections between the Canadian history she was learning in school and [the] Chinese history" with which she was well acquainted.[31] Seixas notes that at least for some students, family histories – including an understanding of one's ethnic identity – can provide frameworks for organizing the history they learn in school.

In the United States, Epstein investigated how students' racialized identities affect their constructions of significance in the context of American history.[32] Epstein determined that students of European descent tended to see

American history from either a "traditional" Eurocentric perspective or a "revisionist" Eurocentric perspective,[33] whereas students of African American descent perceived American history from either an "Afrocentric" or a "double historical consciousness" perspective.[34] Epstein suggests that history teachers need to be aware of "the difficulties of teaching history to students who had constructed perspectives based primarily on the historical experiences of the racial group with which they identified."[35] By incorporating the differing logics of representation into their teaching, Epstein suggests, teachers can help students wrestle with the often contradictory historical perspectives they bring to the classroom.

Levstik's work with Maori and white students in New Zealand found that not only does ethnic identity influence students' understandings of historical significance, but so too does a country's global positioning affect how students ascribe significance to historical events.[36] In this study, students ascribed historical significance to events that helped them understand their own history, that connected New Zealand to the rest of the world, that were symbolic of fairness and peaceful coexistence among diverse groups in New Zealand, and that were examples of New Zealanders' accomplishments. The events to which the students ascribed significance differed with their ethnicity. For instance, white students viewed the Treaty of Waitangi as an instrument for the fair distribution of land, whereas the majority of Maori and Pacific Islander students saw it as a struggle over land that was rightfully theirs in the first place.

In a study comparing conceptions of significance among grade eight students in England and the United States, Yeager, Foster, and Greer found evidence to support the contention that "class, race, family history, popular culture, the media, and other social and cultural forces are important influences" that affect students' understandings of history, including historical significance.[37] While the finding that most of the English students' choices reflected their English background was hardly surprising, some were "influenced by their own [ethnic] cultural upbringing."[38] For instance, for one student whose father lived in Iraq, the Iran-Iraq war was considered significant. For another born in South Africa, the end of apartheid was significant. In these cases, ethnic identity played a key role in determining the significance of events for these students. Identity was important for the American students in this study as well. While their "choices were somewhat less culture bound than the English students," they tended to ascribe significance to events "in terms of American involvement or effects" on the world.[39]

Barton and McCully's work with Protestant and Catholic students in Northern Ireland is a rare example of a study that sought to investigate students' "constructions of historical themes or concepts *and the connection they made between those and their own identities.*"[40] They found that older (compared to younger) students tended to use national, cultural, or religious identifications as a way to select meaningful events in Northern Ireland's history; but they also noted that the majority of students' explanations did not rely on such identifications. And they noted, as well, that gender, geographical location, and other factors can influence students' historical understandings.

Of the many recommendations that can be drawn from this study, two are of particular importance to the current discussion on the relationship between students' socio-cultural identities and their historical understandings. At a policy level, Barton and McCully suggest that individual history departments be given more latitude in developing programs "that take account of individuals and their needs in the communities in which they live."[41] This is not an easy task. Canadian history teachers are already challenged by demanding curricula that span hundreds of years and a multitude of topics. It is impossible to study everyone and everything. Yet research suggests that students in multiethnic societies would be better served by curricula that are tailored to their needs, interests, and prior experiences.

Barton and McCully also note that their "study suggests that history educators need to examine more closely the unintended consequences of their choice of content, particularly the ways in which students from diverse backgrounds may interact differently with the same curriculum."[42] Their suggestions seem especially relevant to students and teachers in the Canadian context, given Canada's diverse society.

In a Canadian study that investigated francophone and anglophone Ontario students' conceptions of historical significance, Lévesque underscores the importance of understanding the relationship between ethnic identity and students' understandings of historical significance: "Students, no less than educational authorities, teachers, and historians, confront the study of the past with their own mental framework of historical significance shaped by their own cultural and linguistic heritage, family practices, popular culture influences, and last, but not least, school history experience."[43]

Lévesque found differences in the events chosen by students in each linguistic group as well as in the criteria they used to determine the significance of events.[44] Anglophone students typically ranked francophone events low on their list of significant events, even though the list was titled "most significant events in *Canadian* history." A parallel finding held for the francophone students, who were more invested in events that predominantly featured francophone history and identity. In terms of criteria used to ascribe significance, anglophone students tended to use disciplinary (historians') criteria, whereas francophone students used more personal criteria such as "symbolic significance" and "intimate interests." Lévesque posits that they "were more likely to use 'intimate interests' than anglophone students precisely because the minority culture with which they identified endorses such connectedness to the collective past."[45] In this study, Lévesque found that the francophone students ascribed significance as a function of – or an expression of – their francophone identity.

Lévesque's research is significant for a number of reasons.[46] It represents the first study in English Canada to replicate well-established research methodologies[47] to investigate Canadian students' understandings of historical significance. It also attempts to understand the role that ethnic identity might play in these understandings. Lévesque attended to the importance of ethnic identity in the analysis of his data; but like other researchers, he missed an opportunity to ask participants directly how they believed their ethnic identity influenced the ways in which they selected and ascribed significance to historical events. This question demands our attention.

### Addressing the Gap

My own work with grade twelve students (seventeen and eighteen year olds) sought to address the gap in the literature identified above. My central research question was this: "What is the relationship between a student's ethnic identity and his/her ascription of significance to phenomena in Canada's past?"

I conducted my research in an urban centre in the Lower Mainland of British Columbia and included Aboriginal, immigrant, and Canadian-born (non-Aboriginal) grade twelve students in my study (twenty-six students in total). VanSledright, Kelly, and Meuwissen contend that "studying ideas about historical significance among learners remains only a partially successful endeavour without collecting sufficient data on their biographies."[48] As a white researcher, I did not want to make assumptions about students' ethnic identities.[49] So I asked students to complete a questionnaire eliciting demographic information and also asked them to write a paragraph describing their ethnic identity "in a way that made sense to them." Then, in small, heterogeneous working groups, students completed a "picture selection" task modelled on well-established American and European research.[50] Students were given thirty event cards that provided brief descriptions of events in Canadian history. The thirty events are commonly found in secondary social studies curricula across Canada.[51] Each event card included the name and date of the event, a brief caption, and between one and three images. The task required students to create a timeline by selecting, out of these thirty, the ten most significant events in Canadian history. Several group and individual interviews were held to elicit students' thinking about the decisions they made during the research exercise. The focus of the individual interview was on the students' understandings of how their ethnic identity may have influenced the decisions they made in the picture selection task. Complex relationships between students' ethnic identities and their understandings of (and ascriptions of) historical significance in Canadian history emerged from the data. In the following vignettes, I explore the relationship between several students' ethnic identities and their understandings of historical significance. I do not have the space to elaborate on all the findings from this study. Rather, I have selected four students to profile, each drawn from one of the subgroups of students who participated in the study: Ariana, an Aboriginal student; Sam, an immigrant to Canada; and Ethan and Will, two Canadian-born students who worked together on the research task but narrated the timeline they created together very differently. I do not claim that these students are representative of their respective subgroups.

## Ethnic Identity and Ascriptions of Historical Significance

### Ariana

Ariana reported that her ancestors were coastal First Nations; she referred specifically to the Nuu-Chah-Nulth Nation and the Cowichen Tribe. She described her own identity as "an urban Aboriginal who learns about other Aboriginal culture because my own isn't offered. Multicultural Canadian Aboriginal." During the research task, Ariana and her partner, Conor, initially ascribed significance to events depicting Aboriginal history. However, as the task went on, Ariana advocated for a wider selection of events. By the end of the research exercise they had created the timeline shown below.

1778: Europeans Arrive on West Coast of Canada
Mid-1800s: Creation of Indian Residential Schools
1858: Fraser River Gold Rush
1881-85: Building of the Canadian Pacific Railway (CPR)

1885: Louis Riel and the Northwest Rebellion
1913: Record Immigration Numbers
1929-39: The Great Depression
1982: Canada Act Passed
1990: Collapse of the Meech Lake Accord
1999: The Marshall Decision

I asked Ariana if she was satisfied with the timeline she and her partner had created. She replied that she felt "less selfish concerning my history because Canada is a multicultural country now." She also explained how she selected events for the timeline: "My perspective of Canadian history is different than everybody else's ... I think if I was born and raised on my reserve I'd try to find all Aboriginal [events] or something. But since I live in an urban setting I've tried to include all of them." Ariana's identity as a "multicultural Canadian Aboriginal" influenced her ideas about historical significance, to the extent that she ascribed significance to events that she felt were representative of her identity.

### Sam

Sam immigrated to Canada from China three years before the study was conducted. When asked to describe his ethnic identity, he wrote:

> I still feel my pride as a Chinese. I defend Chinese history. I am still living in a typical Chinese family, eating typical Chinese food and learning the history of China. But as I live in Canada longer, I think I also have absorbed some Canadian North American culture. But here comes a question: what is Canadian culture? I think it is multiculturalism. So as I become more Canadian, I am more and more tolerant to other cultures. I promote both Canadian and Chinese cultures. So it would be best to describe me as a Chinese-Canadian.

Sam completed the picture selection task with three other students who were also immigrants to Canada and members of ethnic minorities.

1867: Confederation
1881-85: Building of the CPR
1913: Record Immigration Numbers
1919: Winnipeg General Strike

1929: The Person's Case
1939-45: Canada Enters World War II
1957: Pearson Wins Nobel Peace Prize
1971, 1988: Canada Enacts Multiculturalism Policy and Act
1982: Canada Act Passed
1995: The Quebec Referendum

When asked how his ethnic identity may have influenced the decisions he made during the picture selection task, Sam replied: "As I was deciding on these pictures I was kind of putting myself in the mindset of a Canadian instead of a Chinese ... So in some ways during the process of choosing these I shifted my own identity, so not a lot of these things really represent my true identity." Sam was the only person in his group who argued (in vain) to include more issues related to minority rights in their selection of events. The three other group members argued that they preferred to create a timeline that did not show preferential treatment to one ethnic group over another. As a result of this decision, Sam reported that he emphasized his Canadian identity while making decisions about which events were significant. Importantly, Sam added that "it's not like [I'm] Chinese and Canadian. I am in between – but I'm actually, I'm constantly shifting between the two." The notion that one's ethnic identity is always a process – that it is not fixed – is apparent in Sam's reflections on the relationship between his ethnic identity and his ascriptions of significance to events in Canada's past.[52] It also is indicative of a particular use of identity that Sam deployed during the picture selection task. Would Sam deploy his ethnic identity in different ways for different tasks?

### *Ethan and Will*
Ethan completed the timeline activity with Will (profiled below). Ethan, a Canadian-born student, described his ancestry as "half Jamaican, from a Caribbean descent. Also, I have origins from Dutch and Scottish roots. The Scottish part is where I got my last name." One of Ethan's parents was born in Canada, the other in Jamaica. The description he gave of his own ethnic identity was as follows: "I would describe myself as Canadian. My reasons are because of my personal qualities I've inherited from living here ... Being a person with many different racial origins [I] feel as [if] I am the epitome of Canadian culture. I feel as if I am a mosaic, which is what Canada is on a national level."

1670: Granting of Royal Charter for Fur Trade
1759: The Siege of Quebec
1778: Europeans Arrive on the West Coast of Canada
1881-85: Building of the CPR
1867: Confederation
1916-18: The Women's Suffrage Movement
1939-45: Canada Enters World War II
1957: Pearson Wins Nobel Peace Prize
1971, 1988: Canada Enacts Multiculturalism Policy and Act
1982: Canada Act Passed

I asked Ethan to explain the thought process he used to decide which events should be placed on his group's timeline. He said, "When I was going through the picture cards ... I took out all the racial things, right? Because it didn't bother me, right? And hopefully it doesn't bother people now because Canada was in a different place 100 years ago. Canada now is a multicultural place ... and that is the most important thing." Ethan's explanation of how he selected events for his timeline is tied to his perception of his identity as "the epitome of Canadian culture" and "a mosaic." His perception of his own multicultural identity meant that he emphasized, and ascribed significance to, events that depicted Canada as a multicultural nation.

Will was third-generation Canadian. He described his ethnic or cultural origins as "mostly English" and Scottish. Will described his ethnic identity as follows: "Most of my ancestors are Canadian, including my great-grandparents. However, I consider myself a Canadian with British heritage." When asked to reflect on if and how his ethnic identity may have influenced which events he found historically significant, Will offered the following response: "I found a lot of the original establishing things important but – I mean, I can look back and see maybe, maybe some of the stuff in the twentieth century is just as important or more important – but for me, 'cause this [referring to the first five events on the timeline] is sort of when my ancestry came and started to do things, it's important." Will's explanation of the events he and Ethan selected for their timeline stands in stark contrast to the explanation that Ethan offered. Will's identity as a Canadian with British heritage meant he ascribed historical significance to events that were related (in his mind) to his ancestors' arrival in Canada and the founding of the country.

These vignettes present only the briefest of snapshots of the relationship between students' ethnic identities and their understandings of historical significance. In other work I have described this relationship in much more depth.[53] The responses from these students are helpful in that they demonstrate their ability to articulate both their perceptions of their ethnic identities and their awareness of the impact their ethnic identities may have on the ways they think about the past. These vignettes illustrate how a research design focused on students' historical understandings, and that also explicitly attends to issues of identity (ethnic or otherwise), can elicit revealing responses. As the excerpts from Ariana, Sam, Ethan, and Will's interviews indicate, students bring complex identity-related frameworks to their study of history. This finding should serve as a caution against simplistic assumptions about how students in multiethnic societies might operationalize such frameworks when they study the past.

### Educational Implications

Canada's experience with and policy toward ethnic diversity is different from those of other pluralist societies and must be taken into account in any discussion of the nature of ethnicity and ethnic identity in Canada. The first difference is rooted in the country's demographics. On the 2006 Census, more than forty-one percent of Canadians listed multiple ethnic groups when asked to describe their ethnic background.[54] This is quite different, for example, from the black-white dichotomy that characterizes how ethnicity is viewed in the United States.[55]

Kymlicka argues that, though other countries have also begun to wrestle with the tensions associated with living in a pluralist society, Canada is unique in this regard both in terms of the range of diversity present in the country and "in the extent to which it has not only legislated but also *consitutionalized* practices of accommodation."[56] While the Canadian experience is held up by some as a model for multicultural societies, others argue that Canada's approach to ethnic diversity has caused disunity and conflict and has threatened the Canadian identity.[57] These conflicting viewpoints complicate the ways in which educational jurisdictions have responded to the increasing diversity in Canadian schools.[58] History educators and students are obliged to negotiate multiple ways of knowing about the world, all the while teaching and learning variations on a grand narrative of history. A key component in this negotiation is ethnic identity and its relationship to the ways in which students understand historical concepts.

Why should history educators and researchers care about the complex relationships that exist between students' ethnic identities and their historical understandings? I, along with others, believe that this work has important implications for citizenship. Barton and Levstik write that "identity anchored in history provides a more durable commitment to our nation and our fellow citizens ... Regardless of our political inclinations, when our identity is grounded in the nation's history [histories], we have incentives for shared action and public responsibility that would be lacking if we lived only in the present."[59]

Barton and Levstik's argument is that students will have a greater sense of belonging to the nation if their history lessons provide them with opportunities to understand both how the nation developed and how that development has influenced their own identity formation. Many Canadian educational jurisdictions have included an explicit link to identity in history or social studies curricula. However, in most of these curricula, the relationship between identity and history is treated in a unidirectional fashion. This is particularly true for curricula focused on Canadian history. That is, the curricula focus on how learning Canadian history can help students understand their own identity as "Canadians," but do not seem to engage students in questions about how their own identity helps them understand, or may influence, their understanding of Canadian history.

When they ask students to think about their own identity and the relationship it has to their understandings of history, teachers and researchers gain a more complex understanding of the knowledge and values that students bring to their schooling experiences. It is important for teachers to become – and provide opportunities for their students to become – aware of how ethnic identity can have an impact on how students learn history. Though many factors can contribute to this difference in learning (prior knowledge, interest), the relationship between a student's ethnic identity and the learning of history must also be attended to by both the teacher and the student. This opens up many new learning opportunities, such as investigating why different people, or different groups of people, have differing ideas about what is historically significant. Why are there competing accounts of the past? These types of inquiries can lead to deeper historical understanding.

## Conclusion

Canada is a multicultural society, and that will not change. What *will* change, as recent demographic surveys indicate, is the complexity of the diversity present in neighbourhoods across the country.[60] No longer a feature of urban centres alone, diversity is a fact of life in all municipalities in Canada. Educational systems must respond to this diversity. As noted earlier, social studies and history curricula across Canada include "identity" as a core concept and seek to help students understand how their own and others' identities are shaped and nurtured, as well as how identities change over time. Key to developing these understandings is providing opportunities for students to articulate their ideas about their own changing identities (ethnic and otherwise) and the ways in which identity can influence their understandings of educational content generally, and historical content more specifically.

Researchers, too, must also continue their interest in the intersections between identity and understandings of history. Kincheloe contends that

> the development of the individual coupled with the construction of a democratic community is central to a transformative social education. Embracing a critical alterity (awareness of difference) involving responsiveness to others, the new social education works to cultivate an intersubjectivity that develops both social consciousness and individual agency ... Understandings derived from the perspective of the excluded, or the culturally different, allow for an appreciation of the nature of justice, the invisibility of the process of oppression, and the difference that highlights our own social construction as human beings.[61]

In this chapter, I have addressed what I see as two significant gaps in the literature on students' historical understandings. The first gap relates to the nature of ethnicity and ethnic diversity. The process of articulating this comes with an important caveat: just as identity, and ethnic identity in particular, is in constant flux, so must be attempts to define these concepts. Any definitions or other such understandings of ethnicity (and related concepts) must always be considered tentative and open to discussion and elaboration. Otherwise, we run the risk of returning to the problem of essentialized definitions of identity.

The second gap I addressed was the need for researchers to more directly attend to the relationship between students' ethnic identities and their historical understandings. Metacognition, or the ability to think about one's own thinking, is recognized as a significant factor in student learning. According to Donovan and Bransford, metacognition involves "an awareness of the need to ask how new knowledge relates to or challenges what one already knows."[62] Previous studies that examined the relationship between identity (ethnic or otherwise) and students' conceptions of historical significance have not directly asked students to reflect on the intersection between their identity and their historical thinking. My own research with students in a highly multicultural urban centre sought to fill this gap by asking students to reflect on how their ethnic identities may have influenced their ascription of significance to events in Canada's past. Doing so creates an opportunity to develop a deeper understanding of the relationship between a student's ethnic identity and his or her conception of historical significance in the Canadian context. Understanding the values, frameworks, and knowledge that students bring to their understanding of historical significance will help educators better understand how they construct their understandings of the past.

## APPENDIX: LIST OF EVENTS IN PICTURE SELECTION TASK

1670: Granting of Royal Charter for Fur Trade
1755-58: English Expel Acadians
1759: The Siege of Quebec
1778: Europeans arrive on west coast of Canada
1812: The War of 1812
Mid-1800s: Creation of Indian Residential Schools
1858: Fraser River Gold Rush
1867: Confederation
1881-85: Building of the Canadian Pacific Railway
1880s-90s: Recruitment of Chinese workers to build the Canadian Pacific Railway
1885: Imposition of the Chinese Head Tax
1885: Louis Riel and the North-West Rebellion
1907: Anti-Asiatic Riots, Vancouver
1913: Record Immigration Numbers
1914: The *Komagata Maru* Incident
1914-18: Britain (and Canada) enters WWI
1916-18: The Women's Suffrage Movement
1917: The Halifax Explosion
1919: Winnipeg General Strike
1929: The Persons Case
1929-39: The Great Depression
1939-45: Canada enters WWII
1942: Japanese internment during WWII
1957: Pearson wins Nobel Peace Prize
1970: The October Crisis and the War Measures Act
1971, 1988: Canada enacts Multiculturalism Policy (1971) and Multiculturalism Act (1988)
1982: Canada Act Passed
1990: Collapse of the Meech Lake Accord
1995: The Quebec Referendum
1999: The Marshall Decision

## NOTES

This chapter is based on my doctoral research: "Multi-Ethnic High School Students' Conceptions of Historical Significance: Implications for Canadian History Education," PhD diss., University of British Columbia, 2009.

1 Jennifer Kaddatz, "The Ethnic Diversity Survey: Measuring Ethnic Ancestry, Ethnic Identity, and Ethnic Salience in Canada," Association of Canadian Studies Symposium, Toronto, 2005.
2 Statistics Canada, Housing Family and Social Statistics Division, "Ethnic Diversity Survey Questionnaire," http://www.statcan.ca.
3 Ali Rattansi, "Racism, Postmodernism, and Reflexive Multiculturalism," in *Critical Multiculturalism: Rethinking Multicultural and Antiracist Education*, ed. Stephen May (London: Falmer Press, 1999), 79-80, emphasis in original.
4 R.J. Johnston, Derek Gregory, Geraldine Pratt, and Michael Watts, eds., *The Dictionary of Human Geography*, 4th ed. (Oxford: Blackwell, 2000), 235.
5 Ibid.
6 Paul R. Carr and Darren E. Lund, eds., *The Great White North? Exploring Whiteness, Privilege, and Identity in Education* (Rotterdam: Sense Publishers, 2007); Timothy Stanley, "Why I Killed Canadian History: Towards an Anti-Racist History in Canada," *Histoire Sociale-Social History* 33, 65 (2000): 79-103.
7 Johnston, Gregory, Pratt, and Watts, eds., *Dictionary of Human Geography*, 235.
8 Peter McLaren and Rodolfo Torres, "Racism and Multicultural Education: Rethinking 'Race' and 'Whiteness' in Late Capitalism," in *Critical Multiculturalism: Rethinking Multicultural and Antiracist Education*, ed. Stephen May (London: Falmer Press, 1999), 47.
9 George J. Sefa Dei, Leena Luke Karumanchery, and Nisha Karumanchery-Luik, *Playing the Race Card: Exposing White Power and Privilege,* Counterpoints: Studies in the Postmodern Theory of Education, Vol. 244, ed. Joe L. Kincheloe and Shirley R. Steinberg (New York: Peter Lang, 2004), 27.
10 Ibid., 32, emphasis in original.
11 Johnston, Gregory, Pratt, and Watts, ed., *Dictionary of Human Geography*, 236.
12 Rattansi, "Racism, Postmodernism, and Reflexive Multiculturalism."
13 Joanne Nagel, "Constructing Ethnicity: Creating and Recreating Ethnic Identity and Culture," *Social Problems* 41, 1 (1994): 152-53.
14 Chris Barker, "The Construction and Representation of Race and Nation," in *Television, Globalization, and Cultural Identities* (Buckingham: Open University Press, 1999), 62.
15 Ibid.
16 Stuart Hall, "Old and New Identities, Old and New Ethnicities," in *Culture, Globalization, and the World Systems: Contemporary Conditions for the Representations of Identity*, ed. Anthony D. King (Binghamton: Department of Art and Art History, State University of New York, 1991), 49.
17 Edward T. Pryor, Gustave J. Goldmann, Michael J. Sheridan, and Pamela M. White, "Measuring Ethnicity: Is 'Canadian' an Evolving Indigenous Category?" *Ethnic and Racial Studies* 15, 2 (1992): 215.
18 I have purposely omitted "race" from this list of ethnic identity markers due to the contested nature of the term and the caution raised by Johnston, Gregory, Pratt, and

Watts, eds., *Dictionary of Human Geography* concerning the potential conflation of the terms *ethnicity* and *race*.

19  The constructionist versus primordial views of ethnicity are discussed in detail in Carter G. Bentley, "Ethnicity and Practice," *Comparative Studies in Society and History* 29, 1 (1987): 24-55; and Richard Jenkins, "Ethnicity *Etcetera*: Social Anthropological Points of View," *Ethnic and Racial Studies* 19, 4 (1996): 807-22.

20  Yasmeen Abu-Laban and Daiva Stasiulis, "Constructing 'Ethnic Canadians': The Implications for Public Policy and Inclusive Citizenship. Rejoinder to Rhoda Howard-Hassmann," *Canadian Public Policy – Analyse de Politiques* 26, 4 (2000): 481, emphasis in original.

21  Stuart Hall, "New Ethnicities," in *Identities: Race, Class, Gender, and Nationality*, ed. Linda Martín Alcoff and Eduardo Mendieta (Oxford: Blackwell, 2003), 94, emphasis in original.

22  Kelly Tran, Stan Kustec, and Tina Chui, "Becoming Canadian: Intent, Process, and Outcome," *Canadian Social Trends* (2005): 8-23.

23  Reva Joshee, "Citizenship and Multicultural Education in Canada: From Assimilation to Social Cohesion," in *Diversity and Citizenship Education: Global Perspectives*, ed. James A. Banks (San Francisco: Jossey-Bass, 2004), 135.

24  Ibid.; George H. Richardson, "The Death of the Good Canadian," in *The Death of the Good Canadian: Teachers, National Identities, and the Social Studies Curriculum* (New York: Peter Lang, 2002), 51-86. Critics of the "social cohesion" approach to citizenship education argue that such an approach simply recognizes diversity without a critical analysis of power relations, and actually marks a retreat from more activist forms of citizenship education.

25  Keith C. Barton and Linda S. Levstik, *Teaching History for the Common Good* (Mahwah: Lawrence Erlbaum, 2004); Jean-Pierre Charland, *Les élèves, l'histoire et la citoyenneté* (Quebec: Les Presses de l'Université Laval, 2003); Terrie Epstein, "Adolescents' Perspectives on Racial Diversity in US History: Case Studies from an Urban Classroom," *American Educational Research Journal* 37, 1 (2000): 185-214; Jocelyn Létourneau, *A History for the Future: Rewriting Memory and Identity in Quebec*, trans. Phyllis Aronoff and Howard Scott (Montreal and Kingston: McGill-Queen's University Press, 2004).

26  Keith C. Barton, "Students' Ideas about History," in Handbook of Research on Social Studies, ed. Linda S. Levstik and Cynthia A. Tyson (New York: Routledge), 250.

27  Peter Seixas, "Historical Understanding among Adolescents in a Multicultural Setting," *Curriculum Inquiry* 23, 3 (1993): 301-25.

28  Ibid., 319.

29  Ibid.

30  Ibid., 308.

31  Ibid., 316.

32  Terrie Epstein, "Deconstructing Differences in African American and European American Adolescents' Perspectives of US History," *Curriculum Inquiry* 28, 4 (1998): 397-423; Epstein, "Adolescents' Perspectives."

33  Epstein, "Adolescents' Perspectives," 192-94. Epstein explains that the students who held a "Eurocentric" perspective placed Europeans and/or European Americans as

the only noteworthy actors in US history and constructed US history as a narrative of uncomplicated progress. Those who held a "revisionist Eurocentric" perspective constructed similar narratives but did acknowledge the existence of racism in US history.

34 Ibid., 198-200. Students who held an "Afrocentric" perspective on US history were critical about symbolic events such as the Declaration of Independence, arguing that such events led to slavery and discrimination against African Americans. Those who held a "double historical consciousness" perspective claimed that white oppression against African Americans was an integral part of forming the nation and noted that African Americans have resisted such oppression throughout US history.

35 Ibid., 204.

36 Linda S. Levstik, "The Well at the Bottom of the World: Positionality and New Zealand [Aotearoa] Adolescents' Conceptions of Historical Significance," paper presented at the annual meeting of the American Educational Research Association, Montreal, April 1999.

37 Elizabeth A. Yeager, Stuart J. Foster, and Jennifer Greer, "How Eighth Graders in England and the United States View Historical Significance," *Elementary School Journal* 103, 2 (2002): 202.

38 Ibid., 207.

39 Ibid., 209.

40 Keith C. Barton and Alan W. McCully, "History, Identity, and the School Curriculum in Northern Ireland: An Empirical Study of Secondary Students' Ideas and Perspectives," *Journal of Curriculum Studies* 36, 6 (2004): 6, emphasis added.

41 Ibid., 26.

42 Ibid., 27.

43 Stéphane Lévesque, *Thinking Historically: Educating Students for the Twenty-First Century* (Toronto: University of Toronto Press, 2008), 54.

44 Stéphane Lévesque, "'Pour moi c'est pas une fierté pour le Canada mais pour ma famille': The Problems of Canadian Identity and francophone and anglophone Ontario Students' Understanding of Historical Significance," paper presented at the annual meeting of the Canadian Historical Association, University of Western Ontario, London, 1 June 2005.

45 Lévesque, "'Pour moi c'est pas une fierté'"; Lévesque, *Thinking Historically*, 38.

46 Lévesque, "'Pour moi c'est pas une fierté'"; Lévesque, *Thinking Historically*.

47 Keith C. Barton and Linda S. Levstik, "'It Wasn't a Good Part of History': National Identity and Students' Explanations of Historical Significance," *Teachers College Record* 99, 3 (1998): 478-513; Epstein, "Adolescents' Perspectives"; Levstik, "The Well at the Bottom of the World"; "Articulating the Silences: Teachers' and Adolescents' Conceptions of Historical Significance," in *Knowing, Teaching, and Learning History: National and International Perspectives*, ed. Peter Stearns, Peter Seixas, and Samuel S. Wineburg (New York: New York University Press, 2000), 284-305.

48 Bruce VanSledright, Timothy Kelly, and Kevin Meuwissen, "Oh, the Trouble We've Seen: Researching Historical Thinking and Understanding," in *Research Methods in Social Studies Education: Contemporary Issues and Perspectives*, ed. Keith C. Barton (Greenwich: Information Age, 2006), 227.

49 Carr and Lund, *The Great White North?* Dei, Karumanchery, and Karumanchery-Luik, *Playing the Race Card;* Lisa Delpit, *Other People's Children: Cultural Conflicts in the Classroom* (New York: New Press, 1995); Cynthia A. Tyson, "Research, Race, and Social Education," in *Research Methods in Social Studies Education: Contemporary Issues and Perspectives,* ed. Keith C. Barton (Greenwich: Information Age Publishing, 2006), 39-56.
50 Barton and Levstik, *Teaching History for the Common Good;* Epstein, "Adolescents' Perspectives"; Peter Lee and Rosalyn Ashby, "Progression in Historical Understanding Ages 7-14," in *Knowing, Teaching, and Learning History,* 199-222; Lévesque, "'Pour moi c'est pas une fierté'"; Levstik, "Articulating the Silences."
51 See the list of events used in the research task on page 320.
52 Barker, "The Construction and Representation of Race and Nation"; Hall, "New Ethnicities"; Nagel, "Constructing Ethnicity"; Rattansi, "Racism, Postmodernism, and Reflexive Multiculturalism."
53 Carla Peck, "Peering through a Kaleidoscope: Identity, Historical Understanding, and Citizenship in Canada," *Citizenship Teaching and Learning* 5, 2 (2009): 1-15; Peck, "Multi-Ethnic High School Students' Conceptions of Historical Significance"; Peck, "'It's Not Like [I'm] Chinese and Canadian. I am In Between': Ethnicity and Students' Conceptions of Historical Significance," *Theory and Research in Social Education* 38, 4 (2010): 574-617.
54 Statistics Canada, "Canada's Ethnocultural Mosaic, 2006 Census: National Picture," http://www12.statcan.ca.
55 McLaren and Torres, "Racism and Multicultural Education."
56 Will Kymlicka, "Being Canadian," *Government and Opposition Ltd.* 38, 3 (2003): 374, emphasis in original.
57 Neil Bissoondath, *Selling Illusions: The Cult of Multiculturalism in Canada,* rev. ed. (Toronto: Penguin Canada, 2002); J.L. Granatstein, *Who Killed Canadian History?* (Toronto: HarperCollins, 1998).
58 Yvonne Hebert, Lori Wilkinson, and Mehrunnisa Ali, "Second Generation Youth in Canada, Their Mobilities and Identifications: Relevance to Citizenship Education," *Brock Education* 17 (2008): 50-70; Alan Sears and Andrew S. Hughes, "The Struggle for Citizenship Education in Canada: The Centre Cannot Hold," in *The Sage Handbook of Education for Citizenship and Democracy,* ed. J. Arthur, I. Davies, and C. Hahn (London: Sage, 2008), 124-38.
59 Barton and Levstik, *Teaching History for the Common Good,* 60.
60 Statistics Canada, "Canada's Ethnocultural Mosaic, 2006 Census: National Picture."
61 Joe L. Kincheloe, *Getting Beyond the Facts: Teaching Social Studies/Social Sciences in the Twenty-First Century* (New York: Peter Lang, 2001), 179.
62 M. Suzanne Donovan and John D. Bransford, eds., *How Students Learn: History in the Classroom* (Washington, DC: National Academies Press, 2005), 11.

# 16 Learning and Teaching History in Quebec
## Assessment, Context, Outlook

MARC-ANDRÉ ÉTHIER AND DAVID LEFRANÇOIS

This chapter describes the history curriculum in francophone Quebec and assesses the research findings on the teaching and learning of history in schools. It discusses teacher and student characteristics, practices, competencies, and representations.

In the early 2000s, the Quebec government introduced a new curriculum, first at the elementary level, then at the secondary level, an endeavour that has attracted the attention of several history educators.[1] The five parts of this chapter describe the progress of research on the teaching of history in this context. The first synthesizes research on the type of citizenship education that history programs claim to offer. The other parts review the findings of that research, analyzing these programs from various perspectives: type of citizenship education, textbooks, assessment, teachers, and students.

### Citizenship Goals and Types of Citizenship Education in History Programs

According to the Programme de formation de l'école québécoise (Québec Education Program; PFÉQ), one of the major mandates of schools is to educate autonomous individuals capable of acting as engaged, critical citizens.[2] It asserts that at the high school level, this task falls first to Histoire et éducation à la citoyenneté (History and Citizenship Education), even though, as we note further on, it needs the help of other courses to educate "responsible citizens, able to use their minds and skills to support the common good."[3] The PFÉQ mentions the word *citizen* or its derivatives (citizens, citizenship, etc.) 247 times, more than half of these times in relation to history programs. However, several people consider these allusions to be cryptic or elliptical where citizenship education is concerned.[4]

We therefore analyzed the goals of high school history programs, using Westheimer and Kahne's classification.[5] This classification distributes citizens – whom American schools want to educate, too – into three types. The first type, "personally responsible citizens," conform to what "society" requires of them; that is, they identify with their nation's prevailing interests and values. Those standards of behaviour could be represented by the donation of clothes to the poor. The second type, "participatory citizens," contribute toward social and community life, for example, by doing volunteer work for organizations that collect clothing for the poor. The third type, less often encountered, are "justice-oriented citizens." These people try to identify social issues – such as lack of clothing for the poor – and their general causes and then work to reform society by addressing those causes – for example, by organizing an election campaign, a petition, a strike, or a protest march.

The goals of the Quebec history programs cannot be strictly linked to training any one of these citizen types. These programs do not propose that students adopt behaviour that is submissive to authority; nor do they attempt to impose a national identity on students. On the contrary, one of their principal objectives is to teach students to engage in debates on social challenges through the use of orchestrated thought.[6] Thus, these students will not belong to the first type. The programs do contribute toward "structuring students' identity by giving them access to the points of reference they need to understand that they are a part of a community with shared values, particularly those values associated with democracy."[7] But they do not suggest that the principles of democratic civic participation be applied outside the classroom. It follows that these students will not belong to the second type either, even though the programs encourage involvement in public institutions.[8]

Nor do these programs propose that students test the legitimacy of social, legal, or political standards by involving themselves in authentic public debates, or by considering the impact they can have on such standards. Thus, these programs do not belong to the third type, even though they insist that students participate in discussions; even though the memorization of a "series of predefined, decontextualized social concepts, values and requirements"[9] is expressly excluded; and even though students are meant to learn "that in spite of egalitarian democratic discourse, real inequalities persist which they will have to face, regarding which they may have to develop a position."[10] In this sense, these programs are a hybrid of the different types, with the first two dominant and the third recessive.

Despite the equivocal democratic nature of the programs and the fact that their designers took into account that the maximum development level of these competencies cannot be achieved in four years, these programs involve, according to the PFÉQ designers, educating students in Histoire et éducation à la citoyenneté (History and Citizenship Education) so that they will be able to problematize reality, develop their own views, and build their own identity; all of this as an alternative to inculcating a doctrine or ideology by subverting history. History teaching itself should not be subjected to citizenship aims. Rather, civic competence should arise from historical competencies, in the sense that "the fact of determining the contribution of social realities to present-day democratic life" leads students "to wonder about the issues which, in turn, give rise to new interpretations of those realities, whether present or past."[11] Similarly, students should methodically query the social realities so that they can base their opinions and civic consciousness on historical foundations and "understand the effect human actions have on the course of history and ... thus become aware of their responsibilities as citizens." Finally, studying social realities should give students "the opportunity to decontextualize the concepts they have studied and transfer them appropriately"[12] in their lives as citizens.

But according to the program's wording, "good" citizens should also express their competency by embracing predetermined principles ("such as the Constitutional State and universal suffrage"), by opting for values ("such as justice, freedom and equality"), and by adopting behaviours ("such as participation, commitment or taking positions"[13]) supposedly consistent with the established order. To the possible disgust of third-type citizenship education proponents and to the delight of their first-type citizenship education counterparts, several actions are absent, such as *assessing* the consequences that forms of social organization may have for social differentiation, *advocating* for the interests of the most disadvantaged, and *influencing* the lives of adults and young people.

One potential weakness of these programs is that they describe today's Quebec parliamentary system with a fervour that approaches the messianic, almost as if it constituted the standard for liberal democracy, the ultimate political system. Thus, for example, the competence "consolidating the exercise of one's citizenship" is presented merely as an opportunity for students to retrieve their historical knowledge in order to "see," "identify," "define," and "understand" social institutions, values, challenges, identities, and so on.

## Textbooks

Textbooks have been the focus of considerable research, and for good reason: they occupy an important place in teaching – in a way, they embody the program. So this section of the chapter introduces the prevailing processes for distributing textbooks in Quebec and provides a general analysis of the history textbooks used at the elementary and high school levels.[14]

In Quebec, publishing houses – most of them major Quebec media companies and French, British, or American multinationals – recruit authors who write "teaching kits" (print textbooks for students along with print or virtual teaching manuals for instructors). The Bureau d'approbation du matériel didactique (Bureau for the Approval of Teaching Materials) evaluates the teaching kits in terms of the policies and content of the official programs. The ministry approves the kits if they meet program requirements. Government funds for purchasing kits are provided to schools only for approved materials.[15] Seven social science kits have been approved for the second cycle of elementary school, five for the third cycle; five have been approved for history in the first cycle of high school, four for the second.

At a teaching team's request, students' parents may buy activity workbooks to supplement the textbooks. This provides publishing houses with a lucrative sideline. These additional workbooks, which do not need ministry approval, usually include identification and writing exercises. No research has been done to date on how these workbooks affect memorization and comprehension of information, the development of high-level intellectual skills, or the consolidation of attitudes.

In a master's thesis on the resources and methodology offered in high school level history, Boutonnet observed that the history content, iconography, and situations proposed for applying the historical method and developing civic consciousness are the result of a compromise reached by the ministry, the authors, the evaluators, and the publishing houses.[16]

According to the authors quoted by Boutonnet, sixty to ninety-five percent of class time is usually allocated to the manual (all materials and levels taken together); and in the third cycle of primary school, the manuals occupy a decisive place in teaching practices as well as in planning social studies learning situations. Indeed, though the authors did not intend this, the textbooks can easily become surrogate programs for the teachers; and because of their structure, students can come to see them as bearers of "the truth." Moreover, even though the social study program in primary school provides for a competency approach and the progressive building of knowledge, the kits' evaluation criteria do not encourage complex, reflective, critical learning. The same kits also prevent students from absorbing the process of constructing meaning and reconstructing knowledge.

Boutonnet's conclusions regarding first-cycle high school textbooks are just as harsh as those concerning primary school textbooks. The proposed learning situations do not encourage students to cooperate, debate, or engage in democratic actions. Also, sources are often used inappropriately. The instructions are less conducive to reflection than to identification and transcription of the information in the manual. These kits develop a verbal, superficial, or spurious civic consciousness, and they do so mechanically.[17] On the whole, "on the one hand, the program seeks a reflective, critical, autonomous attitude; on the other, the teaching kits are limited to simply transmitting historical knowledge ... A very large gap lies between memorizing knowledge and critically constructing knowledge."[18]

In the second cycle of high school, the content of the teaching kits puts more emphasis on the French than on the First Nations, English, or other cultural communities. Comparisons with other parts of the world often serve as moments to glorify the social standards, lifestyle, and political model of present-day Quebec. Further research is needed to document this and to explore other questions, especially regarding the uses that students and teachers make of this material.

## Assessing Learning

Criticisms of assessment approaches, report cards, competency level scales, and ministerial history examinations have been both many and contradictory. Some of these criticisms have been rigorous, some of them poorly informed, and all kinds have often been driven by ideological goals.[19] This section discusses the pernicious effects of the procedures adopted for establishing outcomes in terms of percentages (the purpose of which is to reassure anxious parents); it then describes the scales and tests being used.

### The General Assessment Method

The initial reform proposal included an innovative measure derived from assessment research: the introduction of descriptive report cards. Some political commentators denounced this measure on the grounds that these report cards would be imprecise, variable, subjective, and full of jargon. The government backed off quickly: in each of the subjects taught, students' academic results would continue to be expressed in percentage grades. But the instructor would no longer determine these grades by totalling the outcomes of several papers or tests. To evaluate all students and provide them with a progress review, the instructor would apply relevant indicators indicating the level of competency as gathered and recorded using various tools (evaluation grids, checklists, etc.). The teacher would then be required to summarize this information by referring to a scale of competency levels established by the ministry.

**The Competency Level Scale**
This scale has five levels for each of the program's competencies: strong, assured, acceptable, somewhat developed, and scarcely developed. There are descriptors for each of these levels. Thus, in the fourth year of high school, a student whose competency 2 *(interpreting social realities using the historical method)* is "strong" can do the following: explain social reality by taking into account causes, consequences, and other components linked to the interpretation; characterize the changes in Quebec society; use concepts linked to social reality appropriately; and propose ways to improve society.[20] However, these constructs have been developed from surveys of a handful of experienced teachers and have not been validated experimentally.

**Methods for Obtaining Outcomes by Percentage**
The descriptive, global, and qualitative nature of this assessment created a problem, which the ministry "resolved" by weighting each of the three competencies. Thus, this year in the fourth year of high school history, competence 1 equals 20 percent, 2 equals 60 percent, and 3 equals 20 percent. Also, numeric conversion tables have been established for each level. Thus, an "always strong" competency 2 equals 60 points out of 60, a "generally strong" competency 2 is worth 54 points, and so on. As an example, let us apply this conversion table to two students: the first has a "generally assured" competency 1, with competencies 2 and 3 always at an "acceptable" level; the second's competency 2 is "hardly developed," but this student is "very strong" with competencies 1 and 3. The quantitative subject matter outcome of the first student would be 72 percent (i.e., 16 + 42 + 14), while for the second student it would be 73 percent (i.e., 20 + 33 + 20).[21] Not every competency needs to be assessed at every educational stage, but all competency components must be assessed at least once per year. Since grades are awarded at every stage of the year, a student can receive a final grade as fallaciously precise as 68.4 percent. The same report card includes the group average. However, the ministry has not stated which studies support the weightings, nor do they state how to interpret the averages of the various competency levels for different competencies (or for various students). This

approach has been criticized as arbitrary and absurd, with conversion methods that overburden, distort, and even invalidate assessments.[22]

### The Ministerial Tests Are Used for Measuring Learning
In history, all fourth-year high school students take a battery of final examinations, which count as half their final grades. These examinations, which last a total of five hours, are referred to as "uniform exams" because they are simultaneously administered in all classes in Quebec. A documentary file for student use comes with the battery of tests.[23]

Ironically, the first editions of these tests segment the three competencies into several smaller components and include several low-level taxonomic questions, most with short answers. However, one of the tests theoretically assesses the competency: "Interroger les réalités sociales [Examining social realities] ..." and consists of two tasks: making a finding, and formulating questions. Another assesses the competency – "Consolider l'exercice de sa citoyenneté [Consolidating the exercise of one's citizenship] ..." – and consists of one task: justifying an opinion.

Much criticism has also focused on these issues: the tests require more reading comprehension skills than competencies in history; they focus on a single "performance"; they are *time consuming for teachers;* and they encourage cramming rather than the development of historical thinking, because the official document explains, notably, the kind of questions the test will contain and which periods and concepts will be covered by it.[24] These issues highlight the Cyclopean magnitude of the approach, which the test designers nevertheless developed swiftly. Teaching methodology research has not yet confronted these issues directly.

## Teachers
A limited (but rapidly growing) number of research projects in French-speaking Quebec universities are looking at history teachers. In this section, we make partial use of those studies in examining initial and continuing teacher education, teachers' views of the reforms, typical practices, and teaching conditions.

### Initial Education
Since 2001, eleven Quebec universities have been offering the teaching certificates required for teaching at the elementary and high school levels.[25] Elementary and secondary teachers must earn 120 university credits. This includes some twenty credits for 720 hours of practice teaching spread over

the four years of the bachelor's degree. All bachelor's degree education courses must develop twelve professional competencies; the first of these is familiarity with the "spirit" of the discipline to be taught.[26] Because quotas have been imposed on them, universities admit few candidates, who will be those with the best (standardized) scores.

Where the social sciences are concerned, one of the major differences between the two curricula relates to the number of courses in the discipline and in teaching methodology. The *baccalauréat en éducation préscolaire et en enseignement primaire* (bachelor's degree in preschool education and primary education), and the *baccalauréat en enseignement en adaptation scolaire et sociale* (bachelor's in teaching educational and social adaptation; elementary school option) usually require one three-credit course, sometimes two, in social studies. A survey conducted by the Comité d'agrément des programmes de formation en enseignement (Educational Training Course Accreditation Committee; CAPFE) of students in those programs, their professors and lecturers both in the field of study and in education, and their fourth teaching practicum supervisors, indicates that these prospective teachers have a poor mastery of the social sciences (except perhaps regarding post-1980 Quebec history), that they seldom teach social sciences during their practicum, and that they – like their supervising teachers – rarely view social sciences as an important subject.[27]

For the bachelor's degree in high school education, students usually have from thirty to forty-five credits in history, fifteen to thirty in geography, and six to fifteen in teaching methodology, with the total never exceeding sixty-three credits. Quite often, education students are enrolled in the same history and geography courses that are offered to students in bachelor's degree programs in history or geography. Fragmentary data indicate that some but not all courses in the discipline are directly related to the material to be taught; in a small number of universities, there are no classes to cover historical subjects of importance to high school curricula. Hence, while teachers are expected to introduce students to, for example, some ancient history, some history of the Orient or Africa, some history of labour, women, or mentalities, and some cultural or social history, they will not have learned about these during their initial baccalaureate. Instead, history classes focus on other subjects, which may be of great interest but are less relevant to the curriculum.

Though the situation varies from one institution and professor or instructor to the next, lecture courses and multiple-choice tests are more frequent than having students work with sources. At best, this provides very indirect preparation for teaching at the high school level. In individual interviews carried out in 2006-7 with fifty-four respondents, senior BES en univers social (Baccalaureat in Secondary Education – Social Studies) undergraduates mentioned research or the historical method as a means for acquiring knowledge, but their descriptions of research or methodology were abstract and scarcely related to the courses they were giving, except for making students more critical of information on the Internet. They acknowledged that they had rarely (if ever) done research with the raw materials of the past in their own university courses. Nevertheless, "research" (on occasion, second-hand summaries of texts) done in history, at any level of teaching, does appear useful to them.[28]

Furthermore, while at the high school level, some experienced teachers have a master's or doctorate in history or in the methodology of teaching history, a number of others, trained before 2001, received only short monodisciplinary preparation (e.g., two or three years in geography or history) and limited teacher education; this, or an eclectic program combining two disciplines taught at the high school level (such as history and chemistry or physical education) with teacher education. Also, more than one-third of history courses are taught by teachers educated to teach another subject (such as geography, ethics, or French), either because they are complementing their assignment or because they were transferred.[29] Having said all this, so far there has been insufficient research to allow us to determine the impact of the various teacher education programs on the development of teachers' historical thinking or their ability to develop their students' thinking.

**Continuing Education**
Once hired, teachers receive little continuing education for acquiring knowledge about the curriculum or deepening their understanding of a subject area. Their primary resources are conferences, professional training sessions offered by the education ministry, and educational advisers. However, ministerial training and teacher education days are rare. As well, funds for attending conferences are shrinking, and so are the number of *conseiller ou conseillère pédagogique* (curriculum consultants) employed by school boards. According to Guay and Jutras, at the beginning of the reform, teachers bitterly felt the absence of any opportunity to clarify their new educational role; the absence of any explanation of the theoretical and ideological bases or the social and political reasons for integrating citizenship education into the teaching of history; and the lack of individualized support,

adapted materials, information on competencies and assessment, and so on.[30] It would appear that this feeling was not unusual, for Moisan found the same thing in her research: teachers of Quebec history hardly ever have the leisure to discuss the theoretical and ideological bases of the program. Instead, they must quickly form an idea of the issue, and then each of them must construct his or her own terms of reference and, based on those, adapt the material to be presented to the students.[31]

**Teachers' View of the Reform**
The uneven support that practising teachers have shown for the reform is hardly surprising. At this writing, criticisms of the programs from second-cycle high school teachers are more extensive than those from first-cycle or primary school teachers. Jutras reports that the teachers expressed uneasiness about the new program – in particular, about the links between history and student citizenship development.[32] Yet most of those finishing their bachelor's degree in high school level social sciences education, when interviewed in 2007, said they supported the reform of high school level programs because it would result in a greater number of history teaching hours. Most of them supported enhancing the importance given to citizenship in the course; according to them, it would provide a heightened awareness of the world and develop critical thinking.[33]

**Usual Practices**
Writings on methodology generally warn against a number of biases that affect studies of observed or stated teaching practices. The available findings are incomplete and tenuous, but they still provide a credible portrait. At the elementary level, many surveys – most of them carried out by Lenoir or Lebrun[34] – have consistently shown that pre-service and in-service teachers assign little importance to the social sciences relative to other subjects. Indeed, the social sciences are generally little taught and are rarely taught as processes. Most often, they serve as contexts for reading or writing.

At the high school level, a significant part of current teaching relies on a sequential view, whereby students pile up knowledge and acquire a chronological understanding of changes in Quebec society before being asked to take a reflective, methodical approach to history concepts. In this respect, Moisan's findings are noteworthy.[35] During the interviews, the teachers (male and female francophone and anglophone teachers in Quebec, in the public and private sectors and in heterogeneous and homogeneous ethnic environments) were asked to define history and citizenship, to discuss how to educate for citizenship in history classes, and to point out various obstacles to this development. In the Montreal area and in a First Nations environment, the identity of the students seemed to be an impediment.

Other observations have concurred with this: the historical heuristics are usually not taught explicitly (by teacher modelling) or inductively, and most students do not practise them; at most, they perfunctorily use isolated aspects in artificial contexts.[36] However, the situation is not uniform. Several Université de Sherbrooke students carried out some research into ways to make familiar educational tools or teaching methods more cohesive, with the objective of developing historical thinking (most often for high school students). Their findings, while not generalizable, are promising.[37]

The usual practices are typically associated with citizenship goals. They often involve inculcating a Westheimer and Kahne type 1 citizenship and transmitting a national identity and Québécois (or Canadian) values, which are always viewed as centred on justice and equality.[38] Nonetheless, certain topics linked to identity are sometimes taboo. For example, teachers at private denominational institutions, be they Catholic or Jewish, claim that they censor themselves regarding constitutional policies, sexuality, homosexuality, secularity, and the theory of evolution.[39]

**Teaching Conditions**

Teachers generally state that research findings on learning and teaching (which seem decontextualized to them) cannot enrich their practice because contextual variables influence it too much.[40] Several of them maintain that poor working conditions prevent them from introducing conditions favourable to student learning. In particular, they mention these: the absence of any way to help handicapped or learning disabled students or those with learning disorders or adaptive difficulties who have been integrated into regular classrooms; the transfer of "better" students from the public to the private sector or to specialized programs; the brevity of the school year in general, and the dearth of time for social sciences in particular; the burden of correcting papers; the lack of computer resources;[41] and factors beyond the education system, such as the difficult living conditions of many students. To date, these significant factors have hardly been taken into account by those who research teaching methodology.

It is often said that good teaching practices in the social sciences will lead students to develop an active relationship to knowledge, to see the social sciences as a reservoir of tools for understanding the world and for self-empowerment, and that this could be accomplished by leading them to question social issues in order to improve society. All of this implies that they must know the content of social studies before they can criticize sources, determine facts, and so on. Some authors, such as Keith Barton and Linda Levstik, stress that very few primary or secondary teachers apply methods encouraged by academics.[42] This being so, several research projects discussed in this chapter have sought to develop instruments for observing how students learn and transfer historical thinking, and to develop learning situations for teacher education.

## Students

Research on how francophone Quebec students narrate the past[43] often highlights how they think about it and refer to it. The focus of research has shifted from the end *product of historical thinking* to the *process* of this thinking. The studies discussed here concern the elementary and high school levels and have not yet been published in English. Their results are in line with numerous earlier findings elsewhere.[44]

### Elementary Level

Research on the ability of elementary school students to deploy historical thinking, and on the types of teaching allowing them to do so, is highly relevant to Quebec educators. Some studies consider how classroom input can contribute toward "thinking historically" before high school; others, how elementary students transfer competencies developed in history classes to other spheres of their lives as citizens. One researcher is conducting speculative/empirical work on various kinds of performance (cooperative, directive, deliberative, etc.) in primary classrooms and the effects of those performances on learning geography, history, and citizenship.[45] Analyses of exchanges about historical problems among small groups of students aged ten to twelve indicate that they compared the gathered data among themselves and listed issues to be covered in their discussions. Generally speaking, though, they showed less competence when it came to explaining social change in history, as opposed to spatial location.

For example, when a team of grade five students tried to describe and explain the living conditions of immigrants to Canada around 1900, based on period photos, the students were unable to adopt a historical perspective. When commenting on the photo of a woman washing clothes by hand, they deduced that she did not have an automatic washing machine and was poor; they did not, for instance, wonder about the existence or rarity of such machines in households at the time. Student reasoning appeared to be linear, with the timeline being the most frequently used tool. The data also show that these students appeared to be content to transcribe what they found in their textbooks, occasionally reformulating it. This involved presenting a chained sequence of facts, which led the students to deal with events or phenomena serially, without necessarily linking them to an explanatory system. These situations led to analyses consistent with recent work on historical thinking.

Among the research targeting the social sciences at the elementary level, a recent study by Déry has provided some evidence that, albeit not often, students at the end of primary school (ages eleven and twelve) are capable of using a competency developed in history class to think historically in their everyday lives.[46] Déry distinguished several elementary-school social sciences teaching practices that appear to favour the acquisition and transfer of this competency by students. Even in this context, where the subjects of the researcher's sample were young, these practices proved effective when the history lessons involved learning simulations that insisted on the problematics of, meaning of, and need for knowledge. This meant offering students in and out of school opportunities to use the new historical learning (concepts, models, skills, etc.) to resolve perplexing issues.

**High School Level**
Research on high school students shows that they share certain trends with students at the primary level when they try to explain past social and political phenomena. Duquette shows us that learning to think historically involves substantial challenges. Indeed, students do seem to have trouble abandoning positivist views of history. Duquette suggests the concept of historical consciousness as a means of helping them overcome these difficulties. That is, she calls for teachers to be actively cognizant of historical thinking and of the consequences of such thinking on how students learn history.[47]

Gagnon is studying how students summon critical thinking during learning activities when confronted with problems that are part of history courses.[48] He recently showed that students usually participate little in a criterion-referenced, contextual, self-correcting, and epistemic manner when they are asked to consider historical concepts or facts. They demonstrate very little critical thinking regarding archives or the discourses of experts, which they see as focused on describing all established, pertinent facts without bias or subjectivity. This view does little to encourage students to carefully review the presuppositions conveyed in those writings.[49] Students are more critical of the discourses of their peers.[50]

In another study, involving a net sample of eight groups of students (N = 217) from the first cycle of high school, a limited number of students (m ≈ 14 years) read in depth, practised source heuristics, contextualized, and corroborated.[51] These students were observed for 110 class hours, during which the researchers noted the verbal content relating to problem-solving methods when teachers assigned problems and helped students acquire the target knowledge for developing competencies in the discipline. During the three problem-solving activities, the students were encouraged to use various sources – for example, they listened to a seven-minute sequence from a feature film *(Da Vinci Code)* and were then expected to assess statements (by checking true or false) and to justify their decisions. While doing this, they were allowed to consult various documents, some of which contradicted one another but all of which were comprehensible to students of that age.[52] After all this, very few students expanded on their answers and only one example of source heuristics was identified. Clearly, they were respecting the tacit contract to which they are usually held, at the conclusion of which they are expected to find "the" right answer on a kind of "reading comprehension" test, as if they were answering a "fill in the gap" question. Documents were seen as texts, all equally true, from which pertinent information was to be extracted. Truth and meaning were seen as givens. The written task showed that the students considered the film to be a source of information with as much reliability as a text. Furthermore, most of the students maintained that historical films present the context of a period well. More specifically, in the pre-test, 106 students stated that they had used one or several texts to answer the questions; 96 asserted that they were referring to the fiction shown in class (or to another feature film they had already seen); and 42 said they had used common sense, their judgment, or their intuitions. In the post-test, 101 students stated that they had referred to one or several texts; 57 to a feature film they had already seen; and 52 to common sense and such like. From all of this, we can infer that under certain conditions, fiction seems as valid to them as a textbook, a journal article, or the interpretation of a professional historian. When there is a contradiction, the students choose the most frequent version.

Moreover, according to research conducted by Charland on the identity that Quebec and francophone fourth-year high school (age sixteen) students claim and on the social representations they evoke relative to political issues, the concept of duration seems to escape most students and the chronology of Quebec history always poses a problem to them, even though they know many aspects of their culture relating to heritage, including several events and names of historical characters.[53] This research also shows that few students of French Canadian origin spontaneously propose that a place be given to the First Nations in the representation of their society, when they are asked to comment on the Fresque des Québécois (a trompe-l'oeil mural, well-known in Quebec City, that represents a hodgepodge of the historical events of the city and the Province of Quebec). The few French Canadian students who talked about adding the Native people all wanted a fresco representing the historical evolution of Quebec society. Most often, they situated Native people at the moment when Europeans and the First Nations met, but without integrating them into any representation of present-day society. This most likely has to do with the impact of the media, which ignore Native people except when they are protesting or have been charged with a crime, but it also has to do with the teaching they receive and the textbooks they use, which reflect the history program currently in use.

The First Nations students surveyed also suggested adding the Native people because they were present before Europeans. But they proposed adding them to another, separate fresco. Young Innu recognized that the Fresque des Québécois represented the majority community. They even suggested additions to make it more representative of Quebecers, but they insisted that this community was alien to them. So there were definitely two sets of "us" and "them" that did not intersect and that the students used to assemble their respective identities.

These findings suggest that more qualitative research is needed in this area, especially concerning student representations and historical thinking and the links between these and student identities, be those assigned by themselves or by others.

## Conclusion

This chapter has briefly presented the contexts of program changes, the components of their content, and the research conducted in Quebec that fits in with recent work on historical thinking and on the teaching of the processing and reasoning methods particular to it.

This has had to be a cursory examination. Nonetheless, three main conclusions stand out: history programs accord great importance to historical thinking on paper, but nothing indicates that the conditions in which the program has been implemented will allow the development of the targeted competencies; researchers are beginning to take an interest in the teaching and learning of historical thinking; and most research continues to focus on the social representations of students and teachers. Clearly, considerable groundwork still needs to be done in this field to enrich our understanding of the actual development of competencies linked to historical thinking and to help curriculum designers achieve a better definition of the competencies.

**NOTES**

This chapter was translated by Yolanda Stern Broad.

1 Most of them are members of the Groupe de recherche sur la citoyenneté et l'enseignement de l'histoire (Research Group on Citizenship and History Teaching; GRECEH) or the Association québécoise pour la didactique de l'histoire et de la géographie (Quebec Association for History and Geography Teaching; AQDHG).
2 MÉQ (Ministère de l'Éducation du Québec), *Programme de formation de l'école québécoise. Enseignement secondaire – 1$^{er}$ cycle* (Quebec: 2004), 4.
3 Ibid., 21. Input is also expected from Ethics and Religious Culture, Geography, and Science and Technology courses, in particular. Other institutions, such as the CLUB 2/3, a youth division of Oxfam-Quebec, have major responsibility for civic education, often in parallel with formal history courses, particularly through "social and community commitment."
4 David Lefrançois, "Sur quelle conception de la citoyenneté édifier un modèle de formation civique? La réponse de la théorie de la démocratie délibérative," in *Quelle formation pour l'éducation à la citoyenneté?* ed. Fernand Ouellet (Quebec: PUL, 2004), 73-100; Marie McAndrew, "Éducation interculturelle et éducation à la citoyenneté dans les nouveaux programmes québécois: une analyse critique," in *Quelle formation*, 27-48.
5 Joel Westheimer and Joseph Kahne, "What Kind of Citizen? The Politics of Educating for Democracy," *American Educational Research Journal* 4, 2 (2004): 237-69. The conceptual framework of this influential article is chosen for reasons of convenience: it fits (albeit partially) our ideology. Of course, there is abundant research on citizenship education in Canada and around the world, but it would be presumptuous, cursory, and irrelevant (considering the limits and the purpose of this short chapter) to undertake any substantial discussion of this literature here.
6 MÉQ, *Programme de formation de l'école québécoise*, 337, 348.
7 Ibid., 95.
8 MÉLS (Ministère de l'Éducation, du Loisir et du Sport), *Programme de formation de l'école québécoise. Enseignement secondaire – 2$^e$ cycle. Parcours de formation générale. Parcours de formation générale appliquée* (Quebec: 2007), 349.
9 MÉQ, *Programme de formation de l'école québécoise*, 499.
10 Ibid., 348.
11 MÉLS, *Programme de formation de l'école québécoise*, 24.
12 Ibid., 32.
13 Ibid., 22.

14 In Quebec, possibly more than elsewhere in Canada, the study of the history text has received significant focus. We especially note the work of Aubin and the extent to which Les Archives Nationales du Québec have mounted exhibits of texts. See Paul Aubin, ed., *300 ans de manuels scolaires au Québec* (Quebec: Bibliothèque et Archives Nationales/Presses de l'Université Laval, 2006).
15 MÉLS (Direction des ressources didactiques), *L'approbation du matériel didactique* (Quebec: 2007). This situation in Quebec is similar to and different from the context in France. Similar, because French textbooks are prepared and published by the private sector (with a turnover of 2.26 billion euros in 2005), but government funds are given to schools for purchasing them. Different, because there are no "official" textbooks, no public institutions for assessing their contents by categorizing them as approved or not. Schools and teachers are responsible for choosing their textbooks in the free market.
16 Vincent Boutonnet, "L'exercice de la méthode historique proposée par les ensembles didactiques d'histoire du 1$^{er}$ cycle du secondaire pour éduquer à la citoyenneté," master's thesis, Montreal: Université de Montréal, 2009, 14-15, 25.
17 Ibid., 91-92.
18 Ibid., 34-35.
19 See, for instance, Robert Comeau and Josiane Lavallée, "Pour une refonte en profondeur des programmes d'histoire," *Le Devoir*, 17 October 2009.
20 MÉLS, *Échelles des niveaux de compétence. Enseignement secondaire. 2$^e$ cycle, 3$^e$ année du secondaire* (Quebec: 2007).
21 MÉLS, *Résultat disciplinaire règle de réussite disciplinaire. Programme de formation de l'école québécoise secondaire, 1$^{er}$ cycle* (Quebec: 2006).
22 These issues affect student academic futures to the extent that the high school diploma can be issued just to students who have achieved a subject matter outcome of at least 60 percent in fourth-year high school history. MÉLS, *La formation générale des jeunes. Instruction 2008-2009* (Quebec: 2008).
23 MÉLS, *Document d'information, épreuves d'appoint, Histoire et éducation à la citoyenneté* (Quebec: 2009), 6. The same type of tests are provided to first- to third-year high school teachers, but the instructor can decide not to count them. Exceptionally, in 2009, the fourth-year high school examination also was a make-up examination.
24 Ibid.
25 MÉQ, *La formation á l'enseignement. Les orientations, les compétences professionnelles* (Quebec: 2001).
26 Ibid.
27 CAPFE, *Rapport annuel 2007-2008 sur l'état des besoins en formation à l'enseignement* (Quebec: 2008), 7-9; MÉLS, *Bilan de l'application du programme de formation de l'école québécoise – Enseignement primaire. Rapport final. Table de pilotage du renouveau pédagogique* (Quebec: 2006).
28 Marc-André Éthier and David Lefrançois, "Trois recherches exploratoires sur la pensée historique et la citoyenneté à l'école et à l'université," in *Histoire, musées et éducation à la citoyenneté: Recherches récentes*, ed. Jean-François Cardin, Marc-André Éthier, and Anik Meunier (Montreal: MultiMondes, 2010).

29 MÉQ, *Réaffirmer l'école: Rapport du Groupe de travail sur la réforme du curriculum* (Quebec: 1997).
30 Luc Guay and France Jutras, "L'éducation à la citoyenneté: quelle histoire!" in *Quelle formation*, 11-26.
31 Sabrina Moisan, "Éduquer à la citoyenneté dans un contexte d'altérité: Le cas de trois enseignants d'histoire," in *Histoire, musées et éducation*.
32 France Jutras, "La délibération sur la pratique: Une expérience de développement professionnel avec un groupe d'enseignantes et enseignants d'histoire et éducation à la citoyenneté au secondaire," in *Histoire, musées et éducation*.
33 Marc-André Éthier and David Lefrançois, "Trois recherches exploratoires." Research financed by the FQRSC.
34 Yves Lenoir, Abdelkrim Hasni, and Johanne Lebrun, "Resultados de vinte anos de pesquisa sobre a importância atribuída às disciplinas escolares que objetivam a construção da realidade humana, social e natural no ensino primário da província de Québec-Canadá," in *O que é interdisciplinaridade?* ed. Ivani Fazenda (São Paulo: Cortez, 2008).
35 Moisan, "Éduquer à la citoyenneté dans un contexte d'altérité."
36 Éthier and Lefrançois, "Trois recherches exploratoires."
37 See, for example Étienne Dubois-Roy and Luc Guay, "La crise d'octobre 1970: Une démarche socioconstructiviste," in *L'enseignement de l'histoire au début du XXI$^e$ siècle au Québec*, ed. Félix Bouvier and Michel Sarra-Bournet (Quebec: Septentrion, 2008), 95-105.
38 Moisan, "Éduquer à la citoyenneté dans un contexte d'altérité," 21-23.
39 Ibid., 20, 22.
40 Jutras, "La délibération sur la pratique," 62.
41 The national service of the Réseau pour le développement des Compétences des élèves par l'Intégration des Technologies du domaine de l'univers social (A Network to Develop Student Competencies Using Information and Communication Technologies; RÉCIT-US) offers many free resources to all Quebec schools: situations d'apprentissage et d'évaluation (learning and assessment situations; SAÉs), image and Website databases, reference documents, technology integration processes, Web 2.0 applications, and so on. For more information, consult the RECIT-US portal at http://www.recitus.qc.ca. Furthermore, Steve Quirion, its principal organizer, and Luc Guay, are the main Quebec educators carrying out basic and applied research on the use of ICT in history. Steve Quirion, "La ligne du temps interactive: Un outil pour la représentation et l'analyse des événements et des processus historiques en enseignement de l'histoire," master's thesis, Université de Sherbrooke, 2008.
42 Keith C. Barton and Linda S. Levstik, *Teaching History for the Common Good* (Mahwah: Lawrence Erlbaum, 2004).
43 Sabrina Moisan, "Mémoire historique de l'aventure québécoise chez les jeunes franco-québécois d'héritage canadien-français: Coup de sonde et analyse des résultats," master's thesis, Université Laval, Québec, 2002. See also Jocelyn Létourneau and Christian Caritey, "L'histoire du Québec racontée par les élèves de 4$^e$ et 5$^e$ secondaire," *Revue d'histoire de l'Amérique française* 62, 1 (2008): 69-93.

44 See, for instance, studies cited in Keith C. Barton, "Research on Students' Ideas about History," in *Handbook of Research in Social Studies Education*, ed. Linda S. Levstik and Cynthia Tyson (New York: Routledge, 2008), 239-58.
45 David Lefrançois and Marc-André Éthier, "The Transfer of Historico-Critical Skills in Québec Classrooms: From Social Studies Class to Political and Community Practice," in *Learning Citizenship by Practicing Democracy: International Initiatives and Perspectives*, ed. Daniel Shugurensky and Elizabeth Pinnington (Newcastle upon Tyne: Cambridge Scholars Press, 2010), 87-104; and "Desarrollo de competencias para la práctica política y comunitaria (educación para la ciudadanía)," *Aula de Innovación Educativa* 170 (2008): 31-36. This research was financed by the Fonds québécois de recherche sur la société et la culture (FQRSC).
46 Chantal Déry. "Étude des conditions du transfert du contexte scolaire au contexte extra scolaire, d'un mode de pensée d'inspiration historienne chez les élèves du 3$^e$ cycle primaire," Ed.D. diss., Université du Québec à Montréal, 2008.
47 Catherine Duquette, "Les difficultés entourant l'apprentissage de la pensée historique chez les élèves du secondaire: La conscience historique comme piste de solution?" in *Histoire, musées et éducation*.
48 Mathieu Gagnon, "Regards sur les pratiques critiques manifestées par des élèves de quatrième année du secondaire dans le cadre de deux activités d'apprentissage par problèmes menées en classe d'histoire au Québec," in *Histoire, musées et éducation*.
49 Ibid., 176-77.
50 Ibid., 177-78.
51 Marc-André Éthier and David Lefrançois, "Investigación sobre el desarrollo de competencias en ciencias sociales a partir de prácticas políticas y comunitarias," *IBER – Didáctica de las ciencias sociales, geografía e historia* 58 (2008): 89-107. This research was financed by the Canadian Council on Learning (CCL).
52 It included a transcription of the sequence, two short newspaper articles on the history of the Templars, and two short excerpts from quasi-contemporary historical studies of the events.
53 Jean-Pierre Charland, Marc-André Éthier, and Jean-François Cardin, "Premier portrait de deux perspectives différentes sur l'histoire Québec enseignées dans les classes d'histoire et leur rapport avec les identités nationales," in *Histoire scolaire*.

# 17 Historical Thinking and Citizenship Education
## It Is Time to End the War

ALAN SEARS

In the late 1980s the education ministries in Canada's three Maritime provinces introduced a new compulsory course titled Maritime Studies. This course focused on understanding the region in its contemporary context. The content was drawn from five social science disciplines: geography, economics, political science, sociology, and cultural anthropology. It was a classic example of a social studies course with a citizenship focus. The provincial social studies consultant charged with implementing the program in Nova Scotia claimed that it would "bring about a much better group of informed students – citizens – than we've ever seen before."[1]

For a variety of reasons, the new course generated considerable controversy across the three provinces, including claims that it was parochial and politically motivated and had been rushed in without adequate resources or teacher in-service. The controversy was most intense in New Brunswick, not because of what Maritime Studies *was* but because of what it was displacing: the long-standing, compulsory grade ten course in Ancient and Medieval History. Groups of teachers and parents began an intense lobbying campaign to either kill Maritime Studies outright, or move it from high school to junior high, or at the very least, allow grade ten students to choose between it and Ancient History. The campaign included letters, petitions, presentations to school boards, and meetings with successive ministers of education.

Throughout all of this, Maritime Studies was vilified as narrow and non-academic. One mother told a consultant hired to assess the controversy that the course would be "ok for kids who are going to stay in New Brunswick and ignore the rest of the world" but not for those with grander ambitions.[2] A group of teachers at the largest high school in the province agreed, writing to the education minister that "an egotistical concern with the very recent past (post 1945) and with the very local scene results in cultural depravation on a grand scale."[3] It was not just Maritime Studies that was being attacked; so also was social studies more generally. In a presentation representing the concerns of a large group of petitioners to a local school board, one parent said, "Social Studies is interdisciplinary – a little bit of this and that and not a whole lot of any one thing. History, on the other hand is a true discipline: an in-depth study with a philosophy, structure, terminology, etc."[4]

At first the province held firm, insisting that Maritime Studies was both substantial and relevant and mandating it as the single, compulsory course for all anglophone grade ten students in the fall of 1987. The public pressure continued, however, and in 1989 the Department of Education backtracked, revising the mandate to allow students in grade ten to take either Maritime Studies or Ancient History. For a variety of reasons, Maritime Studies withered over the next ten years, and today Ancient and Medieval History remains the sole compulsory social studies course for grade ten in New Brunswick.

This incident may not be particularly significant in the overall scheme of curriculum history in Canada, but it is a classic illustration of the kind of skirmishes that have characterized one hundred years of what Ronald Evans has called "the social studies wars."[5] A key front in these wars has been the battle between history and a citizenship-focused social studies for dominance in the social education of students. A number of articles and books have been written about these conflicts, which have spanned the globe and have included battles over curriculum standards in the United States, Aboriginal history in Australia and Canada, and the treatment of the Second World War and its aftermath in the curricula of Germany and Japan, just to name a few.[6]

As Ken Osborne points out in his chapter in this volume, these disputes have often been rancorous. Echoing the language of the New Brunswick debate described above, proponents of history contend that the discipline has lost "its rightful place in the schools"[7] and characterize the subject as demanding and academic whereas social studies is bland and banal. Advocates for social studies and citizenship education fire back that history, at least as taught in schools, is conservative, narrow, exclusive, and unconnected to students' lives.[8] Meanwhile, reports indicate that around the world social education generally is losing space in the curriculum relative to mathematics, language arts, and the sciences.

It is well past time to end this war. In the remainder of this chapter, I will argue that the ongoing conflicts are largely built on false premises, have been destructive for both sides, and undermine social education's already tenuous place in the school curriculum. I will go on to show that history education – in particular, that emanating from scholarship around historical thinking – and current manifestations of citizenship education have considerable common ground upon which to forge a productive relationship that will enhance research, policy, and practice in social education generally.

## Damn Lies and the Truths That Sustain Them

One reason for ending the war is that the rhetoric on both sides is often based on false premises – on specific truths turned into general lies. The "history wars," of which the battle between history and citizenship education for space in school curricula is one front, are part of the broader culture wars that have characterized much of public discourse in many Western democracies over the past several decades. In those battles, "name-calling, insult, ridicule, guilt by association, caricature, innuendo, accusation, denunciation, negative ads, and deceptive and manipulative videos have replaced deliberation and debate."[9] Jocelyn Létourneau, in his chapter in this volume, shows how this was manifested in media coverage of recent reforms to the Quebec curriculum. These practices are neither consistent with democratic dialogue nor a commitment to education but are the tools of indoctrination.

Unfortunately, this kind of discourse has often dominated debates about the relative merits of history and citizenship education. It was pervasive in the Maritime Studies–Ancient and Medieval History debate described above, throughout which advocates of history portrayed the most egregious examples of "soft" social studies content as typical of the field. Another common example is the characterization by some of history taught in schools as static, boring, and irrelevant both to students and to contemporary society more generally. The truth is, there is considerable evidence to support that contention. Forty years ago, the most comprehensive study of history and civics education ever conducted in Canada found that a "bland consensus version of history" was being taught across the country.[10] In her more recent examinations of history education in Australia and Canada, Anna Clark has found essentially the same thing. Students from across both countries told her that they thought national history was important to know but that the history education they experienced was "excessively content-driven and teacher-focused," almost never allowing for the consideration of multiple perspectives, and almost never focused on developing deep understanding.[11] Reports from around the world echo these findings: students claim that in their history classes, "debates are practically nonexistent" and the teaching focuses "on memorization and repetition of teachers' explanations (through taking of class notes) and the contents of textbooks as the core of their history education experiences."[12]

While it is true there is widespread evidence that history teaching across much of the world has followed the patterns described above, the lie often perpetrated in the social studies wars by advocates of social studies and citizenship education has two parts: the generalization that school history is necessarily that way, and the implication that citizenship education is *never* that way. Both parts of this lie are false. As Osborne illustrates in Chapter 2, there are and always have been plenty of counterexamples of history teachers who have involved students in substantial and relevant historical study, including attention to important substantive and procedural concepts in the field. As well, scholars and teachers who advocate developing students' capacities for historical thinking are committed to engaging students as active agents in understanding not only historical materials but also the processes and deliberations that shape those materials. Virtually all see this as a civic enterprise designed to, among other things, "promote reasoned judgment"[13] and involve students in "deliberation over the common good."[14] Furthermore, they have established a substantial foundation of research and program development to support that orientation to the teaching of history.

Recent research in citizenship education undercuts any claims from that field to a superior record in terms of actual classroom practice. In one large international study, teachers reported relying mostly on transmissive approaches to teaching, with rote learning activities far more common than those that promote critical engagement with material. These approaches "frequently consist of encyclopaedic coverage of details of government structures or historical documents that may have little meaning to students and do not connect to their own identity as a citizen with responsibilities and rights."[15]

There are plenty of other examples of how polemicists on both sides of curricular debates between history and citizenship education have made selective use of evidence to bolster false claims. It is not the purpose of this chapter to explore and debunk those claims in detail. Nor is it my purpose to call the culture warriors in this area to peace talks as, frankly, I think that is not likely to be a fruitful enterprise. As Australian historian Stuart Macintyre points out, reasoned debate is not the preferred method of such combatants.[16] I do, however, wish to join Macintyre's call to eschew war in favour of scholarship. "The object of war," he argues, "is to vanquish the enemy. The duty of the scholar is to seek understanding."[17] To that end, as a citizenship educator, I will now turn my attention to what I believe my field can learn from recent work in the field of historical thinking.

## Historical Thinking and Citizenship Education

Just over fifteen years ago, Marker and Mehlinger argued that the field of social studies education as a whole was dominated by advocacy literature and that there was a great paucity of empirical research.[18] Since that time, a significant amount of research has been conducted, most notably in the area of history education, where a number of international scholars in a number of countries have established strong, interconnected research teams and centres. This community has worked to disseminate research results from small and large-scale studies in a range of forums, including publications, conferences, and websites. As this volume illustrates, Canadian scholars have played a key role in these developments. Much of this work in history education has direct implications for civic education in a number of ways, and I will explore these under four general headings: lessons from the cognitive revolution; fostering a sense of civic context and cohesion; specific pedagogical connections; and developing intersecting communities of practice in the field.

### Lessons from the Cognitive Revolution

Howard Gardner contends that in the twentieth century, a "cognitive revolution" radically changed the way we think about teaching and learning.[19] A key tenet of that revolution has been the belief that people come to any learning situation with a set of cognitive structures that filter and shape new information in powerful ways. Gardner calls these structures "mental representations" and argues that they underlie the fact that "individuals do not just react to or perform in the world; they possess minds and these minds contain images, schemes, pictures, frames, languages, ideas, and the like." [20]

The literature uses a range of different terms but generally refers to this phenomenon as prior knowledge, meaning the knowledge that learners bring with them to the classroom or any other learning situation.[21] Research on prior knowledge consistently shows that cognitive schema are persistent as well as resistant to change.

Keith Barton and Linda Levstik provide a clear example from their research on children's understandings of history of how pre-existing frameworks shape new knowledge. A large body of work in this field demonstrates that American students have a conception of the history of the United States framed by the twin themes of freedom and progress. This view allows for slight deviations from the nation's commitment to freedom or minor setbacks on the road to progress in the American story, but the overall direction of national history is toward greater freedom as well as social and economic progress. As part of their work, Barton and Levstik exposed students to historical sources that countered these preconceptions and found that "so powerful was the narrative of progress that it led students to distort the historical evidence to fit their preconceptions."[22]

Barton and Levstik's findings illustrate the central implication of research on prior knowledge: to be effective, curricula and teaching must take the cognitive schema of students into account and operate to create the cognitive dissonance necessary to foster the reframing of those schema in line with more accurate and sophisticated understandings of the concepts and/or processes being studied. If this is not done, teaching all the right information in the world will be largely ineffective. As Gardner writes: "If one wants to educate for genuine understanding, then, it is important to identify these early representations, appreciate their power, and confront them directly and repeatedly."[23]

Effective teaching, then, depends on at least three things: developing an understanding of the conceptual knowledge or cognitive frames children bring with them to school; delineating what sophisticated understandings of key concepts and processes look like in particular fields; and developing pedagogical strategies for moving students from where they are toward more sophisticated understandings. Compared to the areas of mathematics and science, social educators have been generally slow to build a body of knowledge in these three areas.[24] A significant exception to this is history education, where researchers around the world have made a substantial start at building a knowledge base for how both students and professional historians understand historical ideas and processes and the implications of these understandings for policy and practice.[25]

Building on the seminal work by Peter Seixas, Stéphane Lévesque, for example, has set out "a model of historical-knowledge development based on two interrelated forms of historical knowledge: substantive and procedural knowledge."[26] As part of the model, he delineates five procedural concepts that are fundamental to historical understanding – historical significance, continuity and change, progress and decline, evidence, and historical empathy – and argues that "without these concepts, it would be impossible to make sense of the substance of the past."[27] Lévesque and history educators around the world contend that a key component of history education should be to help students develop increasing levels of sophistication in their understanding of key concepts like these.

Will Kymlicka points out that a number of key ideas and concepts "underlie the operation of Western liberal democracies," including "the rule of law, freedom of the press, freedom of conscience, habeas corpus, free elections, universal adult suffrage, etc."[28] Unfortunately, civic educators have not begun work on delineating a core set of concepts that might help describe elements of civic or democratic thinking in the way history educators have done for historical thinking. It is a project worth taking up.

In addition to setting out the elements of historical thinking, scholars in history education have conducted a range of research on how students in a variety of contexts and across levels of schooling think about history generally, as well as how they understand and learn the particular elements of historical thinking. This work is valuable for civic educators in two ways: first, some of the findings have direct implications for civic education; and second, the methodological diversity and sophistication of this work can inform approaches to analogous work in mapping how students understand democratic concepts and ideas.

As discussed above, a significant body of research has demonstrated that a shared cognitive framework of progress and freedom is common and persistent in American students' understandings of their national history. Further work demonstrates that other national and cultural contexts shape historical understanding in particular ways as well. High school students in Northern Ireland, for example, have much different perceptions of their national story. In contrast to American students, these young people do not believe that progress is possible, at least in terms of dealing with the religious and cultural divisions in the territory. For them, history demonstrates that the substantial divisions in the country cannot be changed.[29] In the Canadian context, Létourneau found that francophone Quebec students had very well developed "mythistories" of the history of Quebec and Canada:

"Practically all students I tested, from Grade 11 to the university level, used a narrative that is, in a way, traditional. It refers to the timeless quest of Québécois, poor alienated people, for emancipation from their oppressors."[30] Létourneau contends that this frame is not consistent with the most recent work of historians. Carla Peck's chapter in this volume demonstrates that historical understanding is also shaped by students' particular ethnic and cultural backgrounds.

These kinds of cognitive frames have obvious implications for civic education both in terms of how students see their particular "nation" and in terms of how they might view ideas like the common good or what constitutes appropriate civic engagement. Given that cognitive schema such as these prove persistent as well as resistant to change, the pedagogical implication for citizenship education is that students must be taught to see the internal contradictions in their own narratives and to explore the narratives of others.[31] Helping students develop more nuanced and sophisticated understanding is a long-term and complex process.

This is only a small sampling of a large body of international work on how students understand historical ideas and processes. Other studies have examined students' understandings of historical significance, historical empathy, how historians use sources, and other aspects related to historical thinking and consciousness.[32] A number of research approaches have been used in this work, including interviewing students; observing students engaged in historical problem-solving activities; assessing student products such as essays, drawings, and lists; and engaging students in metacognitive reflection on their work with historical sources.

There has been some research in citizenship education related to how young people understand key civic ideas and processes, but it is not nearly as comprehensive or methodologically rich as the work in history education. The one exception might be understandings of democratic participation or civic engagement, where a fairly wide range of work exists.[33] Other areas of civic understanding remain largely unexplored or underexplored, however, and the field would do well to begin building a corpus of work such as that which exists in history education.

**Fostering a Sense of Context and Cohesion**
The London subway and bus bombings of July 2005 sent shockwaves through the city and around the world. The events themselves were horrific, but the level of concern in Britain was greatly heightened by the discovery that the bombers were not foreigners or immigrants but native-born British

citizens. As then Chancellor of the Exchequer Gordon Brown put it: "We have to face uncomfortable facts that while the British response to July 7th was remarkable, they were British citizens, British born apparently integrated into our communities who were prepared to maim and kill fellow British citizens irrespective of their own religion." Brown went on to lay out how he saw the challenge raised by these facts: "We have to be clearer now about how the diverse cultures which inevitably contain differences can find the essential common purpose also without which no society can flourish."[34]

Following that initial reaction, a number of government-sponsored commissions began to look in more depth at what might be done to foster a deeper sense of social cohesion, especially among immigrant youth, across Britain. One of these concluded in part: "The changing nature of the UK and potential for tension to arise now makes it ever more pressing for us to work towards community cohesion, fostering mutual understanding within schools so that valuing difference and understanding what binds us together become part of the way pupils think and behave."[35] This report spurred calls for teaching "Britishness" in English schools and led directly to reforms of the National Curriculum in citizenship, including much more explicit attention to issues of identity and diversity.[36]

Thankfully, most Western democracies have not experienced terrorist acts similar to those that rocked Britain in 2005; but the sense of crisis around the lack of social cohesion is common, as are calls for citizenship curricula in schools to address it. As Kiwan points out, these all reflect "a central tension in balancing unity and diversity, evident not only in discourses in England, but indeed internationally in a number of different nation-state contexts."[37] There is consensus, then, across democratic states not only that social cohesion is an issue, but also that a key mechanism for dealing with it is through education generally and citizenship education in particular.[38] As the Chief Inspector of Education, Children's Services and Skills for England wrote recently: "Schools have new responsibility to promote community cohesion."[39]

A problem for this, however, is that since the Second World War, citizenship curricula across the democratic world have become increasingly generic, with decreasing focus on national context. This has happened for several reasons, including the recognition that assimilationist approaches to citizenship that dominated citizenship education in earlier years were unjust, harmful, and largely ineffective. In Canada, this has resulted in a widespread educational policy framework that promotes "the pluralist ideal."[40] Central to this is an activist conception of citizenship in which every citizen, or group of citizens, will have the knowledge, skills, and dispositions needed to participate in the civic life of the country and feel welcome to do so. Good citizens in this conception "are seen as people who are: knowledgeable about contemporary society and the issues it faces; disposed to work toward the common good; supportive of pluralism; and skilled at taking action to make their communities, nation, and the world a better place."[41] It is important to note that what citizens are being included in, then, is not citizenship in the ethnic or sociological sense of belonging to a community; rather, they are being included in the community of those who participate, who join in a process.

A broad international consensus exists around this activist/participatory conception of citizenship as the focus for civic education in democratic states.[42] In McLaughlin's terms, for example, initiatives in England call for a "maximal" rather than "minimal" approach to citizenship; that is, citizens are expected to go far beyond minimal requirements of voting and obeying the law and to actively engage themselves in both the formal mechanisms of the political system and the grassroots community involvement of civil society.[43] This largely civic republican approach to citizenship, with its emphasis on the obligation to participate actively in shaping society at all levels, is endemic to definitions of citizenship and citizenship education across the democratic world.

A key feature of this approach to citizenship education is its almost blatant denial of identity as a key aspect of citizenship. Rather, the focus is on process. Citizens' backgrounds and senses of self and others do not matter as long as they engage in liberal-democratic practice. Kiwan found this when she interviewed key policy makers and practitioners in civic education in England. She reports that they universally "underplayed" identity-based conceptions of citizenship in favour of other models, including participatory ones.[44] When asked about this, Professor Bernard Crick, arguably the most influential single individual in the development of England's national curriculum in citizenship, said: "We're not dealing with nationality, we're dealing with a skill, a knowledge, an attitude for citizenship"[45] – an almost perfect description of a generic approach to citizenship.

In discarding the overweening focus on nation – or empire, as the case may be – because it was impractical and assimilationist, citizenship educators may have thrown the baby out with the bathwater. I concur with Barton and Levstik, who write: "Some form of identification is necessary for democratic life, because without attachment to community individuals would be unlikely to take part in the hard work of seeking the common good."[46] I believe that a substantial part of that identification should be with the nation-state, for two reasons.

First, paying attention to specific state contexts is important in citizenship education because, while there are common or generic aspects to democratic citizenship that exist across jurisdictions, it is most often lived out on the ground in specific contexts that give it both form and function. I am not claiming that there is no such thing as democratic theory apart from states; I *am* arguing that democratic citizenship is operationalized and understood differently across jurisdictions and that those differences are important to understand. A combination of factors including history, geography, and demography work together to produce quite distinctive versions of liberal democratic citizenship across countries, even those with relatively similar political heritages such as Britain, Canada, and Australia.[47]

Second, while there have been profound shifts in geopolitics that are causing fundamental changes to the status and role of nation-states, for the foreseeable future they will remain key sites for the formation of identity and the exercise of citizenship. As Barton writes: "If citizens are to work together as members of a democratic society, they must share a sense of identity, and that identity must be parallel to the political system within which citizen action takes place – and in today's world, nations enjoy a privileged position in that regard."[48]

A central question, then, is how to pay close attention to national context and social cohesion in citizenship education – to foster a shared sense of what it means, for example, to be an Australian, Canadian, or British citizen – without slipping back to the assimilationist past. An approach to citizenship education that includes substantial attention to historical thinking offers considerable potential for a way forward.

The Diversity and Citizenship Review Committee in England came to the same conclusion, recommending more explicit connections between citizenship and history in the National Curriculum. In doing so, however, they expressed concern that "teaching Citizenship with History could mean a return to the old curriculum of British constitutional history and civics."[49] Of course, if students are going to pay attention to the British context of English citizenship they must learn about British constitutional history and civics. What the committee was really concerned about was not subject matter but the transmissive pedagogical approach to history discussed above.

Work emerging from scholarship on historical thinking, however, is more consistent with moving from what Kiwan calls a "pedagogy of acceptance" to a "pedagogy of process."⁵⁰ Specifically, this means involving students in the process of constructing the meaning of democratic ideas for their own time and place. In other words, not telling them what it means to be Australian, Canadian, or English but introducing them, in an informed way, to the discussion of what those identities have been in the past, are across various contexts, and should be now and in the future. This can best be done by engaging students with the internal complexity of national identity in their particular context as well as the alternative constructions of national identity across the world. The assimilationist nature of national content can be mitigated by attention to the fluid and contested nature of democratic ideas across both time and place.

Moving forward with this approach will mean paying serious attention to history in citizenship education and citizenship in history education. Democratic ideas have evolved (largely as the result of struggle) across time and context from Ancient Greece to the present, and to be fully educated about those ideas, students have to know something about this long struggle. Part of what is wrong with contemporary generic approaches to civics and citizenship education is that they are disconnected from this historical context, and part of the problem with history education is that it often takes the traditional didactic form discussed above.

Barton and Levstik make a compelling and detailed argument for how teaching history can contribute to building democracies that are "participatory, pluralist, and deliberative."⁵¹ To do this, history can and should be taught in such as way as to "promote reasoned judgment," "promote an expanded view of humanity," and "involve deliberation over the common good."⁵² In particular, they argue that it is possible to teach history in a way that both develops a sense of national identity and explores the contested and complex nature of that identity; and that opens up discussions of difference, exclusion, and inclusion. They posit, for example, that national history should focus in part on the struggles by various groups over time to be included in the national community both in the formal legal and political sense and also in more sociological ways as well. Australia, Canada, and Britain, for example, are all recognized as multinational states. Traditional and conservative approaches to history teaching regard this as a problem that can be fixed through the presentation of single, compelling and heroic versions of the nation's past. The approach that Barton and Levstik propose would see this multinationalism opened up for investigation by asking questions like these: What groups or nations have been included in the state? How did they come to be included? Are all members of those nations satisfied with that inclusion? What, if any, legal and administrative structures are in place to recognize the various nations and to provide them with some autonomy? What issues continue to face the state because of this complexity? And so on.

Kymlicka and Norman point out that national minorities are only one of a range of minority groups that exist in most modern nation-states.[53] Each of these has different characteristics, histories, and relationships with the state. It is important in citizenship education to explore the range of experiences of different groups with the state and to wrestle with questions related to exclusion, inclusion, and social justice. Valuable recent work on history education in states with difficult pasts – including colonialism, war, and genocide – has demonstrated that nuanced history programs "can help to establish a new narrative of the nation, including a new portrayal of the self and those previously designated as Other."[54] We know from recent work in cognition that it is also possible for young children to begin to develop fairly complex understandings of diversity as well as principled approaches to accommodation, but evidence suggests that this requires specific attention to it by knowledgeable and well-trained teachers.[55]

In *Bigger Than Gallipoli: War History and Memory in Australia,* Liz Reed details "the continuing search for a definitive national identity" through the mythologizing of particular events in Australian military history.[56] The search for a sustainable national identity through myth making has often been the central focus of the history taught in schools, but it is not an appropriate project. As Margaret MacMillan points out: "The proper role for historians [and, I would add, history teachers] … is to challenge and even explode national myths."[57] The argument here is that substantial rather than superficial social cohesion depends on a complex and nuanced understanding of the nation and its history rather than a simplistic adherence to a civic religion rooted in myth and ceremony.

**Specific Pedagogical Connections**

Beyond the general themes of attending to the cognitive revolution and fostering substantial rather than superficial social cohesion, many specific elements of work on historical thinking connect directly to significant themes in citizenship education. Space does not permit detailed discussion of many, but I will briefly profile three examples: the fostering of agency; developing understanding of the Other; and enhancing public discourse.

Fostering agency is the central purpose of citizenship education programs across the democratic world.[58] Contemporary approaches to teaching historical thinking emphasize agency at a number of levels, including understanding the agency of historical actors and involving students as agents themselves in constructing their own historical accounts by developing facility with a range of historical processes. As Lévesque points out: "Introducing students to the contested but nonetheless legitimate work of historical investigation and interpretation puts the students in charge of their own learning and encourages them to take pride in and responsibility for their own education and ultimately their future."[59]

Another central goal of citizenship education programs around the world is to develop an understanding of diversity and respect for multiple perspectives. This is a particularly salient part of curricula across Canada.[60] Historical thinking also places a significant emphasis on understanding the Other, albeit a historical rather than present Other. The past has been described as a "foreign country,"[61] and research indicates that many students see residents of that country "as inherently inferior and ignorant."[62] This is exactly the kind of understanding, or misunderstanding, that those interested in contemporary approaches to multicultural education are concerned about. Through addressing the procedural concept of historical empathy or perspective taking, history educators advocate developing students' understanding of and empathy for "conflicting belief systems, and historical actors' differing perspectives."[63] It strikes me that the two projects – developing complex historical *and* contemporary understandings of difference – are entirely complementary.

Fostering deliberative democracy is also an important priority for citizenship education programs across jurisdictions. Barton argues that history education can play a critical role in this regard, particularly by providing students with "experience in public deliberation."[64] There are myriad ways that knowledge of history can enhance public discourse, but I will deal with only two here: one general and one specific.

In terms of the first, Osborne makes the point that history makes possible alternative ways of thinking about the world. Knowing that things have not always been the same opens up the possibility that they could be different now: that the world does not have to be accepted as is, but has been and can be shaped by human actors, including ordinary people. Osborne writes: "History is a critical discipline that historicizes conventional wisdom and thus reveals its contingency."[65] For Osborne, this very contingency goes to the heart of what Canada has been and is as a nation and is an essential underpinning for productive public deliberation:

Perhaps the most fundamental fact about Canada is that it is a country that is continually debating the terms of its own existence. It has been doing so ever since 1763. To participate in this debate, to avoid false solutions, to accept that there might in fact not be any once-for-all solutions at all, and above all not to turn one's back on its frustration, is perhaps the ultimate exercise in democracy.[66]

As for a more specific aspect of public deliberation, MacMillan points out that historical analogy is a ubiquitous and often dangerous part of public debate around the world. She writes, for example, about how demagogues such as Milosevic and Tidjman manipulated history to mobilize their followers during conflicts in the former Yugoslavia, and about "the battle of analogies" that pervaded American deliberations about how to deal with Iraq and Saddam Hussein.[67] She makes the point that "analogies from the past must, of course, be treated with care. Using the wrong one not only can present an oversimplified picture of a complex situation in the present but can lead to wrong decisions."[68] Critical history education can help students understand how to contextualize analogies, consider the degree to which they actually hold, and propose alternative analogies that might better represent the situation.

**Building Intersecting Communities of Practice**
Reform movements have been omnipresent in public education since its beginnings, but there is compelling evidence that schools and teaching have not changed much.[69] I have argued elsewhere, for example, that critical engagement approaches to social education have dominated both teacher education programs and curriculum policy for almost one hundred years but teaching in the field generally continues to conform to traditional didactic patterns.[70] In terms of history education, Osborne has demonstrated that approaches analogous to historical thinking, or at least key aspects of it, have been around since at least the early twentieth century but these have failed to permeate practice to any great degree.[71]

There are a number of reasons for the intransigence of schooling in the face of opportunities and pressures to reform, but a key one is overly prescriptive pronouncements by researchers and policy makers. This approach persistently discounts the experience and role of educational practitioners in shaping policy making and practice. From a purely pragmatic point of view, this has been shown to be disastrous for educational reform. More than a century of evidence clearly demonstrates that teachers, schools, and school systems can and will thwart reform efforts from which they feel alienated.[72] More important, practitioners should not be regarded simply as implementers of policies developed by others but as colleagues in a process of deciding what to do and how to do it. Hargreaves argues that over the past twenty years, educational reformers have discounted teacher professional autonomy to the great detriment of progressive reform. He contends that good teachers have "the competence and confidence to engage critically, not compliantly, with the research that informs their practice."[73]

Work in history education again provides a glimpse of a possible way forward. There has been considerable collaboration between researchers and practitioners in a range of venues for moving ideas from research into practice. The work of The History Education Network (THEN/HiER), and particularly that emanating from the Social Sciences and Humanities Strategic Knowledge Cluster Grant (partly profiled in this volume), is a key example. This work brings together a wide range of scholars and practitioners of history and history education to develop substantial bodies of research to inform and transform practice.

This is exactly the kind of broad community of research, policy, and practice that is needed to foster substantial and lasting reform. It should be noted that this effort in history education was built from the ground up as individual researchers and research centres established national and international networks of collaboration and crossed boundaries to work with a range of practitioners and policy makers before applying for and winning the major funding from SSHRC. The work of the Citizenship Education Research Network (CERN) in Canada has taken some steps in the same direction, but citizenship education in this country does not have the same degree of cross-boundary collaboration either within the academy or with various fields of practice.

## Conclusion

In 1995 a small delegation of teachers and academics met with Manitoba's education minister to lobby for the reversal of a decision to eliminate Canadian history from the province's grade eleven program. The minister, however, said that history must give way so that greater emphasis could be put on literacy. When members of the delegation made the point that history was an excellent vehicle for developing literacy, the minister replied that he was interested in "pure literacy."[74] In other words, history – particularly history focused on developing civic competence – was not functional enough for the minister. Since that time, social education around the world has continued to lose curricular ground vis-à-vis subjects considered more relevant and economically practical, such as literacy, math, science, and career planning. Yet we in the field fight on among ourselves. At the risk of misapplying a historical analogy, we fiddle while Rome burns.

As I have shown above, the war between history and citizenship education is in many ways a false one. I would add here that it is in every way counterproductive to developing substantive and demonstrably sound approaches to social education. Researchers and practitioners interested in historical thinking have made considerable progress in delineating a set of core concepts and processes for the field; in building a knowledge base of how both experts and students understand those; and in fostering intersecting communities of practice that have begun the task of developing usable approaches and materials for nurturing historical thinking. They have done this while acknowledging that a key purpose for history education is to foster civic competence. This body of work has considerable implications for citizenship education, and it is past time that civic educators became aware of it and took up its challenges.

## NOTES

1  Ken Langille, "Maritime Studies: A Political Dream, a Teachers' Reality," *Aviso* 2, 1 (1986): 15.
2  Andrew S. Hughes, "Grade 10 Maritime Studies in New Brunswick: The Report of a Preliminary Assessment," 20, unpublished report for the New Brunswick Department of Education, 1988, copy in possession of the author.
3  Members of the Social Studies Department, Fredericton High School, letter to Hon. Shirley Dysart, Minister of Education, 14 December 1987, author's personal files.
4  Kathy Royama, "To: Board of School Trustees, District 26" (1987), author's personal files.
5  Ronald W. Evans, *The Social Studies Wars: What Should We Teach the Children?* (New York: Teachers College Press, 2004).
6  See, for example, Gary B. Nash, Charlotte Crabtree, and Ron Dunn, *History on Trial: Culture Wars and the Teaching of the Past* (New York: Knopf, 1997); Ken Osborne, "'Our History Syllabus Has Us Gasping': History in Canadian Schools – Past, Present and Future," *Canadian Historical Review* 81, 3 (2000): 404-35; Elizabeth A. Cole, ed., *Teaching the Violent Past: History Education and Reconciliation* (Lanham: Rowman and Littlefield, 2007); and Anna Clark, *History's Children: History Wars in the Classroom* (Sydney: University of New South Wales Press, 2008).
7  Diane Ravitch, *The Schools We Deserve: Reflections on the Educational Crises of Our Times* (New York: Basic Books, 1985), 130.
8  See the special edition of *Social Education* 54, 7 (November-December 1990), on the response to the report of the National Commission on the Social Studies in the United States. Evans, *The Social Studies Wars*.

9 Os Guinness, *The Case for Civility and Why Our Future Depends on It* (New York: HarperOne, 2008), 84.
10 A.B. Hodgetts, *What Culture? What Heritage? A Study of Civic Education in Canada* (Toronto: OISE, 1968), 24.
11 Clark, *History's Children*, 114.
12 Rafael Valls, "The Spanish Civil War and the Franco Dictatorship: The Challenges of Representing a Conflictive Past in Secondary Schools," in *Teaching the Violent Past*, 164. See the other chapters in the same volume for similar reports from a variety of countries.
13 Keith C. Barton and Linda S. Levstik, *Teaching History for the Common Good* (Mahwah: Lawrence Erlbaum, 2004), 36.
14 Ibid., 38.
15 Judith Torney-Purta and Susan Vermeer, "Developing Citizenship Competencies from Kindergarten through Grade 12: A Background Paper for Policy Makers and Educators" (Denver: Education Commission of the States, 2004), 14.
16 Stuart Macintyre and Anna Clark, *The History Wars* (Melbourne: Melbourne University Press, 2004).
17 Ibid., 243.
18 Gerald G. Marker and Howard H. Mehlinger, "Social Studies," in *Handbook of Research on Curriculum*, ed. Philip P.W. Jackson, (New York: Macmillan, 1992), 830-51.
19 Howard Gardner, *The Development and Education of the Mind: The Selected Works of Howard Gardner* (London: Routledge, 2006), 74.
20 Ibid., 76.
21 See, for example, David D.P. Ausubel, *Educational Psychology: A Cognitive View* (New York: Holt, Rinehart and Winston, 1968); Carla Peck and Alan Sears, "Uncharted Territory: Mapping Students' Conceptions of Ethnic Diversity," *Canadian Ethnic Studies* 37, 1 (2005): 101-20.
22 Barton and Levstik, *Teaching History for the Common Good*, 170.
23 Gardner, *The Development and Education of the Mind*, 77.
24 Andrew S. Hughes and Alan Sears, "Macro and Micro Level Aspects of a Programme of Citizenship Education Research," *Canadian and International Education* 25, 2 (1996): 17-30.
25 See, for example, Peter Stearns, Peter Seixas, and Samuel S. Wineburg, ed., *Knowing, Teaching, and Learning History: National and International Perspectives* (New York: New York University Press, 2000); Samuel S. Wineburg, *Historical Thinking and Other Unnatural Acts: Charting the Future of Teaching the Past* (Philadelphia: Temple University Press, 2001); Ruth W. Sandwell, "Introduction: History Education, Public Memory, and Citizenship in Canada," in *To the Past: History Education, Public Memory, and Citizenship in Canada*, ed. Ruth W. Sandwell (Toronto: University of Toronto Press, 2006), 3-10.
26 Stéphane Lévesque, *Thinking Historically: Educating Students for the Twenty-First Century* (Toronto: University of Toronto Press, 2008), 20. See also his chapter in this volume. Peter Seixas, "Conceptualizing the Growth of Historical Understanding," in *Handbook of Education and Human Development: New Models of Learning,*

*Teaching, and Schooling*, ed. David Olson and Nancy Torrance (Oxford: Blackwell, 1996), 765-83.
27 Ibid., 30.
28 Will Kymlicka, "Western Political Theory and Ethnic Relations in Eastern Europe," in *Can Liberalism Be Exported? Western Political Theory and Ethnic Relations in Eastern Europe*, ed. Will Kymlicka and Magda Opalski (Oxford: Oxford University Press, 2001), 13.
29 Barton and Levstik, *Teaching*.
30 Jocelyn Létourneau, "Remembering Our Past: An Examination of the Historical Memory of Young Québécois," in *To the Past*, 71, 72.
31 Barton and Levstik, *Teaching History for the Common Good*.
32 For a general review of some of this work, see Stearns, Seixas, and Wineburg, *Knowing, Teaching, and Learning History*; Wineburg, *Historical Thinking*; Peter Seixas, ed., *Theorizing Historical Consciousness* (Toronto: University of Toronto Press, 2004); and Sandwell, *To The Past*.
33 See, for example, Ottilia Chareka and Alan Sears, "Discounting the Political: Understanding Civic Participation as Private Practice," *Canadian and International Education* 34, 1 (2005): 50-58; and Cliff Zukin, Scott Keeter, Molly Andolina, Krista Jenkins, and Michael X. Deli Carpini, *A New Engagement? Political Participation, Civic Life, and the Changing American Citizen* (New York: Oxford University Press, 2006).
34 BBC News, "Brown's Speech Promotes Britishness" (2006), http://news.bbc.co.uk.
35 Sir Keith Ajegbo, Dina Kiwan, and Seema Sharma, *Diversity and Citizenship Curriculum Review* (London: Department for Education and Skills, 2007), 18.
36 Qualifications and Curriculum Authority, *Citizenship: Program of Study for Key Stage 3 and Attainment Target* (London: Qualifications and Curriculum Authority, 2007).
37 Dina Kiwan, "Citizenship Education in England at the Crossroads? Four Models of Citizenship and Their Implications for Ethnic and Religious Diversity," *Oxford Review of Education* 34, 1 (2008): 42.
38 Alan Reid, Judith Gill, and Alan Sears, eds., *Globalization, the Nation-State, and the Citizen: Dilemmas and Directions for Civics and Citizenship Education* (New York: Routledge, 2010).
39 Ofsted, *The Annual Report of Her Majesty's Chief Inspector of Education, Children's Services, and Skills 2006/07* (London: 2007), 8.
40 Alan Sears, Gerry M. Clarke, and Andrew S. Hughes, "Canadian Citizenship Education: The Pluralist Ideal and Citizenship Education for a Post-Modern State," in *Civic Education across Countries: Twenty-Four National Case Studies from the IEA Civic Education Project*, ed. Judith Torney-Purta, John Schwille, and Jo-Ann Amadeo (Amsterdam: IEA, 1999), 113.
41 Alan Sears and Andrew S. Hughes, "Citizenship Education and Current Educational Reform," *Canadian Journal of Education* 21, 2 (1996): 134.
42 Andrew S. Hughes and Alan Sears, "The Struggle for Citizenship Education in Canada: The Centre Cannot Hold," in *SAGE Handbook of Education for Citizenship and*

Democracy, ed. James J. Arthur, Carole C.L. Hahn, and Ian I. Davies (London: Sage, 2008), 124-38.
43  T.H. McLaughlin, "Citizenship Education in England: The Crick Report and Beyond," *Journal of Philosophy of Education* 34, 4 (2000): 550.
44  Kiwan, "Citizenship Education," 50.
45  Ibid., 46.
46  Barton and Levstik, *Teaching History for the Common Good*, 46.
47  For a much more extensive discussion of this, see Alan Sears, Ian Davies, and Alan Reid, "From Britishness to Nothingness and Back Again," in *Britishness, the View from Abroad*, ed. Catherine McGlynn and Andrew Mycock (New York: Peter Lang, 2011).
48  Keith C. Barton, "History and Identity in Pluralist Democracies: Reflections on Research in the US and Northern Ireland," *Canadian Social Studies*, 39, 2 (2005): 4.
49  Ajegbo, Kiwan, and Sharma, "Diversity and Citizenship Curriculum," 9.
50  Kiwan, "Citizenship Education," 54.
51  Barton and Levstik, *Teaching History for the Common Good*, 34-35.
52  Ibid., 36-38.
53  Will Kymlicka and Wayne W. Norman, ed., *Citizenship and Diverse Societies* (New York: Oxford University Press, 2000).
54  Elizabeth A. Cole, "Introduction: Reconciliation and History Education," in *Teaching the Violent Past*, 20.
55  Carla Peck, Alan Sears, and Shanell Donaldson, "Unreached and Unreachable? Curriculum Standards and Children's Understanding of Ethnic Diversity in Canada," *Curriculum Inquiry* 38, 1 (2008): 63-92.
56  Liz Reed, *Bigger Than Gallipoli: War, History, and Memory in Australia* (Crawley: University of Western Australia Press, 2004), 4.
57  Margaret MacMillan, *The Uses and Abuses of History* (Toronto: Viking, 2008), 39.
58  Hughes and Sears, "The Struggle for Citizenship Education in Canada."
59  Lévesque, *Thinking Historically*, 172.
60  Hughes and Sears, "The Struggle for Citizenship Education in Canada."
61  David Lowenthal, *The Past Is a Foreign Country* (New York: Cambridge University Press, 1985).
62  Lévesque, *Thinking Historically*, 162.
63  Peter Seixas, "What Is Historical Consciousness?" in *To the* Past, 17.
64  Keith C. Barton, "History, Humanistic Education, and Participatory Democracy," in *To the Past*, 61.
65  Ken Osborne, "History and Social Studies: Partners or Rivals?" in *Challenges and Prospects for Canadian Social Studies*, ed. Alan Sears and Ian Wright (Vancouver: Pacific Educational Press, 2004), 73-89.
66  Ken Osborne, "Democracy, Democratic Citizenship, and Education," in *The Erosion of Democracy in Education*, ed. John P. Portelli and R. Patrick Solomon (Calgary: Destelig, 2001), 54.
67  MacMillan, *The Uses and Abuses of History*, 181.
68  Ibid., 175.

69 David B. Tyack and Larry Cuban, *Tinkering toward Utopia: A Century of Public School Reform* (Cambridge, MA: Harvard University Press, 1995).
70 Alan Sears and Jim Parsons, "Towards Critical Thinking as an Ethic," *Theory and Research in Social Education* 19, 1 (1991): 45-68.
71 Ken Osborne, "Fred Morrow Fling and the Source-Method of Teaching History," *Theory and Research in Social Education* 31, 4 (2003): 466-501.
72 Tyack and Cuban, *Tinkering toward Utopia*.
73 Andy Hargreaves, *Teaching in the Knowledge Society: Education in the Age of Insecurity* (New York: Teachers College Press, 2003), 29.
74 Ken Osborne, "Public Schooling and Citizenship Education in Canada," in *Educating Citizens for a Pluralistic Society*, ed. Rosa Bruno-Jofré and Natalia Aponiuk (Calgary: Canadian Ethnic Studies, 2001), 15.

# Contributors

**Penney Clark** is an associate professor in the Faculty of Education, University of British Columbia, and the director of the History Education Network/ Histoire et éducation en réseau. She is associate director of the Centre for the Study of Historical Consciousness, UBC, and a board member for the Benchmarks of Historical Thinking project. She has published on history education in *Theory and Research in Social Education,* the *American Journal of Education,* the *McGill Journal of Education,* the *Canadian Journal of Education,* and the edited collection *Teaching the Violent Past: History Education and Reconciliation* (Rowman and Littlefield, 2007). She contributed pieces on the history of textbook publishing to two volumes in the History of the Book in Canada project (University of Toronto Press, 2005, 2007). She is co-editor (with Roland Case) of two social studies anthologies used widely in teacher education courses.

**Margaret Conrad** is professor emerita at the University of New Brunswick, where she held a Canada Research Chair in Atlantic Canada Studies from 2002 to 2009. She is a fellow of the Royal Society of Canada, recipient of the Queen's Golden Jubilee Medal, and an Officer of the Order of Canada. She was president of the Canadian Historical Association from 2005 to 2007. She has written extensively on Atlantic Canada and women's history and is currently working in the fields of public history and humanities computing.

She recently published (with Alvin Finkel) the fifth edition of a popular Canadian history text, *History of the Canadian Peoples* (Pearson Longman, 2009).

**Nicki Darbyson** is a PhD candidate at the University of Guelph. Her work focuses on Canadian social and women's history. She is currently working on a SSHRC-funded biography of Canadian social activist, writer, and journalist June Callwood. As a former graduate student at Brock University, she was a research associate for Kevin Kee on the "Simulating History: The Best Practices for History Simulations" project and for John Bonnett in the field of digital humanities. An article based on her master's research, "Sadists and Softies: Gender and the Abolition of Capital Punishment in Canada – A Case Study of Steven Truscott," is forthcoming in *Ontario History*.

**Kent den Heyer** is an associate professor in the Department of Secondary Education, University of Alberta. His scholarly contributions include chapters in the edited collections *Theorizing Historical Consciousness* (University of Toronto Press, 2004) and *Curriculum and Pedagogy for Peace and Sustainability* (Educators' International Press, 2003), as well as articles in journals such as *Theory and Research in Social Education* and *Educational Theory*. He is co-editor of the journal *Canadian Social Studies*.

**Marc-André Éthier** is an associate professor of history in the Department of Didactics at the Université de Montréal. His recent research concerns the use of historical method in schools, how it helps young students resolve socio-political problems cooperatively and its contribution to the development of a critical and participative approach to citizenship. He has published extensively with colleague David Lefrançois on citizenship education and curricular implications. Their articles have appeared in journals such as *Revue des sciences de l'éducation*, the *McGill Journal of Education*, and *Revue internationale d'éthique sociétale et gouvermentale*, and in the edited collection *Histoire, musées et éducation à la citoyenneté: Recherches récentes* (MultiMondes, 2010).

**Gerald Friesen** is a distinguished professor at the University of Manitoba, has worked with several community organizations, including the Manitoba Federation of Labour's Education Centre, and is a past president of the Canadian Historical Association and a fellow of the Royal Society of Canada. He is the author (with Royden Loewen) of *Immigrants in Prairie Cities: Ethnic*

*Diversity in Twentieth-Century Canada* (University of Toronto Press, 2009), *Citizens and Nation: An Essay on History, Communication, and Canada* (University of Toronto Press, 2000), and *The Canadian Prairies: A History* (University of Toronto Press, 1984). He also served as chair and general editor for the fifteen-volume series *Manitoba Studies in Native History* (University of Manitoba Press).

**Viviane Gosselin** is the curator of contemporary issues at the Museum of Vancouver and a doctoral candidate in the Faculty of Education, University of British Columbia. Her research is concerned with ways to increase the social relevance of museums. She has led museum exhibition teams for the past fifteen years while serving on peer review committees with the Canadian Museum Association (CMA) and Canadian Heritage. She is on the editorial board of *MUSE*, published by the CMA, has co-published articles in *Museums and Society* and *IBER*, and recently co-edited *National Museums: New Studies from around the World* (Routledge, 2010).

**Kevin Kee** is an associate professor in the Department of History and Centre for Digital Humanities at Brock University, and a Canada Research Chair in Humanities Computing. He was the director and project director of History New Media at the National Film Board of Canada, and presently directs the Ontario Augmented Reality Network from Brock University. He is also president of a company that develops new media products. He has published widely on the use of computer simulations and "serious games" for history and history education, and on Canadian cultural history. His most recent book is *Revivalists: Marketing the Gospel in English Canada, 1884-1957* (McGill-Queen's University Press, 2006).

**David Lefrançois** is an assistant professor in the Département des Sciences de l'Éducation in the Université du Québec en Outaouais. He is also a researcher in the GRECEH (Groupe de Recherche sur la Citoyenneté et l'Enseignement de l'Histoire) and in the CRIFPE (Centre de Recherche Interuniversitaire sur la Formation et la Profession Enseignante). He has published extensively with colleague Marc-André Éthier on citizenship education and curricular implications. Their articles have appeared in journals such as *Educational Philosophy and Theory, Revue des sciences de l'éducation,* the *McGill Journal of Education,* and *Éthique publique,* and in the edited collection *Histoire, musées et éducation à la citoyenneté: Recherches récentes* (MultiMondes, 2010).

**Jocelyn Létourneau** is a professor and Canada Research Chair in the Department of History, Université Laval, Quebec. A member of the Institute for Advanced Study, Princeton, and a fellow of the Royal Society of Canada, he is also a Trudeau Fellow and the principal investigator of "Canadians and Their Pasts," a SSHRC-funded Community-University Research Alliance (CURA) grant. He was a Fulbright fellow at the University of California Berkeley and Stanford University during the winter term, 2010. His recent publications include *A History for the Future: Rewriting Memory and Identity in Quebec Today* (McGill-Queen's University Press, 2004), *Le Québec, les Québécois: Un parcours historique* (Fides, 2004), *Que veulent vraiment les Québécois?* (Boréal, 2006), and *Le Québec entre son passé et ses passages* (Fides, 2010).

**Stéphane Lévesque** is an associate professor of history education at the University of Ottawa and an adjunct research professor at the University of Western Ontario. Active in the national history community, he is a board member of the Virtual Museum of Canada, past president of the Citizenship Education Research Network, and past co-chair of the Teaching History Group of the American Educational Research Association. His recent publications include *Thinking Historically: Educating Students for the 21st Century* (University of Toronto Press, 2008). He is inventor of *The Virtual Historian,* a computer program to teach Canadian history online, and director of the Virtual History Lab at the University of Ottawa.

**Michael Marker** is an associate professor in the Faculty of Education, University of British Columbia, and director of Ts"kel First Nations Graduate Studies. He was teacher education director at Northwest Indian College at the Lummi Reservation in Washington State. He is a member of the editorial advisory board for *BC Studies* and has published on the history of Aboriginal education in *Paedagogica Historica, History of Education,* the *History of Education Review,* the *International Journal of Qualitative Studies in Education,* the *Canadian Journal of Native Education, BC Studies,* the *Anthropology and Education Quarterly,* and in the edited book *Student Affairs: Experiencing Higher Education* (UBC Press, 2004). His present research brings to light ecological education and place-based pedagogies in the Coast Salish region. His forthcoming works are focused on indigenous leadership, traditional knowledge, and modernity.

**Tom Morton** taught for over thirty years at the high school and university levels in Vancouver, Montréal, and Kabala, Sierra Leone. In 1996 he won the

British Columbia Social Studies Teachers' Association Teacher of the Year award, and in 1998 he received the Governor-General's Award for Excellence in Teaching Canadian History. Now retired, he continues to work for the Benchmarks of Historical Thinking project and write curriculum resources.

**Ken Osborne** taught high school history in Winnipeg from 1961 to 1972, when he joined the staff of the Faculty of Education at the University of Manitoba. He retired in 1997 and now holds the rank of professor emeritus. At the University of Manitoba, he won awards for excellence in teaching, interdisciplinary scholarship, and community service. In 1996 he was awarded a Prix Manitoba by the Government of Manitoba for his work in heritage education. In 1999 he received a Distinguished Educator award from OISE/University of Toronto. He has written extensively on citizenship education and the teaching of history, served as editor of *History and Social Science Teacher* and *Manitoba Social Science Teacher,* and been involved in a variety of curriculum development projects, both provincially and nationally.

**Carla Peck** is an assistant professor of social studies education in the Department of Elementary Education at the University of Alberta. She is a board member for the Benchmarks of Historical Thinking project, co-editor of the journal *Canadian Social Studies,* and book review editor for the *Alberta Journal of Educational Research*. In 2010, she received the Pat Clifford Award for Early Career Research in Education from the Canadian Education Association. She is currently principal investigator on a SSHRC-funded research project investigating elementary students' and teachers' conceptions of ethnic diversity. She has published articles on citizenship education and history education in *Theory and Research in Social Education,* the *Canadian Journal of Education, Citizenship Teaching and Learning,* and *Curriculum Inquiry.*

**Ruth Sandwell** is an associate professor and historian of education in the Department of Theory and Policy Studies in Education, University of Toronto, and an instructor in the Initial Teacher Education program at OISE/University of Toronto. In addition to being a historian of rural Canada and the history of the family, she is interested in the intersection of history education and public memory in contemporary Canada. She is co-director and education director of the history education website series *Great Unsolved Mysteries in Canadian History* and the founding co-director of

THEN/HiER. Her recent books are *To The Past: History Education, Public Memory, and Citizenship in Canada* (University of Toronto Press, 2006) and *Contesting Rural Space: Land Policy and Practices of Resettlement on Saltspring Island, 1859-1891* (McGill-Queen's University Press, 2005).

**Alan Sears** is a professor in the Faculty of Education at the University of New Brunswick. His research interests include citizenship education, social studies education, history education, and educational policy. He has directed a number of national studies on the policy and practice of citizenship education in Canada. He is currently principal investigator on a SSHRC-funded research project designed to map young people's understanding of key ideas and concepts related to democratic citizenship. His recent publications include (edited with Alan Reid and Judith Gill) *Globalization, the Nation-State, and the Citizen: Dilemmas and Directions for Civics and Citizenship Education* (Routledge, 2010) and (with Craig Harding) *Voices of Democracy: Action and Participation* (Pearson, 2008). He was recently the guest editor of a special edition of the journal *Citizenship Teaching and Learning* (2009) on citizenship education in Canada.

**Peter Seixas** is a professor and Canada Research Chair in Education at UBC and director of the Centre for the Study of Historical Consciousness. With a doctorate in history from UCLA and twelve years' experience teaching high school social studies, his career spans schools and the academy. He is directing the pan-Canadian history education reform project Benchmarks of Historical Thinking. He is editor of *Theorizing Historical Consciousness* (University of Toronto Press, 2004) and co-editor (with Peter Stearns and Sam Wineburg) of *Knowing, Teaching, and Learning History: National and International Perspectives* (New York University Press, 2000).

**Amy von Heyking** is an associate professor of social studies education at the University of Lethbridge. She is a historian of education as well as a teacher educator and conducts research on the development of young children's historical thinking. As the author of many teaching resources, and in her professional development work with classroom teachers, she provides specific strategies that encourage teachers to integrate best practices in history instruction. She is the author of *Creating Citizens: History and Identity in Alberta's Schools, 1905 to 1980* (University of Calgary Press, 2006).

# Index

Abel, Kerry, 45
Aboriginal peoples: Aboriginal historians, 15-16, 43, 99; assertiveness, and erosion of Canada's nation-building history, 64; in BC Legislature murals, controversy around depiction of, 2, 22, 284; and Christianity, amalgamation into traditional spiritual beliefs, 109; demand for more inclusive approach to history, 43; depiction in Canadian history textbooks, 4, 59, 109; emphasis on local, rather than global society and politics, 98, 105-8; Gitksan-Wet'suwet'en, and *Delgamuukw* decision, 36, 104-5; iconoclastic Native scholarship, questioning Western version of history, 99; languages, and circular notion of time, 102; local traditional knowledge, issues with publication of, 106; omitted from Fresque des Québécois (mural of Quebec history), 339; oral tradition, 33, 36-37, 97-98; perspectives on colonization, 98, 109-11; potlatch, meaning of, 109; relationships with landscape and non-humans, 98, 102-5; residential schools, in social history curriculum, 65; seasonal ceremonies, importance of, 102-3; students, ascription of historical significance to Canadian historical events, 313-14; teaching historical thinking to, in elementary education, 182. *See also* British Columbia; colonization; decolonization; historiography, Aboriginal; oral tradition; past, interpretation of; storytelling, Aboriginal
Abu-Laban, Yasmeen, 308
*Acadiensis*, 43
Afflerbach, Peter, 183
African Canadians, demand for more inclusive approach to Canadian history, 43
agency: in citizenship education, 356-57; and historical thinking, 7, 24, 120, 122, 141, 238, 319; human, 48,

49, 142, 145, 165, 181, 187-88; and museum exhibitions, 249
Alberta: citizenship education, 72; historical thinking, in elementary education, 176-77, 178; social studies curriculum, 5, 61, 72; values education, 68
Alexander, David, 45
American Historical Association, 73, 115
Amherst History Project, 67
Anderson, Benedict, 48
*Annales* school, 42
Ashby, Rosalyn, 7, 118, 181, 227
assessment: components of, according to US National Research Council, 139; developmental model of, 144-45; formative, 139; of historical thinking, 17-18, 19, 139-52; of history teaching, 62, 140-41; summative, 139. *See also* Benchmarks of Historical Thinking Project
Association for Canadian Studies, 6, 7, 47, 75
Association for Values Education and Research, UBC, 68
Atlantic Canada: historical thinking in elementary education, 177-78; Maritime Studies course, 344-46
Audet, Louis-Philippe, 44
Axelrod, Paul, 44

Badiou, Alain: on crisis of fidelity, 162-63; "ethic of truths," 168; on le Mal/Evil, 163; on "truth-processes," 161
Bain, Robert, 255
Bannister, Jerry, 50
Barker, Chris, 307
Barman, Jean, 44, 45
Barthes, Roland, 45
Barton, Keith C.: on historical empathy, 131-32; on role of history education in citizenship education, 24, 318, 353, 354, 355, 357; on students' conclusions after evaluation of evidence, 230-31, 349; on students' historical understandings, 130, 182, 185, 186, 309; on students' view of historical significance, 187; study of Protestant and Catholic students in Northern Ireland, 311; on use of historical fiction in teaching, 183-84; on value of history education, 14, 133
Bass, Randy, 268
Battiste, Marie, 100
Battle of Plains of Abraham, re-enactment cancellation, 1
*BC Studies*, 43
Beard, Charles, 40
*The Beaver: Canada's History Magazine* (now *Canada's History*), 8
Becker, Carl, 123
Begbie Canadian History Contest: participants' reasoning and judgments, 288-97; rules, 287-88; student sample, note on, 298-99
Begbie, Sir Matthew Baillie, 285, 286, 287
Benchmarks of Historical Thinking Project: application of historical thinking in virtual environments, 270-71; assessment for learning strategies, 201-202; and assessment of historical thinking, 17-18, 139-52; benchmark, definition, 195; compared with Osborne's historical concepts, 215-17; critique of, 215-17; goals and assessments, 141-42; and history education, 134; national meetings on incorporating historical thinking into teaching, 12; purpose, 8, 195; sample essay on perspective taking, 147-51; secondary education applications of historical thinking, 195-207; zones of uncertainty, 197, 205-6, 207. *See also* historical thinking concepts; pedagogy, of history

*Index*

Bennet, Alex, 11
Bennet, David, 11
Bercuson, David, 45
Berger, Carl, 39, 49
Berton, Pierre, 47, 221
Bible, as model history text for Europeans, 37
*Bigger Than Gallipoli: War History and Memory in Australia* (Reed), 356
Bliss, Michael, 69
Bogost, Ian, 274
Bouchard, Gérard, 46, 84, 93
Bouchard-Taylor Report, 89-90
Boutonnet, Vincent, 328, 329
Brebner, J.B., 41
British Columbia: Aboriginal oral tradition, 104; Aboriginal response to colonization, 109; Aboriginal view of history, 106-7; controversial murals, in Legislature building, 2, 22, 283-99; history textbooks, 41, 44, 102; removal of Grant's *History of Canada* from classrooms, 3; social studies, 5, 176, 177; Supreme Court of BC ruling on Aboriginal oral tradition in land claims testimony, 36. *See also* University of British Columbia
*British Columbia: A History* (Ormsby), 41
Brock University, Centre for Digital Humanities, 9
Bronfmann Foundation, 7-8
Brown, George, 41, 63
Brown, Gordon, 352
Bruner, Jerome, 66, 68, 116, 133-34, 155
Brunet, Michel, 42
Brymner, Douglas, 39
Buckner, P.A., 45
*Building the Canadian Nation*, 56
*Building the Educational State: Canada West, 1836-1871* (Curtis), 44
Bumsted, J.M., 45
Bureau d'approbation du matériel didactique (Bureau for the Approval of Teaching Materials), Quebec, 328
Butterfield, Herbert, 123

*Canada: A Nation and How It Came to Be*, 56
*Canada: A People's History* series (CBC), 9, 47, 218-20
*Canada and Its Provinces* (Doughty), 40
Canada and Newfoundland Education Association, 60-61
Canada Council, 43
Canada Studies Foundation, 67
*Canada's First Nations: A History of Founding Peoples from Earliest Times* (Dickason), 43
*Canada's History* (formerly *The Beaver: Canada's History Magazine*), 8
Canadian Broadcasting Corporation (CBC): *Canada: A People's History* series, 9, 47, 218-20; *Ideas* series, 8; production of classroom resources, 63
*Canadian Bulletin of Medical History*, 43
*Canadian Encyclopedia Online*, 8
Canadian Historical Association (CHA): discrimination against women, 42; membership, 40; popular booklet series, 47; production of classroom resources, 63
*Canadian Historical Review*, 40, 49
*Canadian Historical Review Forum*, 2
*The Canadian Pageant*, 56
Canadian Public Issues Project, 68-69
Canadian Studies, 67
Canadian University Research Alliance (CURA), 9
Canadian War Museum, 1-2, 48
*Canadian Women: A History* (Prentice et al), 43
*Canadians and Canadiens* (Brunet), 42
"Canadians and Their Pasts" research project (Létourneau), 9
Cannadine, David, 216

Cardin, Jean-François, 342, 343
Careless, J.M.S., 41, 43
Carlson, Keith Thor, 106
Carr, E.H., 123, 125-26, 216
Carson, Don, 269
Case, Roland, 237, 238
Casgrain, Henri-Raymond, 38
Castranova, Edward, 265
Catholic Church, and Quebec history texts, 38
"A Catwalk across the Great Divide: Redesigning the History Teaching Methods Course" (McDiarmid and Vinten-Johansen), 224-26
cause and consequence [historical thinking concept]: compared with Osborne's historical concept, 216-17; definition, 12, 250; and goals of history education, 142; research into children's understanding of, 187-88; use in virtual environments, 271, 273. *See also* historical thinking concepts
CBC. *See* Canadian Broadcasting Corporation (CBC)
*Centenary Series*, 47
Centre for Digital Humanities, Brock University, 9
Centre for the Study of Historical Consciousness, UBC: and Benchmarks of Historical Thinking Project, 8; establishment of, 48; and *Theorizing Historical Consciousness* (Seixas), 9. *See also* Benchmarks of Historical Thinking Project; historical thinking concepts; Seixas, Peter
*Challenge and Survival*, 56
Champlain Society, 40
Chapais, Thomas, 39
Charland, Jean-Pierre, 343
Charlevoix, F.X., 37-38
Charlottetown Accord (1992), 69
*Citizens and Nation: An Essay on History, Communication, and Canada* (Friesen), 49

citizenship education: agency, fostering of, 356-57; citizenship, definition, 14; decreasing focus on nationalist approaches, 352-53; and fostering of deliberative democracy, 356, 357-58; Great Britain, and social cohesion among immigrant youth, 352; and historical thinking, 344-60; and history education, 57, 68, 72, 360; as investigation of public issues and values, 68; need for exploration of alternative narratives, 351; "Other," developing understanding of, 356, 357; research on democratic participation or civic engagement, 351; role of historical thinking in, 354-55; and struggle of immigrant groups for inclusion in national community, 355-56; transmissive approaches to teaching of, 347; Westheimer and Kahne's classification of citizens, 326. *See also* Quebec
Citizenship Education Research Network (CERN), 359
civics, definition, 14
*Civilization* [computer game], 266, 267, 274
Clark, Jeffrey, 273
Clark, Joe, 69
Clark, Penney: on BC secondary school students' reasoning in response to a public history controversy, 22-23; and SSHRC Strategic Clusters Grant for The History Education Network (THEN/HiER), 10
class, addition to Canadian historical canon, 2
classroom contexts. *See* historical thinking; history education, Canada; history education, elementary; history education, post-secondary; history education, Quebec; history education research; history education, secondary; pedagogy, of history

Clements, W.H.P., 58
Coast Salish peoples: division of traditional territory by Canada-US border, 110; labour opportunities under colonization, 109
Coates, Ken, 45
Cochrane, Charles, 57
*The Cod Fisheries* (Innis), 41
Coffin, Caroline, 146, 270
cognition: developmental model of cognition and learning, 142-45; historical cognition, 145-52
Le Collectif Clio, 43
Collectif pour une éducation de qualité (CÉQ), 89-90
colligation, as means of understanding the past, 125-27
Collinghood, R.G., 131
colonization: Aboriginal perspectives on histories of, 98, 109-11; as depicted by students in Begbie Canadian History Contest, 287-97; as ecological as well as cultural revolution, 105; and English Canada's "grand narrative," 158-60; legacy of, as source of present indigenous social conditions, 110; response of Aboriginal people to opportunities under, 109; Western education, as "cognitive imperialism," 100. *See also* decolonization
Comité d'agrément des programmes de formation en enseignement (Educational Training Course Accreditation Committee), 332
*Commercial Empire of the St. Lawrence, 1760-1850* (Creighton), 41
*A Common Countenance: Stability and Change in the Canadian Curriculum* (Tomkins), 44
communities of practice: definition, 246-47; and dynamics of social learning, 247
*A Companion to Museum Studies* (Macdonald), 248

computer games. *See* virtual environments (VEs)
computer technology. *See* online education; virtual environments (VEs)
"Conceptualizing Growth in Historical Understanding" (Seixas), 7
Conley, Marshal, 4
Conrad, Margaret: on Canadian historiography, 15; on centrality of history education, 16; on debate between old-style history and social history, 70; on global citizenship, 16; *History of the Canadian Peoples*, 45
*Contemporary Approaches to Canadian History* (Berger), 49
*Contesting Clio's Craft: New Directions and Debates in Canadian History* (Dummitt and Dawson), 2, 49
continuity and change [historical thinking concept]: colligation, as means of understanding the past, 125-27; definition, 11-12, 250; and goals of history education, 141; progress and decline, 127-29; research into children's understanding of, 184-87; use in virtual environments, 271, 272, 275. *See also* historical thinking concepts
Cook, Ramsay, 43
Cooke, Kim, 204, 206
Cooper, Hilary, 181, 184
Corbin, Alain, 88
*Cours d'histoire du Canada* (Chapais), 39
CRB Foundation, 47, 71
Creighton, Donald, 41, 64
Crick, Bernard, 353
Critical Challenge approach, 237-39
Critical Thinking Consortium (TC2), 237
critical thinking, definition, 164
Cronon, William, 105
Cruickshank, Julie, 101
curriculum, Canadian history: additions to, due to redefinition of historical

studies, 126; and building of strong national identity, 6; Canadian Studies, 67; curriculum theory, definition, 161; and debates over role of history (1990s), 69-73; history as elective subject, 68; identity, as core concept, 319; issues/values approach, 4-5; as opportunity to pursue Badiou's "truth-process," 164; purpose of, 6; push for multicultural diversity over English-French duality, 64; as reflection of "mode of inquiry" of discipline, 66; replacement by social studies, 4, 5; studies of, 62. *See also* history education, Canada; textbooks, Canadian history

curriculum, Quebec history: Aboriginal peoples in, 82; multiculturalism, 82, 83, 87; new history curriculum, 83-86; new history curriculum, introduction (early 2000s), 325; objections to new history curriculum, 74, 86-94; reform of, 81-83. *See also* history education, Quebec; textbooks, Quebec history

Curtis, Bruce, 44

**D**arbyson, Nicki, 21-22
Davis, Bob, 68
Dawson, Michael, 2, 49
de Jong, Michael, 285
Dean, David, 258
decolonization: Aboriginal peoples "writing back" to empire, 98; and self-determination efforts of First Nations, 100; and struggle for alternative, indigenized history, 110
*Delgamuukw* decision, 36, 104-5
Deloria, Vine: critique of Bering Land Bridge theories, 99-100; on sacred ecology, 105
democracy: deliberative, fostered by citizenship education, 356, 357-58; need for core set of concepts to describe, 350; and need for identification with community, 353; research on democratic participation or civic engagement, 351

den Heyer, Kent, 18
Deng, Zongyi, 161
Denos, Mike, 238
Derrida, Jacques, 45
Déry, Chantal, 337
Desjarlais, Chas, 204-5
*The Development of Education in Canada* (Phillips), 44
Dickason, Olive Patricia, 43
*Dictionary of Canadian Biography*, 47
Dominion Education Association, 58
Dominion Institute: founding of, 47, 71; mandate, 5; merger with Historica (2009), 8; Report Card on Canadians' knowledge of history, 5-6; surveys on Canadian lack of knowledge of historical facts, 71. *See also* Historica
Dosanjh, Ujal, 285
Doughty, Arthur, 40
Douglas, James, 285, 286, 287
Dummitt, Christopher, 2, 49
Dumont, Micheline, 43
Duquette, Catherine, 337
Durham, Lord, 38
Durocher, René, 44

*Eastern and Western Perspectives* (Bercuson and Buckner), 45
*Économie et société en Nouvelle-France* (Hamelin), 42
education, in history. *See* curriculum, Canadian history; curriculum, Quebec history; historical thinking; history education, Canada; history education, Quebec; history education research; textbooks, Canadian history; textbooks, Quebec history
Elton, Geoffrey, 157

empathy, historical. *See* perspective/empathy [historical thinking concept]
Engle, Shirley, 227
environment, addition to Canadian historical canon, 2
Epstein, Terrie, 309-10
Ercikan, Kadriye, 143
Erickson, Eric, 276-77
Estates General on Education (Quebec), 82
ethical dimension [historical thinking concept]: compared with Osborne's historical concept, 217; definition, 12, 250; and goals of history education, 142; as point of departure in historical thinking, 158-69
Éthier, Marc-André, 23-24
*The Ethnic Diversity Survey* (Statistics Canada), 305
ethnicity: and changing demographics in schools, 308-9; characteristics, 308; and curricula tailored to student needs, interests and experiences, 311; demographics of, in Canada, 317; difficulty of defining, 306; ethnic groups, depiction in Canadian history textbooks, 4; ethnic groups, inclusion in national community as theme in citizenship education, 355-56; identity, and nationality, 308; identity, and students' historical understandings, 309-20; identity, shift to fluid instead of static, 305-9; and race, 307
Evans, Ronald, 345
evidence, historical [historical thinking concept]: definition, 11, 250; as fostering students' historical understanding, 130; and goals of history education, 141; and Ranke's first principle of scientific history, 129; and records, 129; research into children's understanding of, 182-84; in secondary school assignment on Remembrance Day, 198, 202; sourcing heuristics, 130; in virtual environments, 273, 275. *See also* primary documents

Fahrni, Magda, 2-3
family, addition to Canadian historical canon, 2
feminism: as challenge to prevailing history orthodoxy, 43; and erosion of nation-building history, 64; and male bias of Canada's nation-building story, 59
Fenton, Edwin, 67, 68
Ferro, Marc, 81
Fertig, Gary, 188
Fillmore, Roscoe, 59-60
Finkel, Alvin, 45
First Nations. *See* Aboriginal peoples
Fisher, Peter, 38
Fixico, Donald, 100
Fling, Fred Morrow, 61, 155-56
Forbes, Ernest R., 45
Foster, Stuart J., 310
Foucault, Michel, 44, 45
*The Foundation for the Atlantic Canada Social Studies Curriculum*, 177-78
Francis, Daniel, 158, 200
Fraser, Mariam, 162
Frégault, Guy, 42, 63
Freire, Paulo, 267
Fresque des Québécois (Quebec City mural), 339
Friesen, Gerald: on Canada as historical enterprise, 15; on effective history education, 20; new Western perspective on Canadian history, 45; on revolutions in communication, 49, 50; on students' historical perspective, 146-47
*From Colony to Nation*, 56
"frontier myth," of Canadian history, 40-41, 106
Fulford, Robert, 219-20

*The Fur Trade in Canada* (Innis), 41
Furniss, Elizabeth, 106, 107

**G**addis, John Lewis, 25, 26
Gaffield, Chad, 44, 117
Gagnon, Mathieu, 337
games, computer. *See* virtual environments (VEs)
Garneau, François-Xavier, 38, 39
Gee, James Paul, 267, 276-77
gender, addition to Canadian historical canon, 2, 126
*General History Textbook* (Myers), 4
Gibson, Lindsay, 204
Gidney, Catherine, 3
Gitskan-Wet'suwet'en First Nation, and *Delgamuukw* decision, 36, 104-5
"Giving the Past a Future" conference, 7, 47
Gossage, Peter, 10
Gosselin, Viviane, 21
Governor General's Awards for history teaching, 8
Graff, Harvey J., 44
Grain Growers' Association, 59
Gramsci, Antonio, 44
Granatstein, J.L.: critique of academic teaching of history, 46; critique of new social history, 69; on end of history as school subject, 5, 69; *Who Killed Canadian History?*, 5, 46, 47, 74
Grant, George, 64
Grant, W.L., 3-4
"great men" approach, to history: research into biographical approach to history in elementary education, 187-88; vs "history by numbers," 122
*The Great Unsolved Mysteries in Canadian History* (online education project), 228
Greenhill, Eilean Hooper, 251
Greer, Jennifer, 310
Groulx, Lionel, 39, 40

*Growing Up in British Columbia: Boys in Private Schools* (Barman), 44
Guay, Luc, 333
*La guerre de la Conquête* (Frégault), 42
Gwyn, Sandra, 47

**H**aliburton, T.C., 38, 39
Hall, Stuart, 307-8
Hamelin, Jean, 42
*The Handbook of Education and Human Development: New Models of Learning, Teaching and Schooling*, 7
Hargrave, Joseph James, 38
Harvard Social Studies Project, 68
Haskings-Winner, Jan, 203-4
Hemas Kla-Lee-Lee-Kla (Bill Wilson), 284
Heritage Fairs, 8
*Heritage Minutes*, 7-8
Hirsch, E.D., 214-15
Hirst, Paul, 66
*Histoire du Canada depuis sa découverte jusqu'à nos jours* (Garneau), 38
*Histoire du Québec contemporain* (Linteau et al), 44
*Histoire du syndicalisme Québécois* (Rouillard), 43
*Histoire économique et sociale du Québec, 1760-1850* (Ouellet), 42
*Histoire et description général de la Nouvelle France* (Charlevoix), 37-38
Histoire et éducation à la citoyenneté/ History and Citizenship Education program, 325, 327
Histoire et éducation en réseau (HiER). *See* The History Education Network/Histoire et éducation en réseau (THEN/HiER)
*Histoire Sociale*, 43
historians, Canada: academic/ professional, 34, 39-42, 48, 49-50; accused of abandoning role in national community, 69; amateur,

34, 39; change in approach over time, 216; definition, 13; European, and issue of oral traditions, 36; European, view of history as story of progress, 37; and historical objectivity, 13-14; and history educators, 224-27; inquiry process of turning past into historical narratives, 120-21; public, 13, 48; role of, 33; shift in role from educators to researchers, 66-67; subjective influences, 157-58. *See also* historiography, Aboriginal; historiography, Canadian

historians, Quebec: academic, 39; early narratives, 37; nationalist themes, 38, 41-42; new social history, 43, 44-45; popular, 47; postnationalist, 46

Historica: merger with Dominion Institute, 8, 71; publications, 8; as successor to CRB Foundation, 47. *See also* Dominion Institute

*Historica Minutes,* 8

*An Historical and Statistical Account of Nova Scotia* (Haliburton), 38

Historical Club, University of Toronto, 42

historical empathy. *See* perspective/ empathy [historical thinking concept]

historical fiction, in elementary education, 184

historical societies, 40

*Historical Studies in Education,* 43

historical thinking: assessment of, 139-52; and citizenship education, 344-60; classroom contexts, 18-21; and contextualization of historical analogies, 358; definition, 249; and discipline of history, 73, 133, 213; in elementary education, 19, 175-90; historical consciousness, components of, 141; and historical knowledge, 74; as lab work, 156-58; in museum displays, 21, 245-59; orientations toward, 17-18; and process of doing history, 116-17, 118, 119, 134, 140, 181, 231, 232, 238, 240, 250, 254; progression in, 118-22; in secondary education, 195-207; Seixas' concepts compared with Osborne's, 215-17; sports analogy, 117, 134; use in virtual environments, 21-22, 269-77; using ethical point of departure, 158-69. *See also* historians, Canada; historical thinking concepts; historiography; history education research; pedagogy, of history

historical thinking concepts: cause and consequence, 12, 142, 187-88, 216-17, 250, 271, 273; continuity and change, 11-12, 125-27, 127-29, 141, 184-87, 250, 271, 272, 275; ethical dimension, 12, 142, 158-59, 217, 250; evidence, 11, 129-30, 141, 182-84, 250, 273, 275; perspective/ empathy, 12, 130-33, 142, 144-45, 188-89, 250, 271, 272, 274; significance, 11, 122-25, 141, 187, 215-16, 250, 275. *See also* main entry for each concept

historiography: changes in historical writing, 221; comparative analysis of written texts, 34; definition, 13, 33; historical reasoning, as lab work, 156-58; historization, 91; history of, 34; Western, difficulty of integrating Aboriginal ways of understanding the past, 98. *See also* historians, Canada; historians, Quebec; historiography, Aboriginal; historiography, Canadian; historiography, Quebec

historiography, Aboriginal: as conflicting with "frontier myth," 106-8; emphasis on circular patterns of time, 101; emphasis on moral and spiritual structure of events, 101; indigenous perspectives as conflicting with history of Canada as nation-state, 110-11; mythic forms converging with everyday experience, 104; and oral tradition, 33, 36-37; "progress," as problematic notion, 98, 101, 106. *See also* oral tradition; storytelling, Aboriginal

historiography, Canadian: embedded in cultural traditions of Western world, 34; factors influencing, 35; globalizing trends affecting, 49-50; local history societies, 34; new academic social history, 42-45; postmodernist, 45-46, 70; professional historians, 39-42; public histories, 47-48; secular histories, by Europeans, 37-39. *See also* historians, Canada

historiography, Quebec: early narratives, 37-38; nationalist themes, 41-42. *See also* historians, Quebec

history: archival sources, original restriction to, 36; civic, 34; definition, 13, 125; as discipline, 16, 18-19, 36, 39, 56, 58, 73, 74, 120-21, 141, 155, 156, 177, 213, 217, 221, 233, 250; effect of computer on discipline, 35, 43; "great men" approach to, 122, 187-88; inclusion of oral traditions, 36-37; procedural knowledge, 17, 20, 25, 73, 116, 118, 119, 121, 181, 237, 238, 250, 251, 255, 350; public enthusiasm for, at end of 20th century, 34-35; public vs academic, 35, 221; substantive knowledge, 17, 21, 25, 73, 116-17, 119, 124, 142, 147, 180, 187, 250, 252, 264, 276; von Ranke's scientific principles of, 120. *See also* historians, Canada; historiography; history, Canadian; history education, Canada; history education, Quebec;

history, Quebec; oral tradition; past, interpretation of; pedagogy, of history

history, Canadian: Canadians' lack of knowledge of, 1, 2, 3, 47, 69, 75; Confederation, 58; constitution, as theme, 58, 69; English Canada's "grand narrative," 158-60; "frontier thesis/myth," 40-41, 106; as hedge against globalization and regionalism, 70; "Laurentian thesis," 41, 59; nation-building as theme, 55, 56-67, 97, 110-11; new social history, 42-45, 65, 126; research funding bodies, 43; "staples thesis," 41; survey course, postsecondary, 217-22; use of icons/monuments in teaching of, 282-98. *See also* curriculum, Canadian history; history education, Canada; nation-building, as theme in Canadian history; pedagogy, of history; textbooks, Canadian history

history education: as disciplined "ethic of truths," 154-69. *See also* curriculum, Canadian history; curriculum, Quebec history; history education, Canada; history education, Quebec; pedagogy, of history; textbooks, Canadian history; textbooks, Quebec history.

history education, Canada: British and European history, 55, 56-57; contemporary, 73-75; debates over role of history in curriculum (1990s), 69-73, 345-48; definition, 14; developmental approach, 143-45; disciplinarian approach, critique of, 17, 18, 155-57; experimentation/innovation (1970s-1990s), 55, 67-69; "memorization" method, 63; nation-building (1890-1970s) as theme, 55, 56-67; and provincial examinations, 62, 67; shift from university-based historians to educators, 66-67; social history, inclusion of groups ignored by nation-building narrative (1960s), 2, 65; use of icons/monuments in teaching of, 282-98; *What Culture? What Heritage?* study on teaching of history, 6-7. *See also* citizenship education; curriculum, Canadian history; historical thinking; history education, Quebec; history education research; online education; pedagogy, of history; social studies; textbooks, Canadian history

history education, elementary: assignment examples, 175-76; children's historical thinking, 19, 175-90; goals and assessment, 140; historical thinking, in curriculum, 12, 176-78; historical thinking, limitations of teaching, 178

The History Education Network/Histoire et éducation en réseau (THEN/HiER): aims and motto, 10-11; as community of practice, 247; as example of collaboration between researchers and practitioners, 359; founding of, 10; SSHRC Strategic Clusters Grant, 10

history education, post-secondary: goals and assessment, 140; historical empathy/perspective assignments, 146-47; History Teaching Methods course, for history teachers, 224-40; using historical thinking concepts, 12, 210-22

history education, Quebec: analysis of secondary history programs, 326; approved "teaching kits" funded by province, 328; assessment methods, critique of, 329-31; "conservatists" vs "reformists," 82, 91, 92; current debate on, 81-94; History and Citizenship Education program, 71, 72, 82, 83, 84-86, 325-27, 335; history source book, 63; history teachers, 331-34; Inchauspé Report, 83; *A Journey to the Past: A Quebec Village in 1890/Un voyage dans le passé: Un village québéois à la fin du 19$^{ième}$ siècle* [computer game], 269, 271-73; Lacoursière Report (1996), 73, 82-83; Ministry of Education, 81; nation-building narrative view of history, 41-42, 55, 59, 64, 74-75, 82, 350-51; objections to English-speaking Canada's nation-building history, 60; objections to teaching history featuring cultural pluralism, 83, 87; Parent Commission, 57-58, 59, 64-65; sequential view, followed by reflective approach to history concepts, 334; social sciences, 334-36; students, historical perspective of, 336-39; Task Force on History Teaching, 82; "uniform exams," critique of, 331. *See also* curriculum, Quebec history; history, Quebec; history teachers, Quebec; textbooks, Quebec history

history education research: agenda, significant contributions to, 7-11; analysis of Begbie Canadian History Contest student entries, 287-99; direct implications for civic education, 348; grants from Canadian University Research Alliance (CURA), 9; grants from Social Sciences and Humanities Research Council (SSHRC), 9-10; The History Education Network/Histoire et éducation en réseau (THEN/HiER), 10; revival of, 11; significant publications, 8-9; student ethnicity, and historical understandings, 309-20; students' understanding of historical

thinking concepts, 66, 72-73, 251.
See also Benchmarks of Historical
Thinking Project; historical thinking concepts
history education, secondary: goals and assessment, 140; historical thinking, 12, 22, 195-207, 287-99; historical thinking concepts, 19-20; Quebec, analysis of history programs, 326; socio-cultural identity, and students' historical understandings, 312-20
"History Is a Verb" course (Sandwell), 224-40
*History of Canada* (Grant), 3-4
*History of Canada* (Kingsford), 38
*The History of Canada from Its First Discovery to the Present* (McMullen), 38
*History of the Canadian Peoples* (Conrad et al), 45
*History of the Dominion of Canada* (Clements), 58
history, Quebec: Fresque des Québécois (Quebec City mural), 339; nationalist themes, 41-42, 55, 59, 64, 74-75, 82, 350-51; postnationalist approach to history, 46; redefinition of identity, and new myths of nationhood, 93-94. See also curriculum, Quebec history; historians, Quebec; historiography, Quebec; history education, Quebec; history teachers, Quebec; textbooks, Quebec history
history teachers, Canada: definition, 13; engagement as colleagues by researchers in history education, 358-59; and provincial history examinations, 62, 64; student teachers, teaching historical thinking to, 224-40; working conditions, and teaching of history, 63-64. See also history education, Canada; history education,

Quebec; history teachers, Quebec; pedagogy, of history
history teachers, Quebec: secondary, 332-33; social sciences, neglect of, 332, 334; teaching certificates, 331-32; view of curriculum reform, 333-34; working conditions, 335
"history wars," between history and social studies, 345-48
Hodgetts, A.B., 6-7, 63
Hodkinson, Alan, 185
Hopi people, view of time, 100
Howe, S.L., 285
human rights, addition to Canadian historical canon, 126
Hunt, Martin, 122

icons. See Fresque des Québécois (Quebec City mural); murals, BC Legislature Building
*Ideas* series (CBC), 9
*Images of a Forgotten War: Films of the Canadian Expeditionary Force in the Great War* (NFB), 198
*In Defence of History: Teaching the Past and the Meaning of Democratic Citizenship* (Osborne), 44
indigenous peoples. See Aboriginal peoples
Innis, Harold, 41, 49
Institut d'histoire de l'Amérique français, 40
Institute for the Study of Canada, McGill University, 47, 71

Jaenen, Cornelius, 45
Jain, Genevieve, 4
Jedwab, Jack, 6
Jenkins, Henry, 268-69
Jenkins, Keith, 146
Johnston, R.J., 307
journals: *Acadiensis*, 43; *BC Studies*, 43; *The Beaver: Canada's History Magazine*, 8; *Canada's History*, 8; *Canadian Bulletin of Medical*

*History*, 43; *Histoire Sociale*, 43; *Historical Studies in Education*, 43; *Kayak: Canada's History Magazine for Kids*, 8; *Labour/Le Travail*, 43; *Northern Review*, 43; *Review of Historical Publications Relating to Canada*, 40; *Revue d'histoire de l'Amérique français*, 40; *Transactions* (Royal Society of Canada), 39; *Urban History Review*, 43
*A Journey to the Past: A Quebec Village in 1890/Un voyage dans le passé: Un village québéois à la fin du 19ième siècle* [computer game], 269
Jutras, France, 333, 334

Kahne, Joseph, 326
*Kayak: Canada's History Magazine for Kids*, 8
Kee, Kevin: and student building of historical virtual environments on War of 1812, 274, 275; on virtual environments for learning historical thinking, 9, 21-22
Kelly, Christine, 179
Kelly, Timothy, 312
Kincheloe, Joe L., 319
King, Thomas, 98
Kingsford, William, 38, 39
Kiwan, Dina, 352
*Knowing, Teaching, and Learning History: National and International Perspectives* (Stearns et al), 8, 224
Kohlberg, Lawrence, 68
Kymlicka, Will, 350, 356

*Labour/Le Travail*, 43
Lacan, Jacques, 45
Lacoursière, Jacques, 47, 73, 82
Lacoursière report (1996), 82-83
Lamy, Paul, 4
Lang, S.E., 61-62

*Language, Schooling, and Cultural Conflict: The Origin of French-Language Controversy in Ontario* (Gaffield), 44
Laurel, Brenda, 270
"Laurentian thesis," of Canadian history, 41, 59
Lee, Peter: on children's understanding of causes, 188; on historical thinking concepts, 181; on imagination in history, 131; model of historical knowledge development, both substantive and procedural, 117; on procedural knowledge and notion of progression in history, 118; research into historical thinking in elementary education, 182-83; on "vicarious experience" and historical prediction, 124-25; work of, and development of historical thinking concepts by Seixas, 7, 227, 228
Lefrançois, David, 23-24
Lerner, Gerda, 190
Létourneau, Jocelyn: on identity, and versions of the past, 16-17; on media coverage of reforms to Quebec's history curriculum, 346; on national citizenship, in context of Quebec, 16; and new historiographical approach in Canada, 48; postnationalist approach to Quebec history, 46; on Quebec students internalization of nation-building view of Quebec history, 74-75; on Quebec's national history curriculum, 15; survey on historical consciousness of Canadians, 9
Lévesque, Stéphane: on historical thinking concepts, 17; on progression in historical learning, 17; research into Ontario francophone and anglophone students' conceptions of historical significance, 311-12;

on students as agents in historical process, 356-57; *Thinking Historically: Educating Students for the 21st Century*, 9
Levstik, Linda: on historical empathy, 131-32; on history and citizenship education, 24; on need for identification with community for democratic life, 353; research on children's understandings of history, 349; on role of history education in citizenship education, 318; on students' geographic location and ascription of significance to historical events, 310; on teaching history as contributing to building participatory democracies, 355; on value of history education, 14, 133
Lewin, Kurt, 196
*L'Histoire des femmes au Québec depuis quatre siècles* (Dumont et al), 43
liberalism, 49-50
Library and Archives Canada, 39
Linteau, Paul-André, 44
*The Literacy Myth: Literacy and Social Structure in the Nineteenth-Century City* (Graff), 44
Littlebear, Leroy, 101
Logo programming language, 276
*Louis Riel: Patriot or Rebel/Louis Riel: Patriote ou rebelle?* (Stanley), 47
Lowenthal, David, 130
Lower, Arthur, 41
Luke, Allan, 161
Luther, Martin, 37
Lutz, John, 10

Macdonald, John A., 41
Macintyre, Stuart, 348
MacMillan, Margaret, 356
Maheux, Arthur, 60
*Makers of Canada* (Kingsford), 38
Manitoba: elementary social studies, 178; elimination of Canadian history from Grade eleven curriculum, 359
Maritime Studies course: New Brunswick, as replacement for Ancient and Medieval History, 344-45; portrayed as "soft" social studies course, 346
Marker, Michael: on Aboriginal concerns with local, 16; on inclusion of indigenous world view in history curriculum, 17; on indigenous historical consciousness, 15-16
Marsh, James, 156
Martineau, Robert, 63
Marxism, 43
masculinity, addition to Canadian historical canon, 2, 126
McCallum, Mary, 59
McCully, Alan W., 311
McDiarmid, G. Williamson, 224-26, 227
McDiarmid, Garnet, 4
McGill University, Institute for the Study of Canada, 7, 47, 71
McGregor, Georgia Leigh, 268
McKay, Ian, 2, 15, 49
McKillop, A.B., 46
McLaughlin, T.H., 353
McLuhan, Marshall, 49
McMullen, John Mercier, 38, 39
McTighe, Jay, 165
media, and Canadian history: *Heritage Minutes*, 7-8; research grants, 9-10. *See also* Canadian Broadcasting Corporation (CBC); National Film Board (NFB)
Meech Lake Agreement (1989), 69
Mehlinger, Howard H., 348
Meuwissen, Kevin, 312
Miller, J.R., 43
Mink, Louis, 125
Moisan, Sabrina, 334
Montcalm, Marquis de, 39
monuments, public: controversy, as pedagogical opportunity, 283;

purpose, 282-83; as sites of memory (lieux de mémoire), 282, 297. *See also* Fresque des Québécois (Quebec City mural); murals, BC Legislature Building; past, interpretation of

Morton, Desmond, 47, 74, 198

Morton, Tom, 19-20

Morton, W.L., 41, 59

multiculturalism: addition to Canadian historical canon, 126; as challenge to prevailing history orthodoxy, 43; constitutionalized practices of accommodation, 317; developing understanding of the "Other" in citizenship education, 356, 357; need for educational systems to respond to student diversity, 311, 318-19; in new Quebec history curriculum, 82, 83, 87; in schools, 309; as viewed from English Canada's "grand narrative," 158-60

Mumtaz, Shazia, 266-67

mural of Quebec history (Fresque des Québécois), Quebec City, 339

murals, BC Legislature Building: advisory panel recommendations, 284-85; analysis of student entries in Begbie Canadian History contest, 287-99; as celebration of arrival and progress of European civilization, 283, 284; concealment of, 285; controversy around depiction of Aboriginal peoples and Europeans, 2, 22, 284; history, 285, 287; objection to, by First Nations, 284; panel titles, 285, 287; photographs, 286

*Museum Exhibition, Theory, and Practice* (Dean), 258

*Museum Frictions* (Karp et al), 248

museums: "conceptual historical wayfinders," 21, 258; educational function, as facilitators of learning experiences, 251; exhibitionary practices, research on use of historical thinking, 253-57, 258-59; exhibitionary practices, visitor-centred approach, 252; influence of "cultural turn," in developing more inclusive, explicit and self-conscious practices, 247; research gaps in visitors' historical meaning making, 248-49; school programs, 249; training staff in history-specific tools and culture to create history-considerate exhibitions, 255-57; use of historical thinking in displays, 25, 245-59

Myers, Philip Van Ness, 4

National Film Board (NFB): and "Giving the Past a Future" Conference (1999), 7; *Images of a Forgotten War: Films of the Canadian Expeditionary Force in the Great War*, 198; production of classroom resources, 63

National History Society, 8, 47, 71

nation-building, as theme in Canadian history: challenges, and erosion of (1960s), 64-67; criticisms of, 59-64; in English-speaking Canada (1890-1970s), 55, 56; four principal topics, in history curricula (1890s-1960s), 58; limited portrayal of First Nations, 59; narrative, established by Clements' *History of the Dominion of Canada* (1898), 58; and teaching of British and European history, 56-57; textbooks, 56; viewed as colonizing way of thinking by Aboriginal peoples, 97, 110-11. *See also* Quebec

Neatby, Hilda, 5, 7, 42, 62

*The Neutral Yankees of Nova Scotia* (Brebner), 41

*New England's Outpost* (Brebner), 41

Newman, Peter C., 47

No Child Left Behind legislation, 75
Nora, Pierre, 48, 88, 123, 282
Norman, Wayne W., 356
*North Atlantic Triangle: The Interplay of Canada, the United States, and Great Britain* (Brebner), 41
*Northern Review*, 43
*Northern Visions: New Perspectives on the North in Canadian History* (Abel and Coates), 45

Oakeshott, Michael, 123, 133
OISE. *See* Ontario Institute for Studies in Education (OISE)
online education: *The Great Unsolved Mysteries in Canadian History* course, 228; keyword searches of archives, 229-30; and sources for primary historical documents, 229. *See also* virtual environments (VEs)
Ontario: historical thinking, in elementary education, 177; study of history textbooks, 4
Ontario Human Rights Commission, 4
Ontario Institute for Studies in Education (OISE): Canadian Public Issues Project, 68; and The History Education Network/Histoire et éducation en réseau (THEN/HiER), 10; History Teaching Methods course, for history teachers, 224-40; *Teaching Prejudice*, report on history textbooks, 4; Values Education Project, 68
oral tradition: Aboriginal, and circular nature of time, 98, 101; Aboriginal, as historical memory, 33, 36-37; Aboriginal, recognized by Supreme Court as valid form of legal discourse, 36, 104; European immigrants, 33-34. *See also* storytelling, Aboriginal
Ormsby, Margaret A., 41, 42
Osborne, Kenneth: and "big ideas" that tie historical details together, 214, 220, 221; on Canada and public deliberation, 357-58; on changes in pedagogy of history, 213-14; on "cultural literacy," 214; *In Defence of History: Teaching the Past and the Meaning of Democratic Citizenship (1995)*, 44; definition of "citizenship," 14; on dispute between social studies and history as subjects, 345; on downgrading of history in curriculum, 5; on exercise of citizenship as dependent on understanding of state and society, 16; historical concepts, compared with Seixas historical thinking concepts, 215-17; on national citizenship, in context of Canada, 16; political and military history as "nation-building" narrative, 15; rejection of suggestion that students cannot understand history, 214; on "socialization into discord" of francophone history textbooks, 4; on teaching history using primary documents, 228; "The Teaching of History and Democratic Citizenship," 14; on wonder, 215
Ouellet, Fernand, 41-42

Palmer, Bryan, 43
Papert, Seymour, 267, 276
Parent Commission: on dissociating history from patriotic justification, 57-58, 64-65; report, and changes in Quebec history curricula, 59
Partington, Geoffrey, 122, 132-33
past, interpretation of: Aboriginal ways of understanding the past, 98, 104; analysis of Begbie Canadian History Contest student entries, 287-97, 298-99; circular (Aboriginal) vs linear (Western) thinking, 98, 100-1; colligation, 125-26; as

culturally constituted and narrated, 101; factors in judging historical monuments, 297-98; historical explanations, as constructed, 125, 227; museums, use of historical thinking in displays, 245-59; research into children's grasp of time concepts, 184-86; using primary documents as evidence, 232-40; using virtual environments, 264-77

Peck, Carla, 19, 23

pedagogy, of history: from Aboriginal perspective, 97-111; assessment for learning strategies, 139, 201-2; changes in methodology, 213-14; citizenship education, themes for, 356-58; "cognitive revolution" and prior knowledge, 348-51; Critical Challenge approach, 237-39; critique of, 62; developmental model of cognition and learning, 142-45; discovery and inquiry methods of teaching, 72; elementary, assignment examples, 175-76; elementary, research on teaching, 189-90; evidence-based inquiry, 67; Gaffield's sports analogy, 117, 134; historical cognition, analysis of assessment exercise, 151-52; historical cognition, interpreting evidence of, 147-51; historical cognition, tasks for eliciting, 145-47; historical thinking, cultivation of, 72, 73, 74, 120; historical thinking, importance of teaching, 134; historical thinking, limitations on teaching of, 178, 202-3; history educators, 13; history teachers, 13; innovations, 196-97; "laboratory" methods, 63; "multiple historical narratives," 167; museum professionals, mostly untrained in, 254-55; post-secondary, Canadian history survey course, 217-22; primary documents, creating lesson plans around use of, 232; primary documents, teaching historical thinking to student teachers, 226, 227, 228; problems of relativism of history, 116; procedural knowledge, 118-22, 134; Quebec, sequential view followed by reflective approach, 334; reform of, 63; rejection of nation-building theme, 61; research into students' understanding of history, 72, 180-81; secondary, Remembrance Day assignments, 197-204; sedimentary approach, 142-43; shift from university-based historians to educators, 66-67; "source method," 156; Staley's "future scenarios," 164-67; students, understanding of history, 19, 61, 66, 72, 180-81; substantive knowledge, 117, 119, 134; traditional, characterized by students as static, boring and irrelevant, 346-47; using Badiou's "ethic of truths," 168; using innovative technologies, 147, 200-2; zone of proximal development, 143. *See also* Benchmarks of Historical Thinking Project; curriculum, Canadian history; curriculum, Quebec history; history education, Canada; history education, Quebec; textbooks, Canadian history; textbooks, Quebec history

Peel, E.A., 66

*The Peoples of Canada* (Bumsted), 45

Perry, Adele, 2

Perry, Mark, 206

perspective/empathy [historical thinking concept]: application in virtual environments, 271, 272, 274; contextualizing, 132; definition, 12, 131, 250; developmental approach to assessment of, 144-45; error of dismissal, 144, 145; error of

presentism, 144-45; and goals of history education, 142; imagining, 131-32; judging, 132-33; research into children's understanding of, 188-89; in secondary school Remembrance Day assignment, 200; teaching, using innovative technologies, 147, 200-2
Phillips, Robert, 122
Phillips, Robin, 204
Piaget, Jean, 66, 72, 214, 276
Pierce, Lorne, 62
Portal, Christopher, 7
postmodernist theories, of history: Badiou's "truth-processes" as argument against, 161-62; and deconstruction of meaning, 45-46; as fragmentation of discipline of history, 46, 70; on history as product of particular social systems, 116; view of historians' subjectivity as "discursive conventions," 157
potlatch ceremony, 109
Prang, Margaret, 42
Pratt, David, 4
Prentice, Alison, 43, 44
presentism: as error in historical perspective taking, 144-45; view of elementary school children in understanding of past, 188-89
primary documents: as historical evidence in interpretation of the past, 232-240; online sources for, 229; and possibility of different kind of learning activities, 228-29; student use in classroom, issues, 230-31; use in teaching historical thinking to student teachers, 226, 227, 228. *See also* evidence, historical [historical thinking concept]
*The Process of Education* (Bruner), 66, 155
Programme de formation de l'école québécoise (Quebec Education Program), 24, 325

progress and decline [historical thinking concept]: evaluative judgments of changes, 127-29; and goals of history education, 141; oppositional stance, 127, 128; successional stance, 127, 128
progress, idea of: Aboriginal peoples depicted as victims of, 109; and "frontier myth," as conflicting with Aboriginal perspective on local history, 106-8; as pre-existing framework for American students studying American history, 349; as problematic notion for Aboriginal peoples, 98, 101; research on children's view of history as progress, 186; viewed as impossible by students in Northern Ireland, 350
*The Progressive Party of Canada* (Morton), 41
*The Promise of Schooling: Education in Canada, 1800-1914* (Axelrod), 44
Public Archives of Canada, 39, 63

Quadra, Captain, 285, 286, 287
Quebec: Estates General on Education, 82; Quiet Revolution, 42, 45, 64. *See also* curriculum, Quebec history; historians, Quebec; historiography, Quebec; history education, Quebec; history, Quebec; history teachers, Quebec; textbooks, Quebec history
Queen's University, Sir John A. Macdonald Chair of Political Science, 39

race: addition to Canadian historical canon, 2; and ethnicity, 307; research on effect of ethnicity on students' historical understandings, 310
racism: and depiction of Aboriginal peoples, 109; and English Canada's "grand narrative," 159-60; of

*Index*

immigration policy, in social history curriculum, 65
Raibmon, Paige, 110
Ranke, Leopold von, 39, 120, 129
Rattansi, Ali, 306
records, as first-hand historical information, 129
*Red River* (Hargrave), 38
Reed, Liz, 356
Reform Party of Canada West, 41
Remembrance Day secondary assignments, 197-204
*Report of the Royal Commission on Aboriginal Peoples*, 36-37
*Review of Historical Publications Relating to Canada*, 40
*Revolution* [computer game], 270-71
Richert, J.P., 4
Rioux, Christian, 88
Robert, Jean-Claude, 45
Robinson, Harry, 108
Ross, George, 58
Rouillard, Jacques, 43, 89
Roussos, Maria, 266
Royal Commission on Bilingualism and Biculturalism, 4, 64
Royal Ontario Museum, 47-48
Royal Proclamation (1763), as theme in Canadian history, 58
Royal Society of Canada, 39-40
Rüsen, Jörn, 48, 198, 258, 293
Ryan, Marie-Laure, 266

Sandwell, Ruth, 213; on gap between historians' research methods and teaching of undergraduates, 25-26; on history courses in departments of history and in faculties of education, 20; and The History Education Network/Histoire et éducation en réseau (THEN/HiER), 10; on liberalism, and women in Canada, 50; *To the Past: History Education, Public Memory, and Citizenship in Canada*, 9; on teaching historical practice to teacher education students, 224-40
*The School Promoters: Education and Social Class in Mid-Nineteenth-Century Upper Canada* (Prentice), 44
schools. *See* curriculum, Canadian history; curriculum, Quebec history; history education, Canada; history education, Quebec; history education research; textbooks, Canadian history; textbooks, Quebec history
Schools History Project (UK), 67
Schroeder, Ralph, 265
"Schweigen! Die Kinder!" (Seixas), 116
Scriven, Michael, 155
Sears, Alan, 24
*Second Life* (SL) [virtual environment], 274
Seefeldt, Carol, 185
Segall, Avner, 156
Segger, Martin, 285
Séguin, Maurice, 42
Seixas, Peter: and Benchmarks of Historical Thinking Project, 195, 215; on children's knowledge of the past, 181; on communities of inquiry for history education, 228; "Conceptualizing Growth in Historical Understanding," 7; on "critical disciplinary history" education, 6, 9; on historians' judgments, 132; historical thinking, assessment of, 17-18; historical thinking, concepts, 11-12, 213; historical thinking, conceptualization in Canadian education, 120; historical thinking, need for substantive content, 264; historical thinking, and pedagogy of history, 73; historical thinking, procedural concepts, 238, 350; historical thinking, secondary history education applications, 22-23, 204, 210; *Knowing, Teaching, and Learning History: National and*

*International Perspectives*, 8-9; on postmodern orientation to history education, 272-73; on problem of knowing history, 116; research on student ethnicity, and historical understandings, 309; role in new historiographical approach in Canada, 48; "Schweigen! Die Kinder!", 116; on standards of historical significance, 122; *Theorizing Historical Consciousness*, 9; on transhistorical categories, 126

sexuality, addition to Canadian historical canon, 2

Shemilt, Denis, 183, 184

Shortt, Adam, 39, 40

significance [historical thinking concept]: application in virtual environments, 275; compared with Osborne's historical concept, 215-16; criteria, 122-25; definition, 11, 250; in elementary school history education, 204; and goals of history education, 141; research into children's understanding of, 187, 311-12; research on students' ethnic identity and ascription of historical significance to events, 312-17; in secondary school assignment on Remembrance Day, 198-200

"Simulating History" research project, 9

Six Nations historical society, 40

Skelton, Isabel, 42, 59

*Sketches of New Brunswick containing an account of the first settlement of New Brunswick* (Fisher), 38

*Skyscrapers Hide the Heavens: A History of Indian-White Relations in Canada* (Miller), 43

Slator, Brian, 273

Smith, Andrew, 3

*So Little for the Mind* (Neatby), 5, 7

Social Sciences and Humanities Research Council (SSHRC): funding of historical research, 43; history education research grants, 9-10; Strategic Knowledge Cluster Grant, 359

social studies: battle between history and citizenship-focused social studies, 345-48; blending of history into, 4, 5, 61, 67-69, 72, 190; decreased emphasis on, 46, 346, 359-60; goals and assessment, 140-41; history education, focus on citizenship education, democracy and common good, 119; and history, in elementary education, 176-78; identity, as core concept, 319; interdisciplinary, compared with discipline of history, 345; Maritime Studies, 344-45; "new social studies," shift to, 67; opposition to, 5; research on children's awareness of the past, 180-81

Société des professeurs d'histoire du Québec (SPHQ), 86

Southgate, Beverley, 156, 157

Southwell, George, 285

Spicer, Keith, 69

Stacey, Graeme, 204

Staley, David, 164-65, 167

Stamp, Robert M., 44

Stanley, G.F.G., 47, 159-60

Stanley, Timothy, 158

"staples thesis," of Canadian history, 41

Starowicz, Mark: and *Canada: A People's History* (CBC), 9, 47, 220

Stasiulis, Daiva, 308

Stearns, Peter, 8

Sto:lo Atlas, 106

storytelling: museum exhibitions, 257; virtual environments, 268-69

storytelling, Aboriginal: creation stories, and meaning of local geography, 99; creation stories, implications for land claims, 104-5; erasure of distinction between "story" and "history," 101; importance of stories,

97-98; local narratives of the past, as warnings about industrialization and development, 108. *See also* oral tradition

Strong-Boag, Veronica, 45

students. *See* historical thinking; history education, Canada; history education, elementary; history education, post-secondary; history education, Quebec; history education research; history education, secondary; pedagogy, of history

Talon, Jean, 39

Task Force on History Teaching (Quebec), 82

Task Force on National Unity, 69

TC2 (Critical Thinking Consortium), 237

teachers, history. *See* history education, post-secondary; history teachers, Canada; history teachers, Quebec

*Teaching about Historical Thinking* (Denos and Case), 238

teaching, of history. *See* history education; history teachers, Canada; history teachers, Quebec; pedagogy, of history

*Teaching Prejudice* (McDiarmid and Pratt), 4

textbooks, Canadian history: anglophone and francophone differences, 3, 4; Canadian history source books, 63; challenges, in elementary education, 179-80; contest for national history textbook (1890), 58; controversies over, 3-4; difference in Western and Aboriginal view of plants and animals, 102; English, objections by francophone Canadians, 60; failed attempt at uniform national history textbook, 60-61; featuring historical thinking concepts, 207; and history instruction, 3; inclusion of source tracts and multi-media resources, 67; little provision for practice of historical empathy/ perspective, 146; and nation-building narrative, 55, 56, 57; selection criteria update, 4. *See also* curriculum, Canadian history; history education, Canada

textbooks, Quebec history: anglophone and francophone differences, 3, 4, 60; secondary, more emphasis on French than other cultural communities, 329; "teaching kits," funded by province, 328; "teaching kits," not encouraging of critical learning, 328-29; workbooks, 328

THEN/HiER. *See* The History Education Network/Histoire et éducation en réseau (THEN/HiER)

*Theorizing Historical Consciousness* (Seixas), 9

*Thinking about Exhibitions* (Greenberg et al), 248

*Thinking Historically: Educating Students for the 21st Century* (Lévesque), 9

*To the Past: History Education, Public Memory, and Citizenship in Canada* (Sandwell), 9

Tomkins, George S., 44

*Transactions* (Royal Society of Canada), 39

Treaty of Waitangi, 310

Trevelyan, G.M., 215

Trudel, Marcel, 4, 41, 42, 63

*True Government by Choice Men? Inspection, Education, and State Formation in Canada West* (Curtis), 44

Turner, Frederick Jackson, 40

Underhill, Frank, 40

United Kingdom: history education, change from content acquisition to historical thinking, 119;

National History Curriculum, 70, 73, 75; reforms of the National Curriculum in citizenship, including identity and diversity, 352
United States: Amherst History Project, 67; National History Standards, 70, 73, 75, 119-20, 165; No Child Left Behind legislation, 75
Université de Sherbrooke, 10
University of Berlin, 39
University of British Columbia: Centre for the Study of Historical Consciousness, 6, 9, 48; Department of Curriculum and Pedagogy, 10
University of Toronto: Chair of History, 39; Historical Club, 42; and The History Education Network/ Histoire et éducation en réseau (THEN/HiER), 10
University of Victoria, 10
*Urban History Review,* 43
US National Research Council (NRC), Committee on the Foundations of Assessment, 139

*The Valour and the Horror* (film), 48
values education, 68, 71
Values Education Project, OISE, 68
Vancouver, Captain, 285, 286, 287
VanSledright, Bruce, 116, 120, 179, 183, 207, 312
Veterans Affairs Canada, 7
Vinten-Johansen, Peter, 224-26, 227
*Virtual Archaeologist Educational Environment,* 273-74
virtual environments (VEs): applications for learners, 266-67; biographical recounts, 270-71; *Civilization,* 266, 267, 274; defining goals for history learning, 267-69; definition, 265; designing, 268-69; Disney World, 269; expositions, 274-75; factorial explanations, 273-74; game types, 265, 266; historical recounts, 271-73; as hybrid medium, combining narrative and exploratory activity, 268; immediate feedback, 271; *A Journey to the Past: A Quebec Village in 1890/ Un voyage dans le passé: Un village québéois à la fin du 19ième siècle,* 269, 271-73; *Revolution,* 270-71; *Second Life* (SL), 274; and skills of historical practice, 269-77; student identity options, as conducive to learning, 276-77; use to promote historical thinking, 264-77; *Virtual Archaeologist Educational Environment,* 273-74
Vogt, Erich, 210-11, 213, 221
von Heyking, Amy, 18-19, 25

Walsh, William, 126
Wells, H.G., 60
Wenger, Etienne, 246-47
Westheimer, Joel, 326, 335
*What Culture? What Heritage?* (Hodgetts), 6-7, 63
*What is History?* (Carr), 216
*What is History Now?* (Cannadine), 216
*Who Killed Canadian History?* (Granatstein), 5, 46, 47, 74
Whorf, Benjamin, 100, 101
Wickwire, Wendy, 108
Wiggins, Grant, 165
Williams, Raymond, 97
Wilson, Bill (Hemas Kla-Lee-Lee-Kla), 284
Wilson, J.D., 44
Wineburg, Sam: on challenges posed by study of history, 213; *Knowing, Teaching, and Learning History: National and International Perspectives,* 9; on negotiating the tension between the familiar and foreign past, 256; on odds of achieving mature historical understanding, 115; on students' understanding of historical concepts, 214; on students' view of

*Index*

history as factual, 129; study on what historians do and students' historical thinking, 228
Winnipeg General Strike (1919), 65
Wolf, Eric R., 105
women: addition to Canadian historical canon, 2; demand for more inclusive approach to history, 43; depiction in Canadian history textbooks, 4; discrimination against, in history departments, 42; historical societies, 40
women's movement. *See* feminism
working class, in Canadian history, 43
*Working-Class Experience: The Rise and Reconstitution of Canadian Labour, 1800-1980* (Palmer), 43
Wright, Esther Clark, 42
Wrong, G.M., 39-42, 40

Yeager, Elizabeth A., 310
Young, Robert, 210, 211-12, 213
youth, addition to Canadian historical canon, 2

Printed and bound in Canada by Friesens

Set in Futura Condensed and Warnock by Artegraphica Design Co. Ltd.

Copy editor: Matthew Kudelka

Proofreader: Dianne Tiefensee

Indexer: Annette Lorek